KEY TERMS IN THE WORLD OF AFFAIRS

An English-French Explanatory Dictionary
of Banking, Insurance, the Stock Exchange,
The European Union, Government Policy
and Unemployment and International Trade

by
Jean LOZES and John MURRAY

ellipses

REMERCIEMENTS

ALAIN ROBERT a aidé les auteurs d'une façon remarquable à produire ce texte. Par les conseils et le temps précieux qu'il leur a accordés, il leur a permis d'arriver en temps voulu au formatage définitif exigé par l'éditeur. Ils tiennent, donc, à remercier Alain très chaleureusement de cette grande marque d'amitié.

ISBN 2-7298-4547-X

INTRODUCTION

Le domaine des affaires est l'un de ceux où la langue anglaise exerce aujourd'hui le plus d'influence. Qu'il s'agisse de phénomènes boursiers, de questions bancaires, d'institutions et de réglementations européennes, de relations d'entreprise, d'assurances, d'organismes ou de traités internationaux, c'est-à-dire, en fait, d'activité économique, le recours à l'anglais est général parce que l'internationalisation du marché est devenue le fait marquant de cette fin du XXe siècle.

En raisonnant de plus en plus en termes de blocs commerciaux et non plus seulement de puissances économiques nationales, notre civilisation a encore accru l'utilisation d'une langue dont le pouvoir est d'être comprise et maniée par tous ceux qui ont quelque responsabilité dans ce nouvel ordre économique mondial.

Ce livre s'adresse donc aussi bien aux futurs acteurs économiques, élèves des classes de BTS, des classes préparatoires et des Écoles de Commerce, étudiants des IUT, des filières universitaires d'AES, de Sciences Économiques et de Langues Étrangères Appliquées, qu'à ceux qui, déjà engagés dans la vie professionnelle, cadres des entreprises, des banques, des assurances et des administrations, sont en relation avec les marchés étrangers.

Les uns et les autres y trouveront rassemblées et présentées en langue anglaise bon nombre de données qu'ils devraient sinon aller puiser dans de fastidieuses bibliographies.

Il ne s'agit pas en effet d'un dictionnaire mais d'une véritable petite encyclopédie qui, en suivant un ordre simplement alphabétique, recouvre des sujets aussi variés que la bourse, la banque, l'emploi, les assurances, l'Union européenne et le commerce international. À l'issue de chaque rubrique, des renvois permettent, si on le souhaite, d'intégrer ce que l'on vient de lire dans un ensemble plus vaste. Les spécificités institutionnelles des pays anglo-saxons sont bien entendu prises en compte dans chacun des domaines concernés.

L'utilisation de la langue anglaise peut paraître audacieuse, s'adressant à un public français. Il s'agit au contraire de l'originalité de cet ouvrage qui utilise une langue à la fois simple et rigoureusement idiomatique. Le lecteur peut donc apprendre directement en anglais et mettre ainsi tous les atouts de son côté pour une utilisation ultérieure des connaissances acquises, soit dans un document rédigé en anglais, soit au cours d'un exposé ou d'un séminaire en présence d'anglophones.

Afin qu'il n'y ait pratiquement pas d'obstacle linguistique entre le lecteur et sa lecture, bon nombre de mots ainsi que de très brefs passages sont traduits en français entre parenthèses. De même, la plupart des termes ou expressions faisant l'objet d'une rubrique sont traduits en français, et un lexique français-anglais de tous les mots français utilisés vient clore l'ouvrage. Ainsi l'immersion peut-elle être quasi totale sans que le dépaysement soit exagérément brutal.
C'est l'expérience de l'enseignement de la civilisation économique de la Grande-Bretagne et des États-Unis à des étudiants français qui a nourri la conception de ce livre. Puissent tous ceux qui le consulteront y trouver la satisfaction non seulement d'accroître leur savoir mais aussi de mieux savoir le communiquer.

Jean LOZES

INTRODUCTION

Words, words, words! Yet another book giving more or the same words! We are flooded with dictionaries and textbooks for students of English. But we, the authors, feel this book is a different concept. It is borne out of several years' experience of teaching often complex subjects from the world of business and affairs **in English to French students**, such **as banking, the stock exchange, insurance, unemployment and government policies, the European Union and international trade**, which are covered in this book. In other words, we have written this book to meet the specific needs of the French reader working with the English language.

Our experience has shown that first of all the information pertaining to these subjects is to be found in lots of different books in French or in English, more or less comprehensive and more or less comprehensible. Secondly, there are dictionaries in one, two or more languages, but in most cases these only give a simple word-for-word translation. Thus the French reader seeking to understand well a subject, the principles behind it, which he may not necessarily comprehend in his own language, and the way it is described and referred to **in English**, can be confronted with enormous difficulties. Already we have noticed that it is difficult enough to find a textbook in French or in English which explains these subjects in such a way that even the most disadvantaged beginner has a chance of understanding them.

The problems confronting the French reader or student of economics and business-type subjects in English are twofold. First, there is a linguistic difficulty: The terms used are specialized and the level of competence in English may not always allow a full understanding of readings or lectures in English on the subject. For example, we have noticed among students of *Langues Étrangères Appliquées (LEA)* at the University of Toulouse Le Mirail levels of competence in English ranging from very poor to very good. Furthermore, in these subjects it can be that some terms and expressions are so recent as to have not yet found their way into dictionaries or other reference books, or they may not yet even have an equivalent in French. Secondly, there is the question of **understanding** the mechanics and principles behind the workings of certain institutions, phenomena or behaviour. This is often difficult to arrive at in many textbooks because they are not written with a reader in mind who may not have any background in these subjects. For example, take the term **LEVERAGED BUYOUT** or **LBO**. The French for this is "rachat d'une entreprise par l'effet du levier", or "prise de contrôle par recours à l'emprunt", or "acquisition d'une entreprise par endettement". But what in fact is an LBO? How does it function and in what

circumstances? Who uses it? Why? Can the student or reader explain this to someone else?
It is these two main problems of language and basic comprehension which our work seeks to resolve. We have tried to put ourselves in the shoes of the reader at different levels of linguistic and technical competence and create a reference work that makes his life that bit easier. We have also designed it for those with a good working knowledge of English who simply seek a translation into French of a given term and associated vocabulary.
Each entry contains a) the term in English, with preference for English spelling; b) where known the American version or spelling; c) any abbreviations used for the term; d) the French translation, if known, and any abbreviation; e) a comprehensive explanation and account of the term in English, using expressions and vocabulary typically found in the language and associated with the subject; f) within e) above translations into French of vocabulary, expressions, prepositions, phrases and idiomatic usage in order to facilitate comprehension; and g), for quick reference, a glossary at the end of the main entries of French translations used in the book and their English equivalent.
This work, of necessity, does not claim to be exhaustive. It has been selective, especially seeking to explain the mechanisms behind key aspects in the chosen domains of the world of business and affairs, giving a solid understanding of these. Even if the reader finds the work at times slightly out of date – an unavoidable danger with this kind of book – it is hoped that he will appreciate the care that has been taken to lay open subjects that might otherwise have been difficult to grasp. Once the basic principles have been understood, it is relatively easy then to follow and understand subsequent developments (e.g. the debates following the Maastricht Agreement or the completion of the GATT Uruguay Round).
We have written this book with especially you, the French reader, in mind. We hope it will be of genuine help to you, and perhaps pave the way for other similar works which take into account the problems of learning specialized subjects in a foreign language. As we consider this to be an ambitious approach on our part, we would welcome any comments readers might care to send us via the publishers which could help to improve the usefulness of possible future editions.

John MURRAY

A

"A" SHARE (action ordinaire sans droit de vote)

This is an ordinary share which may only give limited or even no voting rights (droits de vote) at company annual general meetings (assemblée générale annuelle). This contrasts with a **"B" SHARE** (action ordinaire avec droit de vote), which carries full voting rights and is usually reserved for the original owners (propriétaire) or founders (fondateur) of the business to ensure their control. Both "A" and "B" shares are referred to collectively as **MULTIPLE VOTING SHARES** (action à vote multiple ou plural).

☞ See ANNUAL GENERAL MEETING; ORDINARY SHARES; SHARE; SHAREHOLDER.

A RATING See .... CREDIT RATING AGENCY

AA RATING See .... CREDIT RATING AGENCY

AAA RATING See .... CREDIT RATING AGENCY

ABOVE PAR See .... PAR ETC

ACCEPTANCE See .... BILL OF EXCHANGE

ACCEPTANCE BANK See .... MERCHANT BANK

ACCEPTANCE HOUSE See .... MERCHANT BANK

ACCEPTING HOUSE See .... MERCHANT BANK

ACCEPTOR See .... BILL OF EXCHANGE

ACCIDENT INSURANCE (assurance-accidents)

A non-life (non-vie), or casualty/property (biens et personnes) insurance involving (inclure) the following covering or coverage (couverture):

a. **LIABILITY INSURANCE** (responsabilité civile) which covers (couvrir) a person, organisation, institution or business (entreprise) against losses (dommages) due to claims (dommages et intérêts) made against (réclamer) them by third persons (tierce personne) who suffered (subir) a loss because of their actions (de leur fait). **EMPLOYERS' LIABILITY INSURANCE** (responsabilité de l'employeur) covers employers should (dans le cas où) any liability arise (apparaître) for injury (accident) or death (décès) occurring (survenir) to employees at work. Industrial diseases (maladie professionnelle) belong to this section. **PUBLIC LIABILITY INSURANCE** covers individuals (particulier) or businesses against losses or damage occurring to members of the public on their property. Traders (cormmerçant) insure against possible (éventuel) liabilities to customers (client) when on their premises (dans leurs locaux). Homeowners (propriétaire) and tenants (locataire) can do the same (en faire de même) regarding (au regard de) their visitors and neighbours (voisin). Manufacturers (industriel) may insure against claims (sinistre) arising from (dû à) the use (utilisation) of their products. Public authorities (pouvoirs publics) have an obligation to take out (prendre) public liability insurance regarding visitors to administrative buildings (bâtiment public), passers-by (piéton) in the streets etc. Another example is **THIRD PARTY MOTOR INSURANCE** (tiers collision) which is also compulsory (obligatoire) for every driver;

b. **PROPERTY INSURANCE** (biens) which covers theft (vol) or accidental loss on private or other premises (locaux);

c. **PERSONAL ACCIDENT POLICY** (personne, personnelle) which guarantees a lump sum (somme forfaitaire) should (au cas où) accidental death occur or limbs (membre) or eyes be lost through (au cours de) an accident.

The disability to work (incapacité de travail) through an accident or illness (maladie) is also covered in the form of weekly or monthly payments;

d. **FIDELITY GUARANTEE/BOND** (bonne moralité) which covers an employer against the loss of money or inventory (stock) due to employees' dishonesty (indélicatesse). **FLOATING POLICIES** (police flottante, ouverte), i.e. the covering of all employees in the firm may be granted (accorder) by insurers provided (pourvu que) the firm has carefully checked (vérifier) the background (arrière-plan personnel) of its employees. Certain occupations (activité professionnelle), like company liquidator (liquidateur, syndic de faillite), cannot be carried out (exercer) without the covering of a fidelity guarantee policy;

e. **CREDIT INSURANCE** (crédit) which covers losses due to customer's default (défaillance) for goods bought on credit. Traders may take out (prendre) such policies either (soit) for a single (seul, unique) transaction or (soit) for a period of time to cover all transactions up to (jusqu'à) a stated total value (valeur totale indiquée). Only 90% or so (environ) of the possible (éventuelle) debt is generally covered in order not to make the risk utterly (purement et simplement) uninsurable (inassurable) through (en raison de) the creditor's (créancier) possible negligence regarding (vis-à-vis) debtors (débiteur) if 100% of the risk was accepted by insurers.

When several types of accident are covered together within (à l'intérieur) the same policy, the latter (celle-ci) is known as **COMPREHENSIVE** or **ALL-IN POLICY** (tous risques). An example is the **COMPREHENSIVE MOTOR CAR INSURANCE** contract including (comprendre) theft (vol), accidental damage, personal injuries (dommage corporel), liability (responsabilité) to passengers and persons outside (tiers) the vehicle, as well as fire (incendie). However, on account of (en raison de) the rising cost of claims (sinistre), insurers have added (ajouter) **EXCESS CLAUSES** (avenant de franchise) to these all-in policies so that (de sorte que) only the amount of the costs in excess of (dépassant) a fixed sum will eventually (finalement) be repaid (rembourser) to the claimant (assuré sinistré, ayant droit).

☞ See INSURANCE; EXPORT CREDIT INSURANCE.

ACCOUNT DAY, THE See .... SETTLEMENT OF BARGAINS

ACID TEST See .... LIQUIDITY RATIO

ACP COUNTRIES See .... LOME CONVENTION

ACTING IN CONCERT See .... TAKEOVER BID

ACTIVE POPULATION See .... UNEMPLOYMENT

ACTIVE WORKING POPULATION See .... UNEMPLOYMENT

(ACTUAL) TOTAL LOSS See .... MARINE INSURANCE

ACTUAL TRANSACTION See .... SPOT/CURRENT PRICE

ACTUALS See .... SPOT/CURRENT PRICE

ACTUARY See .... INSURANCE

AD VALOREM DUTY See .... CUSTOMS DUTY

AD VALOREM TAXES See .... TAX

ADJUSTMENT (ajustement)

The adaptation of a country's economy to technological changes, shifts (changement) in demand or developments in external trade. The means (moyen) of adaptation may include a reallocation (redéploiement) of labour (main d'oeuvre) and capital away from uncompetitive to competitive sectors. The International Monetary Fund/IMF (FMI) uses the term to define (désigner) the adoption of macroeconomic policies (politique) – monetary, fiscal and exchange rate (taux de change) modifications – in order to (afin de) adjust the level (niveau) of domestic (intérieur) economic activity to conditions prevailing (prépondérant) in the world economy, with the eventual (final) target (but) of correcting (corriger) balance of payments disequilibria and lowering (abaisse) inflation. The IMF grants loans only to countries that accept to adjust their economies as described above.

☞ See BALANCE OF PAYMENTS; FISCAL POLICY; IMF; MACROECONOMICS; MONETARY POLICY; SAFEGUARDS; STRUCTURAL CHANGES.

ADVANCE See .... LOAN

AFBD abbr. for **ASSOCIATION OF FUTURES BROKERS AND DEALERS** See .... SELF-REGULATING ORGANIZATIONS

AFRICAN, CARIBBEAN AND PACIFIC COUNTRIES See .... ACP COUNTRIES

AFTER SIGHT (à X jours de vue)

Usually with reference to a bill of exchange (lettre de change ou traite ou effet de commerce) and meaning payable thirty, sixty or more days after it has been seen by the acceptor (accepteur ou tiré). Such bills of exchange are called **USANCE BILLS** (traite à échéance ou effet à usance).

☞ See AFTER SIGHT; BILL OF EXCHANGE; DRAFT BILL.

AGGREGATE DEMAND (demande globale)

The total demand for all goods and services in an economy. It comprises:

a. public expenditure (dépenses publiques) by government and local authorities;

b. consumers' expenditure on goods and services (biens et services);

c. investment in capital goods (biens d'équipement) and stock (approvisionnement); and

d. exports of goods and services less imports. Government monetary and fiscal policy seeks to influence any combination of the above four elements of aggregate demand in order to stimulate economic growth (croissance) and employment and reduce inflation.

☞ See ECONOMIC GROWTH; FISCAL POLICY; INFLATION; MONETARY POLICY; PUBLIC SECTOR BORROWING REQUIREMENT; UNEMPLOYMENT.

AGM See .... ANNUAL GENERAL MEETING.

AIM See .... INTERNATIONAL STOCK EXCHANGE OF THE UNITED KINGDOM ETC.; UNLISTED SECURITIES MARKET

AIR CONSIGNMENT NOTE See .... BILL OF LADING.

AIRWAY BILL See .... BILL OF LADING.

ALL-IN POLICY See .... ACCIDENT INSURANCE.

ALPHA SECURITIES/SHARES/STOCKS

These are about 130 different shares, which are the most frequently traded (négocié) on the International Stock Exchange (ISE), London, are all quoted on SEAQ and include blue chip companies (sociétés de tout premier ordre) and all the companies listed in the Financial Times-Stock Exchange 100 Share Index. There are three other categories of shares used on the ISE: about 550 **BETA SECURITIES**, which are a little less actively traded, including shares quoted on the Unlisted Securities Market, abbr.USM (l'équivalent en France du Second Marché, un marché Hors-Cote spécial) and have fewer market makers (teneur de marché); **GAMMA SECURITIES** are shares of smaller companies (c. 1,500), which are less actively traded and include most Third Market stocks; and lastly, **DELTA SECURITIES** are stocks which do not change hands very frequently and have very few market makers.

☞ See BLUE CHIP COMPANY; CREDIT RATING AGENCY; INTERNATIONAL STOCK EXCHANGE; MARKET MAKER; SEAQ; SHARE INDEXES; THIRD MARKET; UNLISTED SECURITIES MARKET.

ANDEAN GROUP See .... FREE TRADE AREA.

ALTERNATIVE INVESTMENT MARKET See .... INTERNATIONAL STOCK EXCHANGE OF THE UNITED KINGDOM ETC.; UNLISTED SECURITIES MARKET.

ANDEAN PACT See .... FREE TRADE AREA.

ANNUAL GENERAL MEETING, abbr. **AGM** (assemblée générale annuelle)

The yearly meeting of shareholders (that is, those who hold voting rights) and directors (administrateur) of a company, required by law, also referred to as **ANNUAL MEETING** and in the USA as **STOCKHOLDERS' MEETING**. At this meeting, convened (convoquer) at least three weeks after the company accounts have been published, those present vote on the accounts and the directors' and auditors' (auditeur ou commissaire aux comptes) reports for the past year's activities, decide the fee (honoraires) to be paid to the auditors and the amount of the dividend to go to shareholders, and reappoint (reconduire dans ses fonctions) the auditors and directors. In theory it is through the AGM that shareholders control their company. It is true they vote on the appointment (nomination) of directors and can use the AGM to question the company's policies, the pay awards (hausse de salaire) to directors and so on, but they are presented with a *fait accompli*, as the accounts relate to the previous year's activities and decisions. In addition, voting is usually based on one vote per share, which means that unless (à moins que) shareholders unite with other shareholders and make a point of (mettre un point d'honneur à) being present at the AGM they have little chance of changing things, all the more so if members of the board of directors (conseil d'administration) control the majority of shares. Under British company law, however, certain major resolutions (résolution) like changing the objectives of the company will require (exiger) a 75% vote in favour. Normally shareholders accept the recommendations of the board of directors, but due to the high pay awards directors were giving themselves in both the UK and the USA over the last five years or so, even when their companies were performing badly, the former have brought (exercer) increasing pressure to limit this abuse. AGMs are also held by a range of other business and social organizations such as trade unions (syndicat), clubs etc.

☞ See DIVIDEND; BOARD OF DIRECTORS; SHARE.

ANNUAL MEETING See .... ANNUAL GENERAL MEETING.

ANNUAL PERCENTAGE RATE, abbr. **APR** (taux effectif global/TEG)

The annual rate of interest charged on consumer credit (i.e. when a consumer buys something on credit), and therefore the true cost to the consumer. This true cost is often disguised, as consumers are quoted an attractive monthly rate of interest, say 2% per month; this in itself does not appear to be very much, but when calculated over the whole year it means that in fact the consumer is paying perhaps double or more than the normal rate of interest for his credit. Legislation in both the USA and the UK have now made it obligatory for suppliers of credit to inform consumers of the APR, in other words, the true cost of their credit.

☞ See CREDIT CARD.

ANNUITY BOND See .... BOND.

ANNUITY See .... LIFE INSURANCE.

ANTEDATED CHEQUE (chèque antidaté)

A cheque which has been signed and given an earlier date than the present, thus giving the impression that it was drawn up (établir) and available some time ago (which may have not been the case), but probably got delayed in the post.

☞ See CHEQUE; POSTDATED CHEQUE; BOUNCED CHEQUE; STOPPED CHEQUE.

ANTI-DUMPING CODE (code anti-dumping)

A code of conduct (code de conduite) negotiated under the auspices of GATT during the Tokyo Round. It established strict standards (norme) for anti-dumping proceedings (procédure) in signatory countries. Local (national) legislations may impose special duties (droit) equivalent to the margin (marge) of dumping of imported goods.

☞ See CODES OF CONDUCT; DUMPING; GATT; TOKYO ROUND; STANDARDS.

APEC See .... ASIA-PACIFIC ECONOMIC CO-OPERATION.

APR See .... ANNUAL PERCENTAGE RATE.

ARB See .... ARBITRAGE; TAKEOVER BID.

ARBITRAGE or **ARBITRAGING** (arbitrage)

This is buying a commodity (marchandise), currency (devises), security (titre) or other asset in one market and almost simultaneously selling it in another to make a profit, taking advantage of price differentials or fluctuations in exchange rates (taux de change). It can take the form, for example, of buying a commodity in one market and selling it almost at the same time in another. It can also simply be switching (changer) funds in one investment on the money market to another in order to get a higher profit or yield (rendement). On futures markets (marché à terme) it can be buying a commodity, say, three months forward and at the same time selling it six months forward for a profit. The person carrying out arbitrage is known as an **ARBITRAGER** or **ARBITRAGEUR** (arbitragiste), while those who speculate in the securities of small companies likely to be taken over (reprise), buying them in the hope of an increase in the price are known in the USA mainly as **RISK ARBITRAGEURS** or **ARBS** (arbitragiste-risque).

☞ See BEAR; BULL; COMMODITY; FOREIGN EXCHANGE MARKET; FORWARD CONTRACT; LEVERAGED BUYOUT; MONEY MARKET; OPTION; SPOT/CURRENT PRICE; TAKEOVER BID.

ARBITRAGER/ARBITRAGEUR See .... ARBITRAGE.

ARBITRAGING See .... ARBITRAGE.

ARTICLES OF ASSOCIATION See .... AUTHORIZED/REGISTERED ETC. CAPITAL.

ARTICLES OF GATT (Articles du GATT)

ARTICLE I See .... ENABLING CLAUSE; MOST-FAVOURED-NATION TREATMENT.

ARTICLE II See .... CONCESSION.

ARTICLES III through (à) XXIII See .... CODES Of CONDUCT.

ARTICLE VI See .... BORDER TAX ADJUSTMENTS; COUNTERVAILING DUTIES; DUMPING.

ARTICLE XI See .... QUANTITATIVE RESTRICTIONS; SECTION 22.

ARTICLE XII See .... QUANTITATIVE RESTRICTIONS.

ARTICLE XIII See .... QUANTITATIVE RESTRICTIONS.

ARTICLE XV See .... BALANCE OF PAYMENTS CONSULTATIONS.

ARTICLE XVI See .... BORDER TAX ADJUSTMENTS; EXPORT SUBSIDIES.

ARTICLE XVIII See .... QUANTITATIVE RESTRICTIONS.

ARTICLE XIX See .... ESCAPE CLAUSE; SAFEGUARDS.

ARTICLE XX See .... QUANTITATIVE RESTRICTIONS.

ARTICLE XXI See .... QUANTITATIVE RESTRICTIONS.

ARTICLES XXII, XXIII See .... CONSULTATIONS; DISPUTE SETTLEMENT.

ARTICLE XXIV See .... CUSTOMS UNION; FREE TRADE AREA.

ARTICLES XXXVI, XXXVII, XXXVIII See .... GATT.

ASEAN See .... ASSOCIATION OF SOUTH EAST ASIAN NATIONS.

ASIA-PACIFIC ECONOMIC CO-OPERATION, abbr. **APEC** (Coopération économique des pays d'Asie-Pacifique/CEAP)

The first summit of this eighteen-member forum took place in Seattle, USA, on 20 November 1993. Invited by President Clinton, it pronounced in favour of an "Asia-Pacific economic community" although (bien que) it did not manage (parvenir à) to establish a clear structure. This meeting was above all used by the USA as a "negotiating coin" (pion de négociation) at a time when the Uruguay Round of Gatt talks was in danger of stalling (caler) on account of (en raison de) serious difficulties with Europe. By wielding (brandir) the threat (menace) of a new free-trade area comparable to **NAFTA**, the USA warned the Europeans that it could oppose another fortress to "Fortress Europe". On November 15th 1994 in Indonesia,

APEC's members committed themselves to creating a free trade area stretching from New York to Bangkok and from Chile to China by the year 2020. APEC's members are: Australia, Brunei, Canada, Chile, China, Hong Kong, Indonesia, Japan, Malaysia, Mexico, New Zealand, Papua New Guinea, the Philippines, Singapore, South Korea, Chinese Taipei, Thailand and the United States.

☞ See FREE-TRADE AREA; GATT; NAFTA.

ASSESSOR See .... INSURANCE.

ASSOCIATION OF FUTURES BROKERS AND DEALERS, abbr. **AFBD** See .... SELF-REGULATING ORGANIZATIONS.

ASSOCIATION OF SOUTH EAST ASIAN NATIONS, abbr. **ASEAN** (Association des pays de l'Asie du sud-est/APASE)

A regional association set up (créer) en 1967 of six developing countries (pays en voie de développement) in South-East Asia, including (comprenant) Brunei, Indonesia, Malaysia, the Philippines, Singapore and Thailand. Its main offices (siège central) are in Jakarta, Indonesia. Its aim (but) is to improve (améliorer) co-operation among its members in political, economic and social matters (affaire). It has helped achieve (réaliser) joint (commun) industrial projects in the fields (domaine) of petrochemicals (pétrochimie), fertilizers (engrais), steel (acier) newsprint (papier journal) and rubber (caoutchouc). It has established (instaurer) tariff concessions (concession tarifaire) for intra-**ASEAN** trade in several basic commodities (produit, denrée). The Association also has an emergency oil-sharing scheme (plan d'urgence de partage des ressources pétrolières) to provide assistance to any of its members whose oil supplies (réserves, stock) become dangerously low.

☞ See TARIFF.

ASSURANCE See .... INSURANCE; LIFE INSURANCE.

ASSURED See .... INSURANCE.

ASSURER See .... INSURANCE.

AT A DISCOUNT (avec escompte ou au dessous du pair ou à perte)

This means at a price below a given, face or par value (valeur au pair).

☞ See DISCOUNT.

AT A PREMIUM See .... PAR ETC.

AT CALL MONEY See .... CALL MONEY.

ATM See .... CHEQUE.

AT PAR See .... PAR ETC.

AT SIGHT (à vue ou sur présentation)

This refers to any document indicating a sum of money to be paid, which when presented to the person or organization responsible for paying it, has to be paid immediately, that is, the moment the acceptor (accepteur ou tiré) sees it. Bills of exchange (lettre de change ou traite ou effet de commerce) payable at once in this way are called **SIGHT BILLS** or **BILLS OF SIGHT** (à vue). Traveller's cheques (chèque de voyage) are also payable at sight.

☞ See AFTER SIGHT; BILL OF EXCHANGE; DRAFT BILL; TRAVELLER'S CHEQUES.

AUTHORIZED STOCK See ....AUTHORIZED/REGISTERED ETC. CAPITAL.

AUTHORIZED/REGISTERED/NOMINAL/SUBSCRIBED CAPITAL or **AUTHORIZED STOCK/ISSUE** (capital social/nominal ou actions pouvant être émises ou nombre total d'actions précisé par les statuts)

This is the share capital (capital actions) a company itself defines as being needed, which has to be entered in its **MEMORANDUM OF ASSOCIATION** (acte constitutif d'une société), the legal document required for new companies which also defines the number and value of its shares, its objectives, whether it is limited (responsabilité limitée) or not, its name and where it is registered (enregistrer). This then gives the company the legal right to raise this capital (se procurer ces capitaux) in the form of shares, each of an equal, given value. The other important legal document for the founding of a company is the **ARTICLES OF ASSOCIATION** (statuts), which gives the rules on how the company will be run, how the directors will be elected, the frequency of meetings and so on. Where the company issues (émettre) all the shares they are known as **ISSUED/SUBSCRIBED CAPITAL** (capital souscrit ou actions souscrites); where these issued shares have been paid for they are called **PAID UP/FULLY-PAID CAPITAL**, US **PAID IN/CONTRIBUTED CAPITAL** (capital versé/libéré ou actions entièrement libérées/libérées en totalité); where payment has not yet been demanded for issued shares, those issued shares not paid for are known as **UNCALLED CAPITAL** (capital souscrit et non appelé); where subscribers pay for their shares in instalments (par versement échelonné) this part of the issued capital is known as **CALLED-UP CAPITAL** (capital appelé), until they have completely paid, when such shares become **PAID UP/FULLY-PAID CAPITAL**. Those shares retained by the company and not yet issued (out of the total number of its authorized capital) are known as **UNISSUED CAPITAL** (actions non encore émises/à la souche).

☞ See LIMITED or LIMITED LIABILITY COMPANY; SHARE.

AUTOMATED/AUTOMATIC TELLER MACHINE See .... CHEQUE.

B

B RATING See .... CREDIT RATING AGENCY.

"B" SHARES See .... "A" SHARES.

B/E See .... BILL OF EXCHANGE.

B/L See .... BILL OF LADING.

BACK See .... SETTLEMENT OF BARGAINS.

BACKWARDATION See .... SETTLEMENT OF BARGAINS.

BACKWARDIZATION See .... SETTLEMENT OF BARGAINS.

BALANCE OF CONCESSIONS See .... RECIPROCITY.

BALANCE OF PAYMENTS (balance des paiements)

The record (état) of a country's credit and debit transactions in goods (marchandise) and money (capitaux) with foreign countries and international institutions. The balance of payments is divided into two main sections: the **BALANCE ON CURRENT ACCOUNT** or **CURRENT ACCOUNT BALANCE** (balance des paiements courants) and the **BALANCE ON CAPITAL ACCOUNT** or **CAPITAL ACCOUNT BALANCE** (balance des mouvements de capitaux).

The balance on current account includes (comprendre): visible trade (importations et exportations visibles), i.e. imports and exports of goods, kown as (appeler) the **BALANCE OF TRADE** or **TRADE BALANCE** (balance commerciale); invisible trade or **INVISIBLES** (invisibles), i.e. payments and receipts (recettes) for services such as banking insurance, tourism, shipping (transport maritime), profits (bénéfice) earned (réaliser) overseas (à l'étranger) and interest payments (versement, règlement); private transfers (transfert; virement), i.e. savings (épargne) sent by foreigners working in the country to their country of origin; and public transfers, i.e. payments to international organizations.

The balance on capital account includes: inward and outward long-term flows of money (flux d'entrée et de sortie de capitaux à long terme) for investment, international grants (aide) and loans (prêt, emprunt); inward and outward short-term (à court terme) flows of money for speculative purposes (but).

Governments try to make the two accounts – current and capital – balance (s'équilibrer). Equilibrium is obtained by means of (au moyen de): movements in the gold and foreign exchange (devise) reserves; borrowing from (emprunter à) or lending to (prêter à) other countries or international institutions; and foreign currency (devise) borrowing (emprunté) or lending (prêt) by the public sector, i.e. central government, local government and nationalized industries.

If the imbalance (déséquilibre) is expected to last (durer), then one must resort to (recourir à) adjustments by means of fiscal policy (politique budgétaire), exchange control (contrôle des échanges) and exchange rate changes (modification des taux de change). Import tariffs and quotas as well as export incentives (mesures d'encouragement) may also be applied (appliquer).

The balance of payments may be described as in surplus, active, favorable (excédentaire) or on the other hand in deficit, adverse, passive, unfavourable (déficitaire). A deficit in the balance of payments is not necessarily a bad thing. It may be a form of borrowing used to increase domestic savings (épargne nationale) and thus (ainsi) boost (développer) investment to the benefit of future growth (croissance). But if the deficit results from an excess of demand over supply (offre) in the domestic market (marché intérieur) it will persist until the home market (marché intérieur) has been adjusted. If borrowing is used to finance consumption (consommation) instead of (au lieu de) investment, this will not benefit future growth.

☞ See ADJUSTMENT; BALANCE OF PAYMENTS CONSULTATIONS; BANKING; CUSTOMS DUTY; EQUILIBRIUM; EXCHANGE CONTROLS; EXCHANGE RATE; EXPORT QUOTAS; EXPORT SUBSIDIES; INVISIBLE TRADE; SERVICES; SPECIFIC DUTY; SPECIFIC LIMITATION ON TRADE.

BALANCE OF PAYMENTS CONSULTATIONS (consultations sur la balance des paiements)

Article XV of GATT requires (demander) coordination between the General Agreement on Tariffs and Trade and the International Monetary Fund to ensure that the trade and payments implications of any quantitative restrictions imposed for balance of payments reasons are fully analysed within (au sein de) the respective jurisdictions (juridiction) of both organizations. Any contracting party (partie contractante) that imposes such quantitative restrictions for balance of payments purposes (but, fin) is expected to (devoir) to hold consultations with other interested contracting parties. The Framework agreement (accord cadre) concluded during the Tokyo Round provides (prévoir) that any other trade restrictive measures (mesure commerciale restrictive) imposed for balance of payments purposes should (devoir) also be discussed in such consultations.

☞ See ARTICLES OF GATT; BALANCE OF PAYMENTS; CONSULTATIONS; CONTRACTING PARTY; EXCHANGE CONTROLS; FRAMEWORK AGREEMENT; GATT; IMF; PRIOR DEPOSITS; QUANTITATIVE RESTRICTIONS; TOKYO ROUND.

BALANCE OF TRADE See .... BALANCE OF PAYMENTS.

BALANCE ON CAPITAL ACCOUNT See .... BALANCE OF PAYMENTS.

BALANCE ON CURRENT ACCOUNT See .... BALANCE OF PAYMENTS.

BANK ACCEPTANCE See .... BANKERS'/BANK BILL.

BANK ADVANCE See .... LOAN.

BANK BILL See .... BANKERS'/BANK BILL.

BANK CARD See .... CHEQUE ETC.CARD.

BANK FOR INTERNATIONAL SETTLEMENTS, abbr. **BIS** (Banque des règlements internationaux/BRI)

Was set up (créer) in 1930 with the purpose (dans le but) of acting as (agir en tant que) the central bank of central banks in matters (question) concerning the financial aftermath (répercussions, suites) of World War I. Since the end of World War II, the main functions of a central bank for central banks have been performed (remplir) by the International Monetary Fund. However, the BIS which is headquartered (avoir son siège) in Basle, Switzerland, still achieves (effectuer) a useful task in central banking cooperation.

It acts as a trustee (dépositaire) for international government loans (prêt, emprunt) and carries out (réaliser, effectuer) financial transactions for the OECD, the ECSC, the IMF and the EMS. Since 1986, the BIS has acted as a clearing-house (chambre de compensation) for inter-bank transactions in ECUs. The monthly meetings of the BIS in Basle are attended by representatives of the central banks of Great Britain, France, Germany, Belgium, Italy, Switzerland, The Netherlands, Sweden, the USA, Canada and Japan.

☞ See CENTRAL BANK; EUROPEAN COAL AND STEEL COMMUNITY; EUROPEAN CURRENCY UNIT; EUROPEAN MONETARY SYSTEM; INTERNATIONAL MONETARY FUND; NAFTA; ORGANIZATION FOR ECONOMIC COOPERATION AND DEVELOPMENT.

BANK LOAN See .... LOAN.

BANK/BANKER'S CHEQUE See .... BANK/BANKER'S DRAFT.

BANK/BANKER'S DRAFT or **BANK/BANKER'S CHEQUE** (traite bancaire/sur une banque ou tirage d'un chèque d'une banque sur elle-même)

A cheque drawn (tiré) by a bank on itself (i.e. not by the customer), which is payable immediately on demand (sur demande ou à vue). As it is a bank which has drawn it, the draft is as good as cash (no bank is likely to refuse its own draft) and is used in situations where the creditor will not accept a personal cheque or other forms of payment. In an import/export transaction, for example, the seller may insist on (vouloir ou exiger) receiving a banker's draft before he is prepared to ship the goods. The importer, in this case, will instruct his bank to draw up a banker's draft (for which, of course, he pays) and sends this to the exporter, who then presents it to his own bank for payment.

BANKABLE BILL See .... BANKER'S/BANK BILL.

BANKER'S ACCEPTANCE. See .... BANKER'S/BANK BILL.

BANKER'S CARD See .... CHEQUE ETC. CARD.

BANKER'S CHEQUE. See .... BANK/BANKER'S CHEQUE.

BANKER'S/BANK BILL or **BANK/BANKER'S ACCEPTANCE** or **BANK DRAFT, (US) BANKABLE BILL** (acceptation ou aval de banque)

A bill of exchange (lettre de change) which has been drawn (tirer) by a bank, or accepted (i.e. the bank has agreed to pay it when it matures (parvenir à l'échéance) or endorsed (endosser/avaliser) it. In the UK bank bills mature in up to nine months, and because they are such good security are easily and cheaply discountable. Note that in the US a **BANK BILL** is the English equivalent of a bank-note (billet de banque).

☞ See BILL OF EXCHANGE; DISCOUNT.

BANKING (affaires/opérations bancaires)

This is in essence the business of accepting deposits (dépôt) from customers and making loans (prêt ou emprunt), an activity basically carried out by banks and also today by a range of other financial intermediaries such as building societies (caisse d'épargne/mutuelle de crédit immobilier) and finance houses. The banking system as such will include the central bank, commercial banks (banque commerciale) and merchant banks (banque d'affaires). Banks, especially commercial banks, since de-regulation (libéralisation) in the 1980s have become involved in the provision of a whole range of other services such as insurance and investment advice and broking (courtage), credit cards and foreign exchange; other financial intermediaries like building societies also provide some of these services, as well as cheque and savings accounts (compte courant et compte d'épargne). As most customers use cheques to withdraw money and make payments banks only need to hold small amounts from their customers' deposits to meet daily demands for cash and so are free to lend the rest. Put another way, banks create money: they can lend up to twenty times the amount they hold in cash to meet customers' demands, precisely because experience has shown that depositors will not all want all their money back at the same time. As the system depends entirely on the confidence of customers that they can get their money back when they want to, certain regulations are normally imposed on banks by the central banks and other monetary authorities to ensure this is always possible. For example they may be required to deposit a percentage of their customers' deposits with the central bank, called special deposits (réserves obligatoires), or hold a proportion of these in liquid form, such as government bonds (bon du trésor), the amount being determined by a liquidity ratio (ratio de liquidité). These regulations thus (ainsi) ensure the safety of the banking system, protect depositors (déposant) and regulate money supply (masse monétaire). Banks can be very broadly based with branches (agence) throughout a country, such as commercial banks, or highly specialised, such as merchant banks.

☞ See BORROWING; BUILDING SOCIETY; CENTRAL BANK; COMMERCIAL BANK; CHEQUE; CREDIT CARD; CURRENT ACCOUNT; DEPOSIT ACCOUNT; DE-REGULATION; INTEREST; LENDING; LIQUIDITY RATIO; LOAN; MERCHANT BANK; MONEY SUPPLY; RESERVE ASSET RATIO; RUN ON A BANK; SPECIAL DEPOSITS.

BANKRUPT See .... LIQUIDATION.

BANKRUPTCY PETITION See .... LIQUIDATION.

BANKRUPTCY REFORM ACT, 1978 See .... LIQUIDATION.

BANKRUPTCY See .... LIQUIDATION.

BANQUE DE FRANCE See .... CENTRAL BANK.

BARGAIN or **CONTRACT** (marché ou transaction ou affaire)

The transaction of buying or selling securities (titres) on the London Stock Exchange. An unprofitable transaction is called a bad bargain. Note that each transaction implies two bargains, with someone buying the securities and someone selling them.

☞ See CLOSING PRICE; INTERNATIONAL STOCK EXCHANGE; SETTLEMENT OF BARGAINS; TOUCH.

BARTER See .... COUNTERTRADE.

BB RATING See .... CREDIT RATING AGENCY.

BBB RATING See .... CREDIT RATING AGENCY.

B/E See .... BILL OF EXCHANGE.

BE DECLARED BANKRUPT, TO See .... LIQUIDATION.

BEAR (baissier ou spéculateur à la baisse ou vendeur à découvert)

This is a speculator who sells securities because he expects a fall in prices later, when he will buy them back at the lower price.. More specifically, it is someone who sells securities for future delivery (livraison à terme) he does not yet possess, or, in other words, he sells short (vendre à découvert). The sale of such securities is referred to as a **BEAR SALE** (vente à découvert). He agrees to supply (in other words, to sell) his client with these at an agreed price for future delivery on a certain day. At the same time he hopes to buy these at a lower price than that at which he has contracted to supply them, but before the delivery date. A **COVERED/PROTECTED BEAR** (baissier avec couverture) is a speculator who sells securities he does possess. **A BEAR RAID** (attaque des baissiers) is the selling of securities by a number of investors in collusion (en arrangement collusoire) to push down the price of a security; they are said **TO BEAR THE MARKET** (faire baisser les cours en bourse). This action may be taken to prevent a take-over bid (OPA) in a situation where the predator (prédateur) has offered his own company's shares in exchange for those of the target company (société ou entreprise cible). A **BEAR MARKET** (marché à la/en baisse) is one in which the prices are falling. When bears are forced to buy securities at prices higher than anticipated this is known as a **BEAR SQUEEZE** (étranglement des vendeurs à découvert). A **BEARISH MARKET** (marché baissier/orienté à la baisse) is one which is pessimistic and believes that prices will fall.

☞ See BULL; COMMODITY; CONTANGO; FORWARD CONTRACT; HAMMERING; SETTLING DAY; SPOT/CURRENT PRICE; TAKEOVER BID.

BEAR MARKET See .... BEAR.

BEAR RAID See .... BEAR.

BEAR SALE See .... HAMMERING.

BEAR SALE See .... HAMMERING; BEAR.

BEAR SQUEEZE See .... BEAR.

BEAR THE MARKET, TO See .... BEAR.

BEARER BOND See .... BOND.

BEARER DEBENTURE See .... DEBENTURE.

BEARISH MARKET See .... BEAR.

BELOW PAR See .... PAR ETC.

BETA SECURITIES See .... ALPHA SECURITIES.

BID/BUYING PRICE (prix offert ou prix/cours acheteur)

This is the price at which a buyer of securities (titres), foreign exchange (devises), commodities (marchandises) or unit trusts (SICAV), such as a market maker (teneur de marché), dealer (négociant) or manager (gérant) of a unit trust is prepared to buy. This is, of course, lower than the price at which he offers to sell, the **OFFER/OFFERED**, USA **OFFERING PRICE** (prix de vente/demandé), the difference being his profit. With regard to unit trusts the bid and offer prices contain a sum to cover profit and management charges (frais de gestion).

☞ See COMMODITY; FOREIGN EXCHANGE MARKET; FORWARD CONTRACT; INTERNATIONAL STOCK EXCHANGE; MARKET MAKER; SPOT/CURRENT PRICE; UNIT TRUST.

BIG BANG, THE (le Big Bang de la Bourse de Londres en 1986)

A term used to describe the changes or reforms (réforme) introduced by the International Stock Exchange in London on 27th October, 1986. These included: the introduction of a computerised quotations system (système informatisé de cotations) [see SEAQ and SEAQ International]; the abolition of fixed minimum commissions (commissions ou honoraires minimum fixes) payable to brokers (agent de change ou courtier) for transactions carried out (effectuer) on behalf of clients; the removal (suppression) of the distinction between jobbers (marchand de titres ou négociant en valeurs mobilières) and brokers: jobbers – now called market makers (contrepartiste spécialisé ou teneur de marché) – are now allowed to deal directly with large investors, while stockbrokers – now called broker/dealers (négociant en titres ou négociant courtier) –, previously only permitted to act as agents for their clients (i.e. buying and selling shares for them) are now also allowed to deal on their own account (pour leur propre compte), thus operating in a dual capacity (à double titre) – that is, buying and selling shares with a view to making a profit; and opening membership of the Stock Exchange to outside firms by allowing them to buy in part or wholly existing member firms. These changes, which were ushered in (introduire) at the same time – hence (d'où) the term "Big Bang" – have resulted in an expansion in turnover (chiffres d'affaires) in general and in dealings in international securities (titres) in particular, as well as the virtual cessation (pratiquement la fin de) of dealing on the floor (la corbeille), except for traded options (options négociables), in favour of off-the-floor telephone dealing.

☞ See BROKER/DEALER; FLOOR, THE; INTERNATIONAL STOCK EXCHANGE; MARKET MAKER; PROGRAM TRADING; SAEF; SEAQ; SEAQ INTERNATIONAL; TALISMAN; TAURUS; TOPIC; TRADED OPTIONS.

BIG BOARD, THE See .... STOCK MARKET/EXCHANGE.

BILL See .... BILL OF EXCHANGE.

BILL OF ENTRY, abbr. **B/E** (déclaration en douane)

A written declaration that must be established by the importer or the exporter and sent to the customs authorities (autorités douanières) for the latter (celles-ci) to be able to cross-check (vérifier, comparer) with the ship's report (livre de bord). There are various types of entry (déclaration) according to whether (selon que) commodities (marchandise) are dutiable (passible de droits) or not:

a. **ENTRY FOR FREE GOODS** (déclaration pour marchandises exemptes de droits) must be completed (faire, accomplir) for non-dutiable goods;

b. **ENTRY FOR HOME USE EX SHIP** (déclaration de sortie d'entrepôt pour consommation) required (exiger) for dutiable commodities and where duties (droit) are to be paid at once (immédiatement);

c. **ENTRY FOR WAREHOUSING** (déclaration d'entrée en entrepôt) for dutiable goods too (aussi) but where duties are not paid immediately. In this case commodities are placed in a bonded warehouse (entrepôt sous douane) and will not be released (autoriser à sortir) until duties have been paid, i.e. once (une fois) cleared (dédouaner).

☞ See BONDED WAREHOUSE; CUSTOMS AND ADMINISTRATIVE ENTRY PROCEDURES; CUSTOMS VALUATION CODE; CUSTOMS DUTY.

BILL OF EXCHANGE or **DRAFT BILL,** abbr. **B/E** (lettre de change/traite/effet de commerce)

A written order from one person who is to receive money, the **DRAWER** (tireur) or **PAYEE** (bénéficiaire), to another who has agreed to pay him an agreed sum, the **ACCEPTOR** or **DRAWEE** (accepteur ou tiré), by an agreed date, at sight (à vue ou sur présentation), or after sight (à x jours de vue). The written order may make the sum payable to the writer of the order himself or to the bearer (porteur) of the document. When the drawee or acceptor has agreed to pay under these conditions he signs or accepts the bill, which then becomes an **ACCEPTANCE** (acceptation d'effets). Bills of exchange are now mainly used in international trade, and can be discounted (escompter), i.e. sold on to another party for less than the face value (valeur nominale) in order to have access to the money sooner than the date specified on the **BILL**. There are **INLAND** (sur l'intérieur) and **FOREIGN** (sur l'extérieur) **BILLS**, the former (la première) being used for home trade and the latter (la seconde) for international transactions. The purpose (but) of a bill of exchange in foreign trade is to grant (accorder) credit to the buyer or importer and to provide (fournir) the seller or exporter with payment in an agreed currency (devise donnée). The existence of a foreign bill, especially if other documents such as the bill of lading (connaissement) and the insurance policy are attached (joindre), allows (permettre à) the exporter to obtain finance in advance from a bank. The latter is said to discount (escompter), the bill, i.e. to pay the stated (indiquer) amount less discount (escompte) which is the equivalent of interest plus commission. Foreign bills drawn without shipping documents (document d'expédition) are called **CLEAN** (libre) **BILLS**. The shipping documents are sent directly to the importer for him to claim (réclamer, prendre possession) the goods while the exporter sends the bill to his own bank which presents it to the importer. Bills may be **AT SIGHT** (à vue ou sur présentation); **SIGHT BILLS** or **BILLS OF AFTER SIGHT** (à x jours de vue) or **SIGHT USANCE BILLS** (à échéance ou à usance). Clean bills are used only when the exporter and the importer have already had frequent dealings (relations d'affaires suivies). For safety reasons, exporters generally prefer to send the documents to their buyers only when payment has been made or when the bill has been accepted (accepter) by the drawee.

☞ See ACCEPTANCE, AFTER SIGHT; AT SIGHT; BILL OF LADING; CHEQUE; DISCOUNT; DRAFT BILLS; INSURANCE; SHIPPING DOCUMENTS.

BILL OF LADING, abbr. **B/L** (connaissement)

A shipping document (document de transport, d'expédition) supplied (fournir) by the shipowner (armateur) to the shipper or consigner (expéditeur) or exporter acknowledging formal receipt (accuser officiellement réception) of goods and giving the terms (conditions) under which the shipping company accepts to transport them. The document also mentions name of ship, ports of loading and discharge (embarquement et destination), name and address of consignee (destinataire), description of goods, i.e. weights and measurements, number of cases, markings (marquage) of cases and date. The B/L is usually made out (établir) in triplicate (trois exemplaires). One copy is kept by the captain of the vessel, another is given to the shipper and the third is forwarded (expédier) by mail to the importer or consignee. The consignee uses the B/L to prove his title to the goods (droit de propriété). The shipper or consigner may use the **B/L** as security (garantie) to discount (escompter) a bill of exchange (lettre de change) and as the evidence (preuve) of a shipping contract between him and the carrier (transporteur). A B/L is said to be **DIRTY, CLAUSED, FOUL** or **UNCLEAN** (sous réserve) when the shipowner therein (y) states (indiquer) that the condition of the goods on receipt (à la réception) was not satisfactory. A B/L is said to be **CLEAN** (sans réserve) when no such reservations (réserve) are made. If goods are transported by air, the document is called an **AIR CONSIGNMENT NOTE** or **AIRWAY BILL** (lettre de voiture aérienne).

☞ See BILL OF EXCHANGE; SHIPPING DOCUMENTS.

BILLS OF SIGHT See .... AFTRER SIGHT; AT SIGHT; BILL OF EXCHANGE.

BINDING (consolidation ou à caractère obligatoire)

A provision (disposition) in a trade agreement (accord commercial) that (selon laquelle) no tariff (tarif douanier) rate higher than the rate specified in the agreement will be imposed during the life (durée) of the agreement.

☞ See BOUND RATES; COMPENSATION; CONCESSION; TARIFF.

bk. See .... SETTLEMENT OF BARGAINS.

BLACK KNIGHT See .... TAKEOVER BID.

BLACK MONDAY (le krach du lundi 19 octobre 1987)

On this day world stock market prices (cours boursiers mondiaux) fell (s'effondrer) sharply, creating hugelosses for investors and businesses.

☞ See BLACK TUESDAY.

BLACK TUESDAY (le krach du mardi 29 octobre 1929)

This is the Wall Street (New York) stock market crash (krach ou effondrement des cours boursiers) which took place on 29th October, 1929 and unleashed (déclencher) in America and most countries in the world **THE GREAT DEPRESSION** (la grande crise économique de 1929), causing widespread unemployment, poverty and misery. When this happened the price of securities fell sharply and ruined many investors, at the same time creating a panic among these and other economic agents such as savers and banks.

☞ See BLACK MONDAY; DEPRESSION; RECESSION; TRADE CYCLE.

BLAIR HOUSE COMPROMISE See ....GENERAL AGREEMENT ON TARIFFS AND TRADE.

BLUE CHIPS (valeurs de père de famille/valeurs mobilières de premier ordre)

The shares or stock of major industrial quoted companies with first-class reputations.

☞ See BLUE CHIP COMPANY; SHARE; STOCK.

BLUE CHIP COMPANY (grande société industrielle coté de premier ordre)

A big company with a longstanding (établie de longue date) reputation for good earnings (bénéfices) and stable dividends payments (example: IBM).

Blue chip companies are considered as a very secure investment, with banks lending to them at the best possible rate of interest.

☞ See BLUE CHIPS; PUBLIC COMPANY.

BOARD OF DIRECTORS (conseil d'administration)

These are the men and women elected by the shareholders of a company as **DIRECTORS** (administrateur) to control its management and ensure it is efficiently and profitably run. Those who advise the board and possibly have jobs elsewhere, that is, part-time (à temps partiel) board members, are called **NON-EXECUTIVE DIRECTORS** (directeur administratif ou administrateur). The **CHAIRMAN**, U S **PRESIDENT** (président), heads (diriger) the board and sometimes combines this post with that of **MANAGING DIRECTOR**, abbr. **MD**, US **CHIEF EXECUTIVE** or **CHIEF EXECUTIVE OFFICER**, abbr. **CEO** (Président Directeur Général). This is the person who, with the **MANAGEMENT BOARD** (conseil de direction) runs (gérer) the company on a daily basis, implementing (mettre en oeuvre) the overall policy guidelines (lignes directrices) set out by the board of directors. The combined post is simply chairman and managing director or chief executive (Président Directeur Général). Members of the management board who are also members of the board of directors are known as **EXECUTIVE DIRECTORS** (directeur exécutif).

☞ See ANNUAL GENERAL MEETING; ARTICLES OF ASSOCIATION; ARTICLES OF MEMORANDUM under AUTHORIZED/REGISTERED ETC. CAPITAL; LIMITED or LIMITED LIABILITY COMPANY; SHARE.

BOND (obligation ou bon)

This is a general word to mean a security (valeur ou titre) issued (émis) by a government, local authority (collectivité publique) or business in exchange for a loan (emprunt) to be repaid (rembourser) usually (but not always) at a fixed rate of interest (à un taux d'intérêt fixe). Bonds are very similar to debentures and come in (se présentent sous) two forms: with a **BEARER BOND** (obligation au porteur) the bond and payments belong to whoever holds (détenir) the bond; with a **REGISTERED BOND** (obligation nominative) the bond and payments belong to whoever is registered with (enregistré ou déclaré auprès) the borrower (emprunteur) as being the owner. There are many types of bond, often duplicating debentures. The name of the bond will either indicate the issuer (émetteur) or the way in which interest and principal are to be paid. A **CORPORATE/CORPORATION BOND** (obligation ou effet émis par une société ou bon de caisse ou billet de trésorerie) is one issued by a company as opposed to a **MUNICIPAL/LOCAL AUTHORITY BOND** (obligation des collectivités locales/publiques) or a **GOVERNMENT BOND** (fonds d'Etat ou bon du Trésor). Bonds can have varying dates and terms of repayment (modalité de remboursement) attached to them. A **DEFERRED BOND** (obligation différée) pays a low rate of interest to start with (au début), until this reaches a normal level, when it becomes fixed. **EQUITY** and **PARTICIPATING/PROFIT-SHARING BONDS** (obligation participative) give a share (part) in company profits (bénéfices), but no rights to vote at company annual general meetings (assemblée générale annuelle). An **INDEXED BOND** (obligation indexée) has the interest and sometimes the capital repayment based on (fixé d'après) an index such as the Retail Price Index (indice des prix à la consommation ou de détail) in Britain. An **INTEREST BOND** (obligation émise en paiement des intérêts dus sur un prêt) is a bond offered by the borrower to replace the dividend which he is unable to pay; this form of dividend is known as a **BOND DIVIDEND** (dividende sous forme d'obligation). An **IRREDEEMABLE/ANNUITY BOND** (obligation perpétuelle ou de rente) pays the interest but does not repay the principal (e.g. Consols). A **ZERO COUPON BOND** (obligation à coupon zéro ou différé) pays no interest, but is sold at a huge discount (à perte). This means that when it matures (arriver à l'échéance) the borrower will have a heavy repayment to make.

☞ See ANNUAL GENERAL MEETING; CAPITAL MARKET; CONSOLS; CREDIT RATING AGENCY; DEBENTURE; DISCOUNT; EQUITY; EUROMARKET; GILT-EDGED STOCKS; JUNK BOND under LEVERAGED BUYOUT; MONEY MARKET; PREFERENCE SHARE; SHARE; TREASURY BILL; TREASURY BOND; WARRANT.

BOND DIVIDEND See .... BOND.

BONDED WAREHOUSE (entrepôt sous douane)

A place where imported goods have to be stored (stocker) until relevant (approprié) duties (droit) have been paid. While in a bonded warehouse commodities (marchandise) can however (toutefois) be processed (traiter, transformer) or packed (emballer). Although (bien que) storage charges (frais d'entrepôt/de stockage) have to be paid by the importer, there are compensating advantages. Immediate payment of duties would mean that more of the importer's capital would be tied up (immobiliser) in the goods until processing (traitement, transformation) and packing (emballage) had been completed (effectuer). The importer may even (même) sell the commodities and let the buyer pay for the duties. When imported dutiable (passible de droits) goods are to be re-exported, duties need not (ne pas avoir à) be paid provided (pourvu que) a bonded warehouse is used for storage.

☞ See EX QUAY.

BONDS See .... BOND; DEBENTURE; SHARE.

BONUS ISSUE See .... SCRIP/BONUS ETC. ISSUE.

BOOM (période de forte prospérité/expansion)

This is when aggregate demand (demande globale) in an economy sharply increases and business confidence is high. In this climate, therefore, production, prices and wages rise too, employment increases and the economy expands. This is the top end (le haut) of a trade cycle (cycle économique) and is usually followed by a recession as the economy overheats (surchauffer), inflation appears and measures are taken to reduce it by dampening (freiner) demand.

☞ See AGGREGATE DEMAND; DEPRESSION; INFLATION; RECESSION; TRADE CYCLE.

BORDER TAX ADJUSTMENTS (ajustements de la taxation aux frontières)

The remission (remise, dégrèvement) of indirect taxes on exported goods, including sales taxes (taxe à l'achat) and value added taxes (taxe à la valeur ajoutée) designed to ensure that (concevoir de façon à ce que) national tax systems (régime fiscal) do not impede (entraver) exports; and the imposition of domestic taxes on imported goods, to ensure that the latter (celles-ci) do not receive preferential treatment as compared with domestically produced (produire sur le marché intérieur) goods. Such adjustments are permitted under Articles I and XVI of GATT.

☞ See ARTICLES OF GATT; GATT; TAX; VALUE ADDED TAX.

BORROWING (emprunt)

This is having the use of the money of others for a period – short, medium or longterm (à court, moyen ou long terme) – on the condition that it will be repaid with interest. Borrowers (emprunteur) may be the government, which issues bills (bon du Trésor), local authorities (collectivités locales/publiques), banks which are short of (être à court de) reserves, companies, which can borrow from banks and other financial intermediaries or from the public by issuing debentures (obligations), other financial intermediaries and private individuals (les particuliers).

☞ See BANKING; BOND; BUILDING SOCIETY; CALL MONEY; CAPITAL MARKET; COMMERCIAL BANK; COMMERCIAL PAPER; COUPON; DEBENTURE; EUROCURRENCY MARKET; FINANCIAL INTERMEDIARIES; INTEREST; LENDING; LOAN; MERCHANT BANK; MONEY MARKET; PUBLIC SECTOR BORROWING REQUIREMENT.

BOUNCED/RUBBER/DUD/RETURNED/DISHONOURED CHEQUE (chèque en bois)

A cheque which has been returned to the payee (bénéficiaire) by his bank, as the bank of the person who signed the cheque has refused payment, usually because there is not enough money in the drawer's account.

☞ See CHEQUE; CURRENT ACCOUNT; DRAW/DRAFT, TO.

BOUND RATES (taux consolidés)

Tariff rates (tarif douanier) resulting from GATT negotiations that are incorporated in a country's schedule of concessions (liste de concession) and are thus (donc) enforceable (applicable) as an integral part of GATT. If a contracting party (partie contractante) raises (relever) a tariff to a higher level (niveau) than its bound rate, the major beneficiaries of the earlier (antérieur) binding have a right under (au titre de) GATT to receive compensation, usually in the form of reduced tariffs on other products they export to the country concerned. If the beneficiaries do not receive such compensation they may retaliate (exercer des représailles) by raising their own tariffs against an equivalent value (pour un montant équivalent) of the original country's exports.

☞ See BINDING; COMPENSATION; CONCESSION; CONTRACTING PARTY; GATT; RETALIATION; TARIFF.

BOURSE See .... STOCK MARKET.

BRETTON WOODS CONFERENCE (Conférence de Bretton Woods)

An internationnal meeting of central bank economists and other officials (responsable) which took place in Bretton Woods, New Hampshire, USA, in July 1944. The purpose (but) of the Conference was to discuss alternative proposals (contre-proposition) put forward (émettre) by British, Canadian and US financial experts relating to (avoir trait à) international payments problems, the economic reconstruction needs of Europe, the need to ensure stable exchange rates (taux de change) and free convertibility (convertibilité) of currencies (monnaie). The agreement resulting from this conference led to (conduire à) the establishment (création) of the International Monetary Fund and the International Bank for Reconstruction and Development.

☞ See CONVERTIBILITY; CURRENCY; EXCHANGE RATE; IBRD; IMF.

BROAD MONEY See .... MONEY SUPPLY.

BROKER See .... BROKER/DEALER.

BROKER/DEALER (négociant/courtier en titres)

A firm or individual who either acts solely as an agent (mandataire ou représentant) for clients in buying and selling shares on their behalf (pour leur compte), for which he will be paid a commission, called **BROKERAGE** (frais de courtage), or who combines this latter (cette dernière) function with buying and selling shares on his own account (pour son propre compte). In the former (premier) case he is acting in a single capacity (à un seul titre), and in the latter (second) in a dual capacity (à double titre). He may be considered as a retailer of shares (détaillant en titres), as opposed to the market maker (teneur de marché), who is a wholesaler (grossiste). In the UK, prior to the Big Bang in 1986, the dealer was only permitted to act in a single capacity and was called a **STOCKBROKER** or **BROKER** (agent de change ou courtier en bourse). Any investor wishing to buy or sell securities had to go through (passer par) a stockbroker and had to pay a minimum commission. Now both these restrictions have been abolished.

☞ See BIG BANG, THE; INTERNATIONAL STOCK EXCHANGE; MARKET MAKER.

BROKERAGE FIRM or **STOCKBROKING FIRM** or **STOCKBROKERS** (société de courtage/bourse)

A firm of brokers (agents de change/courtiers en bourse) and/or broker/dealers (négociants en titres ou négociants courtiers) which is a member of a stock exchange. The firm can either buy and sell shares on the instructions of its clients and receive a commission for this service, called **BROKERAGE** (frais de courtage), or it may, in addition, buy and sell shares on its own account (pour son propre compte). In the UK, since the Big Bang in 1986, stockbroking firms have also been allowed to become market makers (teneur de marché) if they so choose to do.

☞ See BIG BANG, THE; INTERNATIONAL STOCK EXCHANGE; MARKET MAKER.

BROKERAGE See ....BROKER/DEALER.

BUFFER STOCKS (stocks régulateurs)

Inventories (stock) or stockpiles (réserve) managed (gérer) so as to moderate price fluctuations. Goods (marchandise) are bought for the stockpile when price floor (plancher) levels (niveau) are reached and sold from the stockpile when price ceiling (plafond) levels are reached. Such goods as rubber, tin (étain) and cocoa (cacao) benefit from buffer stocks through International Commodity Agreements.

☞ See INTEGRATED PROGRAM FOR COMMODITIES; INTERNATIONAL COMMODITY AGREEMENT.

BUILDING SOCIETY (société/caisse mutuelle/d'épargne de financement immobilier/de crédit immobilier/de crédit à la construction et au logement à but non lucratif)

In the UK this is a non-profit making organization, whose purpose is to aid its members, the depositors (déposants), to purchase their own homes. It does this by lending the money received by them to other members at a higher rate of interest than it pays for the deposits. The loan, called a **MORTGAGE** (hypothèque), is secured (garanti) on the property being bought. Since the Building Society's Act, 1986, part of financial de-regulation (déréglementation ou libéralisation), building societies have been allowed to extend their activities to provide banking, insurance and investment services and so compete with commercial banks. Some large building societies like the Woolwich have gone public (s'introduire en bourse) to attract more funds and to compete more effectively in the money-lending market. Building societies are the British equivalent of American savings and loan associations.

☞ See BANKING; COMMERCIAL BANK; DE-REGULATION; FINANCIAL SERVICES ACT, 1986; LOAN; PUBLIC, TO GO; SAVINGS AND LOAN ASSOCIATION.

BULL (haussier)

This is a speculator who optimistically buys securities in the belief that prices will rise, when he will immediately sell them. Thus he buys these not to keep but to hold only long enough to make a profit. Because, for example, on the London Stock Exchange the settlement day (jour de règlement) allows for a maximum of fourteen days before payment has to be made, the bull hopes to sell these securities before, without having yet paid for them, thus merely pocketing (empocher) the profit. Buying securities without ever expecting to pay for them, or selling them without having paid for them is known respectively as **BUYING** or **SELLING IN/FOR THE ACCOUNT** (achat ou vente à terme). The word **"BULLISH"** (orienté à la hausse/en hausse) is often used to describe a stock market which expects a rise in prices, while a **BULL MARKET** (marché en hausse) refers to a market in which prices are rising.

☞ See BEAR; CONTANGO; FORWARD CURRENT; HAMMERING; SETTLING DAY; SPOT/CURRENT PRICE; STAG.

BULL MARKET See .... BULL.

BULLISH See .... BULL.

BUY-BACK ARRANGEMENTS See .... COUNTERTRADE.

BUYING FOR THE ACCOUNT See .... BULL.

BUYING FORWARD See .... FORWARD CONTRACT.

BUYING IN/FOR THE ACCOUNT See .... BULL.

BUYING PRICE See .... BID/BUYING PRICE.

C

C and F See .... COST and FREIGHT.

CAC 40 See .... SHARE INDEX.

CAIRNS GROUP (Groupe de Cairns)

Named after (tirer son nom de) the Australian town of the state of Queensland in which it was created in 1986, the Cairns Group is led by Australia and claims to be (se vouloir) the mouthpiece (porte-parole) of 14 agricultural exporting countries confronted with (face à) the US and the European Union giants. The members of the group are: Argentina, Australia, Brazil, Canada, Chile, Columbia, Fiji, Hungary, Indonesia, Malaysia, New Zealand, the Philippines, Thailand and Uruguay.

CALL MONEY or **MONEY AT/ON CALL/AT SHORT NOTICE** (argent à court terme/au jour le jour)

Money lent which is repayable on demand (payable sur demande) or can be demanded at very short notice (dans un délai très court), such as an overdraft (découvert ou facilités de caisse), a bank loan or bank loans to other financial institutions. It can often also mean money lent on a very short term basis such as day to day (au jour le jour), and such lendings are usually secured (gagé ou contre effets). In the USA the term refers to money specifically lent to stockbrokers (agent de change), who use the securities they hold as collateral (nantissement) for borrowing funds (argent au jour le jour prêté aux agents de change).

☞ See LOAN; OVERDRAFT; SECURITY;

CALL OPTION See .... OPTION.

CALLED-UP CAPITAL See .... AUTHORIZED/REGISTERED ETC. CAPITAL.

CAPITAL (capital)

This is accumulated wealth (la richesse accumulée), which can be in the form of money, buildings (bâtiments) and other assets (actif), which enables the production of further (additionnel) wealth. Capital is in economic theory considered as one of the three factors of production, the other two being land and labour. Thus shareholders provide the capital to start a company.

☞ See AUTHORIZED/REGISTERED ETC. CAPITAL; VENTURE CAPITAL.

CAPITAL ACCOUNT BALANCE See .... BALANCE OF PAYMENTS.

CAPITAL GAIN See .... ORDINARY/COMMON SHARES; YIELD.

CAPITAL GAINS TAX See .... TAX.

CAPITAL MARK

This is a market where funds are lent (prêté) and borrowed (emprunté) for longer terms, especially by industry and commerce for investment and expansion, as opposed to a money market, which is for short-term borrowing (emprunt à court terme). The capital market is served by major financial intermediaries such as the stock exchange, banks, insurance companies and others. The distinction between these two markets, however, in practice is not always clear.

☞ See BOND; BORROWING; COMMERCIAL BANK;COMMERCIAL PAPER; DEBENTURE; EUROCURRENCY MARKET; INTERNATIONAL STOCK EXCHANGE; LENDING; LOAN; MONEY MARKET; SHARE.

CAPITAL TRANSFER TAX (abbr. CCT) See .... TAX.

CAPITALIZATION ISSUE See .... SCRIP/BONUS etc.

CARGO INSURANCE POLICY See .... MARINE INSURANCE.

CARTEL (cartel)

A contractual association of independent business organizations (entreprises ou groupes d'entreprises) located (situer) in one or more countries formed (constituer) for the purpose (but) of regulating the purchasing (achat), production or marketing (commercialisation) of goods (marchandise) by the members. Such activities tend to (avoir tendance) restrict (restreindre) markets and fix distribution and prices. Concerning EC competition policy, Article 85 of the Treaty of Rome declares illegal deals (entente) between companies to fix prices, share out (se partager) markets and limit production. Article 86 of the same treaty outlaws (mettre hors la loi, déclarer illégal) abuses of dominant position by firms or groups of firms.

CASE LAW (jurisprudence)

The codes of conduct (code de conduite) negotiated during GATT Rounds evolve (évoluer) according to (selon) decisions concerning specific cases (cas d'espèce) resulting from allegations (accusation) of violation of GATT rules brought before (soumettre à) the committees (commission) in charge of monitoring (surveiller) the codes. The decisions thus (ainsi) made (prendre) serve as precedents in the resolution of future cases. Case law is also a general legal term for the process (processus) whereby (par lequel) decisions taken by a court (tribunal) are based on past decisions made (prendre) by judges in similar or related cases (affaire). **CASE LAW** in particular forms part of the English legal system.

☞ See CODES OF CONDUCT; DISPUTE SETTLEMENT; GATT.

CASH ISSUE See .... RIGHTS ISSUE.

CASH ON- DELIVERY, abbr. **C. O. D** (paiement contre remboursement)

A trade term meaning that goods must be paid immediately on receipt (dès réception). The phrase (expression) **SPOT CASH** may be used as a synonym.

☞ See INCOTERMS.

CASH DISPENSER See .... CHEQUE.

CASH MACHINE See .... CHEQUE.

CASH POINT MACHINE See .... CHEQUE.

CASH RATIO See .... LIQUIDITY RATIO.

CASH TRANSACTION See .... SPOT/CURRENT PRICE.

CASH WITH ORDER, abbr. **C. W. O** (paiement à la commande)

A trade term meaning that goods must be pre-paid (payer à l'avance). Used especially with items (articles) ordered (commander) by mail (par correspondance).

☞ See INCOTERMS.

CASUALTY/PROPERTY INSURANCE See .... INSURANCE.

CCT (Capital Transfer Tax) See .... TAX.

CD See .... CERTIFICATE OF DEPOSIT.

CENTRAL BANK (banque centrale)

A key part of the monetary system in developed and other countries. Functions vary from country to country, but can include the following:

a. acting as banker to the government by accepting deposits (dépôts) of revenue from taxes, etc. and raising money to finance public indebtedness (where government expenditure is greater than income) through issuing (émettre) various securities;

b. acting as lender of last resort (prêteur en dernier recours/ressort) and banker to the commercial banks and money market; this is a very important function as the holding of government securities by banks and other institutions is very large, and the central discount (escompte) and lending rates (taux) affect other rates of interest: if they go up they increase the cost of borrowing to the banks etc., so the latter increase their interest rates to borrowers, thus making credit more expensive, decreasing money supply (masse monétaire) and reducing aggregate demand (demande globale) and so (ainsi) inflation in the economy; if central bank rates come down banks etc. can lower their rates of interest, thus making credit more freely available (disponible), increasing the money supply and giving a boost (coup de fouet) to the economy;

c. supervising the national banking system (i.e. making sure banks and other financial institutions comply with (obéir) regulations and are not in danger of bankruptcy);
d. issuing (émettre) the national currency;
e. defining interest and discount rates (taux d'intérêt et d'escompte), – see b. above – , liquidity ratios (ratio de liquidité), special deposits and reserve assets (réserves obligatoires)and giving special instructions to banks such as to limit lending for certain purposes;
f. carrying out (effectuer) open market operations (opérations d'open market sur le marché monétaire); and
g. buying and selling national and foreign currencies in order to defend the value of the national currency or pay off national debts (e.g. as with the balance of payments).
Functions b., c., e. and f. are especially associated with monetary policy (politique gouvernementale monétaire). The central banks of the USA, the UK and France, for example, are respectively the Federal Reserve System, the Bank of England and the Banque de France.

☞ See AGGREGATE DEMAND; BANKING; COMMERCIAL BANK; DISCOUNT; FEDERAL RESERVE SYSTEM; INFLATION; LENDER OF LAST RESORT; LIQUIDITY RATIO; MONETARY POLICY; MONEY MARKET; MONEY SUPPLY; MERCHANT BANK; OPEN MARKET OPERATIONS; RESERVE ASSETS; SPECIAL DEPOSITS.

CEO (CHIEF EXECUTIVE OFFICER) See .... BOARD OF DIRECTORS.

CERTIFICATE OF DEPOSIT, abbr. **CD** (certificat de dépôt)

A certificate issued (émettre) by a bank or other financial institution in exchange for a sum of money (usually large) deposited for a fixed time. At the end of the time the bank repays the deposit plus interest. If the depositor (déposant) should want his money back before the time agreed he can sell his certificate to someone else, who will later collect the full sum plus the interest. Both the depositor and the bank benefit from CDs, the former (le premier) by their flexibility (souplesse d'emploi) and earning power (capacité bénéficiaire/rentabilité), the latter (le second) by being guaranteed the use of the deposit for a given period. CDs are negotiable instruments (effet/intstrument négociable) on money markets.

☞ See FINANCIAL INSTRUMENTS; MONEY MARKET; MONEY MARKET INSTRUMENTS; NEGOTIABLE INSTRUMENT.

CERTIFICATE OF ORIGIN, abbr. **C/O** (certificat d'origine)

A document that may be used to replace the consular invoice (facture consulaire). It states (indiquer) the name of the country in which goods mentioned in the export invoice (facture à l'exportation) have been made (fabriquer). It is signed by the exporter and is necessary where preferential tariffs (tarif préférentiel) have been granted (accorder) to the exporting country by the country of destination.

☞ See CONSULAR INVOICE; DOCUMENTATION; EXPORT INVOICE; TARIF.

CHAIRMAN OF THE BOARD OF DIRECTORS See .... BOARD OF DIRECTORS.

CHAPTER 11 See .... LIQUIDATION.

CHARGE CARD See .... CREDIT CARD.

CHECK See .... CHEQUE.

CHECKING ACCOUNT See .... CURRENT ACCOUNT.

CHEQUE BOOK See .... CHEQUE.

CHEQUE GUARANTEE CARD See .... CHEQUE ETC. CARD.

CHEQUE, US **CHECK** (chèque)

This is an order to a bank or other financial institution – the **DRAWEE** (tiré) – in writing by its customer – the **DRAWER** (tireur) – to pay a certain sum to another person or organization – the **PAYEE** (bénéficiaire) – or to the bearer (porteur). In other words, it is a form of bill of exchange (lettre de change). Customers are normally given a **CHEQUE BOOK** (chéquier) containing 25 or more blank (en blanc) cheques. Cheques have come to represent a major way of making payments, instead of using physical money (espèces), but in their turn have seen their role diminished by the advent (avènement) of credit cards and **ELECTRONIC FUNDS TRANSFER**, abbr. **EFT** (transfert électronique de fonds, système de virements informatisés), with which it is possible to transfer money directly from one account (compte) to another. Some large supermarkets and shops have already used the latter (ce dernier) to install (instaurer) a system which enables customers to pay for their purchases (achats) before leaving the shop directly from their current account (compte courant), thus (ainsi) dispensing with (se passer de) the need for cheques and also money. This system is known as **ELECTRONIC FUNDS TRANSFER AT POINT OF SALE** (transfert électronique de fonds ou système de virements informatisés au point de vente), abbr. **EFTPOS**. A very big factor in the reduction of use of cheques has been, of course, the widespread installation and use of **CASH DISPENSERS** (distributeur ou guichet automatique de billets/DAB/GAB), also known as **CASH MACHINES** or **AUTOMATIC/AUTOMATED TELLER MACHINES**, abbr. **ATM**. These enable people to draw out cash 24 hours a day all week, make transfers (virement) and carry out other transactions without putting a foot in the bank.

☞ See BILL OF EXCHANGE; BUILDING SOCIETY; COMMERCIAL BANK; CREDIT CARD; DE-REGULATION; SAVINGS AND LOAN ASSOCIATION; SAVINGS BANK.

CHEQUE/CHEQUE GUARANTEE/BANK/ BANKER'S CARD (carte de garantie d'identité bancaire)

A plastic card issued by British banks to their customers guaranteeing the payment of any cheque signed by the latter (celui-ci) up to at present £50. This means anyone accepting a cheque from a customer presenting this card knows the cheque will not be dishonoured (impayé/refusé/en bois).

☞ See CHEQUE; BOUNCED ETC. CHEQUE.

CHIEF EXECUTIVE See .... BOARD OF DIRECTORS.

CHINESE WALLS See .... CONFLICT OF INTERESTS.

CIF See .... COST, INSURANCE AND FREIGHT.

CIF and C and I See .... CIF.

CIF and C See .... CIF.

CIF and E See .... CIF.

CLAIM See .... INSURANCE.

CLASSICAL UNEMPLOYMENT See .... UNEMPLOYMENT.

CLAUSED BILL OF LADING See .... BILL OF LADING.

CLEAN BILL OF EXCHANGE See .... BILL OF EXCHANGE.

CLEARING AGREEMENT See .... COUNTERTRADE.

CLEARING BANK See .... COMMERCIAL BANK.

CLOSED-END COMPANY See .... INVESTMENT (TRUST) COMPANY.

CLOSED-END FUND See .... INVESTMENT (TRUST) COMPANY.

CLOSED-END INVESTMENT COMPANY See .... INVESTMENT (TRUST) COMPANY.

CLOSING PRICE (cours de/en clôture/ou dernier cours)

This is the last price quoted for a security on a stock exchange towards the end of a given working day (jour ouvrable).

☞ See BARGAIN; FORWARD CONTRACT; SETTLEMENT OF BARGAINS; SPOT/CURRENT PRICE.

COD See .... CASH ON DELIVERY.

CODES OF CONDUCT (codes de conduite)

International instruments (acte, instrument juridique) indicating (spécifier) standards (norme) of behaviour (comportement) thought (juger) desirable by the international community in the attitude of nations and multi-national corporations (société multinationale). Several codes of conduct were negotiated during the Tokyo Round of the GATT with a view to (dans le but de) liberalizing and harmonizing domestic measures (mesure intérieure) that might impede (entraver) trade. They are considered legally binding (soumis à obligation juridique) for the countries that choose to (choisir, décider) adhere to them. Each of these codes is monitored by (placer sous la surveillance de) a special committee which meets under the auspices of GATT and fosters (encourager) consultations and the settlement (règlement) of disputes (différend) arising (survenir) under the code. Countries that are not contracting parties to GATT may adhere to these codes. GATT Articles III through to (à) XXIII also contain commercial policy (politique commerciale) provisions (disposition) known as GATT's code of good conduct. The United Nations (Nations Unies) have also encouraged the negotiation of several "voluntary" codes of conduct, i.e. not legally binding. One of them attempts to specify the rights (droit) and obligations (devoir) of transnational corporations.

☞ See ANTI-DUMPING CODE; ARTICLES OF GATT; CASE LAW; CONTRACTING PARTY; COUNTERVAILING DUTIES; CUSTOMS VALUATION CODE; DISPUTE SETTLEMENT; EXPORT SUBSIDIES; GATT; GOVERNMENT PROCUREMENT POLICIES AND PRACTICES; LIBERALIZATION; LICENSING CODE; MULTINATIONAL CORPORATION; MULTILATERAL AGREEMENT; NON-TARIFF BARRIERS; OFFER LIST; RESTRICTIVE BUSINESS PRACTICES; SAFEGUARDS; STANDARDS; TRANSPARENCY.

COLLATERAL See ....SECURITY.

COMMERCIAL BANK (banque commerciale), sometimes referred to as a **RETAIL** (banque de détail), **DEPOSIT** or **JOINT-STOCK BANK** (banque de dépots)

A bank in the UK which has a network (réseau) of branches (agences) throughout the country and which provides banking services to industry and commerce, institutions, organizations (organismes) and the general public. This type of bank is referred to as a retail bank because it deals with individual customers (persons or organizations) and relatively small sums of money, in contrast with a merchant bank, which deals in very large quantities of money, that is to say, in wholesale financial transactions. In western Europe this type of bank is often referred to as a **CREDIT BANK**, and in the USA as a **MEMBER BANK**. The services offered by commercial banks include accepting customers' money and placing it in a current account, savings account or deposit account, the payment and collection of customers' cheques, standing orders (prélèvement automatique), a credit card facility, personal loans, overdrafts (découvert)and short-term, medium and longterm loans, moving money (transfers de fonds), foreign currency transactions, documentary credit (bills of exchange and letters of credit) and other such services as insurance and investment (buying and selling securities). In the UK commercial banks are sometimes known as **CLEARING BANKS** because of belonging to the London Bankers' Clearing House (chambre de compensation), where cheques from each member bank are exchanged and balances (soldes) settled (although not all British banks are members). **CLEARING HOUSE** (chambre de compensation) is the term used to describe the institution which sorts out the cheques (trier) drawn (tiré) on the different banks and settles the payments between them. The main UK commercial banks are National Westminster, Barclay's, Lloyds and Midland, known as "the big four". All have branches overseas (à l'étranger). Since financial de-regulation (déreglementation ou libéralisation) in the mid-1980s British banks have now offered investment and insurance services, as well as house purchase loans (mortgages), and for the first time face competition from building societies (caisse/société de crédit immobilier). The latter were formerly limited to financing house purchases, but now are also able to offer a wide range of banking services.

☞ See BANKING;BUILDING SOCIETY; CHEQUE; CREDIT CARD; CURRENT ACCOUNT; DE-REGULATION; DEPOSIT ACCOUNT; DOCUMENTARY CREDIT; LENDER OF LAST RESORT; LIQUIDITY RATIO; LOAN; MERCHANT BANK; OVERDRAFT; PERSONAL LOAN; RESERVE ASSETS; RUN ON A BANK; SAVINGS ACCOUNT; SAVINGS BANK; SPECIAL DEPOSITS; STANDING ORDER.

COMMERCIAL PAPER (papier commercial/financier ou bons de caisse à court terme ou billets de trésorerie ou effets de commerce)

Short-term debts (emprunts à court terme) or borrowing instruments (instruments d'emprunt) used by companies to raise capital (trouver des capitaux) or make payments, such as debentures (obligation), bills of exchange (lettre de change ou traite ou effet de commerce) and promissory notes (billet à ordre). In the USA such debt, usually payable in 4-12 months, is called **PRIME COMMERCIAL PAPER** (papier commercial américain de premier ordre), and is sold to the public.

☞ See BILL OF EXCHANGE; BOND; DEBENTURE; FINANCIAL INSTRUMENTS; PROMISSORY NOTE.

COMMISSION (commission)

A fee (honoraire) paid in return for a service. This may be fixed or negotiable. Insurance agents receive a commission from their company on every insurance policy (police d'assurance) they sell. Stockbrokers (agent de change) or broker/dealers (négociant en titres) receive a commission for every securities transaction they arrange for their clients.

☞ See BROKER/DEALER.

COMMODITY (marchandise)

Any substance or article which is considered as useful or necessary for consumption or production, especially raw materials (matières premières), minerals or basic foodstuffs (denrées alimentaires) such as cotton, wool, fur, grain, coffee, tea, fruit, copper, gold and silver. Such commodities are traded on **COMMODITY MARKETS** (bourse des marchandises) or **COMMODITY EXCHANGES** and can be bought and sold anywhere in the world at any time (i.e. for immediate or future delivery) by means of contracts without the necessity of trading from the actual warehouse (dépôt ou entrepôt). The main world commodity markets (or exchanges) are in Chicago, London, New York, Amsterdam, Sydney and Singapore.

☞ See FORWARD CONTRACT; SPOT/CURRENT PRICE.

COMMODITY EXCHANGES See .... COMMODITY.

COMMODITY MARKETS See .... COMMODITY.

COMMON AGRICULTURAL POLICY, abbr. **CAP** (Politique agricole commune/PAC)

The system of agricultural support (soutien) set out (mettre en place) in Article 39 of the Treaty of Rome. It has five main aims (objectif):

a. to raise (augmenter) farm productivity;

b. to guarantee a fair standard of living (niveau de vie) to farmers;

c. to stabilize markets;

d. to ensure regular supplies (approvisionnement);

e. to maintain reasonable consumer prices (prix à la consommation).

It works according to (selon) three principles:

1. a single (unique) market for farm produce which can move (circuler) freely and be traded (échanger) at common prices throughout (à travers) the Union;

2. Community preference (préférence communautaire) involving (comporter) common tariff barriers (barrière douanière) applied to (appliquer à) imports from non-member countries. This common tariff barrier is known as a **COMMON EXTERNAL TARIFF**;

3. common financial liability (responsabilité), each member contributing to a common fund from which expenses are paid. This common fund is the **EUROPEAN AGRICULTURAL GUIDANCE AND GUARANTEE FUND**, abbr. **EAGGF** (Fonds Européen d'Orientation et de Garantie Agricole/FEOGA). The guidance section finances the modernization and improvement (amélioration) of agriculture in a wide range (gamme) of sectors. But by far (de loin) the more costly side of the EAGGF is the guarantee section because its aim (but) is to support (soutenir) prices so as to maintain farmers' income (revenu).

In order to achieve (atteindre) this aim, four different measures are used:

1. support/intervention prices (prix de soutien/d'intervention) which cover 70% or so (environ) of farm output (production), e.g. wheat (blé), maize (maïs), sugar, beef, mutton and lamb, with a guarantee of price and sale (vente). Support prices work as follows: target prices (prix de référence, cible) – prices that will be fair to producers – are fixed by the EU Commission. Intervention prices are set (fixer) slightly (légèrement) below (au-dessous) target prices. If market prices (prix du marché) fall below intervention prices, then the EU intervention boards (commission) buy the products and store (stocker) them for sale at a later date (à une date ultérieure) when market prices have picked up (remonter). This support policy also involves (comprendre) other possibilities such as storage (stockage) aids and subsidies (subvention) to producer organizations for them to buy back surpluses (excédent);

2. import levies (taxe à l'importation) covering about 21% of EU farm produce, such as quality wines, eggs and poultry (volaille), in order to raise import prices to EU price levels (niveau);

3. direct subsidies and export subsidies or restitutions (restitutions) meant to (destiner à) bridge (combler) the gap (différence) between world market prices and guaranteed prices. This concerns for example oilseeds (oléagineux);

4. flat rate (forfaitaire) aid covering less than 1% of EU farm output, such as cotton seed, flax (lin) and hemp (chanvre), granted (accorder) in proportion (au prorata de) the size of land planted and quantities produced.

Due to the enormous costs – financed by taxpayers' money (argent du contribuable) – these policies have generated (engendrer) and to the distortions – dumping, unfair competition, infringement (violation) of GATT rules – they have caused on world markets, limitations on production had to be introduced in the past, such as guarantee thresholds (seuil) – production levels beyond which (au-delà desquels) the intervention system stops operating –, co-responsibility levies (taxe de coresponsabilité) – a tax system penalizing production in excess of authorized amounts –, income aids in favour of the most needy (nécessiteux) farmers, letting large areas of comparatively (relativement) unproductive land lie fallow (laisser en friche) – be "set aside" –, using less fertilizers (engrais) and attempts to match (adapter) agricultural output more closely with actual (réel) demand, thus avoiding (éviter) the accumulation of food mountains.

In view of (dans la perspective de) GATT's latest Round of talks (pourparlers) – the Uruguay Round – the European Commission had proposed a 30% reduction over ten years of subsidies supporting agriculture in the EU as compared with their 1986 levels. However this proposal was severely criticised by the Ministers for Agriculture of the 12 who argued that (faire valoir que) it would mean a 3% annual decrease in farmers' income until 1995. The farm organizations said they would prefer the continuation of the high-price regime combined with supply management (gestion de l'offre) – to restrict the amount which would be produced at these high prices – and tighter (serré) import controls.

On May 21st, 1992, the Union's farm ministers eventually reached an agreement on a reform of the CAP. The centerpiece of the reform was the target price for cereals, the most widely traded farm commodity. This price was to fall by 29% over the next three years. A narrower gap (écart) between the EU target price and prices on world markets meant that export subsidies would fall too. This satisfied one of the demands made by the USA in their dispute with the EU over farm trade, a quarrel that had brought talks on the Uruguay Round to a stop. The deal (accord) on cereals entailed (entraîner) price cuts for other products. It diminished the cost of feed grains (aliments à base de céréales) for beef and dairy farmers (éleveurs de bovins et producteurs laitiers), with a consequence on the price of oil-seeds (oléagineux). In order to discourage beef production even more, the EU decided to cut its purchases of beef. Moreover, support prices for beef and butter were decreased by 15% and 7.5% respectively.

However, a new type of subsidy was introduced to compensate farmers for the price cuts, which means no savings on the EU farm budget. This new subsidy, involving direct payments to cereal farmers, is being paid on condition that farmers take at least 15% of their land out of production. These payments however distort markets less than a system which relies (reposer) on prices entirely. Although domestic support and export subsidies were cut sufficiently to meet the USA's wishes, production was not curbed (diminuer) by enough to satisfy US demands over the volume of exports on each product. Moreover, the compensation payments might infringe (enfreindre) GATT rules. This reform failed to reduce EU cereals production sufficiently and surpluses might soon start accumulating again. The original plan proposed by Ray MacSharry, the EU commissioner for agriculture, was much more vigorous. It intended to pay big farmers much less than small ones while the price for cereals was to be much lower. The British, opposed as they have always been to the size of the EU farm budget and matching (correspondant) cost to UK and EU taxpayers, objected to the first proposal on account of the much lower number of small farmers in Great Britain. EU farmers at large were obviously against the drastic severity of the second. Short of target as the plan eventually adopted may have been (bien que le plan ait été loin d'atteindre son but) concerning EU expenses and world market distortions, the announcement of this reform raised farmers' unrest (agitation) and discontent in many countries of the EU. The EU farmers felt they had been sacrificed on the altar (autel) of the GATT in the negotiations between the EU and the USA. However, further (d'autres) concessions were made afterwards (par la suite) in the field of EU agriculture to satisfy the USA, as can be seen in the GATT entry (article) of this book.

☞ See BUFFER STOCKS; CAIRNS GROUP; COMMON EXTERNAL TARIFF; EU; EUROPEAN COMMISSION; GATT; TREATY OF ROME.

COMMON EXTERNAL TARIFF, abbr. **CET** (Tarif extérieur commun/TEC).

An import duty (droit), levy (taxe) or tariff (tarif douanier) uniformly applied (appliquer) by a customs union (union douanière), such as the EU, to goods (marchandise) imported from outside the union.

☞ See CUSTOMS DUTY; CUSTOMS UNION; EU.

COMMON FUND See .... INTEGRATED PROGRAM FOR COMMODITIES.

COMMON MARKET See .... CUSTOMS UNION; EUROPEAN COAL AND STEEL COMMUNITY; EUROPEAN COMMUNITY.

COMMON SHARES See .... ORDINARY/COMMON SHARES.

COMPARATIVE ADVANTAGE (avantage comparatif)

An international trade theory according to which (selon laquelle) a country or group of countries should (devoir) specialize (se spécialiser) in the production and export of goods and services which it can (pouvoir) produce comparatively more efficiently than others, rather than (plutôt que) seek to (chercher à) produce everything itself. This theory was first developed by the English economist David Ricardo in 1817 in his famous book *Principles of Political Economy and Taxation*, as a basis for raising (éléver) the economic welfare (bien-être) of a nation by means of (au moyen de) international trade.

☞ See STRUCTURAL CHANGE; WELFARE.

COMPENSATION (compensation)
The essential GATT principle through which (selon lequel) any country which increases (augmenter) a tariff (tarif douanier) above its bound rate (taux consolidé) or disrupts (perturber) a trade concession in some way or other, must lower (abaisser) other tariffs or make other concessions to offset (compenser) the disadvantage.

☞ See BINDING; BOUND RATES; CONCESSION; GATT.

COMPENSATORY FINANCE or **FINANCING** (financement compensatoire)
A loan (prêt) granted (accorder) to a country when its exports earnings (recettes à l'exportation) fall below (au-dessous de) a designated (prévoir) level (niveau), and intended (destiner à) to stabilize the country's export receipts (revenu, recettes à l'exportation). Such financial compensation arrangements (accord, système) exist under the International Monetary Fund and the Lomé Convention.

☞ See IMF; LOME CONVENTION.

COMPENSION ARRANGEMENTS See .... COUNTERTRADE.

COMPREHENSIVE MOTOR CAR INSURANCE See .... ACCIDENT INSURANCE.

COMPREHENSIVE POLICY See .... ACCIDENT INSURANCE.

COMPULSORY WINDING UP See .... LIQUIDATION.

CONCERT PARTY See .... TAKEOVER BID.

CONCESSION (concession)
The grant (octroi) of a position (position), privilege, or right (droit) by a negotiator to induce (amener) the other party to yield (accorder, céder) an equivalent position, privilege or right. In GATT trade negotiations, a country normally makes concessions in the forms of reductions of bindings (consolidation) in its tariff and non-tariff import barriers – sometimes called **NEGOTIATING "COIN"** (pion de négociation) – in exchange for reductions in the barriers of other countries to its exports. A country's "schedule of concessions" (liste de concessions), accepted as part of its obligations to other contracting parties (partie contractante), becomes an

integral part (partie intégrante) of GATT under (selon) Article II of the General Agreement.

☞ See BINDING; BOUND RATES; COMPENSATION; CONTRACTING PARTY; ESCAPE CLAUSE; GATT; MOST-FAVOURED-NATION TREATMENT; OFFER LIST; PRINCIPAL SUPPLIER; RECIPROCITY; SAFEGUARDS; TARIFF.

CONFERENCES OF EU HEADS OF STATE AND GOVERNMENT See .... EUROPEAN COUNCIL.

CONFIRMING HOUSE See..EXPORT HOUSE.

CONFLICT OF INTERESTS (conflit d'intérêts)

This is a situation where a financial institution is in a position itself to benefit from the advice it gives clients, and this could be to the disadvantage of the latter (ceux derniers). For example, a securities house (maison de titres) holds a large quantity of shares which it needs to sell and at the same time it advises its client to buy these same shares; or it acts for both parties in a transaction, profiting from this inside knowledge (information priviligiée). The problem of conflict of interests is a difficult one, especially for broker/dealers (négociant en titres) in the UK who have opted (choisis) to operate in a dual capacity (à double titre) – that is, not only obtain securities for their clients but also deal in them on their own account (pour leur propre compte). In financial institutions in order to minimize conflicts of interest, which could be harmful (préjudiciable) or disadvantageous to the interests of clients, communications barriers are set up (créé) between different sections or members of the firm to prevent the leakage (fuite) of price-sensitive information (toute information nouvelle de nature à modifier le cours des titres). These barriers have been referred to as **CHINESE WALLS** (murs chinois).

☞ See BIG BANG; FINANCIAL INSTITUTIONS; INSIDER TRADING; INTERNATIONAL STOCK EXCHANGE.

CONSEQUENTIAL LOSS See.. FIRE INSURANCE.

CONSIGNMENT INVOICE See.. IMPORT AGENT.

CONSIGNMENT NOTE See ....BILL OF LADING.

CONSOLIDATED STOCK See.. GILT-EDGED STOCKS.

CONSOLS See.. GILT-EDGED STOCKS.

CONSTRUCTIVE TOTAL LOSS See .... MARINE INSURANCE.

CONSULAR FORMALITIES AND DOCUMENTATION (formalités et documentation consulaires)

Certain documents or procedures required (exiger) by some countries before their customs authorities (autorités douanières) will allow (permettre, laisser) commodities (marchandise) produced in other countries to enter their markets, such as special invoices (facture) approved by a consul or other official (représentant officiel) of the importing country.

These procedures may impede (entraver) trade, particularly when fees (redevance) are charged (percevoir) for these authorisations. The number of countries resorting to (avoir recours à) consular formalities has declined in recent years and most countries that still (encore) apply (applique) them are developing countries (pays en voie de développement).

☞ See CONSULAR INVOICE; NON-TARIFF BARRIERS; TOKYO ROUND.

CONSULAR INVOICE (facture consulaire)

A document required (exiger) by some importing countries as a proof (preuve) of the true value of the goods (marchandise) traded (échanger). It is used to calculate correct import duties (droit) and has to be signed by the consul of the country of destination.

☞ See CONSULAR FORMALITIES AND DOCUMENTATION.

CONSULTATIONS (consultations)

Formal (officiel) discussions between two or more parties to an agreement, particularly with respect to (surtout en ce qui concerne) their rights (droit) under (dans le cadre de) the agreement. GATT Article XXII makes it an obligation for a contracting party (partie contractante) to consult on any GATT related (se rapporter à) matter (question) whenever any other contracting party requests it to do so. GATT Article XXIII provides (prévoir) that any country that believes (estimer) its trade interests (intérêt commercial) have been adversely affected (subir un préjudice), nullified (annuler) or impaired (compromettre) by changes in the trade regime of another country or by another country's failure to carry out its GATT obligations (manquement à ses obligations dans le cadre du GATT), may request bilateral consultations with the concerned party. If such consultations do not yield (donner, produire) results satisfactory to the concerned parties, the complaining (plaignant) country may ask for the establishment (création) of a special panel (comité) under the aegis (égide, auspices) of GATT to review (examiner) the facts and recommend compensation or any other appropriate action. A GATT contracting party is also expected (être dans l'obligation de) to hold consultations with other interested contracting parties to discuss (s'entretenir de) any trade restrictive measures it imposes for balance of payments reasons.

☞ See BALANCE OF PAYMENTS; BALANCE OF PAYMENTS CONSULTATIONS; COMPENSATION; CONTRACTING PARTY; DISPUTE SETTLEMENT; GATT; PANEL OF EXPERTS.

CONSUMER PRICE INDEX See .... INFLATION.

CONSUMPTION TAX See .... EXCISE TAX.

CONTANGO See .... SETTLEMENT OF BARGAINS.

CONTRA See .... COUNTERTRADE.

CONTRACT NOTE See .... SAEF.

CONTRACT See .... BARGAIN.

CONTRACTING PARTY (partie contractante).

A country that has signed an international convention, such as the GATT, thereby (par là) accepting the body (ensemble) of obligations and advantages stated (spécifié) therein . In GATT documents the signatories are referred to as (être désigné sous le nom de) the contracting parties.

☞ See GATT; PROTOCOL OF PROVISIONAL APPLICATION.

CONTRACTUAL DUTY See .... PRINCIPLES OF INSURANCE.

CONTRIBUTED CAPITAL See .... AUTHORIZED/REGISTERED ETC. CAPITAL.

CONTRIBUTION See .... PRINCIPLES OF INSURANCE.

CONVERGENCE CRITERIA See .... MAASTRICHT.

CONVERTIBLE DEBENTURE See .... DEBENTURE.

CONVERTIBLE LOAN STOCK See .... DEBENTURE.

CONVERTIBLE PREFERENCE SHARES or **CONVERTIBLES, (US) CONVERTIBLE PREFERRED STOCK** (actions priviligiées/prioritaires convertibles)

Preference shares paying a fixed dividend which the issuing company (société émettrice) will convert at a given date into an ordinary share with the right to dividends (when paid).

☞ See DIVIDEND; ORDINARY SHARES; PREFERENCE SHARES.

CONVERTIBLE PREFERRED STOCK See .... CONVERTIBLE PREFERENCE SHARES.

CONVERTIBLES See .... CONVERTIBLE PREFERENCE SHARES.

COREPER See .... EUROPEAN COUNCIL OF MINISTERS.

CORPORATE BOND See .... BOND.

CORPORATE RAIDER See .... RAIDER/CORPORATE RAIDER.

CORPORATE SECTOR See .... PRIVATE SECTOR.

CORPORATION TAX See .... TAX.

COST AND FREIGHT, abbr. **C and F** (Coût et Fret/C et F)

A C and F price in foreign trade contracts (contrat de commerce international) is the seller's price (prix de vente) including (comporter) the cost of the goods (marchandise) and freight (transport) but not the cost of insurance. This type of price quotation (cotation) is used when public authorities (pouvoirs publics) in the importing country require (exiger) that insurance must be supplied from (fournir par) a company subject to (soumis à) their jurisdiction.

☞ See CIF; FAS; FOB; INCOTERMS; INSURANCE.

COST, INSURANCE, FREIGHT, abbr. **CIF** (Coût, Assurance, Fret/CAF)

A CIF price in foreign trade contracts (contrat de commerce international) is a comprehensive (tout compris) seller's price (prix de vente), all relevant (nécessaire) expenses being paid by the seller up to a given point of importation. If the price is quoted (fixer, établir) as **COST, INSURANCE, FREIGHT and EXCHANGE** (change)/**CIF and E** it may mean either that the price will remain the same despite (en dépit de) possible (éventuel) movements in the rate of exchange (taux de change), or that the price includes banker's commission and interest for negotiating the bill of exchange (lettre de change) related to the goods – in which case (auquel cas) the quotation may be CIF and Commission/CIF & C, or CIF and C and I for (mis pour) CIF and Commission and Interest .

☞ See BILL OF EXCHANGE; C and F; EXCHANGE RATE; FAS; FOB; FOR; FOT; INCOTERMS; INSURANCE.

COST, INSURANCE, FREIGHT AND COMMISSION AND INTEREST See COST, INSURANCE, FREIGHT.

COST, INSURANCE, FREIGHT AND COMMISSION See .... COST, INSURANCE, FREIGHT.

COST, INSURANCE, FREIGHT AND EXCHANGE See .... COST, INSURANCE, FREIGHT

COST-PULL INFLATION See .... INFLATION.

COUNTER PURCHASE CONTRACT See .... COUNTERTRADE.

COUNTERTRADE (échanges compensés ou accords de contre-commerce)

A contractual commitment (engagement) arranged between an importing country and an exporting one in order to generate (engendrer) necessary cash flows (flux de liquidités) to finance imports or to avoid using money altogether. These arrangements (accord) characterize 20 to 30% of world trade. They include (comprendre):

a. **COUNTER PURCHASE CONTRACTS** (contrat de contre-achat) providing that (prévoir que) the seller will buy goods from the importer equivalent in value to a certain percentage of the value of the goods sold;

b. **BUY-BACK/COMPENSATION ARRANGEMENTS** (dispositions de rachat ou de compensation) in which an exporter of equipment (matériel), licenses, technology or a turnkey factory (usine clés en main) agrees to accept in full or partial payment (en paiement total ou partiel) products made using the equipment, technology or factory;

c. **CLEARING AGREEMENTS** (accords de clearing ou de compensation) through which two countries which have balance of payments difficulties agree to buy specified quantities of each other's products (leurs produits respectifs) over a certain period of time. All payments are made through their central banks in order to make trade easier;

d. **SWAP SCHEMES** (plans d'échange) through which products from different locations (provenance) are swapped, or traded (échanger) to save (économiser) carriage costs (frais de transport). For example, oil from Azerbaijan can be swapped for (contre) oil from a Latin American producer. Thus the Russian oil is shipped (expédier) to a country in South Asia, while the Latin American oil is shipped to Cuba;

e. **BARTER/CONTRA** or **SWITCH-TRADING** (accords de troc) in which two countries directly exchange commodities (marchandise) of approximately equivalent value, without any flow of money (transfert de fonds) taking place.

☞ See OFFSET REQUIREMENT; TIED LOAN.

COUNTERVAILING DUTIES (droits compensateurs)

Special duties imposed on imports to offset (compenser) the benefits (avantage) of subsidies (aide, subvention) to producers in the exporting country. Such levies (imposition) are allowed under Article VI of GATT and under Section 301 of the US Trade Act of 1974.

☞ See ARTICLES OF GATT; EXPORT SUBSIDIES; GATT; SECTION 301.

COUPON (coupon)

The rate of interest (taux d'intérêt) payable on a fixed interest security (valeur à intérêt fixe).

☞ See BOND; DEBENTURE; GILT-EDGED STOCKS; INTEREST.

COVERED BEAR See .... BEAR.

CREDIT BANK See .... COMMERCIAL BANK.

CREDIT CARD (carte de crédit)

A plastic card issued (émettre) by a bank or other financial institution, which enables its customers to buy on credit by presenting the card to the seller or provider of the goods or services they are buying. Within the next three-six weeks the customer is either sent a bill (facture) for all the credit purchases he has made (in which case he will have to make a payment to the credit company), or his bank will automatically deduct the amount from his current account. Should he fail to pay the bill or not have enough money in his account he will be charged a penal (lourd) rate of interest, known as the annual percentage rate, abbr. APR (taux effectif global, abrégé TEG), usually quoted as a monthly rate. Businesses accepting payment by credit card pay a percentage commission on their sales to the company issuing the card. Some credit cards are issued free to customers by their bank, etc., giving them also the possibility of borrowing money up to a certain limit; other cards, sometimes known as **CHARGE CARDS** (carte de paiement), require an annual payment from card holders and may not offer the possibility of a loan. Well-known credit cards are VISA, Access, Barclay, American Express and Diner's Club. Well-known shops or stores also offer their customers credit cards, known also as **STORE CARDS**, for buying goods and services supplied by the business.

☞ See ANNUAL PERCENTAGE RATE.

CREDIT INSURANCE See .... ACCIDENT INSURANCE.

CREDIT RATING AGENCY (société d'évaluation du crédit/de la stabilité)

This is a company which assesses (noter) the quality of government and corporate debt – bonds, bills (billets de Trésorerie) and debentures (obligations) issued (émis) by state and local authority bodies (collectivité publique) and companies – from the point of view of risk of not being repaid (remboursé). The most famous agencies are two American companies: **MOODY'S** and **STANDARD & POOR'S**, abbr. **S & P**, which dominate the world market. They rate (noter) almost all big debt issued in the USA and about four-fifths of commercial paper and two-thirds of Euro-bonds in Europe (*The Economist*, 30/3/91). Credit rating has become increasingly important to investors, given the recent recession and large number of corporate failures (faillite d'entreprise/de société). The same source cites Moody's as estimating that in 1990 companies defaulted (manquer à ses engagements, ne pas honorer ses échéances, ou être en état de cessation de paiement) on $22 billion of bonds.

The highest rating (notation, cote de crédit ou évaluation des capacités d'endettement) given is **triple A** (i.e. **AAA**), which means the investment is very secure and there is virtually no risk of not being repaid (remboursé); an AA rating is also good, but a little less secure; an **A rating** indicates the investment is still good, but even less secure; this is followed by **BBB**, **BB**, **B** and so on. Companies (including banks) which seek to raise capital (se procurer des capitaux) through issuing (émettre) bonds and debentures or by direct borrowing (emprunt) take the ratings very seriously: a high rating means investors will be attracted, while any borrowing from a bank will be at the lowest interest rates; conversely, low ratings mean more risk and attract less investors, unless the interest offered is high to compensate, as in the case of junk bonds (obligation de pacotille), while bank or other direct borrowing will be at higher rates of interest. The ratings are regularly revised (actualisé) in the light of (en fonction de) changes in events and circumstances likely to (susceptible à) affect the borrower's solvency (solvabilité), such as costs, interest rates, takeover bids (OPA), etc.

☞ See BOND; COMMERCIAL PAPER; DEBENTURE; EURO-CURRENCY MARKET; JUNK BOND under LEVERAGED BUYOUT; MONEY MARKET; TAKEOVER BID.

CREDIT UNION, USA (établissement mutuel collecteur d'épargne, attribuant des prêts à la consommation)

An association of people based on a common tie (lien commun), such as work, hobby, residence, etc., who decide to save money regularly together in a common fund, from which they may borrow at lower rates of interest than offered by banks and other institutions. This is a kind of non-profit making (à but non lucratif) local financial cooperative. Included in the term "thrifts".

☞ See COOPERATIVE; THRIFTS.

CREDITORS' VOLUNTARY WINDING-UP See .... LIQUIDATION.

CROSSED CHEQUE (chèque barré)

This is the usual kind of cheque and has two parallel lines from top to bottom cutting across the writing, in the middle. This simply signifies that the payment can only be made to the bank, which will then credit the amount indicated on the cheque to the customer's account. Payment will not be made over the counter (au comptant/au guichet), the idea being to prevent anyone from dishonestly (malhonnêtement) claiming payment.

☞ See CHEQUE; CURRENT ACCOUNT.

CROWDING OUT See .... UNEMPLOYMENT.

CUM See .... DIVIDEND.

CUM DIVIDEND See .... DIVIDEND.

CUM DIV. See .... DIVIDEND.

CUMULATIVE PREFERENCE/PREFERRED SHARES (actions priviligiées/prioritaires à dividende cumulatif/cumulatives)

Preference shares whose dividend, if not paid in one year, is added to the next and is therefore always payable, even if late.

☞ See NON-CUMULATIVE PREFERENCE SHARES; PREFERENCE SHARES.

CUMULATIVE PREFERRED SHARES See .... CUMULATIVE PREFERENCE SHARES.

CURRENCY FUTURES See .... LONDON INTERNATIONAL FINANCIAL FUTURES EXCHANGE.

CURRENT ACCOUNT BALANCE See .... BALANCE OF PAYMENTS.

CURRENT ACCOUNT See .... BALANCE OF PAYMENTS.

CURRENT ACCOUNT, (US) CHECKING ACCOUNT or **DEMAND DEPOSIT** (compte courant)

A bank account in which customers deposit and withdraw their money at will, using cheques. In some countries certain banks offer interest on this account (the UK, the USA, Germany and Spain, for example), but may make charges (faire payer) for cheques, standing orders (prélèvement automatique) and other services normally given free (gratuitement) if a credit balance (solde créditeur) is not maintained. In the UK and the USA savings banks (caisse/banque d'épargne) now also offer this facility.

☞ See COMMERCIAL BANK; CHEQUE; DE-REGULATION; SAVINGS BANK; STANDING ORDER.

CURRENT EMPLOYMENT STATISTICS See .... UNEMPLOYMENT.

CURRENT POPULATION SURVEY See .... UNEMPLOYMENT.

CURRENT PRICE See .... SPOT or CURRENT PRICE.

CUSTOMS AND ADMINISTRATIVE ENTRY PROCEDURES (formalités douanières et administratives à l'importation)

Clearance (dédouanement) formalities at national ports (point) of entry, such as licensing (licence) procedures, health and sanitary controls, certificates indicating the country of origin, consular invoices (facture consulaire) confirming that the shipment (envoi) corresponds to the contents (contenu) of the export invoice (facture à l'exportation) and the bill of lading (connaissement).

☞ See BILL OF LADING; CONSULAR FORMALITIES AND DOCUMENTATION; EXPORT INVOICE; LICENSING; NON-TARIFF BARRIERS; QUARANTINE; SANITARY AND HEALTH LAWS AND REGULATIONS.

CUSTOMS DRAWBACK See .... RE-EXPORTATION.

CUSTOMS DUTY (droit de douane)

A tax levied (imposer) on imports and exports by the government of a country. A duty may be calculated as a percentage of the value of the goods (marchandise). It is then called an **AD VALOREM DUTY** (droit proportionnel). A duty may also be a fixed sum of money for each unit (unité) of quantity or weight (poids). It is then (alors) called a **FIXED** or **SPECIFIC DUTY** (droit spécifique).

☞ See BILL OF ENTRY; COUNTERVAILING DUTIES; EXCISE TAX; RE-EXPORTATION; TAX.

CUSTOMS UNION (union douanière)

A group of nations which have removed (éliminer) customs duties (droit de douane) and other trade barriers (barrière commerciale) with each other (entre elles), and apply (appliquer) a common external tariff (tarif extérieur commun) on commodities (marchandise) imported from non-members of the union. The European Union is the most famous illustration of this case with its Single Market. Article XXIV of GATT defines the meaning (sens) of a customs union in GATT and the application of other GATT provisions (disposition) to customs unions.

☞ See COMMON EXTERNAL TARIFF; COMMON MARKET; EU; GATT; TRADE DIVERSION.

CUSTOMS VALUATION CODE (code sur l'évaluation en douane)

A code of conduct (code de conduite) negotiated during the GATT Tokyo Round to establish (créer) an international system for the valuation of goods by customs authorities. The code aims to (avoir pour but de) prevent (empêcher) the use of arbitrary national valuation systems as (en tant que) non-tariff barriers (barrière non-tarifaire) to trade. The primary (essentiel) method of valuation is to take into account (prendre en compte) the transaction value (valeur marchande) of the goods. When this is not possible, other methods can be used as specified by the code. The code also provides (prévoir, stipuler) for equitable currency (devise) conversion and quick clearance (dédouanement) of goods when there are delays (retard) in determining their value.

☞ See CODES OF CONDUCT; GATT; NON-TARIFF BARRIER; TOKYO ROUND.

CWO See .... CASH WITH ORDER.

CYCLICAL UNEMPLOYMENT See .... UNEMPLOYMENT.

D

DAWN RAID See .... TAKEOVER BID.

DAX See .... SHARE INDEX.

DE-REGULATION (libéralisation ou déréglementation)

The releasing (desserrement) of legal and other restrictions on the way sectors of the economy, industries and companies can do business, and the services and products they can offer. In the USA this started in the mid-1970s and in the UK from about 1979 with the abolition of exchange control (contrôle des changes), the predominant idea being to increase competition and efficiency. In both countries the financial services sector has been particularly affected, paving the way (frayer le chemin) for banks to enter the investment, insurance and home loans market, insurance companies to enter the lending and property market, and home-financing institutions like building societies (caisse d'épargne mutuelle de crédit immobilier) and thrifts to offer banking, insurance and investment services. This has enormously increased the competition for savers' money and in the lending market, leading to credit booms in the second half of the 1980s in both the UK and the USA. Prior to de-regulation banks were confined to banking services, insurance companies to insurance and so on. Other industries (secteur), such as transport, especially air transport, have also been de-regulated.

☞ See BUILDING SOCIETY; COMMERCIAL BANK; FINANCIAL SERVICES; FINANCIAL SERVICES ACT, 1986; INSURANCE; THRIFTS.

DEAL (coup de bourse ou affaire ou marché ou transaction ou accord)

This is the buying and selling of securities on the stock exchange, often in connection with a merger (fusion), acquisition or friendly or hostile takeover bid (OPA amicale ou hostile). Someone who arranges a deal is known as a **DEALMAKER** (faiseur de "deals" ou marieur d'entreprises ou opérateur en bourse).

☞ See BROKER/DEALER; FINANCIAL INTERMEDIARIES; LEVERAGED BUYOUT; MARKET MAKER; RAID; RAIDER; TAKEOVER BID.

DEATH DUTIES See .... TAX.

DEBENTURE (obligation)

This is another form of **IOU** (reconnaissance de dette),very similar to a bond, being for the most part a fixed-interest security (titre à taux fixe) issued (émise) by limited companies (SARL) or public organizations (l'Etat ou une collectivité publique) in exchange for a loan (prêt ou emprunt), to be redeemed (être amorti) at a future date, the **MATURITY/REDEMPTION DATE** (date d'échéance), usually between ten and forty years later. The interest (intérêt) on a debenture is called a coupon, and this must be paid by the issuing organization, and in the case of companies, regardless of whether they have made any profits or not (qu'elles aient fait ou non des bénéfices), in contrast to a dividend. Debenture-holders (obligataire) can force a company into liquidation if they do not receive their coupon, and in such a case they have priority of payment over shareholders (actionnaire) and bondholders. Debentures, **DEBENTURE STOCK** or **INDUSTRIAL DEBENTURES** are usually secured on (être nanti/gagé/assis sur) all or specific company assets (actif), but not so in the USA. Debentures are negotiable on stockmarkets and exist in different forms, the main ones of which are given below. A **BEARER DEBENTURE** (obligation au porteur) is one which can change hands without the change having to be formally registered (déclaré auprès de) with the issuer (émetteur). The more usual kind, however, is a **REGISTERED DEBENTURE** (obligation nominative), and the holder's name is noted by the borrower as the person to receive payments. A **CONVERTIBLE DEBENTURE** (obligation convertible) is one which can be changed for or converted into an ordinary share or other debenture at some future date. A **FIXED DEBENTURE** (obligation nantie sur un actif particulier) is one secured (garanti) by a particular asset such as a building or machinery. In contrast, a **FLOATING DEBENTURE** is secured on all the assets of the borrower (obligation nantie sur tout l'actif de l'emprunteur). An **INCOME DEBENTURE/BOND** (obligation et intérêt remboursables seulement sur les bénéfices) pays interest and repays the principal only out of company earnings. An **IRREDEEMABLE/PERPETUAL DEBENTURE** (obligation perpétuelle) has no redemption date (date de remboursement) and therefore only pays interest; if issued (émise) by a company, however, the principal will be repaid should it go into liquidation (se mettre en liquidation). With a **MORTGAGE DEBENTURE** (obligation hypothécaire) payment of interest and principal is secured on specific property (propriété). A **REDEEMABLE DEBENTURE** (obligation remboursable à une date fixe ou en avance à la demande de l'emprunteur) allows the borrower to repay the loan at a fixed date or before. **LOAN/UNSECURED STOCK** (obligations non garanties), another form of debenture, in contrast to most of the others, are unsecured loans. **CONVERTIBLE LOAN STOCK** (obligations convertibles non garanties) can be converted at some future date to ordinary shares; if during the **CONVERSION PERIOD** (délai de conversion) the stock are not converted then they revert (redeviennent) to being ordinary unsecured stock.

☞ See BOND; BORROWING; CAPITAL MARKET; COUPON; CREDIT RATING AGENCY; GILT-EDGED STOCKS; LENDING; LOAN; MERCHANT BANK; MONEY MARKET; PREFERENCE SHARE; SHARE; TREASURY BILL; TREASURY BOND; WARRANT.

DEBENTURE STOCK See .... DEBENTURE.

DEBENTURES See .... DEBENTURE.

DEFERRED BOND See .... BOND.

DEFERRED SHARES or **ORDINARY DEFERRED SHARES** (actions différées)

Shares which pay dividends only after all other kinds of shares have been paid their dividends (i.e. after ordinary, preference, etc. shares). Deferred shares are usually held by founders (fondateur) or others closely connected with the business and can often receive a large proportion of the profits which remain after other shareholders have been paid an agreed dividend rate (taux de dividende convenu).

☞ See DIVIDEND; FOUNDERS' SHARES; ORDINARY SHARES; PREFERENCE SHARES; SHARE; SHAREHOLDER.

DEFLATION (déflation)

This is a continued reduction in the general price level, often together with declines in output and employment. Governments with high inflation in their economies will carry out deflationary policies (politique de déflation) using monetary and fiscal policies to reduce the amount of money circulating in the economy.

☞ See INFLATION; FISCAL POLICY; MONETARY POLICY; TAX.

DE-INDUSTRIALIZATION (désindustrialisation)

A decrease (baisse) in the share (part) of manufacturing (production industrielle) in the income (revenu) of a nation. Most industrialized countries are affected (toucher) by this decline which takes place to the advantage of (au bénéfice de) services. As manufactures (produit manufacturé) make up (constituer) the bulk (gros) of exports, this process (processus) might in the future (à terme) create a large imbalance (déséquilibre) between visible trade and invisible trade, and cause a loss (perte) of income for the nations concerned.

☞ See INVISIBLE TRADE; SERVICES; VISIBLE TRADE.

DEL CREDERE AGENT See .... IMPORT AGENT.

DEL CREDERE COMMISSION See .... IMPORT AGENT.

DELTA SECURITIES See .... ALPHA SECURITIES.

DEMAND DEPOSIT See .... CURRENT ACCOUNT.

DEMAND-PULL INFLATION See .... INFLATION.

DEPARTMENT OF TRADE AND INDUSTRY (l'équivalent en France du ministère du Redéploiement industriel/de l'Industrie et du Commerce extérieur)

British government department responsible for: international trade policy (e.g. helping exporters), promoting industry (especially in the poorer regions of the country) and small firms, research and development in science and technology, competition law (mergers (fusion), monopolies and acquisitions), fair trade, consumer protection, and the regulation of the financial services sector (e.g. insurance, Lloyd's, The International Stock Exchange and financial intermediaries such as banks, building societies (société/caisse d'épargne mutuelle de crédit immobilier), investment and unit trusts (SICAV) etc. through (par l'intermédiaire) Self-Regulatory Organizations, abbr. SROs (organisation indépendante).

☞ See FINANCIAL INTERMEDIARIES; FINANCIAL SERVICES ACT, 1986; INTERNATIONAL STOCK EXCHANGE; LLOYD'S; SELF-REGULATORY ORGANIZATIONS.

DEPOSIT ACCOUNT, also (US) TIME/NOTICE ACCOUNT (compte de dépôt/d'épargne)

A bank account which receives customer deposits (dépôts), for which they receive interest. Cash may be withdrawn, but usually with notice (préavis), say seven days or longer, and not by using cheques. The account must be kept in credit (maintenir un solde créditeur) to receive interest. A deposit account is usually used by bank customers to earn interest on money they do not need immediately. A **FIXED DEPOSIT ACCOUNT** (compte de dépôt à terme fixe) is for a fixed sum of money placed with a bank or financial institution for a given length of time at a fixed rate of interest, which is higher than that earned by a deposit account. Such accounts may also be offered by other financial institutions such as building societies and savings and loans associations.

☞ See BUILDING SOCIETY; COMMERCIAL BANK; CURRENT ACCOUNT; DE-REGULATION; SAVINGS AND LOAN ASSOCIATION; SAVINGS BANK.

DEPOSIT BANK See .... COMMERCIAL BANK.

DEPOSITOR (déposant)

Someone who places money in an account, usually with a bank or similar or other financial institution for safekeeping (en garde), convenience (commodité), or as a way of saving or investing.

☞ See BANKING; COMMERCIAL BANK; CURRENT ACCOUNT; DEPOSIT ACCOUNT; SAVINGS ACCOUNT; SAVINGS BANK.

DEPRESSION (dépression)

This is a severe fall (chute ou baisse) in output (production) and aggregate demand (demande globale), accompanied by high unemployment and low prices, levels of investment and business confidence. A depression is the bottom end (le fond) of a trade cycle (cycle économique).

☞ See AGGREGATE DEMAND; BLACK TUESDAY; FISCAL POLICY; INFLATION; MONETARY POLICY; RECESSION; UNEMPLOYMENT; TRADE CYCLE.

DIRECT TAXES See .... TAX.

DIRECTORS See .... BOARD OF DIRECTORS.

DIRTY BILL OF LADING See .... BILL OF LADING.

DISCLOSURE OF SHAREHOLDINGS RULE See .... TAKEOVER BID.

DISCOUNT (escompte)

In banking and finance this is the amount deducted from the face value (valeur nominale) of commercial paper (effets de commerce) or short-term money market instruments (effets financiers du marché monétaire à court terme) such as bills of exchange (lettre de change ou traite ou effet de commerce), trade acceptances (acceptation d'effets), treasury bills (billet/bon du trésor à court terme) and promissory notes (billet à ordre), when they are bought before they are due to mature or be paid (parvenir à échéance). This **DISCOUNT RATE** (taux d'escompte) is normally expressed as a percentage, being the amount deducted as a percentage of the par value (valeur au pair) of the paper. The buyer pays the seller the value of the bill, etc. less the discount; when the bill etc. is due to be repaid he collects its par value; his profit is the difference between what he bought the bill for (le prix qu'il a payé l'effet) and the face or par value that he receives when it is due to be repaid. The **DISCOUNT RATE** set (fixer) by central banks indicates the discount at which they are prepared as lender of last resort (prêteur en dernier ressort) to buy treasury and other bills back from commercial banks and other financial instututions which are short of (manque de) cash in the discount market. In commerce discounts are a reduction in the price of goods and services or an invoice or bill (facture) to persuade customers to buy more or pay sooner (rabais/remise, escompte de règlement).

☞ See BILL OF EXCHANGE; CENTRAL BANK; COMMERCIAL PAPER; DISCOUNT HOUSE; DISCOUNT MARKET; FEDERAL RESERVE SYSTEM; FINANCIAL INSTRUMENTS; LOMBARD RATE; MONEY MARKET; PAR VALUE; PROMISSORY NOTE; TRADE ACCEPTANCE; TREASURY BILL.

DISCOUNT HOUSE (banque d'escompte, maison de réescompte)

This is a unique (spécifiquement) British financial institution which operates as a specialist bank. Discount houses are so called because they discount (escompter) bills of exchange (lettre de change) which have been accepted (accepté) by banks, that is to say, they buy them at less than their face value (valeur nominale). They function by borrowing surplus short-term money from commercial banks and use this to buy financial instruments (effets financiers) such as Treasury bills (bon du Trésor), bills of exchange and sterling certificates of deposit (certificat de dépôt). The banks which lend to the discount houses can demand their money back at any moment – it is at call money (argent à court terme/au jour le jour). If they do this and the discount houses do not have enough money they are entitled (autoriser) to borrow from the Bank of England as lender of last resort (prêteur en dernier recours). The Bank will buy their financial instruments at a discount; the discount houses are said here **TO RE-DISCOUNT** (réescompter) the bills with the Bank (because they have already discounted them once when they bought them in the first place) or to sell them at a discount (vendre à perte) to the Bank. This special facility is only open to the discount houses (of which there are about eight) and recently to a few other financial institutions. As a result of this favoured (privilégié) relationship discount houses are required (exiger) to tender for (soumissionner pour) all the Treasury bills issued (émis) each week by the government to ensure that the latter (ce dernier) gets the funds it needs, even if other institutions such as banks and brokers (courtier) do not tender. Discount houses operate in what is known as the discount market.

☞ See AT CALL; BILL OF EXCHANGE; BOND; CERTIFICATE OF DEPOSIT; COMMERCIAL BANK; COMMERCIAL PAPER; DEBENTURE; DISCOUNT; DISCOUNT MARKET; FINANCIAL INSTRUMENTS; PUBLIC SPENDING BORROWING REQUIREMENT; TREASURY BILL; TREASURY BOND.

DISCOUNT MARKET (marché du réescompte)

This is a special UK financial market for borrowing and investing short-term money. It involves discount houses (banque d'escompte ou maison de réescompte), accepting houses (maison d'acceptation ou banque d'affaires spécialisée dans l'acceptation des traites) and commercial banks which invest in treasury bills (bon du trésor à court terme), bills of exchange (traite) and short-dated bonds (obligation à court terme), which change hands at a discount (à perte).

☞ See CENTRAL BANK; DISCOUNT; DISCOUNT HOUSE.

DISCOUNT RATE See .... DISCOUNT.

DISHONOURED BILL See .... SHIPPING DOCUMENTS.

DISHONOURED CHEQUE See .... BOUNCED ETC. CHEQUE.

DISINFLATION (désinflation)

This is simply cutting back, reducing or eliminating inflation.

☞ See DEFLATION; FISCAL POLICY; INFLATION; MONETARY POLICY; TAX.

DISPUTE SETTLEMENT (règlement des différends)

Resolution of conflict, generally through (au moyen de) a compromise between opposing claims (thèses divergentes), sometimes eased (faciliter) through the efforts of an intermediary. GATT Articles XXII and XXIII set out (définir) consultation procedures a contracting party (partie contractante) may follow to obtain legal redress (réparation) if it thinks its benefits (avantage) under (dans le cadre de) GATT are impaired (léser). Each contracting party may negotiate solutions to trade problems bilaterally within the framework (dans le cadre de) of GATT. If bilateral consultations fail (échouer), the matter (question) may be referred to (porter devant) all contracting parties. The latter (celles-ci) may establish (constituer) a special panel (comité) to arbitrate the matter. Such procedures may lead to (mener à) recommendations (recommandation) or rulings (décision) from the contracting parties directed to (adresser à) the disputants (parties en présence, adversaires), or even (même) to other countries as well (également).

☞ See CASE LAW; CODES OF CONDUCT; CONSULTATIONS; CONTRACTING PARTY; FRAMEWORK AGREEMENT; GATT; GOVERNMENT PROCUREMENT POLICIES AND PROCEDURES; PANEL OF EXPERTS; TOKYO ROUND.

DIVIDEND (dividende)

This is the part of the profits of a company distributed to ordinary shareholders, once holders (détenteur) of preference shares (action à dividende prioritaire) and debentures (obligation) have been provided for. The decision as to how much the dividend will be is taken by the board of directors (conseil d'administration). The amount (montant) is usually expressed as either a percentage of the nominal value of the ordinary share capital of the company (e.g. if the nominal value of the share was £5 and the dividend 50p then the dividend could be expressed as 10% – [50 /500] x 100), or as a given sum of money per share (e.g. 50p per share). The value of the dividend decided by the board of directors will depend on the profitability (rentabilité) of the company and the need for retained earnings (bénéfices non distribués) for future needs (e.g. investment, higher interest rates, anticipated downward trend in the market for the company's products, etc.). Sometimes companies still maintain or increase dividends when a given year's performance has been poor. They do this out of (sur) reserves (réserves/provisions) – accumulated earnings from the past – if they consider the future outlook to be good, and also to maintain shareholders' confidence. Dividends can be paid quarterly (trimestriellement) or bi-annually (semestriellement), when they are called **INTERIM DIVIDENDS** (dividende provisoire/intérimaire ou acompte sur dividende); the last dividend to be paid in the financial year (exercice financier) is the **FINAL DIVIDEND** (solde de dividende). Where share prices are quoted with the words **CUM DIVIDEND**, abbr. **cum div.** (avec le dividende ou coupon attaché) this indicates the buyer of the share also gets the next dividend; **EX DIVIDEND**, abbr. **ex div.** or **x.d.** (ex dividende, coupon détaché) means the seller gets the dividend. The word **CUM** attached to other types of security simply indicates additional benefits to the buyer, while **EX** will indicate an absence of such benefits (e.g. **EX COUPON** (coupon détaché), abbr. **ex cp.** or **x. cp.** means the seller of the bond, and not the buyer, gets the coupon). **EX ALL**, abbr. **x.a.** means the buyer buys without any of the rights the company is offering at the moment (e.g. bonus or scrip issue shares, dividend, etc.).

☞ See ANNUAL GENERAL MEETING; BOND; COUPON; DEBENTURE; ORDINARY SHARE; RESERVES; RETAINED EARNINGS; RIGHTS ISSUE; SCRIP ISSUE; SHARE; WARRANT; YIELD.

DIVIDEND SPLIT See .... SCRIP/BONUS ETC. ISSUE.

DIVIDEND YIELD See .... YIELD.

DOCUMENTARY BILL See .... SHIPPING DOCUMENTS.

DOCUMENTATION See .... SHIPPING DOCUMENTS.

DOCUMENTS FOR COLLECTION See .... SHIPPING DOCUMENTS.

DOCUMENTS-AGAINST-ACCEPTANCE See .... SHIPPING DOCUMENTS.

DOCUMENTS-AGAINST-PAYMENT See .... SHIPPING DOCUMENTS.

DOUBLE OPTION See .... OPTION.

DOW JONES INDUSTRIAL AVERAGE See .... SHARE INDEX.

DOW JONES See .... SHARE INDEX.

D/P BILL See .... SHIPPING DOCUMENTS.

DRAFT See .... BILL OF EXCHANGE.

DRAFT BILL (traite/effet/lettre de change)

A bill of exchange or written order to someone to pay money before it has been signed by the debtor (débiteur), that is, the one who is going to pay, and therefore before it has been agreed. Often used as a synonym for bill of exchange.

☞ See BILL OF EXCHANGE

DRAGONS (Dragons) or **TIGERS** (Tigres)

The nickname (surnom) given to the four newly industrializing or industrialized countries (nouveau pays industriel ou industrialisé) of South-East Asia – Hong Kong, Singapore, South Korea and Taiwan – which in recent years have achieved (réaliser) the most outstanding (remarquable) economic performance, thus (ainsi) obtaining an export capacity which is a growing (grandissant) threat (menace) to the old industrialized world notably (notamment) because of the very low cost of labour (main-d'oeuvre) in the region.

☞ See HIGH PERFORMING ASIAN ECONOMIES; NEWLY INDUSTRIALIZING OR INDUSTRIALIZED COUNTRY.

DRAW/DRAFT, TO (tirer)

In banking to write out and sign a cheque or bill of exchange. The person who draws or drafts is the **DRAWER** (tireur, quelquefois souscripteur [d'une traite]), he who is asked to pay (usually a bank) is the **DRAWEE** (tiré ou accepteur [d'une traite], while he who receives the payment is the **PAYEE** (bénéficiaire).

☞ See BILL OF EXCHANGE; CHEQUE.

DRAWBACK See .... RE-EXPORTATION.

DRAWEE See .... BILL OF EXCHANGE; CHEQUE; DRAW/DRAFT, TO.

DRAWER See .... BILL OF EXCHANGE; CHEQUE; DRAW/DRAFT TO.

DUD CHEQUE See .... BOUNCED ETC. CHEQUE.

DUMPING (dumping, vente à bas prix)

The sale of a commodity (marchandise) in a foreign market at less than fair value (à une valeur inférieure à sa valeur équitable), i.e. a price lower than the selling price (prix de vente) within (à l'intérieur) the exporting country or in third countries (pays tiers). Fair value can also be the cost of production plus an 8% or so (environ) profit margin (marge bénéficiaire). Dumping is generally considered as an unfair trade practice (pratique commerciale déloyale) likely to (susceptible de) disrupt (perturber) markets and injure (léser) producers in the importing country.

☞ See ANTI-DUMPING CODE.

DUTY PAID See .... EX QUAY.

E

EARLY DELIVERY See .... PROMPT/EARLY DELIVERY.

EARNINGS PER SHARE See .... YIELD.

EU See .... EUROPEAN COMMUNITY.

ECGD See .... EXPORT CREDITS GUARANTEE DEPARTMENT.

ECONOMIC AND MONETARY UNION See .... EUROPEAN MONETARY SYSTEM; MAASTRICHT.

ECSC See .... EUROPEAN COAL AND STEEL COMMUNITY.

ECU See .... EUROPEAN CURRENCY UNIT.

EDF See .... EUROPEAN DEVELOPMENT FUND.

EEA See .... EUROPEAN ECONOMIC AREA.

EEC See .... EUROPEAN COMMUNITY.

EFT See .... CHEQUE.

EFTA See .... EUROPEAN FREE TRADE ASSOCIATION.

EFTPOS See .... CHEQUE.

EIB See .... EUROPEAN INVESTMENT BANK.

ELECTRONIC FUNDS TRANSFER AT POINT OF SALE See .... CHEQUE.

ELECTRONIC FUNDS TRANSFER See .... CHEQUE.

ELIGIBLE LIABILITIES See .... RESERVE ASSETS.

EMPLOYEE SHARE/STOCK (US) OWNERSHIP PLAN, abbr. **ESOP** (actionnariat du personnel)

These are schemes (système) intended to motivate the workforce (main-d'oeuvre ou salariés) by giving them the possibility of acquiring shares in the company that employs them. Such schemes have existed since the 1950s, but became more prominent in the 1980s. In the USA this was due to a favourable tax climate created by the government to encourage them and to their subsequent usefulness as a means of warding off (échapper à/éviter) hostile take-over bids (OPA hostile). In the UK they were encouraged by the government's privatization policy, which gave employees an opportunity to buy shares before the public in the companies being sold off, and its desire to promote wider share-ownership (élargir ou agrandir le nombre d'actionnaires).

In 1989 it was estimated that the percentage of workers owning shares in their employing company was as follows: Canada: 25%; USA: 23%; UK and Sweden: 20%; and France, West Germany and Switzerland: 9%. ESOPs have been set up (instauré) in such companies in Britain as Road Chef, a catering firm (restauration) and NFC – National Freight Consortium – a transport group, and in the USA in Polaroid, which produces photographic equipment, and Texaco, an oil company.
It should be noted that ESOPs vary (varier) in scope (étendue) and form (forme): they can give (distribuer gratuitement) or sell shares to employees and therefore result in a wide or limited ownership of shares by employees; they also bring with them varying degrees of employee participation in running (fonctionnement) the company. The general view is that the performance of the company in terms of productivity and customer satisfaction improves with an ESOP, but the actual benefits to employees can vary considerably. This is because the success of their company does not only depend on their input (contribution) but also on external factors over which they have no control, such as government policy, inflation, interest rates and market conditions. In addition, their motivation to work harder may be limited if they are not genuinely encouraged to participate in the running of the company.

☞ See ANNUAL GENERAL MEETING; AUTHORIZED/REGISTERED ETC. CAPITAL; INFLATION; LEVERAGED BUYOUT; LIMITED or LIMITED LIABILITY COMPANY; MONETARY POLICY; SHARE; TAKEOVER BID.

EMPLOYERS' LIABILITY INSURANCE See .... ACCIDENT INSURANCE.

EMPLOYMENT See .... UNEMPLOYMENT.

ENABLING CLAUSE (clause d'autorisation)

Formally (officiellement) named the "Decision on Differential and More Favourable Treatment, Reciprocity, and Fuller Participation of Developing Countries" (Décision sur le traitement différentiel et plus favorable, la réciprocité et l'accroissement de la participation des pays en voie de développement), the Enabling Clause was negotiated during the GATT Tokyo Round. It legalized (entériner) the extension by developed contracting parties of GATT of preferences (préférence) to developing countries, despite the multi-lateral non-discrimination in trade terms required of contracting parties under GATT Article I.

☞ See CONTRACTING PARTY; FRAMEWORK AGREEMENT; GATT; GENERALIZED SYSTEM OF PREFERENCES; MOST-FAVOURED-NATION TREATMENT; TOKYO ROUND.

ENDOWMENT POLICY See .... LIFE INSURANCE.

ENTREPÔT PORT See .... RE-EXPORTATION.

ENTREPÔT TRADE See .... RE-EXPORTATION.

ENTRY FOR FREE GOODS See .... BILL OF ENTRY.

ENTRY FOR HOME USE EX SHIP See .... BILL OF ENTRY.

ENTRY FOR WAREHOUSING See .... BILL OF ENTRY.

EQUILIBRIUM (équilibre)

This is a theoretical concept used by economists to indicate a situation of stability and minimum change, as the forces affecting the situation are in balance (en équilibre). An equilibrium price, for example, is one at which the quantity demanded of a good is equal to that suppliers are prepared to supply. If less were demanded then suppliers would have to lower their price in order to sell more (thus competing among themselves). This would then result in a new equilibrium price. If a labour market is in equilibrium then the amount of labour demanded will equal the amount offered at given salary or wage levels. Equilibrium can be general or partial, and also dynamic (as opposed to static), when the variables involved continue to change, but in a regular way (e.g. a continuing 2 % increase in exports).

☞ See CLASSICAL UNEMPLOYMENT under UNEMPLOYMENT; SUPPLY AND DEMAND.

EQUITY BOND See .... BOND.

EQUITY CAPITAL See .... SHARE.

ERM See .... EUROPEAN MONETARY SYSTEM.

ESC See .... EUROPEAN ECONOMIC AND SOCIAL COMMITTEE.

ESCAPE CLAUSE (clause d'exemption, de sauvegarde)

A provision (disposition) in a bilateral or multilateral trade agreement (accord, traité commercial) allowing (permettre) a signatory nation to suspend tariff or other concessions (concessions tarifaires ou autres) where imports jeopardize (menacer) the domestic producers (producteur national). Article XIX of GATT authorizes such safeguard measures (mesure de sauvegarde) so that (de sorte que) firms may have time to adjust to (s'adapter à) the rising level (niveau) of import competition (concurrence à l'importation).

☞ See CONCESSION; GATT; SAFEGUARDS.

ESOP See .... EMPLOYEE SHARE/STOCK OWNERSHIP PLAN.

ESTATE DUTIES See .... TAX.

EU See .... EUROPEAN COMMUNITY; EUROPEAN UNION.

EU COMPETITION POLICY (Politique de la concurrence de l'Union européenne)

EU competition policy is dealt with (traiter, aborder) in Articles 85 and 86 of the Treaty of Rome. The first mainly (essentiellement) forbids companies to practice price collusion (entente illicite sur les prix), to share out (se partager) markets and to limit production. The second outlaws (proscrire, interdire) "abuses of dominant position" (abus de position

dominante) by companies or groups of companies. Moreover (de plus), Articles 92-94 ban (interdire) government subsidies (subvention de l'État) distorting (fausser) or likely to (susceptible de) distort competition.
In order to prevent (empêcher, prévenir) such abuses, the European Commission can act either (soit) on its own initiative, without reference to (sans en référer à) the European Council of Ministers, or (soit) following (à la suite de) complaints (plainte) lodged (déposer) directly before national courts (tribunaux nationaux) by EU members, companies or individuals (particulier). The Commission has almost unlimited powers of investigation (enquête). It can visit companies unexpectedly (à l'improviste), demand (exiger) access to documents and take away (emporter) photocopies as evidence (preuve).
The several hundred cases (affaire) which are thus (ainsi) dealt with every year are often resolved (résoudre) by means of (au moyen de) voluntary policy changes (changement de politique). If policy changes ordered (ordonner) by the Commission are not made, offenders (contrevenant) are imposed fines (amende). The Commission's decisions may be challenged (attaquer, contester) in the European Court of Justice. EU competition legislation prevails over (primer sur) national law and is directly enforceable (applicable) in the member states.
The Commission has jurisdiction (avoir compétence à) to approve mergers (fusion) and takeovers (rachat, prise de contrôle) affecting (toucher) more than one member state and exceeding certain financial thresholds (seuil). State-owned enterprises (entreprise publique) must comply with (se conformer à) EU competition legislation exactly as privately owned (privé) ones. Government subsidies can be exempted by the Commission from the rules of the Treaty of Rome when they concern natural disasters, depressed (en déclin, en crise) regions, the promotion of new economic activities or industries (secteur) seriously affected by recession. In the past decade (décennie), such exemptions have been granted (accorder) in favour of shipbuilding (construction navale), textiles, synthetic fibres and steel (acier). In general, the Commission is of a view that (considérer que) all kinds of state aid (soutien de l'État) should be kept as low as possible. National governments often tend to radically disagree on this point as they have to face (faire face à) serious difficulties in the field (domaine) of employment.

☞ See EUROPEAN COMMISSION; EUROPEAN COMMUNITY; EUROPEAN COUNCIL OF MINISTERS; EUROPEAN COURT OF JUSTICE; MERGER; MONOPOLIES AND MERGERS COMMISSION; RESTRICTIVE BUSINESS PRACTICES; SUBSIDY; TAKEOVER; TREATY OF ROME.

EURATOM See .... TREATY OF ROME.

EUROBOND See .... EUROCURRENCY MARKET.

EUROCRATS See .... EUROPEAN COMMISSION.

EUROCURRENCY MARKET or **EUROMARKET** (marché des euro-devises)

This is a capital market in Europe and elsewhere (especially in Canada and Japan) for currencies and various financial instruments (effet financier) held in Europe but deposited in countries in which the depositor (déposant) is not physically located (e.g. a European business with dollars in a bank account in America). Such currencies are known as **EUROCURRENCIES** (euro-devises), hence (d'où) the **EURODOLLAR**, Euroyen, Eurofranc, Euromark etc., and are lent on by banks holding them. The **EUROMARKET** also includes trade in **EUROBONDS** (euro-obligation), which are longer term loans (emprunt à plus long terme), issued (émis) by banks on behalf of (pour le compte de) companies or governments in currencies outside the latter's (ces derniers) country of origin and traded (négocié) internationally. For example, a German bank raises (lancer/émettre) a loan for a French or British company by issuing a dollar bond, which is then sold internationally – this is a **EUROBOND**. The Eurobond market is a very large one, but as it is not located in one centre it is largely unregulated (non contrôlé).

☞ See BOND; CAPITAL MARKET; COMMERCIAL PAPER; DEBENTURE; LIBOR; LONDON INTERNATIONAL FINANCIAL FUTURES EXCHANGE; MONEY MARKET.

EUROCURRENCY See .... EUROCURRENCY MARKET.

EURODOLLAR See .... EUROCURRENCY MARKET.

EUROMARKET See .... EUROCURRENCY MARKET.

EUROPEAN AGRICULTURAL GUIDANCE AND GUARANTEE FUND See .... COMMON AGRICULTURAL POLICY.

EUROPEAN ASSEMBLY See .... EUROPEAN PARLIAMENT.

EUROPEAN BANK FOR RECONSTRUCTION AND DEVELOPMENT, abbr. **EBRD** (Banque Européenne pour la Reconstruction et le Développement/BERD)

Inaugurated in April 1991 the **EBRD** – both (à la fois) a merchant bank (banque d'affaires) and a development bank – aims at (viser à) promoting (promouvoir) development and democracy in Eastern Europe. It operates (fonctionner) according to (selon) three rules (règle):

a. lending (prêter) only to countries with a good record (palmarès, image de marque) in market economics (économie de marché), human rights (droits de l'homme) and multi-party democracy;

b. letting no one country (aucun pays à lui seul) take more than 20/25% of the bank's total lending;

c. forbidding (interdiction à) the former Soviet Union – for a five-year transitional (transitoire) period – to borrow (emprunter) more than it has subscribed in capital. The former Soviet Union's provisional (provisoire) share (part) of the total capital of $12 billion (milliard) is 6%. These borrowing rules cannot be changed without the agreement of 85% of the shareholders (actionnaire) – which (ce qui) gives the USA and Japan a joint veto (droit de veto en commun). The USA is the biggest shareholder while

EU countries and institutions together (ensemble) hold (détenir) 51% of **EBRD**'s capital. There are 41 shareholding countries as a whole (en tout). The bank is managed (gérer) by a chairman and a Board (conseil) of 23 directors, including the former Soviet Union and the popular democracies. The bank's energy (efforts) and money (capital) are directed at (concentrer sur) a few (quelques) sectors: finance, telecommunications, roads, energy and the environment. Loans at very low rates (taux) and investment are primarily (en priorité) directed at the private sector, state companies (secteur public) coming second (venir après).

☞ See EU; MERCHANT BANK.

EUROPEAN CENTRAL BANK See .... MAASTRICHT.

EUROPEAN COAL AND STEEL COMMUNITY, abbr. **ECSC** (Communauté Européenne Charbon Acier/CECA)

Established by the Schuman Plan – so-called after (d'après) the name of the then (d'alors) French Foreign Minister (ministre des affaires étrangères) – it was set up (mettre en place) on April 18, 1951 when Belgium, France, West Germany, Italy, Luxembourg and The Netherlands (Pays Bas) signed the Treaty of Paris. The ECSC existed as such (en tant que telle) until July I, 1957, the date of the "Treaty of Fusion", when it was formally (officiellement) amalgamated with the other two Communities, EURATOM and the EEC. Since then (depuis lors) the three Communities have jointly (conjointement) been known as the European Community, or sometimes the European Communities. The Treaty of Paris, ratified by the six countries in 1952, suppressed all import duties (droit de douane) and quota (contingent, quota) restrictions on coal, iron ore (minerai), steel and scrap (ferraille) metal in trade between member countries. The treaty also set up (instaurer) a control over restrictive business practices (pratiques commerciales restrictives) and mergers (fusion, concentration d'entreprise) considered as obstacles to free competition (libre concurrence). Power was vested in (confier à) a High Authority to raise funds (réunir des fonds) by levying (percevoir) a tax on producers. This finance goes into the European Coal and Steel Fund (Fonds Européen Charbon Acier) whose functions are to make loans (prêt) for capital investment (dépenses d'investissement) and to give assistance to redundant (licencié) or redeployed (reconvertir) workers. The High Authority may also fix price levels (niveau) and production quotas at the request of (à la demande de) the European Council of Ministers. The parliamentary common assembly and the court of justice also established by the treaty were to serve as models for the institutions of the EC, now called the European Union, whose High Authority now is the European Commission.

☞ See EU; EURATOM; EUROPEAN COMMISSION; EUROPEAN COUNCIL OF MINISTERS; EUROPEAN UNION; MERGER; RESTRICTIVE BUSINESS PRACTICES.

EUROPEAN COAL AND STEEL FUND See .... EUROPEAN COAL AND STEEL COMMUNITY.

EUROPEAN COMMISSION (Commission européenne)

Is based in Brussels (Bruxelles) in the Berlaymont building, where it meets once a week, usually on Wednesdays. Has 20 members reputed for their independent, non-party (non partisan, libre de toute appartenance politique) stance (position) and appointed (nommer) by member governments for 4 years. This term of office (mandat) is renewable (renouvelable). Decisions are made (prendre) on a one-man-one-vote (une voix par personne) basis, but the biggest five members – Germany, France, Italy, Britain and Spain – have two commissioners (commissaire) instead of (au lieu de) just one, like the other ten. Headed by its President appointed for two years, the Commission is the motor of the EU. Its tasks, as stipulated in Article 155 of the Treaty of Rome, are those of initiative, supervision (surveillance) and implementation (mise en oeuvre). In charge of ensuring that the provisions (disposition) of the Treaty are carried out (exécuter), its main (essentiel) role is to submit proposals (proposition) to the European Council of Ministers. The latter (celui-ci) would be unable (incapable) to make decisions otherwise (autrement). Once (une fois) taken by the Council of Ministers, these decisions are implemented (mettre en oeuvre) by the Commission. The Commission also has powers to act on its own (de son propre chef) in a number of areas (domaine): coal and steel industries, competition policy (politique de la concurrence) and Common Agricultural Policy. Moreover (de plus), it administers EU funds, prepares a budget bill (projet), negotiates international agreements on behalf of (pour le compte de) the EU and decides whether (si) actions should (devoir) be brought (intenter) in the European Court of Justice against one member state for non-compliance (non-respect) with EU law (droit). After receiving advice (avis) from the European Parliament and if necessary from the European Economic and Social Committee, the European Commission and the European Council of Ministers issue (publier) **regulations** (règlement), which are immediately enforceable (applicable) in all member states, **directives** (directive) assigning (fixer) targets (objectif) to members which are free to select (choisir) the form and method of achieving (atteindre, réaliser) them, **decisions** (décision) which are binding (exécutoire) on the member, firm or individual (particulier) to whom they are addressed, **recommendations** (recommandation) and **opinions** (avis) which addressees (destinataire) are free to follow or not. As the heart of the EU, the European Commission has a staff (personnel) of 12, 000 or so (environ) including *eurocrats* of all ranks and types, from directors general (directeur général) – only 27, each dealing with (s'occuper de) an important sector: competition, farming, external relations – to interpreters and translators (interprète/traducteur) – about 3,000 – dealing with the 11 official languages: English, Finnish, French, German, Italian, Dutch (hollandais), Danish (danois), Greek, Swedish, Spanish and Portuguese, English and French being those in which most day-to-day (journalier) business is conducted.

☞ See BINDING; COMMON AGRICULTURAL POLICY; EU; EU COMPETITION POLICY; ECSC; EUROPEAN COUNCIL OF MINISTERS; EUROPEAN COURT OF JUSTICE; EUROPEAN ECONOMIC AND SOCIAL COMMITTEE; EUROPEAN PARLIAMENT; MAASTRICHT; TREATY OF ROME.

EUROPEAN COMMUNITY, abbr. **EC (Union européenne/CE)** or **EUROPEAN ECONOMIC COMMUNITY,** abbr. **EEC** (Communauté Économique Européenne/CEE)

From the start, a principal objective of the Community was the establishment of a customs union, other types of economic integration and political cooperation among its members. The Treaty of Rome in 1957 provided for (prévoir) the progressive suppression of customs duties (droit de douane) on internal trade, the establishment of a **COMMON EXTERNAL TARIFF** (tarif extérieur commun) and guarantees of free movement (libre circulation) of labour (main d'oeuvre) and capital within (à l'intérieur de) the Community. The original "six" – Belgium, France, West Germany, Italy, Luxembourg and The Netherlands (Pays-Bas) – were joined by the United Kingdom, Denmark and Ireland in 1973, by Greece in 1981 and by Spain and Portugal in 1986. Austria, Finland, and Sweden became members on 1st January 1995. Norway declined entry in a popular referendum held on 28th November 1994. In compliance with (conformément au) the Treaty of Maastricht, the name European Community was changed to European Union on 1st November 1993.

☞ See COMMON AGRICULTURAL POLICY; COMMON EXTERNAL TARIFF; CUSTOMS UNION; EU COMPETITION POLICY; EURATOM; EUROPEAN COAL AND STEEL COMMUNITY; EUROPEAN COMMISSION; EUROPEAN COUNCIL; EUROPEAN COUNCIL OF MINISTERS; EUROPEAN COURT OF JUSTICE; EUROPEAN COURT OF AUDITORS; EUROPEAN ECONOMIC AND SOCIAL COMMITTEE; EUROPEAN ECONOMIC AREA; EUROPEAN INVESTMENT BANK; EUROPEAN PARLIAMENT; INSURANCE; LOME CONVENTION; MAASTRICHT; SINGLE EUROPEAN ACT; TREATY OF PARIS; TREATY OF ROME.

EUROPEAN COUNCIL (Conseil européen) or **EUROPEAN SUMMITS** (Sommets européens) or **CONFERENCES OF EUROPEAN HEADS OF STATE AND GOVERNMENT** (Conférences des chefs d'État et de gouvernement européens)

Has/have met since 1974 and were given legal recognition (reconnaissance légale) by the Single European Act (Acte Unique Européen) in 1985. Deliberations are informal (officieux). Meetings take place at least (au moins) twice a year in the member state whose turn it is (dont c'est le tour de) to chair (présider) the Council of Ministers. Countries are represented by their prime ministers, except France whose president attends (participer, assister). Meetings are also attended by foreign ministers (ministre des affaires étrangères) together with (ainsi que) the president and one vice-president of the European Commission. Discussions bear on (porter sur) major (essentiel) EU issues (question) – the European Monetary System, Common Agricultural Policy, institutional reforms, foreign policy – and also on technical matters (affaire) on which lower EU officials (responsable) have failed to agree (ne pas parvenir à s'entendre). The

European Council often takes over from (remplacer, prendre le relai) the European Commission as the motor of the EU of which it is the executive head. The most important of these conferences in the recent past was the Maastricht summit in December 1991.

☞ See COMMON AGRICULTURAL POLICY; EU; EUROPEAN COMMISSION; EUROPEAN COUNCIL OF MINISTERS; EUROPEAN MONETARY SYSTEM; MAASTRICHT; SINGLE EUROPEAN ACT.

EUROPEAN COUNCIL OF MINISTERS (Conseil des ministres européens)
Is based in Brussels (Bruxelles) in the Charlemagne building but also meets in Luxembourg in April, June and October. Is chaired (présider) in turn (chacun à son tour) by member governments every six months. The composition of the Council changes with (selon) the subject discussed. Foreign ministers meet once a month. So do (de même que) farm (agriculture) and finance ministers. So-called (que l'on nomme) "Specialist Councils" also take place involving (comprendre) ministers of industry, transport etc., but less often. The 80 or so (environ) Council sessions convened (réunir) every year are prepared by the Committee of Permanent Representatives, known by its French acronym (sigle) **COREPER** (Comité des représentants permanents). Since the coming into effect (mise en application) of the Single European Act in July 1987, the majority-voting system (scrutin majoritaire) has replaced unanimity (vote à l'unanimité) for many decisions. Unanimity is still (encore) needed (requérir) for passing (voter) "directives" (directive) or "regulations" (règlement) in three main fields: foreign policy, taxation and the revision of treaties. Member countries have a power of veto if they consider vital national interests are at stake (en jeu). The majority-voting system works (fonctionner) on a weighted (pondéré) or qualified (qualifié) basis. The Council had 76 votes (voix), each member state being allocated (se voir attribuer) a number of votes in proportion to its size (importance): Germany, Britain, France, Italy (10 each); Spain (8); The Netherlands, Belgium, Greece, Portugal (5 each); Ireland, Denmark (3 each); and Luxembourg (2). As 54 votes were required to pass (voter) a law by qualified majority, a blocking minority (minorité de blocage) then had to pool (réunir) 23 votes. With the entry of Austria (4 votes), Finland (3 votes) and Sweden (4 votes) in January 1995, a blocking minority has to muster (réunir) 26 votes as the Council now has 87 votes as a whole (en tout) and needs 62 votes for a measure to be agreed. The powers of the Council are as follows: il sets (fixer) EU policies (politique) by adopting, amending or refusing draft legislation (projet de loi) initiated by the Commission; it adopts EU budget jointly with (conjointement avec) the European Parliament and it appoints (nommer) members of other EU institutions such as the Economic and Social Committee and the Court of Auditors.

☞ See EU; EU COMPETITION POLICY; EUROPEAN COMMISSION; EUROPEAN COURT OF AUDITORS; EUROPEAN ECONOMIC AND SOCIAL COMMITTEE; EUROPEAN PARLIAMENT; MAASTRICHT; SINGLE EUROPEAN ACT.

EUROPEAN COURT OF AUDITORS (Cour des comptes européenne)

Is based in Luxembourg. Consists of 15 members appointed (nommer) by the Council of Ministers for a renewable (renouvelable) six year term of office (mandat). Audits or checks (vérifier) EU revenue (recettes) and spending (dépenses). Plays a highly influential role as it has frequently uncovered (mettre à jour) cases of mis-spending (gaspillage) in the fields (domaine) of agricultural support (soutien), aid to the third world or financial misconduct (fraude). Publishes an annual report, as well as (ainsi que) specific surveys (étude) either (soit) at the request of (à la demande de) other EU institutions or on its own (de sa propre) initiative.

☞ See EU; EUROPEAN COUNCIL OF MINISTERS.

EUROPEAN COURT OF JUSTICE (Cour de justice européenne)

Founded in 1953, it sits (avoir son siège) in Luxembourg and consists of 16 judges. Each EU country has 1 judge. The 16th member ensures an uneven balance. The judges are assisted by advocates-general. Members of the Court are chosen by the Council of Ministers and appointed (nommer) for a renewable (renouvelable) term (mandat) of 6 years. Half of the Court is renewed every 3 years. The working language (langue de travail) is French. The Court may sit (siéger) as a single body (en formation plénière) for most important cases, or as one of the Chambers (chambre) which have been set up (créer).

Cases (affaire) brought before (porter devant) the Court may concern: litigations (litige) between member states, between the EU and member states, between EU institutions, between individuals (particulier), legal entities (personne morale) and the EU, and interpretations of international agreements and rulings (arrêt) on how national courts should apply EU rules.

The European Court of Justice is the Community's only court. Judgements have to be unanimous (pris à l'unanimité) and are final (sans appel). Hearings (audience) are public. As the Court's function is to ensure that EU law (droit) is correctly applied, most cases are brought up by the Commission. Union law (droit européen) prevails (prévaloir) over national law should (si) interests be conflicting (les intérêts se heurtent). The number of cases is constantly growing – over 350 a year – the most important ones being connected with EU competition and trade policy.

The Single European Act created a Court of First Instance, that began to work (fonctionner) in October 1989, to ease the workload (alléger la charge de travail) of the European Court.

☞ See EC; EC COMPETITION POLICY; EUROPEAN COMMISSION; EUROPEAN COUNCIL OF MINISTERS; SINGLE EUROPEAN ACT.

EUROPEAN CURRENCY UNIT See .... EUROPEAN MONETARY SYSTEM.

EUROPEAN DEVELOPMENT FUND See .... EUROPEAN INVESTMENT BANK.

EUROPEAN ECONOMIC AND SOCIAL COMMITTEE, abbr. **ESC** (Comité économique et social européen)

Is based in Brussels (Bruxelles) where its members – 200 or so – meet once a month. Members are appointed (nommer) on the nomination (sur proposition) of governments, by the Council of Ministers for a renewable (renouvelable) term (mandat) of 4 years. Is an advisory body (instance consultative) to the Commission and the Council of Ministers. It has the right (droit) under (selon) the provisions (disposition) of the Treaty of Rome to be consulted before "directives" (directive) and "regulations" (règlement) in some areas (dans certains domaines) can be approved. The Economic and Social Committee is made up of 3 interest groups: representatives of employers, of workers and of various interests such as consumers (consommateur), farmers, the self-employed (travailleur indépendant) and academics (universitaire). The influence of the Committee is particularly useful on technical issues (question) such as farming (agriculture), transport, social policy and the EU's internal market.

☞ See EUROPEAN COMMISSION; EUROPEAN COUNCIL OF MINISTERS; EUROPEAN INTERNAL MARKET; TREATY OF ROME.

EUROPEAN ECONOMIC AREA, abbr. **EEA** (Espace économique europeen/EEE)

Set up (instaurer) by a new treaty signed on 22 October 1991 in Luxembourg between the European Community and the European Free Trade Association, the EEA came into effect (entrer en vigueur) in 1993 after ratification by the European Parliament and the 19 signatory countries. The latter (celles-ci) are the 12 EU nations and the at the time 7 members of the EFTA except Switzerland (see below). The EEA is the world's largest free-trade area (zone de libre échange), with 380m consumers (consommateur) and 46% of world trade. Each EFTA member already had its own free-trade agreement with the EU for most goods (marchandise). But the new treaty goes further (aller plus loin). It removes (supprimer) non-tariff barriers (barrière non tarifaire) such as technical standards (norme), and extends (étendre) free trade to services and to the movement (circulation) of capital and workers. However (cependant), energy, coal, steel and food are excluded. The EFTA has not adopted the **COMMON AGRICULTURAL POLICY**. Its members are allowed (permettre) to retain (conserver) their own farm policies (politique agricole).

In return for (en échange de) better access to the EU's Single Market, the EFTA has adopted many of its rules on consumer protection, the environment, and competition policy. Mergers (fusion), public procurement (passation des marchés de l'Etat) policies and state subsidies (subvention) have to comply with (satisfaire à) Brussels requirements (exigence). The EFTA also has had to make more difficult concessions such as bigger fishing quotas for the EU in EFTA countries' waters (eaux territoriales), access for heavy lorries (poids lourds) through Alpine passes (col) in Austria and Switzerland and a pledge (engagement) of 2 billion ecus of aid from EFTA countries to help finance development in the poorer countries of Southern Europe.

EFTA countries have not adopted the full Single Market programme. The EEA is not a **CUSTOMS UNION** (union douanière) with a **COMMON EXTERNAL TARIFF** (tarif extérieur commun). Its members maintain border (frontière) controls with the EU, denying them (priver de) the full benefits (avantage) of the Single Market. However, EFTA countries thus save the cost of harmonizing their taxes and are able to retain their external tariff and quota systems which are more liberal than the EU's.

Nonetheless (cependant), many EFTA countries saw the EEA as a first step (pas) towards full membership (appartenance à part entière) of the EU. Although (bien que) better average economic results were obtained by the EFTA than by the EU in the past, concerning unemployment, inflation and income, some countries of the EFTA stagnated while others suffered from high inflation. In 1990, Finland, Norway and Sweden pegged (rattacher) their currencies to the ECU while (tandis que) Austria had long tied its chilling to the Deutschemark. Several governments were keen to (être impatient de) become members of the European **EXCHANGE RATE MECHANISM**, which theoretically allowed them to become associate members of the EU.

The main benefit to EFTA members of access to the European Single Market will come through fiercer (féroce) competition within their home markets (marché intérieur), offering bigger potential gains in efficiency when they are exposed to more competition. EFTA members can also look forward to (espérer) more inward direct investment from American and Japanese firms. Finally, the EEA will also allow (permettre) EFTA companies to compete on equal terms (sur un pied d'égalité) with EU firms for public sector contracts. Without the EEA, EFTA countries were likely to (être susceptible de) feel economically disadvantaged after 1992.

Switzerland rejected EEA entry by 50.3% on December 6, 1992, arguing that (faire valoir que) its sovereignty and neutrality were at stake (en jeu). The Swiss also feared that the free movement (libre circulation) of workers would increase the foreign population (20% at the time of the vote) in the country and eventually result in (avoir pour conséquence) a decrease in salaries.

As said above (ci-dessus), for some EFTA countries, EEA entry served as a staging post (relais, étape) to full EU membership. Austria, Finland and Sweden became members of the EC, now called the European Union (EU), on 1st January 1995.

☞ See COMMON AGRICULTURAL POLICY; COMMON EXTERNAL TARIFF; CUSTOMS UNION; EU; EFTA; EUROPEAN CURRENCY UNIT; EUROPEAN PARLIAMENT; EUROPEAN SINGLE MARKET; EXCHANGE RATE MECHANISM; FREE TRADE AREA; GOVERNMENT PROCUREMENT POLICIES AND PRACTICES; SERVICES; STANDARDS; SUBSIDY.

EUROPEAN FREE TRADE ASSOCIATION, abbr. **EFTA** (Association européenne de libre échange/AELE)

A regional association established in 1960 by the Stockholm Convention. It is headquartered (avoir son siège) in Geneva and now comprises (comprendre) Iceland, Liechtenstein, Norway and Switzerland.

Denmark and the United Kingdom withdrew from (se retirer de) **EFTA** when they joined (entrer dans) the EU in 1973. So did Austria, Finland, and Sweden in January, 1995 when they entered the European Union.

EFTA members have gradually eliminated tariffs (droit de douane) on manufactured goods originating from (provenir de) and traded (échanger) within (à l'interieur de) EFTA. Most (la plupart) agricultural produce are not included in the EFTA schedule (plan) for internal tariff reductions. Each member maintains its own (son propre) external tariff vis-à-vis non-members.

EFTA countries have all concluded a trade agreement with the EU providing for (prévoir) the mutual elimination of tariffs for most manufactured goods. Thus (ainsi), the EU and EFTA form a free trade area (zone de libre échange) which, following (à la suite de) a treaty signed in Ootober 1991, is now called the European Economic Area.

☞ See CUSTOMS UNION; EU; EUROPEAN ECONOMIC AREA; FREE TRADE AREA; TARIFF.

EUROPEAN INTEGRATED OPERATIONS (opérations intégrées européennes)

Intended to (avoir pour but de) provide financial and technical assistance to specific areas (région) of the European Union which are particularly deprived (démuni), these operations may be focused (cibler) on very limited sections – for instance Naples, Belfast or the Lozère department of France – or bear on (porter sur) much larger parts of the **EU**, like several regions of France, Italy and the whole of (l'ensemble de) Greece, i.e. the Southern parts of the **EU** suffering from a lack of (un manque de) adjustment (adaptation) to the enlargement (élargissement) of the Union. The latter operations (les opérations décrites en dernier) are named **INTEGRATED MEDITERRANEAN PROGRAMMES** (Programmes intégrés méditerranéens/PIM). These integrated operations come on top of (s'ajouter à) the other EU sources from which regions benefit (profiter).

☞ See EUROPEAN AGRICULTURAL GUIDANCE AND GUARANTEE FUND; EU; EUROPEAN COAL AND STEEL COMMUNITY; EUROPEAN COMMISSION; EUROPEAN MONETARY SYSTEM; EUROPEAN REGIONAL DEVELOPMENT FUND; EUROPEAN SOCIAL FUND; NEW COMMUNITY INSTRUMENT.

EUROPEAN INTERNAL MARKET (grand marché intérieur européen)

The name given to the Single (unique) Market EU authorities wanted to have achieved (réaliser) by (d'ici, pour) 1992, but which could not be largely completed until January 1993. The measures to be adopted in view of (dans la perspective de) this goal (objectif) are contained in the white

paper (livre blanc) drawn up (rédiger, établir) by the European Commission and approved by the European Council in 1985. They consist in removing (supprimer) three categories of barriers to the achievement (réalisation) of the Single Market:
a. physical barriers, i.e. the full abolition of frontier controls. The so-called (que l'on nomme) **SINGLE ADMINISTRATIVE DOCUMENT**, abbr. **SAD** (Document administratif unique/DAU) introduced in 1988 is an illustration of this action. Indeed, this single document now replaces (remplacer) no less than (non moins de) 70 forms (formulaire) that used to be necessary for lorry drivers (transporteur par route) going through internal EU borders (frontière). All restrictions on goods and individuals were to be removed (lever, supprimer) by 1992;

b. technical barriers, i.e. the abolition of national standards (norme) and regulations (réglementation). As a first stage (dans un premier temps), these should be replaced by a system of mutual recognition (reconnaissance) of national standards. Then (ensuite) European standards should be adopted. The EU intends to lay down (établir) minimum health and safety requirements (exigence) compulsory (obligatoire) for all member states, to liberalize public procurement (marchés de l'Etat), to establish a single market for services, to remove legal restraint (obstacles juridiques) to the formation (constitution) of EU-wide companies and to adopt a Union trade mark (marque, label);

c. fiscal barriers, i.e. the harmonization of Value Added Tax (TVA) and excise duty (impôt indirect) rates (taux) by means of (au moyen de) an authorized variation of + or - 2.5% against (par rapport) the target rate (taux de référence). A minimum 15% norm was set for VAT as of (à compter de) January 1993 while (tandis que) free movement (circulation) of capital and labour had been achieved earlier. One of the main stumbling blocks (pierre d'achoppement) remains the issue (question) of border control. Although (bien que) the white paper was drawn up by an Englishman, Lord Cockfield, the then (d'alors) Commissioner (commissaire) for the internal market, the United Kingdom is one of the most determined opponents (adversaire) to the removal (suppression) of frontier controls. It is preoccupied with terrorism, drug trafficking (trafic de stupéfiants) and by animal-borne diseases (maladie transmissible par les animaux). Ireland is another example of a member state facing (se trouver confronté à) the same difficulties in those fields (domaine). In order to by-pass (éviter, contourner) these oppositions, 5 members of the EU – Belgium, France, Germany, Luxembourg and The Netherlands – signed the **SCHENGEN AGREEMENT** (accords/convention de Schengen) in 1990. They were soon joined (rejoindre) by Greece, Italy, Spain and Portugal. The agreement consists in suppressing internal frontiers but increasing checks (contrôle) at external borders (frontière). It came into effect in March 1995 by harmonizing visa requirements (exigences en matière d'obtention des visas), pooling (mettre en commun) police resources, co-operating closely to fight narcotic trafficking and to detect offences (délit, infraction) in the field of taxation and customs duties. However, Greece and Italy are not yet in position to apply the agreement. Neither is Austria which adhered to it in April 1995.

☞ See EU; EUROPEAN COMMISSION; EUROPEAN COUNCIL; EUROPEAN COUNCIL OF MINISTERS; SINGLE EUROPEAN ACT.

EUROPEAN INVESTMENT BANK, abbr. **EIB** (Banque européenne d'investissement/BEI)
Is based in Luxembourg where its board (conseil d'administration) of governors (gouverneur), consisting of the ministers of finance of the **EU**, meets once a year. Since it was established in 1958, under Article 130 of the Treaty of Rome, the EIB which is both an EU institution and a bank has financed projects by making loans (consentir des prêts) and giving guarantees (donner sa caution, son aval) in three different fields (domaine):
a. aid programmes to the less developed EU areas and associated countries;

b. plans involving modernization, conversion and development considered necessary in order to promote (promouvoir) the harmonious development of the Common Market;

c. contributions to programmes in which member countries have a common interest, i.e. transport and other infrastructures, advanced technology (secteurs de pointe), energy and environmental protection (protection de l'environnement).

The EIB is a non-profit-making (à but non lucratif) institution. Its capital has been collectively subscribed by EU members and its financial resources are raised (se procurer, obtenir) on capital markets (marché des capitaux ou/et marché financier). Loans usually do not exceed 50% of the cost of the project and cannot be more than two and a half times (deux fois et demie) the subscribed capital (capital souscrit) of the bank. They are repayable (remboursable) over (sur) seven to twelve years. In order to apply these policies, three funds (fonds) have been established:
i. the **EUROPEAN REGIONAL DEVELOPMENT FUND** (Fonds Européen de Développement Régional/FEDER) dealing with the development of the poorer regions of the Union, such as Greece and Ireland;
ii. the **EUROPEAN SOCIAL FUND** (Fonds Social Européen) dealing with the redeployment (reconversion) of workers who have lost their jobs, more particularly young people in the neediest regions (les régions les plus nécessiteuses ou défavorisées) and;
iii. the **EUROPEAN DEVELOPMENT FUND** (Fonds de Développement Européen) providing (apporter) aid to countries of the Lomé Convention.

☞ See CAPITAL MARKET; COMMON MARKET; EU; LOME CONVENTION; TREATY OF ROME.

EUROPEAN MONETARY COOPERATION FUND See .... EUROPEAN MONETARY SYSTEM.

EUROPEAN MONETARY INSTITUTE See .... MAASTRICHT.

EUROPEAN MONETARY SYSTEM, abbr. **EMS** (Systeme monétaire européen/SME)
Was set up (instaurer) in 1978 and inaugurated in March 1979 to replace the so-called (que l'on nomme) **SNAKE** (serpent) which dated back to (remonter à) 1972.
Under the "snake", member countries agreed to manage (gérer) their currencies (monnaie) so that their exchange rates (taux de change) moved in relation to one another (les uns par rapport aux autres) plus or minus 2.25% and with the US $ plus or minus 4.45%. The "snake" was largely unsuccessful because countries kept going in and out (entrer et sortir) of it, as they were unable to maintain their currencies within (à l'intérieur) the predetermined limits and as, after 1973, commitment to (rattachement à) the US $ was abandoned, due to the breakdown (faillite, rupture) of the fixed exchange rate system (système de taux de changes fixes) set up by the Bretton Woods agreement in 1944. The EMS requires (exiger) countries to contain (maintenir) variations in their exchange rates within specified limits in relation to one another. These limits are set (fixer) against (par rapport à) a common currency unit (unité de compte) called the European Currency Unit/**ECU**.
Under this so-called (appelé) **EXCHANGE RATE MECHANISM/ERM** (Mécanisme du taux de change), each currency has a central rate (taux pivot, moyen) against the ECU. This central rate varies according to (selon) the weight (valeur pondérée) of each currency, i.e. the share (part) of the country's output (production nationale) in the EU total. Using the ECU central rate of each currency, bilateral rates are calculated for each currency against the others. The authorized fluctuation margins (marge) around these central rates originally were plus or minus 2.25% for all EU members except plus or minus 6% for Italy, Portugal, Spain and the United Kingdom. Greece does not belong to the EMS. Like the Special Drawing Rights in the International Monetary Fund, the ECU is therefore (donc) a basket (panier) of currencies, i.e. here the weighted average (moyenne pondérée) of EU currencies.
Since the creation of the EMS, several realignments of central rates have had to take place by mutual agreement. Financial solidarity mechanisms are available (disponible) to members when their currencies reach their floor (plancher) or ceiling (plafond) rates. Central banks have to intervene to maintain currencies within the predetermined limits or "bands"(bande). Intervention means selling the currency that is at its ceiling rate to increase the supply on the market and thus lowering its exchange value vis-à-vis other currencies, or purchasing the one that is at its floor rate to create the opposite effect. Short-term support (soutien) may be provided through various forms of credit. A realignment takes place only when a currency has stayed at its floor or ceiling for too long.
The advantage of the EMS is to stabilize EU currencies, to avoid (éviter) the sudden, trade-oriented (pour raison commerciale) devaluations of the past, and thus to reduce inflation rates. It is also to avoid fluctuations in currency values, which create uncertainties and difficulties for importers,

exporters and investors. Besides (par ailleurs), the ECU, which has become a reference, almost an exchange standard (étalon) for the EU currencies, is backed (soutenir) by the **EUROPEAN MONETARY COOPERATION FUND/EMCF**, a large financial reserve fueled (alimenter) by member states with 20% of their gold reserves and 20% of their US $ reserves. The EMCF acts as (faire fonction de) a clearing house (chambre de compensation) for the EU central banks in the EMS operations. It is assisted in this task by the Bank for International Settlements.

The ECU is now also used for many dealings (opération) both private and commercial – bank deposits (dépôt bancaire), travellers cheques, payments (règlement) and bond issues (émission d'obligations) – because its value is less likely (susceptible) to vary than any other EU currency individually.

As a whole (en somme) the EMS slowly paves the way (ouvrir la voie) to European Economic and Monetary Union/EMU (Union économique et monétaire/UEM), but serious difficulties remain. Indeed, the United Kingdom – which had eventually joined the ERM in October 1990 – defected from (quitter) it in September 1992, due to severe disturbances on European exchange markets created by the aftermath (retombées, suites) of Maastricht. Italy, which had left the wide "band" of the ERM in January 1990 to join the narrow "band", eventually had to leave the EMS at the same date as the United Kingdom for the same reasons, thus letting its currency float freely (flotter librement). Thus, both countries chose to let their domestic needs prevail: lower interest rates, implying lower exchange rates, to pull their economies out of recession and boost exports. In August 1993, due to renewed severe speculative attacks against the system, the authorized fluctuation margins of EU currencies around their central rates were widened to plus or minus 15%. However, some countries like France still adhere to plus or minus 2,25% margin in order to maintain the strength of their currencies.

In spite of the difficulties, the ultimate goal (but final) is twofold:

a. to transform the EMCF into a European Monetary Fund which would become the central bank of the EU and;

b. to create a single (unique) European currency. The achievement of this goal would make the EU a much more manageable (gérable) trading bloc, facilitating trade and putting the ECU on an international footing as a world currency like the Deutsche mark, the US dollar, the Sterling pound or the yen, thus encouraging investments.

☞ See BANK FOR INTERNATIONAL SETTLEMENTS; BOND; BRETTON WOODS; CLEARING HOUSE; EU; EXCHANGE RATE; INTERNATIONAL MONETARY FUND; MAASTRICHT.

EUROPEAN PARLIAMENT (Parlement européen ou assemblée européenne)
Formal title (apellation officielle): **EUROPEAN ASSEMBLY**.

Holds its full (plénier) sessions in Strasbourg, France, has its secretariat in Luxembourg while most of its 45 committees (commission) – which achieve (effectuer) much of the Assembly work – sit (siéger) in Brussels,

... uffrage universel) for the first time ... place every five years. Originally had 518 ... the European Parliament (député européen). The number ... MEPs is in keeping with (proportionnel à) the population figure (nombre d'habitants) of each member country.

The European Parliament has nine different political groups: Left Unity group/LU 13; Greens, 22; Mainly regionalist Rainbow group/RBW, 8; European Socialist Party/PES, 199; Independents and Non-attached/NA (non-inscrits), 96; Liberal, Democratic and Reformist group/LDR, 43; European People's Party/EPP, 148; European Democratic Alliance/EDA, 24 and European Right/ER, 14. In order to set up (constituer) a group, 26 MEPs are needed if they are nationals (ressortissant) of one country; 21 if they are nationals of two countries; 16 if they represent three member states and only 13 if they belong to four or more states of the Union.

The powers of the Assembly are as follows:

a. amends (amender) and votes on the European Commission's bills (projet de loi);

b. can reject measures backed (soutenir) by the European Council of Ministers and the European Commission;

c. adopts or rejects the EU budget, a responsibility it shares (partager) with the European Council of Ministers;

d. rules on (statuer sur) EU trade pacts (traité commercial) with non-members;

e. passes (voter) non-binding (sans caractère obligatoire) resolutions;

f. and can dissolve (dissoudre) the European Commission through (au moyen de) a vote of censure if a majority of two thirds of the votes (voix) is reached.

Points one and four on this list are recent contributions to the Assembly's responsibilities as rearranged (revoir, remanier) in 1985 when the Treaty of Rome was revised. These changes are embodied (contenir) in the Single European Act of 1985. The Treaty of Maastricht slightly extended the Assembly's right of veto, gave it the right to vote on the appointment of the president of the European Commission, but did not grant (accorder) it the authority to make laws.

At the Edinburgh summit of 12-13 December 1992, two important decisions were taken (prendre une décision):

i. The Parliament's seat (siège) is to remain in Strasbourg, France;

ii. As of (à compter) the parliamentary election of June 1994, the number of MEPs was raised to 567 in order to take into account (tenir compte de) both population increases and German unification which took place in October 1990. The respective number of MEPs are now as follows: Belgium, 25; Denmark, 16; France, 87; Germany, 99; Great Britain, 87; Greece, 25; Ireland, 15; Italy, 87; Luxembourg, 6; Portugal, 25; Spain, 64 and The Netherlands, 31. The number of MEPs has now been raised to 626 to take into account the entry of Austria, Finland and Sweden as of January 1st,

1995. The next important task of the European Parliament will be to prepare the special 1996 inter-governmental conference on Europe's future after the Maastricht treaty.

☞ See BINDING; EUROPEAN COMMISSION; EUROPEAN COUNCIL OF MINISTERS; EU; MAASTRICHT; SINGLE EUROPEAN ACT; TREATY OF ROME.

EUROPEAN REGIONAL DEVELOPMENT FUND See .... EUROPEAN INVESTMENT BANK.

EUROPEAN SINGLE MARKET See .... EUROPEAN INTERNAL MARKET.

EUROPEAN SOCIAL FUND See .... EUROPEAN INVESTMENT BANK.

EUROPEAN UNION, abbr. **EU** (Union européenne/UE)

The new name of the European Community since November 1st 1993 as provided by (comme prévu par) the Treaty of Maastricht.

☞ See EUROPEAN COMMUNITY; MAASTRICHT.

EUROPOL See .... MAASTRICHT.

EUROSCEPTICS See .... MAASTRICHT.

EU SUMMITS See .... EUROPEAN COUNCIL.

EX ALL See .... DIVIDEND.

EX COUPON See .... DIVIDEND.

EX DIVIDEND See .... DIVIDEND.

EX DOCK See .... EX QUAY.

EX FACTORY See .... EX WORKS.

EX MILL See .... EX WORKS.

EX QUAY (à quai ou franco à quai)

A price quotation (cotation, calcul de prix) in which the customs clearance (dédouanement) charges (frais) are included. Synonyms: ex dock, duty paid and ex wharf. Not to be mistaken (à ne pas confondre) with "ex quay, duty on buyer's account" (à quai, droits à la charge de l'acheteur), a quotation which does not include customs clearance charges.

☞ See EX SHIP; INCOTERMS.

EX See .... DIVIDEND.

EX SHIP, abbr. **X ship, X shp** or **X sh** (prix marchandises au débarquement)

A price quotation (cotation, calcul de prix) including (comprendre) all costs but neither unloading (déchargement) nor customs clearance (dédouanement) charges (frais).

☞ See EX QUAY; INCOTERMS.

EX STORE See .... EX WORKS.

EX WAREHOUSE, abbr. **EX WHSE,**
X WHSE (prix sortie d'entrepôt, de magasin) See .... EX WORKS; INCOTERMS.

EX WHARF, abbr. **EX WHF,**
X WHF. (prix départ quai, entrepôt maritime) See .... EX QUAY; INCOTERMS.

EX WORKS, abbr. **X wks** (prix sortie d'usine)

The price quotation (cotation, calcul du prix) of the goods (marchandise) at the place (endroit) stated (indiqué), here (ici) the works (usine) or factory.

☞ Synonyms: EX FACTORY; EX MILL; EX STORE/Xstre; EX WAREHOUSE/ex whse.

ex cp. See .... DIVIDEND.

ex div. See .... DIVIDEND.

EXCESS CLAUSE See .... ACCIDENT INSURANCE.

EXCHANGE CONTROL (contrôle des changes)

Government rules limiting the purchase and sale of currencies (devise) by residents of a country and the freedom of movement (circulation) of money to other countries. These regulations are adopted to protect the exchange value of the country's currency by preventing a flight of capital (fuite des capitaux), thus (ainsi) improving (résoudre) serious balance of payments difficulties. When such measures are applied (appliquer), importers must require (demander) prior (préalable) authorization from public authorities (pouvoirs publics) to obtain the foreign currency necessary to pay for the foreign goods (marchandise) they wish to bring into (faire entrer) the country. As (étant donné que) these steps (mesure) restrict imports, they are considered non-tariff barriers (barrière non tarifaire) to trade. Similarly, tourists wishing to go abroad cannot take out (emporter) more than the amount specified by the central banking authority of the country.

☞ See BALANCE OF PAYMENTS; BALANCE OF PAYMENTS CONSULTATIONS; CURRENCY; NON-TARIFF BARRIERS; SPECIFIC LIMITATIONS ON TRADE.

EXCHANGE RATE (taux de change)

The rate at which a currency (monnaie) is exchanged for (contre) another currency, for gold, or for Special Drawing Rights.

☞ See CURRENCY; IMF; PAR VALUE; SPECIAL DRAWING RIGHTS.

EXCHANGE RATE MECHANISM See .... EUROPEAN MONETARY SYSTEM.

EXCISE DRAWBACK See .... RE-EXPORTATION.

EXCISE TAX (Droit de consommation, d'accise ou de régie ou impôt indirect)

Sometimes called a **CONSUMPTION TAX**, it is imposed on certain goods (marchandise) produced within (à l'intérieur) – e. g. tobacco and spirits (spiritueux) – or imported – e. g. petroleum – into a country.

☞ See BORDER TAX ADJUSTMENTS; INDIRECT TAX; ROAD TAX.

EXECUTIVE DIRECTORS See .... BOARD OF DIRECTORS.

EXERCISE/STRIKE PRICE See .... OFFER FOR SALE; OPTION.

EXIMBANK See .... EXPORT-IMPORT BANK OF THE UNITED STATES.

EXPORT AGENT (Commissionnaire exportateur)

Represents the exporter or even (même) the foreign buyer. Helps find purchasers or sellers and receives a commission on sales transacted (conclure). May achieve (effectuer, s'occuper de) all exporting formalities, such as arranging (s'occuper de) insurance, shipping space (tonnage nécessaire), credit and documentation (documents d'expédition). Small exporters who cannot afford (ne pouvoir se permettre de posséder) their own (propre) export department resort to (avoir recours à) such services.

☞ See CONFIRMING HOUSE; DOCUMENTATION; INSURANCE.

EXPORT CREDIT INSURANCE (assurance des crédits à l'exportation)

A section of Accident Insurance designed (concevoir) to guarantee the exporter will be paid for his goods (marchandise) after delivery (livraison). The underwriter (garant de l'assurance ou assureur) of the export credit insurance is then (alors) responsible for (de) the collection (recouvrement) of payment from (auprès de) the importer. On account of (en raison de) the tremendous (énorme) variety of risks involved (concerner) in international trade, many countries have created public corporations or agencies (organisme d'Etat) acting as (faire fonction de) insurers either (soit) directly or in cooperation with commercial banks (banque commerciale). Indeed, governments have an interest in helping their industries to win these extremely valuable overseas contracts which are capital for a country's earnings (rentrée, gain) and balance of payments. Export credit policies give companies confidence (confiance) to sell abroad, knowing that they are covered against non-payment and also enable (permettre) them to offer potential customers attractive credit terms (conditions), thus (ainsi) making them more competitive.

☞ See ACCIDENT INSURANCE; EXPORT CREDITS GUARANTEE DEPARTMENT; EXPORT-IMPORT BANK OF THE UNITED STATES; INSURANCE; UNDERWRITER.

EXPORT CREDITS GUARANTEE DEPARTMENT, abbr. **ECGD** (Service du gouvernement britannique qui garantit les exportations; équivalent de la Compagnie française d'assurance du commerce extérieur/COFACE)

A government department in Great Britain, set up (créer, mettre en place) in 1919 to foster (promouvoir) exports by providing (fournir) British businesses with export credit insurance (assurance des crédits à l'exportation), especially against non-payment by overseas (étranger) buyers. Here is (voici) a list of some of the more important risks covered (couvrir): insolvency (insolvabilité) of the buyer – 90% of loss (perte, sinistre); buyer's failure to pay (défaut de paiement) within (dans les) six months – 90% of loss; défault (manquement, défaillance) of buyer on his contract after shipment (expédition) of goods: exporter bears (supporter) 15% of price of goods, ECGD 85% of remaining (restant) loss. If buyer is a government and default occurs (survenir) before shipment, ECGD covers 90% of loss. In the following seven cases, coverage (couverture) is 90% if loss occurs before shipment and 95% if afterwards (par la suite):

i. government action blocking or delaying (retarder) transfer of payment;

ii. imposition of new import licensing restrictions (restriction sur les licences d'importation) or cancellation (annulation) of an import licence;

iii. cancellation or non-renewal (non-renouvellement) of a British export licence or imposition of new export licensing restrictions;

iv. war, revolution or civil disturbances (troubles de l'ordre public) in the buyer's country;

v. war between buyer's country and Great Britain;

vi. additional (supplémentaire) handling (manutention), transport or insurance charges (frais) arising from (du fait de) the interruption or diversion (changement de route) of voyage (traversée, voyage) when these (ceux-ci) cannot be recovered (récupérer) from (auprès de) buyer;

vii. any other loss occurring outside (hors de) Great Britain and not within the control (hors du contrôle) of either (soit) exporter or purchaser (acheteur), and not normally insurable (assurable) with (auprès de) insurance companies.

The policies (police) offered (proposer) by ECGD are as follows: **comprehensive** (tous risques) **policies** in which the period of credit does not exceed six months (exceptionally five years), for instance for equipment (matériel) to be used in capital improvement projects (projet d'amélioration de l'équipement). The whole (ensemble) of the exporter's trade must be insured, or the whole for an agreed (déterminé) group of markets, for twelve months ahead (à venir). The exporter makes monthly declarations of the business done (transactions effectuées). In 1991 arrangements (disposition) were made by the ECGD for the sale to the private sector of these policies covering exports sold on short-term credit; **medium-term** (à moyen terme) **policies** in which the normal period of credit is five years – exceptionally the Bank of England accepts to re-finance (assurer le refinancement) bank-lending (prêt bancaire) to enable (permettre) exporters to face (faire face à) competition (concurrence) when credit exceeding five years is being offered (proposer) by competitors (concurrent).

The so-called (que l'on appelle) "contract policies" (police de contrat) cover from date of contract and include pre-shipment (préalable à l'expédition) risks. The so-called "shipment policies" (police d'expédition) cover from date of shipment; **finance guarantee policies** (police de cautionnement) for special cases where credit arrangements (modalités) mentioned above (ci-dessus) are not sufficient. The buyer makes an initial down-payment (payer un acompte) and the ECGD guarantees the full repayment (remboursement) by instalments (à tempérament) of any loan (prêt) granted (accorder) to him to finance the balance (solde); **dollar Market** (marché en dollars) **policies** designed (concevoir) to assist exports to North America. They cover a proportion of possible (éventuel) losses arising from advertising (publicité), stock in hand (marchandises en magasin) and distribution activities. They may even (même) guarantee some of (une part de) the expenditure (dépenses) required (nécessaire) to speed up (accélérer) production; other policies such as **Small Exporter** (petits exportateurs) **policies** intended (destiner) for small export turnover firms (société dont le chiffre d'affaires à l'exportation est petit) and offering favourable terms (conditions) as (en guise de) an introductory trade-in (droit d'entrée réduit) to ECGD services. Many other risks may also be covered such as the insurance of overseas subsidiaries (filiale) and of inventories (stocks) held (détenir) abroad against the possibility of confiscation or prohibition of re-exportation.

☞ See ACCIDENT INSURANCE; EXPORT CREDIT INSURANCE; EXIMBANK; RE-EXPORTATION; RISK; SUBSIDIARY.

EXPORT DOCUMENTS See..SHIPPING DOCUMENTS.

EXPORT HOUSE (maison/société d'exportation)

A merchant (société de négoce) knowing the market where the goods are produced, the market where they are sold, and with influence in both (l'un et l'autre). Such a company, acting as (agissant en qualité de) an agent (commissionnaire, mandataire) receives a commission to establish a link (lien) between the buyer and the seller and serves as an advisor (conseiller) for both. It can also see to (s'occuper de) all customs and transport arrangements (formalités). A **CONFIRMING HOUSE**, US **INDENT HOUSE** (maison, société spécialisée dans le commerce extérieur), is a type of export house which – on top of (en plus de) the services mentioned above – confirms (confirmer) that the order (commande) placed (passer) will be remitted (régler) and may even pay the exporter – the seller – immediately for the commodities (marchandise) sold, thus acting as the buyer.

☞ See SHIPPING DOCUMENTS; FACTORING.

EXPORT INVOICE (facture à l'exportation)

Part of export documentation. Is a document of title (titre de propriété) established when the goods (marchandise) are sent to a specific buyer (à un acheteur déterminé). On top of (en plus de) prices and costs, it contains specifications (caractéristiques) of the weights (poids), shipping marks (marque d'expédition), freight (fret), insurance and other charges (frais) such as commission to the agent (agent, commissionnaire, mandataire) and dock charges (frais, droits de bassin). Copies (duplicata) are sent to the addressee (destinataire) for him to (afin qu'il puisse) check against (comparer à) his original contract (contrat de départ).

☞ See DOCUMENTATION; INSURANCE; EXPORT AGENT; IMPORT AGENT.

EXPORT QUOTAS (contingents ou quotas d'exportation)

Restrictions imposed by an exporting country on the value (valeur) or volume (volume) of certain exports in order to (afin de) protect domestic (national) producers and consumers (consommateur) from provisional (provisoire) shortages (pénurie) of the commodities (produit) concerned or to support (soutenir) their prices in world markets (sur les marchés mondiaux).

These quotas are used within the framework (dans le cadre de) of International Commodity Agreements (accords internationaux sur les matières premières), of Orderly Marketing Agreements (accords de commercialisation régulière) and of Voluntary Restraint Agreements (accords d'autolimitation), They also aim at (viser à) promoting (promouvoir) domestic processing (traitement sur place) of raw materials (matière première) in countries that produce them.

☞ See INTERNATIONAL COMMODITY AGREEMENT; ORDERLY MARKETING AGREEMENT; VOLUNTARY RESTRAINT AGREEMENT.

EXPORT SUBSIDIES (subventions à l'exportation)

Government payments (versement, allocation) or other financial benefits (avantage) granted to (accorder à) domestic producers (producteurs nationaux) for the export of their goods (biens, marchandises) and services (services). Article XVI of GATT stipulates that export subsidies distort (fausser) normal trade activities – e.g. the long running dispute between the USA and the EU over agricultural subsidies – and impede (gêner) the achievement (réalisation) of GATT objectives. Indeed, producers can produce without loss and yet at a low price, thus breaching (enfeindre) the main principles of the GATT: reciprocity, non-discrimination and transparency.

The Tokyo Round prohibited the use of export subsidies by developed countries for manufactured and semi-manufactured goods, but allowed (permettre) it under certain conditions provided that (à condition que) the subsidies did not enable (permettre) the country that used them to obtain more than a fair share (juste part) of world exports of the product concerned.

☞ See ARTICLES OF GATT; CODES OF CONDUCT; COUNTERVAILING DUTIES; GATT; SERVICES.

EXPORT WHOLESALE MERCHANT (grossiste à l'exportation)

Acts (agir) on his own behalf (pour son propre compte), i.e. buys goods (marchandise) in bulk (en gros) and finds his own buyers abroad (à l'étranger).

EXPORT-IMPORT BANK OF THE UNITED STATES, abbr. **EXIMBANK**

A US public corporation (société d'Etat) created by executive order (ordonnance) of the President in 1934 and given a statutory basis (statut juridique) in 1945. The Eximbank makes (accorder) guarantees (caution) and insures (assurer) loans (prêt) to help finance US exports. The bank also covers short-term political risks (risque politique à court terme). The risks guaranteed are much the same (en gros les mêmes) as with other corporations of that type, like **ECGD** in Great Britain or Compagnie Française d'Assurance du Commerce Extérieur/**COFACE** in France.

☞ See ECGD; EXPORT CREDIT INSURANCE.

F

F. P. A See .... FREE OF PARTICULAR AVERAGE under MARINE INSURANCE.

FACE VALUE See .... PAR ETC

FACTOR See .... FACTORING/FACTORIZING.

FACTORING COMPANY See .... FACTORING/FACTORIZING.

FACTORING/FACTORIZING (affacturage ou factoring)

This is an activity in which a company which supplies (fournir) goods to customers and which has not yet been paid for these, pays another, the **FACTOR** or **FACTORING COMPANY** (agent à la commission qui recouvre les créances des entreprises ou société de factoring) to collect the money it is owed. The factor pays its client company immediately the value of goods supplied, usually less a small charge of 2-3% plus interest for any trade credit given to the debtor, and then has the responsibility of obtaining payment for these. In other words, he takes the risk away from his client company of not being paid, of having bad debts (créance douteuse).

Factoring companies can be independent or owned by (propriété de) merchant banks (banque d'affaires), commercial banks, finance houses (société de crédit) and export houses (maison ou société d'exportation), as is the case in Britain. They may, especially international factoring companies, play a special role with exporting companies, protecting by insuring against bad debts, facilitating payment or even lending money to suppliers over a short term at market rates of interest.

☞ See COMMERCIAL BANK; ECGD; EXPORT HOUSE; MERCHANT BANK.

FAIR TRADING ACT, 1973 See .... MONOPOLIES AND MERGERS COMMISSION.

FAS See .... FREE ALONGSIDE SHIP.

FAT MAN See .... TAKEOVER BID.

FED See .... FEDERAL RESERVE SYSTEM.

FEDERAL RESERVE BOARD See .... FEDERAL RESERVE SYSTEM.

FEDERAL RESERVE SYSTEM, abbr. **FED** (institut d'émission de la monnaie aux Etats-Unis)

The central banking system of the USA. Because of the large geographical area covered it has 12 regional **RESERVE BANKS** (banque de la Réserve fédérale), not one central bank, as in most other countries, 25 branches (succursales) and 11 offices (agences), all controlled by the **FEDERAL RESERVE BOARD** (Conseil d'administration de la Réserve Féderale Américaine) in Washington. The capital of the above banks is owned by the 5,978 member banks. The **FED** has the normal functions of a central bank: it is lender of last resort (en dernier recours ou ressort), sets (fixer) the discount (escompte)and other rates of interest, carries out open market operations (opérations d'open market), supervises the American banking system and generally sets out (définir ou fixer) the broad lines of government monetary policy.

☞ See BANK OF ENGLAND; CENTRAL BANK; DISCOUNT; LENDER OF LAST RESORT; MEMBER BANK; MONETARY POLICY; OPEN MARKET OPERATIONS.

FIDELITY BOND See .... ACCIDENT INSURANCE.

FIDELITY GUARANTEE See .... ACCIDENT INSURANCE.

FIMBRA abbr. **for FINANCIAL INTERMEDIARIES, MANAGERS AND BROKERS REGULATORY ASSOCIATION** See .... SELF-REGULATING ORGANIZATIONS.

FINAL DIVIDEND See .... DIVIDEND.

FINANCE HOUSE or **FINANCE/HIRE-PURCHASE/CREDIT COMPANY** (société/établissement spécialisé(e) dans la vente à tempérament ou société de crédit/prêts)

This is a company whose main business is to finance hire-purchase (location-vente, vente à tempérament ou crédit à la consommation) and related activities such as debt factoring (affacturage) and leasing (crédit-bail), which it does by borrowing large sums from commercial banks and the general public.

☞ See FACTORING; HIRE-PURCHASE; LEASING.

FINANCIAL FUTURES See .... LONDON INTERNATIONAL FINANCIAL FUTURES EXCHANGE.

FINANCIAL INSTRUMENTS (effets/instruments financiers)

A general term for most forms of short-term and long-term investments traded (négocier) on money markets and stock exchanges at a discount (avec escompte). It includes bills of exchange (lettre de change), bonds, certificates of deposit (certificat de dépôt), promissory notes (billet à ordre) and stocks and shares.

☞ See BILL OF EXCHANGE; BOND; CERTIFICATE OF DEPOSIT;COMMERCIAL PAPER; DISCOUNT; MONEY MARKET; PROMISSORY NOTE; SHARE; STOCK EXCHANGE; TREASURY BILL; WARRANT.

FINANCIAL INTERMEDIARIES (intermédiaires financiers)

A broad term to include institutions which receive and hold funds from individuals and other institutions for the purpose of making loans or investments. Financial intermediaries include banks, building societies (société/caisse d'épargne mutuelle de crédit immobilier), insurance companies, stockbroking firms (société de courtage) and investment and unit trusts (SICAV). Their overall function is to channel (canaliser) funds from lenders to borrowers.

☞ See BANKING; BROKERAGE FIRM ETC.;BUILDING SOCIETY; FINANCIAL SERVICES ACT, 1986; INSURANCE; INVESTMENT TRUST; MARKET MAKER; SELF-REGULATING ORGANIZATIONS; UNIT TRUST.

FINANCIAL INTERMEDIARIES, MANAGERS AND BROKERS REGULATORY ASSOCIATION, abbr. **FIMBRA** See .... SELF-REGULATING ORGANIZATIONS.

FINANCIAL SERVICES (services financiers)

A general term referring to banking (activités bancaires), investment (investissement), insurance (assurance) and accounting (comptabilité). The financial services sector started to be de-regulated in the USA and the UK in the second half of the 1970s.

☞ See BANKING; DE-REGULATION; FINANCIAL SERVICES ACT, 1986; INSURANCE; INVESTMENT.

FINANCIAL SERVICES ACT, 1986

This is a British law intended to make financial services in the UK more competitive internationally, maintain adequate protection for the investing public and at the same time reduce government involvement in regulating this industry. It coincided with the Stock Exchange's "Big Bang". It set up the Securities and Investment Board, abbr. SIB (l'équivalent de la Commission des Opérations de Bourse en France, abrégé COB) as a private (privé) body, financed and run by (géré) professionals themselves from the securities industry to authorize and regulate the latter (celle dernière); in addition, each area of financial activity such as unit trusts (SICAV), pensions funds (caisse de retraite), life insurance (assurance-vie) etc. is regulated by its own self-regulatory organization, abbr. SRO (organisation indépendante). The Act makes it illegal for anyone to run an investment company (société d'investissement) without permission (autorisation) from the Securities and Investment Board (SIB) or a relevant (approrié) self-regulatory organization (SRO), while certain investment markets to function will also need approval. In addition, financial intermediaries, such as insurance brokers (courtier), are required to tell their clients whether they are independent or **"TIED"** (astreint aux ventes exclusives), advising the client only on the financial products of the company they represent (the sale of which gives them a handsome commission).

This Act came fully into operation in 1988, but discussion and debate still continues about the efficacy and efficiency of the self-regulatory organizations as a means of regulating the UK financial services industry.

☞ See BIG BANG; BROKER/DEALER; DEPARTMENT OF TRADE AND INDUSTRY; FINANCIAL INTERMEDIARIES; INSURANCE; INTERNATIONAL STOCK EXCHANGE; MARKET MAKER; SECURITIES AND INVESTMENT BOARD; SELF-REGULATORY ORGANIZATIONS.

FINANCIAL TIMES ALL-SHARE INDEX See .... SHARE INDEX.

FINANCIAL TIMES-STOCK EXCHANGE INDEX See .... SHARE INDEX

FIRE INSURANCE (assurance incendie)

A non-life (non-vie) or casualty/property (biens et personnes) insurance involving (inclure, comprendre) two supplementary (complémentaire) sections (chapitre). The first is **MATERIALS** or **MATERIAL DAMAGE** (dommages matériels) covering material damage caused by fire to buildings (locaux), furniture (meubles) etc. Floods (inondation), storms (tempête), earthquakes (tremblement de terre), explosions and frost (gel) also come under (faire partie de) this section. The insurer, especially in the case of industrial buildings (locaux commerciaux), imposes such precautions as fire alarms, sprinklers (sprinkler) and extinguishers (extincteur). The second is **CONSEQUENTIAL LOSS** (dommages indirects) which covers other than material losses (dommages autres que matériels) due to fire, such as a loss of net profit (bénéfice net) caused to a business (affaire) by a fire. Indeed (en effet), the business may have to wholly (complètement) or partly (partiellement) close down (fermer). Salaries, rents (loyer) and interest rates which it may still (encore) have to pay while (pendant que) it is temporarily shut down, increased working costs (frais d'exploitation) which may arise (survenir) if it continues to operate (fonctionner) – all these can be covered, as well as (de même que) book debts (comptes fournisseurs) because records (traces comptables) of the debtors (débiteur) have been destroyed by the fire or by any of the causes included in a fire policy (police incendie).

☞ See INSURANCE.

FISCAL POLICY (politique budgétaire/fiscale)

One of the two main tools (instrument) of government (the other being monetary policy) to influence a country's level of economic activity. It concentrates on altering (modifier) levels of taxation and government or public expenditure (dépenses publiques). Tax cuts (réduction d'impôts), for example, in the form of tax allowances (exonération fiscale ou crédit d'impôt) such as for investment, tax rebates (remises d'impôt ou réductions d'imposition) and other tax incentives (incitation/aide fiscale), taking into consideration (prendre en compte) a time lag (temps de latence), will give firms and people more money to spend and therefore boost (gonfler) aggregate demand (demande globale) and employment, as will an increase in government spending. The main danger here is the risk of inflation (people will have more money to spend, but the economy may not be able to meet the increase in demand for goods that this causes, and this could lead to a rise in prices and also imports). On the other hand, both an increase in taxes and cuts (réduction) in government expenditure reduce the amount of money in circulation in the economy, and therefore reduce aggregate demand, and more than likely (très probablement), employment as well, all with a view to curbing (juguler) inflation.

☞ See AGGREGATE DEMAND; ECONOMIC GROWTH; INFLATION; MONETARY POLICY; MONEY SUPPLY; PRIVATIZATION under PUBLIC SECTOR; PUBLIC SECTOR BORROWING REQUIREMENT; TAX; UNEMPLOYMENT.

FIXED DEBENTURE See .... DEBENTURE.

FIXED DEPOSIT ACCOUNT See .... DEPOSIT ACCOUNT.

FIXED DUTY See .... CUSTOMS DUTY.

FIXED PRICE OFFERS See .... OFFER FOR SALE.

FLOATING CARGO INSURANCE POLICY See .... MARINE INSURANCE.

FLOATING DEBENTURE See .... DEBENTURE.

FLOATING POLICY See .... ACCIDENT INSURANCE; MARINE INSURANCE.

FLOOR, THE, (US) THE PIT (corbeille/salle de cotations)

The area in stock exchanges where traditionally buyers and sellers of securities (titres) meet to trade (négocier). In the International Stock Exchange, London, dealings (transactions) on the floor have largely been replaced by electronic information and trading systems (systèmes informatisés d'information et de transactions), whereby deals (transactions) are made over the telephone, thus eliminating the need for buyers and sellers to meet in person, except in the case of the traded options market (marché d'options négociées).

☞ See BIG BANG, THE; INTERNATIONAL STOCK EXCHANGE; PROGRAMME TRADING; SAEF; SEAQ; SEAQ INTERNATIONAL; TALISMAN; TAURUS; TOPIC; TRADED OPTIONS.

FOB See .... FREE ON BOARD.

FOB VESSEL See .... FREE ON BOARD.

FOOTSIE See .... SHARE INDEX.

FOQ See .... FREE ALONGSIDE SHIP.

FOR See .... FREE ON BOARD.

FOREIGN BILL OF EXCHANGE See .... BILL OF EXCHANGE.

FOREIGN EXCHANGE MARKET (marché des changes)

This is a market where foreign convertible currencies (devises) such as the pound sterling, the US dollar and the French franc are traded (négocié). It comprises two activities: first, the spot market (marché au comptant/du disponible), in which currencies are traded (se négocier) for immediate delivery (livraison immédiate); and second, the forward market (marché à terme), in which they are bought and sold for future delivery (livrable pour une date ultérieure ou à terme).

☞ See COMMODITY; FORWARD CONTRACT; LONDON INTERNATIONAL FINANCIAL FUTURES EXCHANGE; SETTLEMENT OF BARGAINS; SPOT/CURRENT PRICE.

FOREIGN TRADE ZONE See .... RE-EXPORTATION.

FORM 10K See .... SECURITIES AND EXCHANGE COMMISSION.

FORWARD BUYING See .... FORWARD CONTRACT.

FORWARD CONTRACT (contrat à terme ou engagement d'acheter ou vendre à une date ultérieure à un prix fixé)

This is a contract in which the seller guarantees to provide the buyer with a specific quantity of a commodity (marchandise) at a fixed price for delivery on an agreed future date. Forward contracts can also be used for foreign exchange (devises). **FUTURES** (opérations/livraisons ou cotations à terme) are similar to **FORWARD CONTRACTS**, except they are contracts for standard (normal) quantities regularly traded (négocié) in commodity markets. **FUTURES** can also be a means of buying and selling forward foreign exchange, financial instruments (instruments financiers) and options (option négociable), where they can also be bought and sold in specialized markets – **FORWARD/FUTURES MARKETS** (marché à terme) –, such as the **LONDON INTERNATIONAL FINANCIAL FUTURES EXCHANGE**, abbr. **LIFFE**. Both **FORWARD CONTRACTS** and **FUTURES** are used to hedge (mettre à couvert) the investor or reduce his risk against fluctuations in price or availability (disponibilité). **BUYING FORWARD** or **FORWARD BUYING** (achat à terme) means the buying of materials, commodities, shares, securities, foreign exchange etc. well in advance (bien à l'avance) in anticipation of future need or shortages or in order to make a profit or prevent a real or potential loss should prices change. **SELLING FORWARD** (vendre à terme) is the selling for delivery at a future date (livrable pour une date ultérieure) at an agreed price. At the time of the contract to do this the seller may or may not be in possession of that which he has agreed to supply. The **FORWARD/FUTURES PRICE** (prix à terme) is the price to be paid for a commodity, security or foreign exchange which is to be delivered at an agreed date in the future., and is contrasted with the spot price, which is for immediate delivery (livraison immédiate).

☞ See BEAR; BULL; COMMODITY; HEDGE; LONDON INTERNATIONAL FINANCIAL FUTURES EXCHANGE; FOREIGN EXCHANGE MARKET; OPTION; SETTLEMENT OF BARGAINS; SPOT/CURRENT PRICE.

FORWARD PRICE See .... FORWARD CONTRACT.

FORWARDING AGENT See .... SHIPPING AND FORWARDING AGENT or BROKER.

FOT See .... FREE ON BOARD.

FOUL BILL OF LADING See .... BILL OF LADING.

FOUNDERS' SHARES (parts de fondateur)

Shares often issued to those who have founded the company. These will usually keep the control of the company in the hands of the founders, who stand a good chance to receive greater dividends than other shareholders, but who may have to wait longer for these.

☞ See "A" SHARES;DEFERRED SHARE; SHARE; SHAREHOLDER.

FOURTH MARKET, USA (quatrième marché)

A market for buying and selling unlisted securities (titres hors cote) in which brokers (négociant en titres) and clients deal privately without using the more usual channels (voies) such as stock exchanges.

☞ See LISTING; OVER-THE-COUNTER MARKET; PLACING; THIRD MARKET; UNLISTED SECURITIES MARKET; UNLISTED/UNQUOTED SECURITIES.

FRAMEWORK AGREEMENT (accord-cadre relatif au commerce international)

The four separate agreements concluded during the GATT Tokyo Round, which constitute the so-called (que l'on nomme) "Framework Agreement" dealing with (porter sur):
a. the legal reconciliation (conciliation sur le plan juridique) of differential and more favourable treatment for exports of developing countries with the GATT most-favoured-nation principle (clause de la nation la plus favorisée), the legal acceptance (acceptation, reconnaissance) of non-reciprocity in trade relations between developed and developing (développé et en voie de développement) countries, and the greater participation of developing countries in the GATT treaties;

b. the trade restrictive measures (mesures commerciales restrictives) which may be taken by developing countries for balance of payments purposes (raison liée à);

c. adequate safeguard (sauvegarde) actions to promote (promouvoir) the start and extension of domestic industries (industrie nationale) in developing countries; and

d. an understanding (accord) on notification of decisions, regular consultation on new problems, enforcement dispute settlement (règlement des différends sur l'application) and surveillance of trading compliance (conformité de l'activité commerciale) with the agreement.

☞ See BALANCE OF PAYMENTS CONSULTATIONS; DISPUTE SETTLEMENTS; ENABLING CLAUSE; GATT; PREFERENCES; RECIPROCITY; SAFEGUARDS; SPECIAL AND DIFFERENTIAL TREATMENT; TOKYO ROUND.

FREE ALONGSIDE SHIP, abbr. **FAS** (franco le long du navire ou rendu sous palan)

The FAS price of a commodity (marchandise) in foreign trade contracts (contrat de commerce international) is the seller's price (prix de vente) including (comporter) all costs and risks up to the point of embarkation (embarquement) from which the vessel (vaisseau) or plane selected by the buyer will transport the goods (marchandise). But this price does not include the cost of loading the goods on the ship or plane. The term **FREE ON QUAY/FOQ** may also be used.

☞ See C & F; CIF; FOB; FOR; FOT; INCOTERMS.

FREE OF PARTICULAR AVERAGE See .... MARINE INSURANCE.

FREE ON BOARD, abbr. **FOB** (franco à bord)

The FOB price of a commodity (marchandise) in foreign trade contracts (contrat de commerce international) is the seller's price (prix de vente) including (comprendre) all charges (frais), packaging (emballage, conditionnement), carriage (port) up to (jusqu'à) the point of delivery (livraison) on board (à bord) the ship or plane and at the point of shipment (point d'embarquement) named (désigner) by the buyer. The term **FOB VESSEL** is sometimes used – especially in the USA – to stipulate that the transport charges (frais) up to the quay and the cost of loading (charger) the goods on to the vessel are fully included. The same rules apply (s'appliquer) to **FREE ON RAIL/FOR** or **FREE ON TRUCK/FOT** (franco wagon).

☞ See C & F; CIF; FAS; INCOTERMS.

FREE ON RAIL See .... FREE ON BOARD.

FREE ON TRUCK See .... FREE ON BOARD.

FREE PORT See .... RE-EXPORTATION.

FREE TRADE AREA, abbr. **FTA** (zone de libre-échange)

An area including (comprendre) at least (au moins) two countries that have eliminated tariff (tarifaire) and most (la plupart) non-tariff (non-tarifaire) barriers concerning trade among themselves (entre eux/elles), while (tandis que) each participating country applies (appliquer) its own (ses propres) tariffs to imports from countries which are not members.

The most famous examples are: the European Free Trade Association/EFTA (Association européenne de libre échange/AELE) formed in 1960; the European Economic Area/EEA (Espace économique européen/EEE) created through the 1991 treaty concluded between the EU and EFTA; the North American Free-Trade Agreement/NAFTA (Accord de libre échange nord-américain/ALENA) that took effect (entrer en vigueur, prendre effet) in 1989 between the USA and Canada, and was joined by Mexico in 1992; and the **ASIA-PACIFIC ECONOMIC CO-OPERATION/APEC** whose first summit took place in November 1993.

The **ANDEAN GROUP** (Groupe Andin) that has existed to no great effect (sans grand succès) since the late 1960s (1a fin des années 60) when (époque à laquelle) the **ANDEAN PACT** (Pacte Andin) was signed between Peru, Bolivia,

Ecuador, Colombia and Venezuela, recently relaunched its plans for economic integration.
Argentina, Uruguay, Paraguay and Brazil hope to unify their economies in the group they call **MERCOSUR** which they established through a treaty in March 1990.
The USA is interested in signing free trade agreements with members of these two groups.
Article XXIV of GATT defines the meaning of a free trade area in (au sein de) GATT and explains how other GATT provisions (disposition) are applicable to free trade areas.

☞ See APEC; COMMON EXTERNAL TARIFF; CUSTOMS UNION; EU; EFTA; EEA; GATT; NAFTA.

FREE TRADE ZONE See .... RE-EXPORTATION.

FREE ZONE See .... RE-EXPORTATION.

FREIGHT FORWARDER See .... SHIPPING AND FORWARDING AGENT or BROKER.

FREIGHT INSURANCE POLICY See .... MARINE INSURANCE.

FREIGHT NOTE (bordereau de transport)

Established by the shipping company (compagnie de transports); shows the charge (coût) for shipping the commodities (marchandise). Is sent to the exporter who may pay immediately, in which case (auquel cas) the freight note is returned to him receipted (acquitté) by the shipping company together with (ainsi que) signed copies (exemplaire) of the bill of lading (connaissement). If freight payment is to be made later, by the exporter or the importer, the freight note is also returned to the exporter but not receipted.

☞ See BILL OF LADING.

FRICTIONAL UNEMPLOYMENT See .... UNEMPLOYMENT.

FRIENDLY TAKEOVER See .... TAKEOVER BID.

FRONT-RUNNING (prise d'avance)

This is the practice by some market makers (teneur de marché), broker/dealers (négociant en titres) and brokers (courtier) of buying or selling securities on the basis of prior information received from the investment analysists they employ. For example, an analyst may be going to advise certain of the firm's clients to buy company X's shares. If the firm's market makers then buy these shares before the clients, and are therefore able then to sell them to the clients at a profit, but at a higher price, this is called front-running. Such an action is considered unfair and therefore controlled in many countries.

☞ See INSIDER TRADING; INTERNATIONAL STOCK EXCHANGE; SECURITIES AND EXCHANGE COMMISSION; SECURITIES AND INVESTMENT BOARD.

FTA See .... FREE TRADE AREA.

FULL EMPLOYMENT BUDGET BALANCE (équilibre budgétaire de plein emploi)

This is a way of calculating the benefits to be gained by the government from a given additional amount of government expenditure to lower unemployment or prevent it from increasing. A comparison is made between the sum to be invested by the government to lower unemployment and the revenue to be saved through having to make less social security payments (because of less unemployed people) and to be gained through additional tax receipts (coming from those who are now newly employed).

☞ See UNEMPLOYMENT; FISCAL POLICY; MONETARY POLICY; TAX.

FULL EMPLOYMENT See .... UNEMPLOYMENT.

FULL LISTING See .... LISTING.

FULLY PAID SHARES See .... SHARE.

FULLY-PAID CAPITAL See .... AUTHORIZED/REGISTERED ETC. CAPITAL.

FUND MANAGER See .... INSTITUTIONAL INVESTOR.

FUTURE DELIVERY (livraison à terme)

A trade term mentioned on a sales contract (contrat de vente) bearing on (porter sur) either (soit) crops (récolte) which are not yet (pas encore) harvested (ramasser, récolter, moissonner) or (soit) securities (valeur mobilière) dealt (échanger, traiter) on the so-called (que l'on nomme) futures market (marché à terme).

☞ See BUYING FORWARD; COMMODITY; FORWARD/FUTURES PRICE; FORWARD CONTRACT; INCOTERMS; SELLING FORWARD; SPOT PRICE.

FUTURES MARKETS See .... FORWARD CONTRACT.

FUTURES PRICE See .... FORWARD CONTRACT

FUTURES See .... FORWARD CONTRACT.

G

GALLOPING INFLATION See .... INFLATION.

GAMMA SECURITIES See .... ALPHA SECURITIES.

GATS See .... GENERAL AGREEMENT ON TARIFFS AND TRADE.

GATT See .... GENERAL AGREEMENT ON TARIFFS AND TRADE.

GDP See .... GROSS DOMESTIC PRODUCT.

GEMM See .... GILT-EDGED MARKET MAKER.

G7 See .... GROUP OF SEVEN.

GENERAL AGREEMENT ON TARIFFS AND TRADE, abbr. **GATT** (Accord général sur les tarifs douaniers et le commerce)

A multilateral trade agreement aimed at (avoir pour but de) expanding international trade as a means of (en tant que moyen de) increasing world welfare (bien-être). Over (plus de) 100 countries accounting for (représenter) 80% of world trade are Contracting Parties (parties contractantes) to GATT, and some 30 countries associated with it benefit from the application of its provisions (dispositions) to their trade (échanges commerciaux).

The acronym (sigle) GATT also refers to (désigner) the organization headquartered (avoir son siège) in Geneva, Switzerland, which is responsible for the enforcement (mise en application) of the General Agreement. This organization provides a framework (servir de cadre) within which international negotiations – known as "Rounds" (cycles) – are conducted in order to lower (abaisser) tariffs and other barriers to trade. It is also a consultative mechanism to which governments may resort (avoir recours) when seeking to (chercher à) protect their trade interests (intérêts commerciaux).

The GATT was signed in 1947 as (en tant que) an interim (provisoire) agreement. It was then (par la suite) internationally recognized (reconnaître sur le plan international) as the most important international institution in matters (question) of trade negotiations after the US Senate (le Sénat des EU) refused to ratify the 1948 Havana Charter (Charte de La Havane) which would have created the International Trade Organization/ITO as a specialized agency of the United Nations, like (à l'instar de) the International Monetary Fund and the World Bank.

The Articles of the GATT pledge (engager) member countries to the expansion of multilateral trade through the reduction of import tariffs and quotas (contingent, quota) and the abolition of preferential trade agreements.

The three guiding principles (principe fondamental) embodied (contenir) in the Articles of the GATT are:
i. **RECIPROCITY**. If one country lowers its tariffs, it can expect other countries to lower theirs (les leurs). This principle regards (considérer) a market-opening measure as a concession, for which concessions in return are required (demander). It does not allow a governement to threaten (menacer) to raise its tariffs, even if (même si) such a threat might force other governments to lower theirs;

ii. **NON-DISCRIMINATION**. This principle is known as the Most-Favoured-Nation/MFN rule (loi de la nation la plus favorisée). It says that countries should not grant (accorder) one member or group of members preferential trade treatment over (par rapport à) the others. Every country is to be treated as favourably as the most favoured;

iii. **TRANSPARENCY**. This principle urges (inciter) countries to replace (remplacer) non-tariff barriers – such as quotas – with (par) tariffs, and then to bind (considérer comme irrévocable) those tariffs, i.e. promise not to raise them again. Tariffs foster (favoriser) a climate of greater certainty among nations. Their impact on trade is easier to judge and they are also more easily negotiated than non-tariff barriers.

Here are the names and dates of GATT Rounds that have taken place since the General Agreement was passed: Geneva (1947), Annecy (1948), Torquay (1950), Geneva (1956), Dillon (1960-61), Kennedy (1964-67), Tokyo (1974-79), and Uruguay (1986-1993). It is to be noted that the duration (durée) of negotiations has tended to be longer since the 1960s. This is a sure sign of the growing difficulties members have met in trying to resolve their differences (différend).
The first major revision of the GATT was made in 1955, when (date à laquelle) provisions concerning subsidies (subvention) designed to (destiner à) reduce imports or increase exports – export incentives (soutien à l'exportation) – were strengthened (renforcer). Members are required to give details of any subsidies. If the latter (ceux-ci) affect the interests of any other member, they must be discussed with a view to (dans la perspective de) their possible (éventuel) reduction or elimination. Members "should seek to avoid" (devoir chercher à éviter) the use of subsidies on the export of primary products (produit de base). For other products, direct or indirect subsidies should be stopped "as soon as practicable" (dès que possible) if they result in (avoir pour conséquence) export prices lower than the home prices (prix sur le marché intérieur, national) of the product.
In 1965, another major revision was adopted. It forms Part Four of the General Agreement (Articles XXXVI, XXXVII and XXXVIII) and contains explicit commitments (engagement) to ensure appropriate

recognition of (reconnaissance due à) the specific needs of developing countries (pays en voie de développement). This new approach allowed the waiving of (dérogation à) the MFN principle in agreements with developing countries.

With the 1980s recession in world trade and the rise of unemployment, countries tended to become more protectionist, imposing non-tariff barriers – such as **VOLUNTARY RESTRAINT AGREEMENTS/VRAS** (accords d'autolimitation) or **SECTION 301** – while economic blocs signed preferential trade agreements with other countries.

After being brought to a halt (arrêter, suspendre) in December 1990 for want of (par manque de) any possible settlement (règlement) of the issues (question) on its agreed agenda, i.e. farm export subsidies, restrictions on trade in services – known as the **GENERAL AGREEMENT ON TRADE IN SERVICES/GATS** (Accord général sur le commerce des services) -, the protection of intellectual property (propriété intellectuelle) and restrictions on direct foreign investment, the Uruguay Round was resumed (reprendre) in March 1991.

In May 1992, the EU's farm ministers agreed on a reform of the Common Agricultural Policy/CAP, which was a first necessary step (pas) in the negotiations with the USA. In November 1992, after the USA threatened (menacer de) a transatlantic trade war due to begin in December, a breakthrough (percée, avancée) was achieved (réaliser) in the GATT talks (pourparlers). The EU signed the so-called **BLAIR HOUSE COMPROMISE** (accord de **BLAIR HOUSE**) by which it agreed on a 21% cut in the volume of its subsidized (subventionner) exports – in the six years to 1999 – thus allowing US cereal farmers to push into (s'introduire, accéder) new markets. In exchange for this, CAP reform compensation measures (mesure compensatoire à la reforme de la PAC) were to be safeguarded under the GATT agreement, while the oilseeds (oléagineux) deal was to focus on (porter, être centré sur) land area (surface arable) rather than volume of production as was originally demanded (comme l'exigeaient à l'origine) by the USA. 10% of the EU's oilseed acreage (terre consacrée à la culture des oléagineux) were to be set aside (mettre en jachère, geler) during the six years covered by the agreement.

The 21% reduction of the EU's subsidized exports was to entail (entraîner) the following cuts in EU exports: 500,000 tons of beef meat, 150,000 tons of poultry (volailles), 350,000 tons of pork meat, 130,000 tons of cheese, 250,000 tons of citrus fruits (agrumes) and 450,000 hectolitres of wine.

The other main elements of the farm deal included:

a. "rebalancing" (rééquilibrage). The USA agreed that it would consult the EU about some form of corrective action if its exports of cereal substitutes (produit de remplacement) into the EU undermined (saper, miner) the CAP reform agreement;

b. "the peace clause". The EU secured (s'assurer de, obtenir) the commitment (engagement) from the USA that the latter (ceux-ci) would not unilaterally use its strong trade legislation to impose new tariffs against the EU;

c. "US farm supports". These were to be cut by about 20% under the proposed deal, although (encore que, bien que) the Americans were allowed to retain (conserver) one important support system known as "deficiency payments" (paiement differentiel).

After some changes at France's request due to French farmers' unrest (agitation), this agreement – then called **BLAIR HOUSE 2** – was approved by the EU Council of Ministers just before the Uruguay Round was eventually (finalement) brought to an end (mener à son terme) in Geneva on its newly fixed deadline (date limite) – 15 December 1993.

Here are the main points of the Uruguay deal whose Final Act was signed in Marrakesh, Morocco, on 15 April 1994 by 125 countries and which went into effect (prendre effet) in January 1995:

WORLD TRADE ORGANIZATION/WTO (Organisation mondiale du commerce/OMC): the name of the new body (organisme) to replace the GATT. It will have stronger powers to police (maintenir l'ordre dans) world trade and settle (régler) disputes. It will implement (mettre en oeuvre) the results of the Uruguay Round.

Agriculture: import bans (interdiction) – rice (riz) in Japan and South Korea (Corée du Sud) – and quotas are replaced by import duties (droit à l'importation). These are to be decreased by (de) 36% over six years. Government supports (soutien) to farmers that increase production and surpluses (excédent) are to be cut by an average 20%. Spending (dépenses) on export subsidies (subvention à l'exportation), mainly European and American, which price efficient farmers out of world markets (qui privent, en raison des prix pratiqués, les agriculteurs compétitifs de l'accès aux marchés mondiaux) is to be cut by 33% over six years for developed countries and by 24% for developing countries over ten years. Developed countries are to reduce their subsidised (subventionné) exports by 21%.

Textiles and clothing: the **MULTI- (GB) FIBRE (US) FIBER ARRANGEMENT** quotas used by rich countries to limit developing country imports are to be progressively dismantled (démanteler) over ten years and tariffs reduced. Developing countries reduce trade barriers.

Services: a framework accord (accord cadre) for basic fair-trade principles such as non-discrimination. Special provisions (disposition) are to be negotiated for each sector.

Intellectual property: an extensive agreement on patents (brevet), copyright (droits d'auteur), trademarks (marque de fabrique), geographical indications (provenance), industrial design (création), microchip (puce) design and trade secrets. The establishment of international standards (norme) of protection and the requirement (exigence) for effective enforcement (application). Developing countries will have extra time to put rules in place.

Anti-dumping: clear rules for conduct of investigations and criteria (critères) for determining dumping and injury (dommage) to industry. Anti-dumping duties lapse (devenir caduc) after five years.

Industrial tariffs: will be cut by rich countries by more than a third. Over 40% of imports of industrial goods will enter duty-free. Major trading countries will suppress duties for pharmaceuticals, construction equipment, medical equipment, farm equipment, steel, beer, furniture, spirits (spiritueux), wood, paper and toys.

This long list of measures in a wide range of sectors explains why negotiators have taken so much time finding an agreement. The European film-making industry remains out of the deal and should continue to be protected against the entry of US films by means of its former subsidies and quotas. This example shows how difficult it has been to achieve (réaliser) an advance in free trade. In spite of this "cultural exemption" (exception culturelle) and of a few other exclusions, the Uruguay Round is to be remembered as the most ambitious trade liberalisation package (train de mesures) in history. New difficulties now arise (apparaître) though (toutefois) as signatories have to examine (étudier) the possible entry of China into the WTO and the links (lien) between labour standards (normalisation du travail) and trade.

☞ See ARTICLES OF GATT; BINDING; BOUND RATES; CODES OF CONDUCT; COMMON AGRICULTURAL POLICY; COMPENSATION; CONSULTATIONS; CONTRACTING PARTY; EU; FREE-TRADE AREA; GENERAL AGREEMENT ON TRADE IN SERVICES; GENERALIZED SYSTEM OF PREFERENCES; GRANDFATHER CLAUSE; IMF; INTERNATIONAL TRADE CENTER UNCTAD/GATT; LIBERALIZATION; LICENSING; MOST-FAVOURED-NATION TREATMENT; MULTI-FIBER ARRANGEMENT; MULTILATERAL TRADE NEGOTIATIONS; PRINCIPAL SUPPLIER; PROTOCOL OF PROVISIONAL APPLICATION; QUANTITATIVE RESTRICTIONS; SECTION 301; SERVICES; SPECIAL AND DIFFERENTIAL TREATMENT; STATE TRADING NATIONS; SUBSIDY; SUPER 301; VOLUNTARY RESTRAINT AGREEMENTS; WELFARE; WORLD BANK.

GENERAL AGREEMENT ON TRADE IN SERVICES, abbr. **GATS** (Accord général sur le commerce des services) See GENERAL AGREEMENT ON TARIFFS AND TRADE; SERVICES.

GENERAL AVERAGE See .... MARINE INSURANCE.

GENERAL INSURANCE See .... INSURANCE.

GENERALIZED SYSTEM OF PREFERENCES, abbr. **GSP** (Système généralisé de préférences/SGP)

A system developed by the **UNITED NATIONS CONFERENCE ON TRADE AND DEVELOPMENT/UNCTAD** (CNUCED) to promote (promouvoir) the expansion of manufactured and semi-manufactured exports from developing countries by means of (au moyen de) tariff preferences (préférences tarifaires). These preferences are temporary and non-reciprocal. Some developing countries – such as members of the **ORGANIZATION OF PETROLEUM EXPORTING COUNTRIES/OPEC** (OPEP) or other cartels for example – are ineligible to receive (ne pouvoir bénéficier de) GSP benefits (avantage). The Enabling

Clause (clause d'autorisation) adopted during the Tokyo Round, legally established (donner une existence légale) the GSP within GATT, in spite of (en dépit de) the existence of the Most-Favoured-Nation rule.

☞ See CARTEL; ENABLING CLAUSE; GATT; LOME CONVENTION; MFN; SPECIAL AND DIFFERENTIAL TREATMENT; UNCTAD.

GILT-EDGED MARKET MAKER, abbr. GEMM (contrepartiste général en fonds d'Etat)
An accredited (agrée) stockbroking firm (maison de titres), nominated by the Bank of England to deal in (opérer sur) gilt-edged stocks (fonds d'Etat). There are more than twenty GEMMS, whose main function is to set (fixer) prices for supply and demand in gilts to other Stock Exchange members and to outside investors they know.

☞ See GILT-EDGED STOCKS.

GILT-EDGED STOCKS/GILTS (fonds d'Etat, dits valeurs dorées sur tranche)
British government securities (titres) issued (émettre) by the Bank of England to raise money to meet the deficit in the government budget. Referred to popularly as "gilts" not because the certificates are edged (border) with gold, but because they represent excellent security - the government always guarantees to (s'engage à) pay the interest and repay the stocks on maturity (rembourser le montant total de la somme empruntée à une date spécifiée). Gilts are broadly divided into three categories, according to when they are due to be redeemed (en fonction de l'éloignement de leur échéance ou remboursement): short-term (à court terme), within seven years (known as **SHORTS** [valeurs à court terme]); medium-term (à moyen terme), seven to fifteen years (known as **MEDIUMS** [valeurs à moyen terme]; and long-term [à long terme], over fifteen years **LONGS** [valeurs à long terme]). Some gilts are **INDEX-LINKED** (indexé), which means the government changes the interest and the sum borrowed in line with (en fonction de) inflation, as measured by the Retail Price Index (indice des prix de détail). A small number of undated stocks exist (titres non remboursables); for example, stocks originally issued (émettre)) in 1883 to replace stock issued in 1855, which are known as **CONSOLIDATED STOCK**, or **CONSOLS**. Interest for gilts is in most cases fixed and payable every six months, and is known as the coupon (le coupon). Gilts are negotiable instruments (effets négociables), traded at a discount (avec escompte). They are bought and sold in large quantities by institutional investors - insurance companies (compagnies d'assurance), pensions funds (caisses de retraite) and building societies (caisse d'épargne / mutuelle de crédit / financement immobilier) because of their solidity and high degree of liquidity. As well as raising money the issuing (émission) of gilts can serve as a tool (instrument) of government monetary policy: buying or selling gilts, because they exist in such vast quantitities, will have the effect

of increasing or reducing the money supply (masse monétaire) and will influence long-term interest rates in the economy.

☞ See BOND; CENTRAL BANK; FISCAL POLICY; INSTITUTIONAL INVESTORS; INTEREST RATE; LIQUIDITY; MONETARY POLICY; MONEY SUPPLY; NEGOTIABLE INSTRUMENTS; OPEN MARKET OPERATIONS; PUBLIC SECTOR BORROWING REQUIREMENT; SECURITIES; TREASURY BILL; TREASURY BOND.

GILTS See .... GILT-EDGED STOCKS.

GNP See .... GROSS NATIONAL PRODUCT.

GO BANKRUPT, TO See .... LIQUIDATION.

GO INTO LIQUIDATION,TO See .... LIQUIDATION.

GOVERNMENT PROCUREMENT POLICIES AND PRACTICES (politiques et pratiques de passation des marchés de l'Etat).

The ways (procédés) through which (selon lesquels) governments purchase (acheter) goods (marchandises) and services. These ways are considered as non-tariff barriers (barrières non-tarifaires) by the GATT if they favour domestic suppliers (fournisseur national) even though (alors même que) imported goods and services are cheaper or of better quality. Most governments indeed (en effet) generally used to award contracts (passer un marché) on the basis of bids solicited from (appel d'offres lancé auprès de) domestic suppliers only. The Government Procurement Code (Code de passation des marchés de l'Etat) signed during the GATT Tokyo Round seeks to (chercher à) reduce unfair practices (pratique déloyale) in that field (domaine) by improving transparency and equity with regard to foreign suppliers.

☞ See CODES OF CONDUCT; GATT; MOST-FAVOURED-NATION TREATMENT; DISPUTE SETTLEMENT; NON-TARIFF BARRIERS; SERVICES; TOKYO ROUND; TRANSPARENCY.

GOVERNMENT THINK TANK See .... THINK TANK.

GO PRIVATE, TO See .... LEVERAGED BUYOUT.

GO PUBLIC, TO See .... LEVERAGED BUYOUT.

GO SHORT, TO See .... HAMMERING.

GOVERNMENT See .... BOND; TREASURY BOND.

GRANDFATHER CLAUSE (Clause d'antériorité ou des droits acquis)

A provision (disposition) in a legal instrument (instrument juridique) allowing (permettre) countries acceding to it to maintain pre-existing domestic (national) legislation inconsistent with (incompatible avec) the provisions of that instrument.

☞ See GATT; PROTOCOL OF PROVISIONAL APPLICATION.

GREAT DEPRESSION See .... BLACK TUESDAY.

GREEN CURRENCY See .... MONETARY COMPENSATORY AMOUNT.

GREENMAIL See .... TAKEOVER BID.

GROSS DIVIDEND See .... YIELD.

GROSS DOMESTIC PRODUCT, abbr. **GDP** (Produit Intérieur Brut, abrégé PIB)
This is the total value of all goods and services produced by an economy (but not goods which go into the making of other goods, such as plastic or sheet steel (tôle d'acier) for cars, such goods being known as INTERMEDIATE **GOODS/PRODUCTS** or **PRODUCER GOODS** (produits intermédiaires) at market prices.

GROSS NATIONAL PRODUCT, abbr. **GNP** (Produit National Brut, abrégé, PNB)
This is GDP plus income or revenues obtained from investments and possessions held abroad (à l'étranger), less income or revenues from assets held in the country but owned by foreigners (and thus leaving the country). GDP and GNP are measures used internationally to indicate economic progress and compare economic growth rates (taux de croissance) of different economies. In analysing figures for GDP and GNP it is important to make the difference between nominal values (en monnaie courante), which reflect the effect of inflation, and real or constant terms (en monnaie constante), whereby (par quoi) nominal values are deflated to show whether the actual volume of goods and services produced in the economy has grown or only been inflated by price increases. In the latter case, obviously, if GNP or GDP figures show an increase of say, 5%, but inflation has increased by 3%, then real growth has only been 2%. Where inflation is greater, say at 10%, this suggests that the economy has experienced a *negative* growth rate of -5%, bearing in mind (tenir compte de) the way in which inflation is measured.

☞ See INFLATION; RECESSION.

GROSS INTEREST See .... YIELD.

GROUP OF SEVEN, abbr. **G7** (Groupe des Sept/G7)
The group includes (comprendre) Britain, Canada, France, Germany, Italy, Japan and the USA. These countries are the seven most industrialized nations belonging to (appartenir à) the Organization for Economic Co-operation and Development/OECD. The G7 was formed (constituer) in 1987 for the purpose of (dans le but de) stabilizing the currencies (monnaie) of its members in order to promote (promouvoir) a better world economic growth (croissance). The G7 is also interested in helping to solve (résoudre) such political conflicts as the war in Bosnia or the nuclear attitude of North Korea.

☞ See ORGANIZATION FOR ECONOMIC CO-OPERATION AND DEVELOPMENT.

GROUP OF TEN See .... INTERNATIONAL MONETARY FUND.

H

HAMMER THE MARKET, TO See .... HAMMERING

HAMMERING (exclusion de la Bourse pour cessation de paiement ; entraînement de la baisse des cours par vente à découvert)

In the UK this means the bankruptcy (faillite) of a member of the Stock Exchange, which up to 1976 was usually announced in public, preceded by striking a hammer (frapper avec un marteau) to call everyone's attention.

In the US this refers to the widespread (répandu) selling by bears (baissier ou spéculateur à la baisse) of securities which they have promised to deliver at an agreed price and on a certain date, but which they themselves do not yet possess nor have they yet bought. They do this in the expectation of lowering the market price and so hoping to being able to purchase them at a price lower than that at which they have promised to deliver. Thus, if their strategy (stratégie) is correct they will make a profit, this being the difference between the price at which they have now bought the shares and the one at which they promised to deliver, the latter (ce dernier) being higher. The expression **TO HAMMER THE MARKET** (faire baisser les prix) by extension has come to mean simply selling large quantities of shares at the same time, which results in a sharp fall in price. The action by bears of selling securities they do not yet possess, known as **SHORTS** (valeurs mobilières vendues à découvert), is referred to as **SELLING SHORT, SHORT SELLING, SHORT/BEAR SALE** or **SHORTING** (vente à découvert). The person who does this is referred to as a **SHORT SELLER** (vendeur à découvert). The word "short" is used because the seller is short of (il lui manque) the securities he has contracted to deliver. The expression **TO GO SHORT** (vendre à découvert) simply means to sell securities the seller does not possess. Where a seller buys or is forced to buy securities he has promised to deliver, even when at a higher price than he is going to sell them, thus making a loss, he is said **TO SHORT COVER** (racheter à découvert ou faire une opération servant à couvrir un découvert en bourse), hence **SHORT COVERING** (rachats de vendeurs à découvert, opération servant à couvrir un découvert en bourse ou couvert de position à découvert). Being committed to delivering the securities when he does not yet possess them he is in a **SHORT POSITION** (à découvert). By buying the securities he needs to meet his contractual requirements he is said to close his short position (déboucler ou liquider sa position).

☞ See BEAR; BULL; BACKWARDATION; COMMODITY; CONTANGO; FOR/IN THE ACCOUNT; FORWARD CONTRACT; LONDON FINANCIAL FUTURES EXCHANGE; SECURITIES; OPTION; SHARE; SPOT/CURRENT PRICE; WARRANT.

HARD (UK) FIBRES (US) FIBERS (fibres dures)

Sisal (sisal), abaca (chanvre de Manille) and coir (fibre de coco).

☞ See INTEGRATED PROGRAM FOR COMMODITIES.

HAVANA CHARTER See................................GENERAL AGREEMENT ON TARIFFS AND TRADE.

HEDGE (protection ou valeur refuge) or **HEDGING** (couverture ou arbitrage)

A hedge (literally "la haie") is a way for a buyer of securities (titres), commodities (marchandise) or foreign exchange (devises) to protect himself against a loss or loss of profit from his purchase, due to fluctuations in exchange rates (taux de change), market prices or inflation.

For example, a dealer in shares (négociant) in April agrees to supply a client with a quantity of shares for delivery (livraison) in July at price X. When July comes the price of the shares has risen, say, to X + Y. If he had not sold his shares in April but hung on to (conserver) them he could have sold them in July for X + Y, the spot price (cours du disponible), thus making himself an extra profit of Y. So, in order not to lose this potential profit, the dealer in April hedges himself (se mettre à couvert ou se couvrir) by buying forward (acheter à terme) the same number of shares he has agreed to supply his client, at the same price, also for delivery in July. Thus, in July he delivers to the client his shares at price X, as agreed, and at the same time he sells the shares he has bought forward at price X for himself at price X + Y, the July spot price. In this way he has not lost the profit Y. If, however, in July the spot price is lower than the April forward price of X, say X - Y, he will make a loss of Y on the shares he bought for himself at price X, but this will be offset (compensé) by the sale of shares to the client at price X, which is higher than the July spot price by Y, the net result being no loss.

☞ See BEAR; BULL; FORWARD CONTRACT; OPTION; SETTLEMENT OF BARGAINS; SPOT/CURRENT PRICE.

HIGH PERFORMIING ASIAN ECONOMIES, abbr. HPAEs (économies asiatiques à hautes performances)

Indonesia, Hong Kong, Japan, Malaysia, the Republic of Korea, Singapore, Taiwan Province of China and Thailand.

☞ See DRAGONS; TIGERS.

HIRE-PURCHASE, US INSTALMENT CREDIT/BUYING (vente à tempérament)

A form of consumer credit in which the buyer of a good (article ou bien) pays for it over a period of time on a regular basis, say monthly, after having paid a deposit (verser des arrhes). In this time he has the use of the article but does not legally own it (devenir propriétaire) until he has paid the last instalment (le dernier versement). Thus, if the consumer fails to pay all the instalments the provider of the credit, usually a finance house (société de crédit) working in conjunction (en collaboration) with the seller of the good, has the right to repossess (reprendre possession de ou faire saisir un article ou bien non entièrement payé) or take back the good.

☞ See FINANCE HOUSE

HOLDER (détenteur, porteur, possesseur, titulaire)

Someone who is in possession of a financial asset (actif) such as a bank account, insurance policy (détenteur ou titulaire) or shares (porteur ou possesseur).

HOSTILE TAKEOVER BID See .... TAKEOVER BID.

HOT MONEY See .... MONETARY POLICY.

HOUSE See .... MERCHANT BANK.

HPAEs See .... HIGH PERFORMING ASIAN ECONOMIES

HULL INSURANCE POLICY See .... MARINE INSURANCE.

HYPER-INFLATION See .... INFLATION.

I

IBMBR See .... LIBOR.

IBRD See .... INTERNATIONAL BANK FOR RECONSTRUCTION AND DEVELOPMENT.

ICA See .... INTERNATIONAL COMMODITY AGREEMENT.

IMF See .... INTERNATIONAL MONETARY FUND.

IMPORT AGENT (commissionnaire importateur)

Deals with (s'occuper de) the marketing (commercialisation) of goods (marchandise) sent abroad (à l'étranger) on consignment (en consignation, en dépôt), i.e. not to a definite buyer, and for which a consignment invoice (facture en consignation) – an export invoice (facture à l'exportation) for goods to be sold by an agent abroad at the risk of the exporter – is drawn up (établir). May also offer the exporter a guarantee against bad debt (créance douteuse), in which case he is called a **DEL CREDERE AGENT** (agent ducroire). For accepting this risk he is paid an extra commission called **DEL CREDERE COMMISSION** (commission ducroire).

☞ See EXPORT INVOICE.

IMPORT QUOTAS (contingents ou quotas d'importation)

Restrictions imposed by an importing country on the value – for balance of payments purposes – or volume – for the protection of the domestic market – of certain imports.

☞ See BALANCE OF PAYMENTS; PROTECTIONISM.

IMPORT SUBSTITUTION (substitution d'importation)

An attempt (tentative) by a country to decrease (diminuer) its imports and thus (donc, ainsi) its foreign exchange (devises) spending (dépenses) by fostering (promouvoir) the development of domestic (national) industries.

☞ See INDUSTRIAL POLICY; INFANT INDUSTRY ARGUMENT; MERCANTILISM.

IMPORT TARIFF See .... TARIFF.

IMRO, abbr. **for INVESTMENT MANAGERS' REGULATORY ORGANIZATION** See .... SELF-REGULATING ORGANIZATIONS.

IN BOND (en dépôt ou en entrepôt sous douane)

A price quotation (cotation ou calcul de prix) in international trade contracts (contrat de commerce international) including all charges (frais) up to (jusqu'à) delivery (livraison) in a bonded warehouse (entrepôt sous douane) at a named (désigner) port. Customs duties (droit de douane) are to be paid by the buyer.

☞ See BONDED WAREHOUSE; CUSTOMS DUTY; INCOTERMS.

IN LIQUIDATION See .... LIQUIDATION.

INC See .... LIMITED or LIMITED LIABILITY COMPANY.

INCOME DEBENTURE See .... DEBENTURE.

INCOME TAX See .... TAX.

INCOME YIELD See .... YIELD.

INCORPORATED See .... LIMITED or LIMITED LIABILITY COMPANY.

INCOTERMS (incotermes)

Trade terms used in foreign trade contracts (contrat de commerce international), published by the **INTERNATIONAL CHAMBER OF COMMERCE** in Paris, defining a set (série) of international rules (règle) that describe clearly the duties (obligation) of the parties and thus (ainsi) avoid (éviter) disagreements (désaccord).

☞ See C & F; CIF; CIF and C; CIF and C and I; CIF and E; COD: CWO; DUTY PAID; EX DOCK; EX QUAY; EX SHIP; EX WAREHOUSE; EX WHARF; EX WORKS; FAS; FOB; FOQ; FOR; FOT; FUTURE DELIVERY; IN BOND; PROMPT CASH; PROMPT DELIVERY; READY DELIVERY; SAILING; SPOT CASH.

INDEMNITY See .... PRINCIPLES OF INSURANCE.

INDENT (commande reçue de l'étranger)

A foreign order (commande), an order placed (passer) from abroad (de l'étranger) by an importer or an import agent (commissionnaire importateur).

☞ See IMPORT AGENT.

INDENT HOUSE See .... EXPORT HOUSE.

INDEX-LINKED (indexé)

Anything whose value changes with changes in a given index (indice). For example, the consumer price index (indice des prix à la consommation ou de détail) is used by some companies to give their employees an increase in salary at regular intervals when the index moves up in value. Trade unions may use the consumer price index to demand higher wages for their members. The interest and capital repayment on some gilts are index-linked.

☞ See BONDS; GILT-EDGED STOCKS; INFLATION.

INDEXED BOND See .... BOND.

INDIRECT TAXES See .... TAX.

INDUSTRIAL DEBENTURE See .... DEBENTURE.

INDUSTRIAL POLICY (politique industrielle).

Government policies aimed at (destiner à) fostering (favoriser) the development of industry. Such policies may include (comprendre): tax incentives (incitation fiscale) to promote (promouvoir) investment (investissements) or exports; direct or indirect subsidies (subvention); special financing arrangements (accord spécial de financement); protection against foreign competition (concurrence); worker training programmes (programme de formation du personnel); assistance for (assistance, aide à) Research and Development/R & D (recherche et développement) and measures to help small businesses.

☞ See INFANT INDUSTRY ARGUMENT; FISCAL POLICY; IMPORT QUOTAS; INVESTMENT PERFORMANCE REQUIREMENTS; MANAGED TRADE; MERCANTILISM; TAX.

INFANT INDUSTRY ARGUMENT (argument de l'industrie naissante)

Temporary protection for a new industry (industrie, secteur industriel) in a country by means of (au moyen de) tariff and non-tariff barriers (barrières tarifaires et non tarifaires) to imports in order to (afin de) help it settle (s'installer, se mettre en place) and eventually (finalement) become competitive (concurrentiel) in world markets.

☞ See GATT; GENERALIZED SYSTEM OF PREFERENCES; IMPORT QUOTAS; NON-TARIFF BARRIERS; SUBSIDY; TARIFF.

INFLATION (inflation)

A continuing increase (augmentation) in the general level of prices, measured by the changes in the consumer price index, known in the UK as the **RETAIL PRICE INDEX** or **RPI** (indice des prix à la consommation ou de détail). This is calculated by taking a number of common items (article) on which most families are assumed to spend money (e.g. food, drink, clothes, lodging (logement), electricity, gas and transport) and noting the percentage change in price of these items in total, weighted (pondéré). The causes of inflation are several and often inter-related:

a. too much money circulating in the economy (caused by monetary and fiscal policy, credit facilities and economic growth), which stimulates demand, and not enough goods and services available to meet this demand, thus pulling prices up – what economists call **DEMAND-PULL INFLATION** (inflation par (l'augmentation de) la demande); and

b. rising costs of production (caused by, say, wage and salary increases, increases in the cost of raw materials (matières premières), oil and money), which lead to companies putting up their prices in order to recover (récupérer) these costs and or maintain their profit margins – **COST-PUSH INFLATION** (inflation par les coûts). If the rise in prices is very high, making it preferable to barter (troquer) rather than use money as a means of exchange, as was the case in Weimar Germany in the early twenties, this is known as **HYPER-INFLATION** or **GALLOPING INFLATION** (hyperinflation, inflation galopante). Where inflation is combined with low industrial production and high unemployment, as was the case in the UK in part of the 1970s, this is known as **STAGFLATION** (stagflation ou inflation dans la stagnation), a word formed from the words "stagnation" and "inflation".

Governments attempt to control inflation by using monetary and fiscal policy with varying degrees of success. High interest rates in the USA and UK in the late 1980s and beginning of the 1990s, part of monetary policy designed to reduce the money supply, for example, resulted in unprecedented levels of bankruptcy and, it is believed, have actually contributed to the economic depression experienced in both those countries.

☞ See AGGREGATE DEMAND; CREDIT CONTROL: ECONOMIC GROWTH; FISCAL POLICY; MONETARY POLICY; MONEY SUPPLY; PUBLIC SECTOR BORROWING REQUIREMENT.

INHERITANCE TAXES See .... TAX.

INLAND BILL OF EXCHANGE See .... BILL OF EXCHANGE.

INSIDER TRADING/DEALING (délit d'initié)

In the securities (titres) industry this is using privileged, inside information for one's personal profit, and in countries like the UK, the USA and France is illegal. For example, a director (administrateur) of Company A knows that his company is shortly going to take over (racheter) Company B and therefore buys a large quantity of shares in the latter (celle dernière), knowing in advance and before the general public that with this takeover (OPA) the price of Company B's shares will go up, when he can sell them at a profit. With the advent (avènement) of screen-based trading (échanges informatisés) any unusual movements in share price have become much more easily detectable, making it easier to identify insider trading. Financial regulators (organisme de contrôle) such as the UK Securities and Investment Board, the US Securities and Exchange Commission and the French Commission des Opérations de Bourse also collaborate much more closely in cases of suspected fraud.

☞ See INTERNATIONAL STOCK EXCHANGE; SEAQ; SECURITIES AND EXCHANGE COMMISSION; SECURITIES AND INVESTMENT BOARD.

INSTITUTIONAL INVESTORS (investisseurs institutionnels ou zinzins)

These are collective savings and investment institutions such as pensions funds (caisses de retraite), insurance companies and investment and unit trusts (société d'investissement à capital fixe et SICAV) which invest a large part of their funds in securities (titres). The choice of investment for an institutional investor is made for it by its own professional **FUND MANAGER** (gérant de fonds). Institutional investors are very important as buyers of securities. It is estimated that they own something like 40% of all the shares quoted on Wall Street, while in the UK they probably hold 70% of all the shares of UK companies quoted on the London Stock Exchange (*The Penguin Dictionary of International Finance*, 1989). Institutional investors have sometimes been accused of "short-termism" (politique à court terme/à courte portée) in that (en ce que) they are only interested in companies making a profit now, and this prevents them from investing in good companies which require more long-term investment and so re-invest (réinvestir) a higher proportion of their profits instead of paying out higher dividends.

☞ See COUPON; DIVIDEND; INTERNATIONAL STOCK EXCHANGE; INVESTMENT TRUST; SECURITY; SHARE; UNIT TRUST; YIELD.

INSURABLE INTEREST See ....PRINCIPLES OF INSURANCE.

INSURANCE (assurance)

An agreement (accord) or contract (contrat) commonly called a policy (police) between the **ASSURED**, the **INSURED** or **POLICYHOLDER** (assuré, titulaire d'une police) and the **ASSURER** or **INSURER** (assureur). The former (le premier) pays a premium (prime) to the latter (le second) who in return (en échange) promises to compensate (dédommager, indemniser) him should he (dans le cas où il) suffer (subir) losses (perte, dommage). Contracts are sold either (soit) directly by insurance companies and their agents such as, in the UK, banks and building societies (société d'investissement et de crédit immobilier), or (soit) through (par l'intermédiaire de) brokers (courtier) who may be "tied" (astreint à la vente exclusive des contrats d'une compagnie) or self-employed (indépendant), selling insurance for a variety of companies. Brokers act as (agir en tant que) agents (mandataire) for their clients, negotiate the most favourable terms (conditions) for them and receive commissions from insurers. The four broad categories of insurance are:

i. FIRE (incendie), including (comprendre) flood (inondation) and storm (tempête) damage;

ii. ACCIDENT (accident), including theft or burglary (vol) and liability (responsabilité);

iii. MARINE (maritime), including a share (part) of aviation insurance;

iv. LIFE (vie, ou sur la vie), including endowment (assurance en cas de vie, viagère, à capital différé). The first three categories are known as **NON-LIFE** (non-vie) or **GENERAL** (générale) or **CASUALTY/PROPERTY** (biens et personnes), as distinct from life **ASSURANCE** or – more commonly today, especially in the USA – life insurance.

The premiums are so (de telle façon) calculated that the total amount paid by all insured should (devoir) enable (permettre) the insurer to pay claims (sinistre) and administrative costs (frais de dossier) and to make a profit (bénéfice). The calculation of premiums is made by **ACTUARIES** (actuaire) on the evidence of (sur la base de) existing statistical information regarding (concernant) past losses. **ASSESSORS** (assesseur) establish losses in money terms (en termes financiers). The basis of insurance consists in spreading (répartir) risk so that an individual who suffers loss is compensated at the expense of (aux dépens de) all those who insure against (s'assurer sur, pour) it. In 1992, the magazine *The Economist* published a list of European and American top insurance and reinsurance (réassurance) companies in declining order (par ordre décroissant) of gross premium income (revenu brut sur primes). The top insurance companies in Europe are: Allianz, Zurich, UAP, Prudential, Generali, Royal Insurance, Winterthur, Axa-Midi, Nationale-Nederlanden and Sun Alliance. The biggest reinsurance companies are: Munich Re, Swiss Re and Hannover Re. America's top ten insurance companies by premium income are: Prudential, State Farm, Metropolitan, Allstate, Aetna Life and Casualty, CIGNA, American International Group, Travelers, New York Life and CNA Financial. There have been enormous difficulties in the world's non-life insurance industry. In 1989 and 1990, over (plus de) 100 insurers in the USA went into liquidation (faire faillite).

☞ See ACCIDENT INSURANCE; CAPITAL MARKET; EXPORT CREDIT INSURANCE; FINANCIAL SERVICES ACT, 1986; FIRE INSURANCE; INSURANCE PREMIUM; LIFE INSURANCE; LLOYD'S; MARINE INSURANCE; NATIONAL INSURANCE; PRINCIPLES OF INSURANCE; REINSURANCE; RISK; SERVICES; UNDERWRITER.

INSURANCE BROKER See .... INSURANCE.

INSURANCE PREMIUM (prime d'assurance)

A regular (régulier) or original lump (global, forfaitaire en une seule fois) sum paid for an insurance policy (police d'assurance) that provides (assurer, fournir) protection against a risk.

☞ See INSURANCE.

INSURED See .... INSURANCE.

INSURER See .... INSURANCE.

INTEGRATED MEDITERRANEAN PROGRAMMES See .... EUROPEAN INTEGRATED OPERATIONS.

INTEGRATED PROGRAM FOR COMMODITIES, abbr. **IPC** (Programme intégré des matières premières/PIMP).

A plan adopted at the **UNITED NATIONS CONFERENCE ON TRADE AND DEVELOPMENT/UNCTAD** in 1976 for promoting (promouvoir) the adoption of International Commodity Agreements (Accords internationaux sur les matières premières) and other measures aimed at (destiner à) strengthening (renforcer) export earnings (recettes à l'exportation) for 18 key commodities (produits essentiels) exported by some developing countries. The 18 commodities include 10 major products which are storable (stockable) and suitable for buffer stock arrangements (pouvoir faire l'objet de constitution de stocks régulateurs) – cocoa (cacao), coffee, copper (cuivre), cotton, hard fibres (fibres dures), jute, rubber, sugar, tea and tin (étain) – and 8 additional products of particular export interest to developing countries – bananas, bauxite, iron ore (minerai de fer), manganese, meat, phosphates, tropical timber (bois exotique) and vegetable (végétal) oil –. The centerpiece (pièce maîtresse) of the Program is the Common Fund (Fonds commun) with two provisions (disposition) or "windows":

i. window 1, financed by mandatory (obligatoire) contributions of member governments, provides funds to help finance buffer stocks (stocks régulateurs);

ii. window 2, largely financed by voluntary contributions, supports (soutenir) research and development/R & D and export promotion for selected commodities.

☞ See BUFFER STOCKS; COMMODITY; HARD FIBRES; INTERNATIONAL COMMODITY AGREEMENT; MANAGED TRADE; UNCTAD.

INTER-BANK MARKET BID RATE See .... LIBOR.

INTER-BANK MONEY See .... LIBOR.

INTER-BANK MONEY MARKET See .... LIBOR.

INTER-BANK RATE See .... LIBOR.

INTEREST (intérêt)

This is the price to be paid by a borrower (emprunteur) of money to the lender (prêteur). The **INTEREST RATE** or **RATE OF INTEREST** (taux d'intérêt) determines the amount to be paid by the borrower and is expressed as a percentage of the sum borrowed (emprunt ou prêt). This may be fixed (fixe) or floating or variable (flottant ou variable).

There are different types of interest rate, depending on the economic agents involved. For example, governments fix a central interest rate (taux directeur) which in turn determines the interest rate commercial banks offer to their customers; banks borrowing from each other or from the central bank are subjected to special interest rates; discount rates (taux d'escompte) for financial instruments like treasury bills (bons de trésor à court terme) and bills of exchange (traite) are a form of interest. Interest rates will vary according to whether (selon que) the borrowing (emprunts) is short-term, medium or long-term, the risk involved and the nature of any security (nantissement) offered.

☞ See BANKING; BORROWING; CENTRAL BANK; COUPON; DEBENTURE; DISCOUNT; DISCOUNT HOUSE; DISCOUNT MARKET; LENDING; LIBRO; LOAN; LOMBARD RATE; MONETARY POLICY; MONEY MARKET.

INTEREST BOND See .... BOND.

INTEREST RATE See .... INTEREST.

INTERIM DIVIDEND See .... DIVIDEND.

INTERMARKET TRADING SYSTEM See .... OVER-THE-COUNTER MARKET.

INTERMEDIATE GOODS See .... GROSS DOMESTIC PRODUCT.

INTERMEDIATE PRODUCTS See .... GROSS DOMESTIC PRODUCT.

INTERNATIONAL TRADE ORGANIZATION See .... GATT.

INTERNATIONAL ARRANGEMENT ON EXPORT CREDITS (Accord international sur les crédits à l'exportation)

An agreement among 22 OECD members not to lower (abaisser) interest rates (taux d'intérêt) for export credits below (au-dessous) predesignated (préétablir) levels (niveau) without informing other OECD members. Although (bien que) it is not binding (à caractère obligatoire), this arrangement encourages transparency in that field.

☞ See BINDING; EXPORT SUBSIDIES; OECD; SUBSIDY; TRANSPARENCY.

INTERNATIONAL BANK FOR RECONSTRUCTION AND DEVELOPMENT, abbr. **IBRD** (Banque internationale pour la reconstruction et le développement/BIRD)

The IBRD, commonly known as the World Bank (Banque mondiale), is an intergovernmental financial institution headquartered (avoir son siège) in Washington, D.C. Its aims (objectif) are to help increase productivity and incomes (revenu) and reduce poverty in developing countries (pays en voie de développement). It was established (créer) in December 1945 on the basis of a plan developed (élaborer, mettre au point) at the Bretton Woods Conference of 1944. The Bank lends (prêter) financial resources to credit-worthy (solvable) developing countries. It raises funds (lever, se procurer des capitaux) by selling bonds (obligation) in the world's major capital markets (marché financier). Over the years (au fil des années), these bonds have earned (acquérir) a quality rating (réputation) enjoyed only by (dont jouissent seulement) sound (aux finances saines) governments and leading companies (entreprises de premier ordre). The profits (bénéfice) earned (réaliser) by the Bank are ploughed back (réinvestir, reverser) into its capital.

☞ See BOND; BRETTON WOODS; CAPITAL MARKET.

INTERNATIONAL CHAMBER OF COMMERCE See .... INCOTERMS.

INTERNATIONAL COMMODITY AGREEMENT, abbr. **ICA** (Accord international sur les matières premières/AIMP)

Provisions (disposition) intended (destiner à) to defend a price range (échelle, éventail de prix) for some commodities through the use (utilisation) of buffer stocks (stock régulateur) and/or export quotas (contingent d'exportation). Such provisions are applied (appliquer) through (par le biais de) existing agreements between most producers of coffee, cocoa (cacao), natural rubber, sugar and tin (étain). The term ICA also applies to commodity agreements – for jute and jute products (jute et ses dérivés), olive oil and wheat (blé), for example – that seek (chercher à) to foster (promouvoir) cooperation among producers and consumers through improved (améliorer) consultations, exchange of information, research and development/R & D and export promotion.

☞ See BUFFER STOCKS; COMMODITY; EXPORT QUOTAS; INTEGRATED PROGRAM FOR COMMODITIES.

INTERNATIONAL MONETARY FUND, abbr. **IMF** (Fonds monétaire international/FMI)

Was established by the Bretton Woods Agreement of 1944 and came into effect (entrer en vigueur) in March 1947. Its purpose (but) is to stabilize the international monetary system in order to promote (promouvoir) the harmonious expansion of international trade. This involves the removal (suppression) of foreign exchange controls (contrôle des changes), the stabilization of exchange rates (taux de change) and the operation (utilisation) of a multilateral payments system (système de paiements multilatéraux) between member countries – now over (plus de) 150. Originally, members were required (être tenu de) to maintain an exchange rate within a limit of + or - 1% around its par value (parité). This par value was priced (évaluer) in terms of (par rapport à) the US dollar which in turn was linked (lier) to gold. In December 1971 the so-called (que l'on appelle) **GROUP OF TEN** or **PARIS CLUB** – the USA, the UK, Germany, France, Belgium, The Netherlands, Italy, Sweden, Canada and Japan – adopted new central values (taux pivot, taux moyen) so as to achieve (effectuer) a dollar devaluation of 10%, with allowed (permettre) fluctuation margins (marge de fluctuation) of + or - 2.25%. Each member country was asked to subscribe to the IMF a quota consisting of 25% in gold and 75% in their national currency (monnaie). Members' balance of payments temporary difficulties are eased (atténuer) by the Fund, thus helping to stabilize exchange rates. A member in temporary difficulty receives foreign exchange (devises) from the IMF in return for (en échange de) its own currency which it must buy back (racheter) within (dans un délai de) three to five years. Members with overdue debts (arriérés) must confer with the IMF on the policies (politique) they apply (appliquer) or should adopt to straighten (redresser) their balance of payments deficit. Stand-by credit (crédit relais) may also be negotiated. Supplementary international monetary reserve assets (avoirs) are available (disponible, à la disposition de) to members by means of (au moyen de) **SPECIAL DRAWING RIGHTS/SDRs** (Droits de tirage spéciaux/DTS). The latter (ceux-ci) were created by the IMF in 1969 and may be used both in transactions between the Fund and members and in the settlements (règlement) of members' international accounts. The value of an SDR is calculated with reference to the foreign exchange value of a basket (panier) of the currencies of the five major trading countries – the US Dollar, the German Mark, the French Franc, the Japanese Yen and the British Pound. The SDR is the unit of account (unité de compte) of the Fund. Its value is revised every five years. As of (à compter de) January 1991, the share (part) of the British Pound, the French Franc and the US Dollar has been slightly (légèrement) reduced while (tandis que) the weight (poids) of the Deutschemark and the Japanese Yen has been raised in order to take into account (prendre en compte) the changing economic importance of each of these countries. Borrowing ability (possibilité d'emprunt) and voting rights (droit de vote, nombre de voix) of members are in proportion to the quota they subscribed. Borrowing is limited to twice (deux fois) the amount (montant) of the quota. The USA currently (à l'heure actuelle) holds (détenir) 22% of the voting rights and the European Union about 27%, giving them veto power as (étant donné que) an 85% majority is necessary to adopt major changes in IMF procedures. An important revision was made in 1976. Subscribing 25% of the quota in gold is no longer required, while commitment (lien) to par values (parité) has been abolished. The Fund is administered by a board (conseil) of executive directors, including representatives of the world's five biggest economies and Saudi Arabia (Arabie Saoudite) which is one of the largest creditors. There are 21 executive directors as a whole (en tout) plus one managing director (directeur général). The Fund largely publicizes (donner une large publicité) its views through speeches and an annual report which is a very important document on the state of the world economy.

☞ See BALANCE OF PAYMENTS; BRETTON WOODS; EXCHANGE CONTROLS; EXCHANGE RATE; PAR VALUE.

INTERNATIONAL SECURITIES REGULATORY ORGANIZATION, abbr. **ISRO** See................ SELF-REGULATORY ORGANIZATIONS.

INTERNATIONAL STOCK EXCHANGE OF THE UNITED KINGDOM AND THE REPUBLIC OF IRELAND LTD. London, abbr. **ISE** (La Bourse internationale des valeurs du Royaume-Uni et de la république d'Irlande)

Previously known as the **LONDON STOCK EXCHANGE**, a name which informally (officieusement) continues to be used, it was reorganised into its present form at the time of the Big Bang ("le Big Bang", déréglementation des opérations financières à la Bourse de Londres) in October, 1986, to take advantage of international opportunities. It is said to be Europe's foremost centre for international finance and investment, and is distinguished by its use of high technology, which was largely introduced in 1986 and has been undergoing continual perfection (amélioration). The electronic price and trading information system (système informatisé de cotation et de transaction), which includes SEAQ, SEAQ International, TOPIC, TALISMAN, TAURUS (which has now been abandoned) and SAEF, enables instant communication between buyers and sellers on a 24 hour basis (24 heures sur 24); the floor (la corbeille/salle de cotations) has largely been replaced by television screens (see TOPIC) linked (relier à) with the Stock Exchange's computers, which connect (mettre en relation) market makers (teneur de marché) – those who sell and buy large quantities of specific shares – with brokers' offices (bureaux des firmes de courtage) in the UK and all over the world. The high technology used has led to "program(me) trading" (courtage par ordinateur) – the automatic buying and selling of certain securities by means of computers when prices reach certain levels – thus avoiding the necessity for buyers and sellers to meet in person.

The ISE provides three main markets for UK company securities:

i. the listed market (la cote officielle) for established companies prepared to adhere to strict demands (exigence) for information and transparency; such companies have to offer (mettre à la disposition du marché) at least 25% of their shares to the general public and until recently had to show five years of profitable accounts (exercice bénéficiaire), but a ruling by the European Union has reduced this to three; this is a primary or new issue market for raising new or additional capital, or a secondary market for re-selling and buying existing securities of quoted (cotées) companies;

ii. the Unlisted Securities Market, abbr. USM (correspond au Second Marché en France), created in 1980 for companies seeking to raise capital, but not ready yet for a full listing (cotation officielle) or not wanting to comply with (se conformer à) the strict regulations for listed companies (société cotée); to be quoted on the USM companies have to offer a minimum of 10% of their shares to the general public and before the EU ruling had to show three years of profitable accounts, but now it is only two; at the time of writing the USM is being threatened (menacer) with extinction, due to the poor liquidity of shares in this market; it is to be replaced by the Alternative Investment Market/AIM with less strict regulations; and

iii. the Third Market (troisième marché), created in 1987 for even smaller companies seeking to raise capital.

In addition, the ISE provides a market for gilts and other government securities (fonds d'Etat), company fixed interest securities (obligations à intérêt fixe), traded options (options négociables), the transactions for which are still conducted on the floor, and international equities (actions étrangères).

Membership of the Stock Exchange before 1986 was limited to individual members of member firms, the latter (celles-ci) being stockbroking or jobbing firms (sociétés de courtiers ou de marchands de titres); only members could buy and sell securities on the Stock Exchange. Also, at the time (à l'époque) there was a fixed minimum commission payable to the broker on each transaction he conducted for his client, while jobbers were not allowed to deal directly with the public – the buying and selling of stocks and shares by private individuals or non-member organizations and institutions could only take place through (par l'intermédiaire de) a broker. Brokers then operated in a single capacity (à un seul titre) – that of agent (mandataire ou représentant) for their client, payment for which was the commission received. With the Big Bang membership was made wider by permitting outside companies to buy member firms, and UK and foreign banks and overseas securities firms (société de placement/d'investissement en valeurs mobilières) took advantage of this. The old distinction between jobbers and stockbrokers (non-existent on other stock exchanges) was abolished: the jobber has now become a market maker (contrepartiste spécialisé ou teneur de marché), specialising in the wholesale buying and selling (achat et vente en gros) of certain shares, and large investors can negotiate directly with him for the best price without using the services of a broker; the stockbroker has now become a broker/dealer (négociant en titres/négociant courtier), who can act as an agent for his client or buy and sell shares on his own behalf (pour son propre compte), thus operating in a dual capacity (à double titre); furthermore, he can elect to (choisir de) become a market maker. The fixed minimum commission has been abolished and replaced by a negotiable fee (honoraires négociés).
The ISE is managed (dirigée) by a Council (le Conseil, organisme directeur), which sets rules (mettre en place des règles de fonctionnement) and enforces standards (veiller au respect des normes de qualité), as well as supervises the activities of the Exchange staff (personnel de la Bourse). For example, there is the **PANEL ON TAKEOVERS AND MERGERS** or **TAKEOVER PANEL**, whose function is to ensure that takeovers (offre publique d'achat, abbr. OPA) and mergers (fusion) conform to the rules laid down in *The City Code on Takeovers and Mergers*. This Panel (commission) and the Monopolies and Mergers Commission, a government body, between them ensure that potential takeovers and mergers are not against the public interest. While the ISE has its own body (organisme) – the insider trading (délit d'initié) group – and procedures for ensuring that investors are protected against fraud and dishonest dealing (transactions malhonnêtes), the government's Department of Trade and Industry (l'équivalent du ministère de l'Industrie et du Commerce extérieur) is also responsible for this through its Securities and Investment Board, abbr. SIB (l'équivalent de la Commission des Opérations de Bourse en France, abrégé COB). The latter carries out these functions through (par l'intermédiaire de) Self-Regulating Organizations, abbr. SROs (organisations indépendantes). Prior to 1988 the Council had a special compensation scheme (système

d'indemnité) for investors who lost money through a member of the Stock Exchange going bankrupt (faire faillite) or being negligent and giving bad advice. This covered them for up to £250,000 of losses due to a member firm directly and up to £500,000 for losses due to a member firm's subsidiary (filiale). Now this scheme has been abandoned and replaced by one run by the Securities and Investment Board, which covers all investment advisers, but which only provides cover for a maximum of £48,000 – the **INVESTORS COMPENSATION SCHEME** .

The Council directs a number of standing commissions (commissions permanentes), which are responsible for the day-to-day running (fonctionnement ou gestion) of the Stock Exchange, which includes its computer systems (systèmes informatisés d'information et de transactions) and services offered to members, and it employs in all some 3,000 people.

☞ See ALPHA SECURITIES; BIG BANG, THE; BROKER/DEALER; DEBENTURE; DEPARTMENT OF TRADE; FLOOR, THE; GILT-EDGED STOCK; INSIDER TRADING; LIQUIDITY; LISTING; LOAN STOCK; MARKET MAKER; MONOPOLIES AND MERGERS COMMISSION; OVER-THE-COUNTER MARKET; PLACING; PRIMARY MARKET; PROGRAMME TRADING; SAEF; SEAQ; SEAQ INTERNATIONAL; SECONDARY MARKET; SECURITIES AND INVESTMENT BOARD; SELF-REGULATING ORGANIZATIONS; STOCK BROKING FIRM; STOCK MARKET; TALISMAN; TAURUS; THIRD MARKET; TOPIC; TRADED OPTIONS; UNLISTED SECURITIES MARKET; UNLISTED/UNQUOTED SECURITIES.

INTERNATIONAL TRADE CENTRE UNCTAD/GATT, abbr. **ITC** (Centre du commerce international CNUCED/GATT)

An international organization based (avoir son siège) in Geneva, Switzerland, which serves (servir les intérêts de) both the United Nations Conference on Trade and Development/UNCTAD and GATT. It provides (offrir, fournir) a wide range (gamme) of technical assistance to developing countries (pays en voie de développement) seeking (chercher) to promote (promouvoir) their exports.

☞ See GATT; UNITED NATIONS CONFERENCE ON TRADE AND DEVELOPMENT.

INTRODUCTION (introduction en bourse)

This is a way for a private company about to (être sur le point de) go public (s'introduire en bourse) to issue (émettre) shares. It is done through a broker or issuing house (agent de change ou banque de placement) buying the shares in small lots as and when demanded by clients. This method, although not as common as placing and offer for sale, is the cheapest for raising capital and is used by companies which already have an established spread (éventail) of shareholders and are seeking permission for their shares to be dealt in on the stockmarket. Companies on the Unlisted Securities Market, abbr. USM, have often used an introduction to move up to full listing (cotation officielle).

☞ See INTERNATIONAL STOCK EXCHANGE; LISTING; OFFER FOR SALE; PLACING; SPONSOR; STOCK MARKET; UNLISTED SECURITIES MARKET.

INVESTMENT BANK See .... MERCHANT BANK.

INVESTMENT CLUB (club d'investissement)

A small group of generally inexperienced people who regularly contribute a sum of money, which they then use to acquire a portfolio (portefeuille) of shares. These clubs are helped by investment specialists, who teach the members how the stock exchange works and how to invest and spread the risks (répartir les risques), and the difference between growth (croissance) and safety (securité) and quick or high returns (rendement élevé), which involve a short-term approach and an increased degree of risk. These clubs started in the USA in the 1940s and then spread to Europe.

☞ See PORTFOLIO; SECURITIES; SHARE; STOCK EXCHANGE; YIELD.

INVESTMENT MANAGERS' REGULATORY ORGANIZATION, abbr. **IMRO** See .... SELF-REGULATING ORGANIZATIONS.

INVESTMENT PERFORMANCE REQUIREMENTS (exigences en matière de performance des investissements)

Special conditions imposed on direct foreign investment (investissements directs à l'étranger) by recipient governments (gouvernements qui les reçoivent, en bénéficient), such as to export a certain percentage of the output (production) or to ensure the employment of a specified percentage of local labour force (main d'oeuvre).

☞ See INDUSTRIAL POLICY.

INVESTMENT TRUST or **INVESTMENT (TRUST) COMPANY** or **CLOSED-END COMPANY/FUND/INVESTMENT COMPANY** (Société d'investissement à capital fixe ou fonds de placement fermé)

This is a limited company whose objective is to make a profit from the buying and selling of securities (titres) and from dividends and interest received. It issues (émettre) shares and uses its capital, in other words, to buy shares in other companies. Shares in the investment trust company can be bought and sold, as with any other quoted company, and their value on the stock market will depend on the value of the shares it holds and the level of dividend payments. Investment trusts are also referred to as closed-end funds because, unlike unit trusts, their size is limited to their initial share capital (capital actions), and the only way they can grow is by increasing this by means of, for example, a rights issue (émission de droits de souscription ou d'attribution).

☞ See DIVIDEND; LIMITED or LIMITED LIABILITY COMPANY; RIGHTS ISSUE; SECURITIES; SHARE; STOCK EXCHANGE; UNIT TRUST; YIELD.

INVESTMENT-LINKED ASSURANCE See .... LIFE INSURANCE.

INVESTORS COMPENSATION SCHEME See .... INTERNATIONAL STOCK EXCHANGE.

INVISIBLE TRADE or INVISIBLES (commerce invisible ou échanges invisibles)

The exportation and importation of intangible (incorporel) items (article) such as freight (fret ou prix du transport des marchandises), insurance (assurance) and financial services, which are included in the current account (paiements courants) section of a country's balance of payments. Intangible or non-tangible items also include tourism, while financial services include banking, stock exchange transactions, accounting (comptabilité) and technical know-how (savoir-faire) relating to financial services.

☞ See BALANCE OF PAYMENTS; INSURANCE; SERVICES; VISIBLE TRADE.

INVISIBLES See .... INVISIBLE TRADE.

IPC See .... INTEGRATED PROGRAM FOR COMMODITIES.

IRREDEEMABLE BOND See .... BOND.

IRREDEEMABLE DEBENTURE See .... DEBENTURE.

IRREDEEMABLE PREFERENCE SHARES (actions priviligiées/prioritaires irrachetables ou irremboursables)

Preference shares which the company has no right to buy back. In other words, holders of irredeemable preference shares will only receive their fixed dividend; the money they have paid for the shares is a kind of permanent loan, and the only way they can get it back is to sell the shares to someone else, as is the case with ordinary shares.

☞ See ORDINARY SHARE; PREFERENCE SHARE; REDEEMABLE PREFERENCE SHARES.

ISRO, abbr. **for INTERNATIONAL SECURITIES REGULATORY ORGANIZATION** See .... SELF-REGULATING ORGANIZATIONS.

ISSUED CAPITAL See .... AUTHORIZED/REGISTERED ETC. CAPITAL.

ISSUING HOUSE See .... MERCHANT BANK.

J

JOB TURNOVER (instabilité d'emploi ou rotation/mouvement du personnel)

This is defined as the number of times a job is held by different people in a given period. This will be higher in occupations which pay little and/or whose conditions of work are difficult or disagreeable, such as in the hotel and catering industries (industries de l'hôtellerie et de la restauration).

☞ See UNEMPLOYMENT.

JOBBER See .... MARKET MAKER.

JOINT-STOCK BANK See .... COMMERCIAL BANK; JOINT-STOCK COMPANY.

JOINT-STOCK COMPANY (société par actions)

The concept of the joint-stock company originated (naître) in England in the seventeenth century in response to the enormous needs for capital to finance ventures (risque) and projects which demanded more money than most single individuals had or were prepared to risk. A number of investors contributed varying amounts of capital, thus becoming stockholders (actionnaire), and shared in the profits according to the proportion of the capital they provided. The term "joint-stock company" is little used today in the modern context, but is the basis behind the development of different forms of shares to finance commercial activity and the forms of commercial organization which followed (e.g. limited companies (SARL), public limited companies (plcs), etc.).

☞ See ANNUAL GENERAL MEETING; AUTHORIZED/REGISTERED ETC. CAPITAL; CAPITAL; LIMITED or LIMITED LIABILITY COMPANY; LIQUIDATION; SHARE..

JUNIOR DEBT See .... LEVERAGED BUYOUT.

JUNK BOND See .... LEVERAGED BUYOUT.

JUST IN TIME (juste à temps, à flux tendus)

A form of inventory control (contrôle ou gestion des stocks) which enables (permettre) factories to order (commander) or produce just enough to fulfill (faire face à) immediate needs or orders (commande). Thus (ainsi), the factory produces completed (fini) products – as opposed to (par opposition à) semi-finished (semi-fini) ones – and reduces manufacturing time (temps de fabrication) as well as the expense (coût) of keeping large supplies (stock) on hand (disponible).

K

KENNEDY ROUND See .... GATT.

KEY-MAN INSURANCE POLICY See ....PRINCIPLES OF INSURANCE.

L

LAISSEZ-FAIRE (laisser-faire)

An economic principle which originated (naître) in France in the first half of the 18th century and was later developed by Adam SMITH as a rule of practical economic conduct. It means letting things proceed (avancer, se faire) without interference. A. SMITH applied (appliquer) the principle of laissez-faire to foreign trade and advocated (prôner) the withdrawal (retrait, suppression) of the restrictions imposed by mercantilism. In domestic affairs (affaires intérieures) too the principle was expressed that the individual is most productive when allowed to follow his own self-interest (son intérêt personnel) without external restrictions, thus achieving (réaliser) the common interest of the nation.

☞ See MERCANTILISM.

LAUTRO, abbr. **for LIFE ASSURANCE AND UNIT TRUST REGULATORY ORGANIZATION** See .... SELF-REGULATING ORGANIZATIONS.

LBO See .... LEVERAGED BUYOUT.

LEAN MANUFACTURING (production industrielle “maigre”)

A phrase (expression) coined (créer, inventer) by the Massachusetts Institute of Technology/MIT to define the methods of production of Japanese carmakers (fabricant d’automobiles) that economize on (faire des économies sur) production means (moyen).

LEASE-BACK See .... LEASING.

LEASING (leasing, crédit-bail [entreprises], location avec option d’achat, abrégé LOA, [particuliers], location à bail)

This is a contract (called a lease [bail]) in which the owner of material, property (propriété) or equipment (outillage), say a building, an aeroplane or machine, the **LESSOR** (bailleur ou loueur), allows another party, the **LESSEE** (locataire ou preneur à bail), to use (employer) this for a given time and for a given rent (loyer). The **LESSEE** in this situation leases **from** (prendre à bail) the **LESSOR**, who leases **to** (louer/mettre à bail) or who leases **out to** the former (donner à bail au premier). The **LEASING COMPANY** (société de crédit-bail) at the end of the contracted period for using the equipment etc. may include in the leasing contract, especially as regards machines and equipment, the right for the lessee to buy (racheter) the leased (loué) equipment at a price which reflects its value after the wear and tear (usure ou détérioration) which has taken place. This method of financing, first developed in the USA, has found increasing favour in Europe as a form of investment, due to the fact that the leasing charges can be considered as a business expense and therefore reduce liability (assujettissement) to corporation tax (impôt sur les sociétés). **LEASE-BACK** (crédit-bail adossé ou cession-bail) is a contract in which the owner of the property, etc. sells it to another party, the buyer, on condition that the latter (celui-ci) can lease it back to the former for an agreed time and for an agreed rent. As regards buildings and property (immobilier) the owner may choose simply to lease (louer à bail) these for a given time, after which ownership (propriété) reverts (revenir à) to him or his estate (succession).

☞ See FINANCE HOUSE.

LEASING COMPANY See .... LEASING.

LENDER OF LAST RESORT (prêteur en dernier recours/ressort)

A bank which is prepared to provide funds to other banks and financial institutions which are short of (manquer de) cash. This is an important function of a central bank, as the rate at which it lends and/or its discount rate (taux d'escompte) for bills and securities are set (fixer) above the market rate and influence interest rates in the economy, and hence (donc) the money supply (masse monétaire).

☞ See CENTRAL BANK; DISCOUNT; DISCOUNT HOUSE. DISCOUNT MARKET; FEDERAL RESERVE SYSTEM; INTEREST; LIQUIDITY RATIO; MONEY SUPPLY; RESERVE ASSETS; RUN ON A BANK; SECURITIES; SPECIAL DEPOSITS; TREASURY BILL.

LENDING (prêts ou prêt)

The provision of money to others on a temporary basis – short, medium or long term (à court, moyen ou long terme) – on the understanding (étant entendu que) that it will be returned with interest. Lenders (prêteur) of money are usually banks, finance houses (société de crédit), companies with surplus cash, the general public and financial intermediaries (e.g. insurance companies) and housing finance organizations such as UK building societies (société/caisse d'épargne mutuelle de financement immobilier), which specialize in lending money for house purchase, but now also are allowed to branch out (diversifier ses activités) into banking and other financial activities.

☞ See BANKING; BORROWING; BUILDING SOCIETY; CAPITAL MARKET; COMMERCIAL BANK; COUPON; DE-REGULATION; EUROCURRENCY MARKET; INTEREST; FINANCE HOUSE; FINANCIAL INTERMEDIARIES; INTEREST; LOAN; MERCHANT BANK; MONEY MARKET; SECURITY.

LESSEE See .... LEASING.

LESSOR See .... LEASING.

LEVERAGED BUYOUT (or **BUY-OUT**), abbr. **LBO** (rachat d'entreprise avec effet de levier ou acquisition d'une entreprise par endettement)

This is a financial technique originating in the USA which enables individuals or companies to take over other companies without necessarily possessing much of the capital required to do this. It is based on heavily borrowing (fort degré d'endettement). A company or group of investors finds up to 10% of the capital required, a bank or group of banks lends say (disons) 50-70%, accepting the assets (actif) of the company to be taken over as security (garantie) for the loan (emprunt) and charging a high rate of interest for taking a risk in lending so much, and the remaining 20-40% is obtained by issuing (émettre) debt, or, in other words, by inviting the general public to lend the new company money.

This debt, in the form of bonds (obligation ou bon) and other commercial paper (effets de commerce ou billets de trésorerie), has varying degrees of security behind it. For example, **SENIOR DEBT** (dette de premier rang) has a reasonable level of security behind it: when it matures (parvenir à échéance) the holder (détenteur) can more or less rely on being paid his money back, especially if the company should go bankrupt. **JUNIOR DEBT** (dette de deuxième rang) has less security behind it (it is more risky). In the USA a prominent financial instrument in facilitating LBOs has been the **JUNK BOND** (obligation de pacotille/pourrie), so-called because there is very little security behind it and investors risk losing their money if anything goes wrong with the issuer (émetteur). Junk bonds have been in existence since the 1920s, but came into prominence in the 1980s in connection with LBOs, despite the fact that famous credit rating agencies (société d'évaluation du crédit/de la solvabilité) like Moody's and Standard & Poor's have classified (classer) them as below investment grade (i.e. not reliable as investments). Their re-launch was very much associated with the New York stockbroking (société de courtage), banking and investment firm Drexel, Burnham and Lambert, which in 1990 filed for bankruptcy (déposer son bilan), and Michael Milken, the founder of their junk bond trading department, the so-called "junk-bond king", who himself received a ten year prison sentence for violating federal securities law and tax laws. The attraction of junk bonds for investors, however, is that they offer interest rates which can be as much as seven or more percentage points above that obtainable on US Treasury bonds (bon du trésor à long terme) and, despite the enormous publicity attached to the failure (faillite) of a few large companies issuing such bonds, the default rate (taux de non-paiement) in general has not been inhibitive (décourageant) to investors.

The term **MEZZANINE FINANCE** (financement mezzanine ou intermédiaire ou hybride ou strapotin) is used to describe debt issued by companies which also includes a degree of participation in the company's equity (capitaux propres). It is not pure debt and it is not pure equity, but a mixture of the two, such as an equity loan (prêt participatif). This gives investors some share in the profits as well interest and repayment.

The fact that 80% or more of the finance for an LBO often comes from borrowing at a high rate of interest makes the manoeuvre a very risky undertaking. To survive, LBOed companies usually sell off non-core (non-essentiel) parts of the business to reduce the burden of debt. But in order to continue to service their debt (payer les interêts d'un emprunt) and eventually repay the capital borrowed they must maintain sales and cash flow (marge brute d'auto-financement). Such companies are in deep trouble when there is a recession and the government's policy is high interest rates to fight inflation. In such circumstances many of them do not survive.
The 1980s saw a spate (afflux) of takeovers and buyouts in the USA and UK, a large number of them using leverage (effet de levier ou endettement). The LBO technique has enabled managers to buy out their employing company – known as a **MANAGEMENT BUYOUT** (rachat de l'entreprise par ses cadres); managers and employees together to buy their own company – a **MANAGEMENT-EMPLOYEE BUYOUT** (rachat de l'entreprise par ses salariés, ou RES); managers to buy back from the public their company's shares – a **MANAGEMENT BUYBACK** (rachat de ses propres actions par l'entreprise); and managers from outside the company (de l'extérieur) to take it over – a **MANAGEMENT BUY-IN** (rachat d'une entreprise par les cadres extérieurs).
The investors in a buyout in its various forms usually seek **TO TAKE A COMPANY PRIVATE** or to **TO GO PRIVATE** (acquérir toutes les actions d'une entreprise cotée afin de la retirer de la Bourse), that is, take the company shares off the market so it is no longer a public (société anonyme par actions), quoted (coté) company; then, once profitability has been established, they will want the company **TO GO PUBLIC** (s'introduire en Bourse). **TO TAKE A COMPANY PUBLIC** (introduire une société en Bourse) means the same thing. This is with a view to making handsome profits (de beaux bénéfices) on the sale of shares to the public.

☞ See ARBITAGE; BOND; CASH FLOW; COMMERCIAL PAPER; CREDIT RATING AGENCY; DEBENTURE; EQUITY; INFLATION; INTEREST; INTRODUCTION; INVESTMENT BANK; LIMITED or LIMITED LIABILITY COMPANY; MERCHANT BANK; RAIDER/CORPORATE RAIDER; RECESSION; SECURITY; SHARE; STOCKBROKING FIRM; STOCK EXCHANGE; TAKEOVER.

LIABILITY See .... INSURANCE.

LIABILITY INSURANCE See .... ACCIDENT INSURANCE.

LIBERALIZATION (libéralisation du commerce)

Reductions in tariffs (tarif douanier) and other measures that restrict (entraver) trade, unilaterally or multilaterally. Trade liberalization has been the target (objectif) of all Rounds of GATT. The term also refers to the removal (suppression) of government controls and restrictions within (à l'intérieur de) the financial sector with a view to (en vue de) increasing competition and flows of funds (flux financiers).

☞ See CODES OF CONDUCT; DEREGULATION; FINANCIAL SERVICES ACT, 1986; GATT.

LIBOR, abbr. **for LONDON INTER-BANK OFFERED RATE,** also called the **INTER-BANK RATE** (taux d'intérêt directeur sur le marché des eurodevises de Londres, taux interbancaire offert à Londres, abrégé TIOL)

This is the rate of interest for loans on the London **INTER-BANK MONEY MARKET** (marché monétaire interbancaire), a market where banks attract funds to lend to other first-class banks for usually up to six months. Banks borrow on this market to cover liquidity problems (i.e. shortage of (manque de) cash), and the deposits (dépôts) and loans (prêts) are in euro-currencies (eurodevises). Because there is so much trading (volume des transactions) on the London inter-bank money market, LIBOR is used widely as the basis for (servir de référence) setting (fixer) other major interest rates. The interest rate for funds deposited in this market is the inter-bank market bid rate, abbr. **IBMBR.** Other financial centres also have an inter-bank money market. The Paris equivalent of LIBOR, for example, is **PIBOR,** the Paris Inter-Bank Offered rate, (taux interbancaire offert à Paris, abrégé TIOP).

☞ See CAPITAL MARKET; DEPOSIT; EUROCURRENCY MARKET; LIQUIDITY; LIQUIDITY RATIO; LOAN.

LICENSE See .... LICENSING; LICENSING CODE.

LICENSING (octroi d'une licence)

The requirement (exigence) by a country for a formal application (demande officielle) for a special permit, usually called a (GB) licence (US) license, as a prior condition (comme condition préalable) to importing or exporting certain goods (marchandise). An **OPEN GENERAL LICENCE** (licence permanente) is a standing (permanent) permit. A **SPECIFIC IMPORT LICENCE** (licence spéciale) must be applied for (demander) and granted (accorder) for a particular value (valeur) of goods. **OPEN INDIVIDUAL LICENCES** (licence particulière) are granted to individual importers for a particular commodity (marchandise, denrée, produit).

☞ See CUSTOMS AND ADMINISTRATIVE ENTRY PROCEDURES; LICENSING CODE; NON-TARIFF BARRIERS; PRIOR DEPOSITS; QUANTITATIVE RESTRICTIONS; SPECIFIC LIMITATIONS ON TRADE.

LICENSING CODE (Code des licences)

A Tokyo Round Code aimed at (viser à) simplifying import licensing procedures (procédure de licence d'importation) and at ensuring (assurer) their fair (loyal) application. The Code also seeks (chercher) to improve (améliorer) the transparency (transparence) of these proceedings (procédure) by requiring (demander) the publication of relevant (adéquat) national laws (loi) and regulations. Adherence to (adhésion à, respect de) the Code is monitored (surveiller) by a Committee on Import Licensing under the aegis (égide, aupices) of GATT.

☞ See CODES OF CONDUCT; GATT; LICENSING; NON-TARIFF BARRIERS; TOKYO ROUND; TRANSPARENCY.

LIFE ASSURANCE AND UNIT TRUST REGULATORY ORGANIZATION, abbr. **LAUTRO** See .... SELF-REGULATING ORGANIZATIONS.

LIFE INSURANCE or **ASSURANCE** (assurance-vie)

One of the four broad (grand) categories of insurance which includes (comprendre) life cover (couverture) – less than (moins de) 20% of premiums (prime) – as well as a form of savings (épargne) – more than (plus de) 80% of premiums – pensions and health insurance. The word "assurance" is used because most **LIFE POLICIES** (police) do not indemnify (indemniser) but undertake to (s'engager à) pay. The main kinds (catégorie) of insurance policy are **WHOLE LIFE** (en cas de décès), **ENDOWMENT** (en cas de vie, à capital différé), **TERM** (à durée limitée, temporaire) and **ANNUITY** (rente viagère, annuité). A **WHOLE LIFE** – also called **PURE LIFE** - policy provides (garantir) dependents (ayant-droit) with a lump sum (règlement forfaitaire) or a regular income (revenu) on (à) the death of the person whose life has been assured.

An **ENDOWMENT POLICY** provides for payment (versement) to be made (effectuer) at death of person assured or at the end of (au terme de) a predetermined period of time, whichever is earlier (au premier des deux évÉnements qui se produit). Thus (ainsi, donc) the contract benefits the policyholder (détenteur de la police, assuré) and/or only his dependents. **ENDOWMENT** and **WHOLE LIFE** policies can be either (soit) **WITH PROFITS** (avec intéressement ou participation aux bénéfices) or (soit) **WITHOUT** – or **NON-PROFITS** (sans intéressement). The first option is more costly (coûteux) as the policyholder has a right (droit) to a share (part) of the profits (bénéfice) made by the life investment fund (fonds d'investissement) on which the policy is assessed (asseoir). When a policy is said to be **INVESTMENT-LINKED** or **UNITLINKED** (lié aux résultats de l'investissement), it is because it is tied (lier) to the performance (résultat) of a unit trust (société d'investissement à capital variable/SICAV) or investment trust (société d'investissement à capital fixe). A **TERM POLICY** is a contract granted (accorder) for a fixed period (à terme fixe) only. If the policyholder survives the term (échéance), he receives nothing. A popular kind of term policy is **MORTGAGE PROTECTION** (assurance prêt hypothécaire) in which the policyholder covers the risk of not being able to repay (rembourser) a mortgage loan (prêt hypothécaire) by (à) the date fixed should (si) he die earlier.

In return for (en échange de) a determined total premium (prime), an **ANNUITY POLICY** provides for the payment of a fixed or variable sum of money at regular dates (échéance) for a predetermined period or for the life of the annuitant (rentier, détenteur de rente). Terms (condition) vary according to (selon) the various sub-categories: "annuity certain", "certain annuity" or "terminable annuity" (rente certaine) in which fixed amounts are paid at stated (fixe) dates for a fixed number of years. Those contracts remain (rester) unaffected (inchangé) by death of annuitant or of any other person (tout autre personne);

"cash-refund annuity" (rente avec remboursement en espèces) in which at death of annuitant the company pays his representatives (ayant-droit) a sum in cash amounting to (s'élever à) the difference between the original total premium (prime initiale totale) and the amounts (montant, somme) the annuitant has received up to (jusqu'à) his death. The lump cash refund (remboursement global en espèces) may be replaced (remplacer) by regular payments to a named (désigner) person;
"contingent annuity" (rente contingente, conditionnelle, aléatoire, accident, casuelle) in which payments start at death of a named person other than (autre que) the annuitant;
"deferred annuity" (rente différée) providing for payment to take place at a certain date, i.e. when the annuitant reaches a certain age;
"immediate annuity" (rente immédiate) providing for payment of annuity either immediately or a half year (semestre) later;
"life annuity" (viagère, à vie) in which annuity is paid only during a person's life;
"retirement annuity" (rente retraite) in which annuitant receives a pension as soon as (dès que) he retires (prendre sa retraite), until his death;
"reversionary annuity" or "annuity in reversion" (rente réversible) in which payments begin at death of annuitant and are made to a named person for the latter's life (durée de la vie de celle-ci);
"survivorship annuity" (rente viagère avec réversion) in which payments continue after death of annuitant and are made to a named person, i.e. widower/widow (veuf/ve);
"temporary annuity" (rente temporaire) paid for a predetermined number of years but stopped by annuitant's death before the end of that period;
"variable annuity" (rente variable) tied (lier) to performance of Stock Exchange (marché boursier) as (étant donné que) the premium paid by annuitant (rentier, détenteur de rente) is invested (placer) by the insurer (assureur) in stocks and shares (valeurs mobilières).
Almost all countries give (accorder) tax relief (abattement fiscal) for life insurance premiums. Great Britain no longer does (ne le fait plus) but has brought in (introduire) new tax breaks (réduction d'impôt) for personal supplementary pensions (retraite complémentaire) instead (à la place).

☞ See INSTITUTIONAL INVESTORS; INVESTMENT TRUST; INSURANCE; STOCK EXCHANGE; UNIT TRUST.

LIFE POLICY See .... LIFE INSURANCE.

LIFFE See .... LONDON INTERNATIONAL FINANCIAL FUTURES EXCHANGE.

LIMITED LIABILITY COMPANY See .... LIMITED or LIMITED LIABILITY COMPANY.

LIMITED or **LIMITED LIABILITY COMPANY** (société à responsabilité limitée, abrégé SARL)
In the UK this is a joint-stock company (société par actions) whose owners, the shareholders (actionnaires) have limited financial liability (responsabilité) should the company incur (contracter) debts it cannot pay

or go bankrupt (faire faillite). This means their financial liability is limited to the amount of capital they have invested or agreed to invest in the company. This is contrasted with an **UNLIMITED (LIABILITY) COMPANY** (société à responsabilité illimitée), in which the owners (propriétaires) are liable not only up to the capital they have brought to the company or agreed to bring but also to the extent of their personal fortune (e.g. their home, car, television, jewelry, etc.), as is the case with the names at Lloyd's, the UK specialized insurance market.

LIMITED LIABILITY COMPANIES exist in two forms in the UK:

i. the **PRIVATE** or **PRIVATE LIMITED COMPANY** (SARL), which usually has the word "LIMITED" or its abbreviation **"LTD"** at the end of its name or title (raison sociale); this form of company is not allowed to invite the general public to buy its shares or debentures (obligations) [ne pas avoir le droit d'annoncer une émission d'actions ou d'obligations au public]; its size is limited to 2-50 shareholders, who cannot transfer (transférer) their shares to someone else without the agreement of the other owners of the firm; and

ii. the **PUBLIC LIMITED COMPANY** (société anonyme), which must have these words or their abbreviation **"PLC"** in their name; for the **PLC** there is no limit to the number of shareholders it can have and no restriction on their right to transfer their shares; the **PLC** has the right to offer its shares and debentures to the public and to be quoted on the London Stock Exchange and the Unlisted Securities Market. In the USA there is no such legal distinction between private and public companies, both of which bear the word **INCORPORATED** or the abbreviation **INC.** in their name.

☞ See ANNUAL GENERAL MEETING; ARTICLES OF ASSOCIATON and ARTICLES OF MEMORANDUM under AUTHORIZED/REGISTERED ETC. CAPITAL; JOINT STOCK COMPANY; INTERNATIONAL STOCK EXCHANGE; LISTING; LLOYD'S; SHARE; UNLISTED SECURITIES MARKET.

LIQUID ASSETS (disponibilités)

Cash and assets (actif) which can be readily (aisément, facilement) turned into cash or money, such as bank deposits and quickly saleable investments, such as government bonds (bon du trésor).

☞ See ASSETS; BOND; GILT-EDGED STOCKS; INVESTMENT; LIQUIDITY; LIQUIDITY RATIO.

LIQUID See .... LIQUIDITY.

LIQUIDATION or **WINDING-UP** (liquidation ou dissolution)

This is the voluntary (volontaire) or compulsory (forcé) closing of a company, often because it is unable to pay its debts, or because its members, the shareholders (actionnaires), no longer wish it to continue. It therefore is said **TO GO** or **TO BE PUT INTO LIQUIDATION** (se mettre en liquidation ou déposer son bilan)), which means its assets (actif) are sold off, debts paid and any remaining money, if there is any, distributed among the members. When an official **LIQUIDATOR** (liquidateur judiciaire) is appointed (nommé) the company is said to be **IN LIQUIDATION** (en liquidation). A liquidator can be appointed by a court (cour) in the case of a compulsory winding-up (liquidation forcée), that is, by order of the court. If it is by the wish of the shareholders (actionnaire) or board of directors (conseil d'administration) it is called a **MEMBERS' VOLUNTARY WINDING-UP** (liquidation par les actionnaires); if it is as a result of action (procédure) taken by the creditors it is known as a **CREDITORS' VOLUNTARY WINDING-UP** (liquidation par les créanciers). The liquidator's job is to get hold of all the company's assets, sell them as quickly as possible for cash for the best price he can get, pay off the creditors in order of preference (i.e. tax and national insurance (Sécurité Sociale) contributions first) and, if anything is left, divide this among the shareholders. A **RECEIVER** (administrateur judiciaire ou syndic de faillite), on the other hand, represents a particular creditor and is put into a company to recover a specific debt or debts which it has failed to pay. For example, where a bank has lent money to a company secured on (être nanti sur) the latter's (ce dernier) property and has not obtained repayment it is likely to insist that a receiver be called in. In that case the company is said to have passed into, gone into (entrer en liquidation) or be in **RECEIVERSHIP** (règlement judiciaire). The receiver will exercise the same functions as a liquidator, except that he represents the interests of **SECURED CREDITORS** (créancier nanti ou privilégié) who has called him in, the bank in this example. This means in practice that after he has finished there will be little left to repay the **UNSECURED CREDITORS** (créancier sans garantie ou chirographaire). Calling in the receiver usually (but not always) means the beginning of the end for the company.

BANKRUPTCY (faillite ou banqueroute) is a declaration by a court of law that an individual or company cannot pay his/its debts, and is the result of a **PETITION IN BANKRUPTCY** or **BANKRUPTCY PETITION** (demande de dépôt de bilan ou de mise en liquidation judiciaire), which is made either by the debtor (débiteur) or person who is insolvent (insolvable), or by a creditor (i.e. the person who is owed the money). As a result, the person has **TO GO BANKRUPT** (faire faillite) or **TO BE DECLARED BANKRUPT** (être déclaré/mis en faillite) and becomes a **BANKRUPT** (failli ou banqueroutier). In the case of a company it is then said to go into liquidation. Under American law this can be avoided if the company applies to the court for protection from its creditors so that (afin de) it can re-organize its affairs to pay off its debts. The law allowing it to do this is **CHAPTER 11** of the **BANKRUPTCY REFORM ACT**, 1978.

☞ See ANNUAL GENERAL MEETING; BOARD OF DIRECTORS; LIMITED or LIMITED LIABILITY COMPANY; PREFERENCE SHARE; SHARE.

LIQUIDATOR See .... LIQUIDATION.

LIQUIDITY (liquidité)

The extent to which available money or assets (actif) can easily and quickly be turned into cash. A company or bank having **LIQUIDITY PROBLEMS** means it is having difficulty in finding cash to meet its current commitments (tenir ses engagements). Assets can be very liquid (liquide/disponible), the most liquid being by definition money, or less liquid – a building, for example, which will take time to sell.

☞ See LIQUID ASSETS; LOAN; LIQUIDITY RATIO; SECURITY.

LIQUIDITY PROBLEMS See .... LIQUIDITY.

LIQUIDITY RATIO (ratio de liquidité)

a. In order to make sure banks will always have enough cash on hand (disponible) to meet the demand for withdrawals (retraits) by customers and not lend out too much, they are encouraged or required by central banks and financial authorities to maintain a certain amount of **LIQUID ASSETS** (disponibilités), variously defined by them, but generally including cash, money lent out at call (à vue ou sur demande) and at short notice (call money) and short-term government bonds (bons du trésor) as a proportion of their total deposit liabilities (passif). Deposits by customers are a bank's liabilities because the bank must repay them, while loans form part of its assets. The ratio is intended to prevent runs on banks (ruées sur les banques pour demandes de remboursement) and maintain confidence in the banking system. It can also be used as part of government monetary policy to control the money supply (masse monétaire). Increasing the liquidity ratio forces banks to put aside as reserves more of their liquid assets, thus reducing the amount of money they can lend out, and hence the money supply. Reducing the ratio has the opposite effect.

b. For businesses this is an accounting term (also called **CASH RATIO**) which indicates the ratio (rapport) of liquid assets (actif liquide/disponibilités) to liabilities (passif). Liquid assets for a company are usually cash in hand (encaisse disponible), bank deposits, money owed to the company by customers and assets which can be quickly sold. This ratio, also referred to as the **ACID TEST RATIO** (ratio de liquidité immédiate), is a rough measure (évaluation approximative) of the solvency (solvabilité) of a company.

☞ See ASSETS; BANKING; BOND; CALL MONEY; CENTRAL BANK; LIABILITIES; LIQUIDITY; MONETARY POLICY; MONEY SUPPLY; RESERVE ASSETS; RUN ON A BANK; SPECIAL DEPOSITS.

LISTED SHARES See ....LISTED/QUOTED SECURITIES.

LISTED/QUOTED COMPANY (société inscrite ou cotée en bourse)

A company whose shares have been accepted for listing (cotation) by a stock exchange. Its shares subsequently will be traded on the stock exchange and changes in their price publicly noted. To be accepted for listing companies are submitted to careful inspection by the stock exchange and have to meet certain requirements (remplir certaines conditions). Companies seek to become listed (cotée) in order to have access to cheaper

finance than that offered by banks and other financial institutions. For example, if they issue (émettre) shares, these are sold, the company receives the money, which it does not have to pay back, and pays out a dividend according to its possibilities and needs; if they issue debentures (obligation) they choose themselves the rate of interest and the date of repayment (remboursement). In becoming quoted (or going public) in this way they are exposed to the disadvantage of having to continually provide information about their activities and of having the share price subjected to factors outside their control (e.g. supply and demand, rumours and state of the economy), as well as to the danger of takeover bids (OPA).
Companies seeking finance in this way, that is, by a full listing (cotation officielle), but not wanting or able to meet all the requirements of the stock exchange can resort to other financial markets within or outside the system of the stock exchange, such as in the UK the Unlisted Securities Market, abbr. USM, and the Third Market (troisième marché), and more generally placing and over-the counter markets (marché hors cote), abbr. OTC.

☞ See FOURTH MARKET; INTERNATIONAL STOCK EXCHANGE; INTRODUCTION; LIMITED OR LIMITED LIABILITY COMPANY; LISTED/QUOTED SECURITIES; LISTING; MERCHANT BANK; OFFER FOR SALE; OVER-THE-COUNTER MARKET; PLACING; PUBLIC COMPANY; STOCK MARKET; THIRD MARKET; UNLISTED SECURITIES MARKET.

LISTED/QUOTED SECURITIES (valeurs cotées)

Securities which have been accepted for listing (cotation) by a stock exchange, thus enabling them to be traded on the exchange. Shares may also be referred to as being listed or quoted.

☞ See LISTED/QUOTED COMPANY; LISTING.

LISTING (cotation en bourse)

The act of putting the shares of a company on the official list (Cote officielle) of shares traded on a stock exchange, which in the case of the International Stock Exchange, London, can be on a primary, secondary, unlisted securities (hors cote) or third market (troisième marché) for shares. Being listed (cotée) on a stock exchange list gives a company a wider exposure (plus grand contact avec) to investors, and therefore a greater chance of raising the capital (se procurer/trouver les capitaux) it requires. To obtain **FULL LISTING** or be fully listed (inscrite à la Cote officielle) on the London Stock Exchange (as opposed to being listed on the USM) at least 25% of a company's shares must be offered to the general public (mettre à la disposition du marché), the company must be able to show profits (bénéfices) for the last three years and comply with stringent requirements (se conformer aux conditions sévères) to communicate all share-price sensitive information (toute information nouvelle de nature à modifier le cours des titres). A full listing gives a company high visibility and wide exposure to the public, thus providing the opportunity to raise large capital sums; but in exchange the company sacrifices its privacy and must submit to continual analysis from outside.

☞ See INTERNATIONAL STOCK EXCHANGE; LISTED/QUOTED COMPANY; LISTED/QUOTED SECURITIES; PRIMARY MARKET; PUBLIC COMPANY; SECONDARY MARKET; UNLISTED SECURITIES MARKET.

LLOYD'S (La Lloyd's)

Lloyd's is not an insurance company. It is a market where underwriters (souscripteur de risques, assureur) and brokers (courtier) meet. It is a unique (unique en son genre) structure. This market started at the end of the 17th century in the coffee shop of Edward Lloyd, Tower Street, London. In 1774, the market moved to the Royal Exchange but retained (garder) its original name "Lloyd's", formerly (auparavant) "at Lloyd's". Since 1985 the market has been taking place in a very modern building especially built for the purpose (à cet effet) by Richard Rogers and nicknamed (surnommer) "the percolator" on account of (en raison de) its shape.

Lloyd's has about 28,400 members called **NAMES** of whom (dont) 5,000 are non-British and only 50 are French. Names accept unlimited liability (responsabilité illimitée) for claims (sinistre). They are not connected necessarily with the insurance industry, but some of them are insurance professionals or work in the industry (secteur). They pledge (engager) their personal wealth (fortune) which must be very significant and partly liquid. A name's financial position (surface financière) decides how much premium income (revenu sur primes) can be accepted on his behalf (pour son compte). Members are co-opted after approval by a 28-strong Council. Membership is personal, not transferable but can be revoked at any moment if the name does not comply any more with criteria (critères) of wealth and solvency (solvabilité). In recent Lloyd's history, Sir Freddy Laker had his name struck off (radier) following the bankruptcy of his airline.

With their capital members support some 350 competing syndicates to which they delegate full authority to subscribe risks and manage claims. Each name can be a member of several syndicates which may have from a few hundred to several thousands participants. Thus a syndicate is a curious sort of partnership in which the sleeping partners (commanditaire) have unlimited responsibility while the everyday work is done by almighty (omnipotent) active partners (commandité). These active partners are called underwriters. There are 4 to 6 of them for each syndicate. Each team of underwriters holds a stall (box) in Lloyd's so-called (que l'on appelle) Underwriting Room where they meet independent Lloyd's brokers.

Brokers have a special status comparable to a solicitor's practice (charge d'avoué) with a limited membership (numerus clausus). Lloyd's brokers have no direct contact with the public of clients but receive underwriting applications (demande de garantie) from local brokers all over the world who specialize either in direct risk or business (assurance) or in indirect business (réassurance). As for any policy in any company an agreement is reached (conclure) according to (selon) underwriting terms (conditions de garantie) and the premium (prime) to be paid by the client. The contract is signed by the underwriter.

Two-thirds of Lloyd's premiums are dollar-denominated (libellées en dollar) and two-fifths of its risks are located in the USA. However, the main share of Lloyd's US market is done in reinsurance contracts because Lloyd's is authorized to deal in direct insurance in only two states of the USA.

Lloyd's is present though (toutefois) in most of the complex insurance technical arrangements (montage). For instance, when a country makes the underwriting (souscription) of policies with national companies mandatory (obligatoire), the latter (celles-ci) make a fronting arrangement (montage en façade) and are fully reinsured with Lloyd's.

Lloyd's is divided into four markets – marine, non-marine, aviation, motor – to which are to be added advanced technology (de pointe) sectors related to war damage, nuclear issues and satellites. Among the risks underwritten (garantir, assurer) exclusively by Lloyd's are: kidnapping, oil-rigs (plate-forme pétrolière), refineries, space shuttles (navette spatiale) and the huge reward (récompense) promised by such or such (tel ou tel) industrialist (industriel) to the person who captures the Loch Ness monster. Lloyd's does not handle (s'occuper de) life assurance.

The economic role of Lloyd's is not only to collect premiums but of course to pay claims (indemniser les sinistres) of which (dont) here are (voici) some unusual (exceptionnel) ones in the recent years: the obsolescence of equipment rented (louer) by IBM – rapid, successive technological advances entailed (entraîner) heavy replacement costs which were borne (prendre en charge) by Lloyd's –; the death of workers because of cancer due to asbestos (amiante); the Piper Alpha oil rig which exploded in 1988, followed by Hurricane Hugo and the San Francisco earthquake in 1989.

The growing cost of claims, the insistence of clients on cheaper premiums, the huge losses that have affected the management of some syndicates – recently entailing (entraîner) legal actions (poursuites en justice) successfully taken by members ($800 million have been awarded to them in compensation) against underwriters for incompetence or fraud – and the reduction of tax breaks (déduction d'impôt) that names and syndicates used to enjoy, together with competition – all these factors make it necessary for Lloyd's to change its syndicate structure and to reform its methods of capital-raising (levée de capitaux), accounting (comptabilité) and creating reserves (constitution de réserves). Lloyd's has a special three-year accounting system (système de comptabilité sur trois ans) which leaves accounts (compte) open-ended (ouvert) for losses (perte) endured (subir) over last three years and not finished yet. The recent opening to corporate capital (capitaux des sociétés) is believed to make Lloyd's a more attractive investment for new names and to maintain its long-standing (de longue date) reputation as a payer. Recent reports indeed show that as many as 6,000 names have quit (partir) in the past few years and that another 5,000 might soon follow. Despite its very serious difficulties, Lloyd's attempts to remain the leading insurer of oil, marine and big-catastrophe risks, with a quarter of the world market. It is a leader in new risks and crucial to world reinsurance. It has a symbolic value to the City of London as the largest single (à lui/elle seul/e) City contributor to invisible trade for Britain's balance of payments.

Some reforms have already started in order to attract more customers, with the writing (établissement) and sale of multirisk policies that many individuals (particulier) and companies want, the opening of six offices around the European continent to tackle (affronter, s'attaquer à) the Single Market (Marché unique), and the recent permission given to syndicates to deal directly with the public – instead of (au lieu de) going through (passer par) registered Lloyd's brokers (courtier "maison") – to write motor insurance (assurance automobile).

In April 1995, in order to reassure the City of London, Lloyd's had to publicly deny rumours of its possible closing down as financial circles thought that it would fail its next credit rating test (test de solvabilité) to which all insurers are put (soumettre).

☞ See BALANCE OF PAYMENTS; EUROPEAN INTERNAL MARKET; INVISIBLE TRADE; REINSURANCE.

LOAN or **ADVANCE** (prêt, emprunt ou avance de fonds)

A sum of money lent by a bank or financial institution, usually against security or collateral (garantie ou nantissement), referred to as a **SECURED LOAN** (emprunt garanti/gagé/nanti) for a short-term, medium term or long-term period, defined respectively (but this definition varies) as up to one or two, three to five or more than five years in length. Interest is payable from the day the loan is received. Whereas loans of a personal nature (prêt personnel), say (disons) to buy a video tape recorder, may not necessarily require security (nantissement), business and large loans in general do, to cover the possibility of the lender (prêteur) not being paid back. There are a variety of different loans and ways of paying the interest and repaying the capital borrowed (e.g. capital and interest by instalments [par versements échelonnés], interest regularly and capital at the end of the term of the loan [échéance], etc.). The interest payable will depend on the situation of the borrower (his reputation, the liquidity of the collateral he offers, his ability to meet the payments, his line of business (branche d'activité) etc.), and the economic climate (conjoncture économique), the period of the loan and other factors which affect the risk attached to lending the money.

☞ See BORROWING; CAPITAL; CAPITAL MARKET; INTEREST; LENDING; LIQUIDITY; LIQUIDITY RATIO; MONEY MARKET; SECURITY.

LOAN STOCK See .... DEBENTURE.

LOCAL AUTHORITY BOND See .... BOND.

LOCAL CONTENT (composants de fabrication locale)

Locally produced components (pièces détachées) which foreign manufacturers are required (se voir demander) to use in their transplants (unité de production délocalisée) in order to give local or domestic (national) producers of such components fair (loyal) trade treatment. For example, the USA imposes local content requirements (exigence) on Japan in the car industry. France demands a certain percentage of local content in Japanese cars produced in the United Kingdom and exported to other member countries of the European Union. Such requirements help to avoid (éviter) the so-called (que l'on appelle) **SCREW-DRIVER PLANTS** (usine tournevis) in which workers simply assemble (monter) parts (pièce) made abroad. Such requirements thus ensure that some of the additional benefits of a plant setting up in a foreign country go to that country. Imports are reduced and local businesses benefit from supplying the foreign company. Otherwise (sinon) all the benefits go abroad (apart from hiring local employees).

☞ See COUNTERTRADE; OFFSET REQUIREMENTS; TRANSPLANT.

LOCAL FINANCIAL COOPERATIVE See .... CREDIT UNION.

LOMBARD RATE (taux Lombard, taux des avances sur titres de la banque centrale d'Allemagne, la Bundesbank)

In the German banking system this is the rate of interest at which the Bundesbank is prepared to lend to commercial banks and other financial institutions, but always against security (sur gage/nantissement), which is usually in the form of financial instruments (effets/instruments financiers) such as bonds (obligation), bills of exchange (lettre de change), treasury bills (billet/bon du trésor) etc. This rate of interest is usually half a percentage point above the discount rate at which the Bundesbank, as lender of last resort (prêteur en dernier recours), will buy back financial instruments from the banking system.

☞ See CENTRAL BANK; COMMERCIAL BANK; DISCOUNT; DISCOUNT HOUSE; FINANCIAL INSTRUMENTS; LIBRO.

LOME CONVENTION (Convention de Lomé)

A convention originally signed in 1975 at Lomé, the capital of Togo, by the members of the European Economic Community/EEC – now called the European Union/EU – and 46 "Associated Countries of Africa, the Caribbean and the Pacific" – now commonly known as the ACP countries. It replaced earlier agreements between the original six members of the EEC and former (ancien) colonies, the Yaoundé Convention, Cameroun. It unified and expanded the systems of preferences of EEC members with these countries.

Under (selon) the Lomé Convention, all ACP countries are provided (se voir accorder) duty-free entrance into the EU for all their industrial products and 96% of their agricultural produce. A notable feature (caractéristique) of the Convention is an export scheme (système, plan) aimed at (viser à) stabilizing the agricultural export earnings (recettes, revenus à l'exportation) of the ACP countries. This scheme is known as STABEX. The European Development Fund was created by the EEC to grant (accorder) and manage (gérer) financial and technical help to these countries.

The agreement was superseded (remplacer) by a revised Lomé Convention in 1979 which increased the number of ACP countries to 66, raised the finance available for STABEX and eased (faciliter) the conditions of the loans (prêt). In 1981, a scheme similar to STABEX was set up (instaurer) to stabilize the production and exports of certain ores (minerai). The scheme is known as SYSMIN. As well as for STABEX, compensatory payments from the EU are based on the amount by which a country's income from exports falls below designated levels (niveau pré-établi). Another round of negotiations took place in 1984 – Lomé III – with more emphasis on aid, and Lomé IV, signed in 1990, has enlarged even more (encore) the scope (perspective) of support (soutien) to industrial enterprise by means of (au moyen de) joint initiatives between EU economic operators and ACP states, and to cooperation programmes in the fields (domaine) of energy, shipping (transports maritimes), fisheries (pêcherie) and social and cultural advance. For the period 1990-2000, the Lomé IV convention covers 69 countries.

Although (bien que) the EU devotes (consacrer) a larger share of its GNP (PNB) to development aid than either (soit) the USA or Japan, some of its policies, notably the CAP/Common Agricultural Policy, are said to increase the difficulties of Third World countries. The EU is also accused of reaping (récolter) more gains than its ACP partners from the aid programmes as (étant donné que) EU firms receive the bulk (le gros) of the contracts awarded (accorder).

☞ See COMMON AGRICULTURAL POLICY; COMPENSATORY FINANCE; INDUSTRIALPOLICY; EU; EUROPEAN INVESTMENT BANK.

LONDON INTER-BANK OFFERED RATE See .... LIBOR.

LONDON INTERNATIONAL FINANCIAL FUTURES EXCHANGE, abbr. **LIFFE**

Created in 1982, under the supervision of the Bank of England, this is a market for trade in **FINANCIAL FUTURES** (instruments financiers à terme ou contrats à terme d'instruments financiers). These are contracts for the purchase or sale of a standard (normal) quantity of a financial asset such as titles (droit de propriété) to bank deposits, certificates of deposit, abbr. CDs (certificat de dépôt), foreign currency (devises), ordinary shares (actions ordinaires), treasury bonds (bon du trésor) and other income-generating securities, at an agreed price for delivery on a specific future date. **FINANCIAL FUTURES** differ from **FORWARD CONTRACTS** (engagement d'acheter ou vendre à une date ultérieure à un prix fixé) in financial assets in that they are in standard (normal) quantities, traded regularly, while the latter (ces derniers) are for once-only (unique) transactions. Dealings (transactions) in foreign currencies on this market are known as **CURRENCY FUTURES** (devises à terme). The main financial futures exChanges in the world are in Chicago, London and Sydney.

☞ See ARBITRAGE; BEAR; BULL; FORWARD CONTRACT; COMMODITY; FOREIGN EXCHANGE MARKET; HEDGE; OPTION; SPOT/CURRENT PRICE; WARRANT.

LONDON MONEY MARKET See .... MONEY MARKET/LONDON MONEY MARKET.

LONDON STOCK EXCHANGE See .... INTERNATIONAL STOCK EXCHANGE OF THE UNITED KINGDOM ETC.

LONDON TRADED OPTIONS MARKET See .... OPTION.

LONGS See .... GILT-EDGED STOCKS.

LTOM See.. OPTION.

M

M0, M1, M2, M3 and M4 See .... MONEY SUPPLY.

MAASTRICHT

The Dutch town host to (ville d'accueil de) December 1991 EU summit. The name of the Treaty the Twelve signed in February 1992 calling for cooperation on monetary, economic, foreign policy and security matters. The Treaty, which amends the 1957 Treaty of Rome, proclaims the birth of the **EUROPEAN UNION**. Among the key points of the Maastricht treaty:

a. **CURRENCY**: adoption of a single EU denomination, the ECU, by 1999 at the latest;

b. **FOREIGN AND SECURITY POLICY**: creation of a European defence pillar to serve as a bridge between NATO (OTAN) and the EU, along with new measures to enhance (renforcer) foreign policy coordination;

c. **SOCIAL AFFAIRS**: a protocol allowing all member countries to establish common labour policies. Britain refused to participate;

d. **EUROPEAN UNION**: a statement on eventual (à venir) European citizenship (citoyenneté) to permit every EU national (ressortissant) the right to vote, no matter (quelque soit) where he or she lives in the Union.

Agreement on Economic and Monetary Union/EMU (Union économique et monétaire/UEM), involving a single (unique) currency, was the summit's outstanding (majeur) achievement (réalisation). The Twelve outlined **CONVERGENCE CRITERIA** (critères de convergence) to be met (respecter) before adopting the ECU, possibly on January 1st 1997:

i. total government debt must fall below 60% of Gross Domestic Product/GDP while budget deficits may not surpass 3% of GDP;

ii. national currencies (monnaie) must remain within the narrow band (marge de fluctuation étroite) of the Exchange Rate Mechanism/ERM of the European Monetary System/EMS for at least two years prior to adoption of the ECU;

iii. and interest rates must fall within two percentage points of those in the three EU countries with the lowest inflation.

To help lagging (en retard) EU economies catch up (rattraper), the Maastricht participants agreed to create a cohesion fund available to pay for transportation infrastructure, environmental clean up and other projects. If on January 1st, 1997 fewer than (moins de) seven countries meet the requirements, introduction of the single currency will be delayed until 1999. At that point, qualifying nations will automatically put the ECU into circulation as their legal tender (monnaie à cours légal). Countries unable to switch to the ECU by 1999 will do so as their economic performance (résultats) improves according to the EU requirements. A **EUROPEAN MONETARY INSTITUTE** was created in 1994 as a precursor of the **EUROPEAN CENTRAL BANK**, which will be set up in 1997 or in1999 at the same time as the single currency. In 1997, Britain will have the choice of "opting in or out" (choisir d'entrer ou de rester en dehors) by means of a vote of the British Parliament on whether or not to accept the single currency later in the decade. However, after much hesitation, the House of Commons (Chambre des Communes) eventually (finalement) ratified the other provisions (dispositions) of the Treaty in June1993 except the social ones (see below). The Prime Minister John Major, had to ask for a vote of confidence (vote de confiance) in his government on the issue (question) of ratification. The main opponents (adversaire) were the members of the Labour Party and the so-called (que l'on nomme) **EUROSCEPTICS** of the Conservative Party.

Denmark, whose constitution requires a popular vote on such issues, pronounced against the ratification by a referendum held in June 1992. However, it was decided that Denmark should be given a second chance. Another popular vote was held in 1993. This time the answer was positive. The Irish voted in favour of Maastricht in June 1992 as well as the French who went to the polls (aller aux urnes) in September of the same year and gave it a very short majority. The other EU members ratified the Treaty with a vote of their parliaments in 1993. In December 1991, only three EU countries satisfied the strict conditions for monetary union mentioned above: France, Luxembourg and Denmark. By mid-1993, only one did – Luxembourg.

Agreement on majority voting in the area of a common foreign and security policy could not be reached. Britain insisted on unanimous support for important EU initiatives. The **WESTERN EUROPEAN UNION/WEU** (Union de l'Europe occidentale/UEO), a long-inactive consultative group that now includes nine EU members, was designated as the EU's military pillar to act in coordination with NATO. The WEU was created in 1948 by Belgium, Britain, France, Luxembourg and the Netherlands, joined in 1954 by Germany and Italy, and reactivated in 1984. Spain and Portugal have been members since 1986. The **WEU** had been largely superseded (supplanter) by the creation of NATO in 1949.

The Maastricht Treaty extended EU competence to other more ordinary areas, including industrial affairs, health, education and the environment. The treaty also calls for increased cooperation on matters ranging from asylum (droit d'asile) policy to immigration. **EUROPOL**, intended to serve as the precursor of a Continental police intelligence service, will lead the fight against Europe-wide organized crime and narcotics trafficking. The EU

Parliament won the right to veto several categories of Union legislation, but did not gain the authority to make laws although (bien que) it should gradually become the joint manager of the Union together with the Council of Ministers. The first manifestation of this new authority was its vote on the appointment of the new president of the European Commission in July 1994. The **SOCIAL CHARTER** of the Treaty, covering minimum wages, dismissals (licenciement) and union-management (patronat-syndicats) consultation, was opposed by Britain on account of (en raison de) the decade-long fight against union power led by the Conservatives. Low-wage countries like Spain, Portugal and Greece also had reservations (réserve), fearing that tighter EU-wide labour regulations could undercut (diminuer) their competitive advantage. In the end, a compromise was found, allowing 11 EU members to sign a separate agreement on labour policy. This **CHARTER** is not part of the revised Treaty of Rome nor has it force (être en vigueur) in Britain.

Maastricht marked a major milestone (étape) in a process (processus) that started more than three decades ago. However, the European Monetary System is being continually attacked and economic difficulties of all kinds affect trade within the Union and outside its frontiers. This situation, together with (ainsi que) the hesitations in foreign and security policy matters – concerning for example the armed conflict in former (ex) Yugoslavia – is bound to slow down (ralentir) the implementation (mise en oeuvre) of this very ambitious Treaty which is to be examined again (institutional aspects) at an intergovernmental conference/IGC scheduled (prévoir, programmer) for 1996.

☞ See EUROPEAN CURRENCY UNIT; EUROPEAN MONETARY SYSTEM; EUROPEAN PARLIAMENT; EXCHANGE RATE MECHANISM; TREATY OF ROME.

MACROECONOMICS (macroéconomie)

The section (branche) of economics concerned with (s'intéresser à) the study of relationships between broad economic aggregates (agrégat), such as national income (revenu national), savings (épargne), investment (investissements), consumption (consommation), employment (emploi), the money supply (masse monétaire), the average price level (niveau moyen des prix), exports, imports, and the balance of payments. This is constrasted with (ceci par opposition à) microeconomics, which studies economic behaviour (comportement) at the individual level.

☞ See AGGREGATE DEMAND; BALANCE OF PAYMENTS; MICROECONOMICS.

MAJORITY HOLDING See .... TAKEOVER BID.

MANAGED TRADE (commerce dirigé)

The application by governments of selective protectionist measures under the guise of (sous couvert de) a supposedly (prétendument) more efficient management of their industrial policy. The phrase (expression) may also describe stabilization arrangements (accords) such as Stabex in the Lomé Convention.

☞ See INDUSTRIAL POLICY; LOME CONVENTION; PROTECTIONISM.

MANAGEMENT BOARD See .... BOARD OF DIRECTORS.

MANAGEMENT BUYBACK See .... LEVERAGED BUYOUT.

MANAGEMENT BUY-IN See .... LEVERAGED BUYOUT.

MANAGEMENT BUYOUT See .... LEVERAGED BUYOUT.

MANAGEMENT-EMPLOYEE BUYOUT See .... LEVERAGED BUYOUT.

MANAGEMENT/MANAGERS' SHARES (parts de fondateur)

Deferred shares given to managers as an incentive for them to make the company perform well.

☞ See DEFERRED SHARES.

MANAGING DIRECTOR See .... BOARD OF DIRECTORS.

MANDATORY BID See .... TAKEOVER BID.

MARCHE DES OPTIONS NEGOCIABLES See .... OPTION.

MARINE INSURANCE (assurance maritime)

A non-life (non vie) or casualty/property (biens et personnes) category of insurance which is divided into four different sections:

i. **HULL POLICY** (sur corps) covering the hull (coque), superstructure and machinery (machines) of the ship (navire) or aircraft (appareil, avion) against such hazards (risque) as fire (incendie), storm (tempête) and collision. May also include (comprendre) liability (responsabilité) for damage (dommage) to other ships or aircrafts. The policy may be taken out (souscrire) for a period of time or for a specific voyage (voyage, traversée);

ii. **CARGO POLICY** (sur facultés) taken out for a particular voyage. Covers the cost of the cargo if the latter (celle-ci) has been totally destroyed or lost as well as the profit (bénéfice) that would have been made if the goods (marchandise) could have been sold. Should (si) the goods have already been sold, the buyer then (alors) receives the full amount (montant total) of his purchase (achat). When transport charges (frais) have been pre-paid (payer d'avance), this cost forms a part of the value of the cargo. When the goods are to be (devoir être) paid only after they have been received, the buyer does not of course have to pay for the goods, but the cargo policy covers the bank which had granted (accorder) the credit terms (conditions, facilités). A cargo policy may be taken out for a single (unique) amount or can be **FLOATING** (flottante), i.e. cargo can be shipped (acheminer, expédier) up to (jusqu'à) a certain amount (montant). In the latter case (dans ce dernier cas), once (une fois que) the full amount (le montant total) has been used (utiliser), the policy has to be renewed (renouveler) and a new premium (prime) paid. For each shipment (expédition), the insured (assuré) informs the insurer (assureur) of the value involved (concerner) and receives a certificate. Aircraft cargo (cargaison aérienne) insurance is placed in (relever de) the broad category of insurance known as **ACCIDENT**.

iii. **FREIGHT POLICY** (fret, prix du transport des marchandises) covers the amount charged (facturer) by shipping firms (expéditeur) for transport. If freight charges (frais) have not been pre-paid, they have to be insured separately by the shipping company. If the goods are not delivered (livrer) the freight charges cannot be claimed (réclamer);

iv. **SHIPOWNER'S LIABILITY POLICY** (responsabilité de l'armateur) covers claims (sinistre) caused by the shipowners' or their employees' negligence in dealing with (traiter, s'occuper de) the cargo or the passengers, if any (s'il y en a). Liability to aircraft passengers is placed in the **ACCIDENT** category. The types of marine loss are as follow:

a. **(ACTUAL) TOTAL LOSS** (perte totale réelle) where the ship sinks (couler) and/or the cargo is totally lost;

b. **CONSTRUCTIVE TOTAL LOSS** (perte censée totale) where the ship has been abandoned or the cargo is so damaged (endommager) as to be (jusqu'à être) worthless (sans aucune valeur);

c. **PARTIAL LOSS** (perte partielle):

– **GENERAL AVERAGE** (avarie commune) or **FREE OF PARTICULAR AVERAGE/F.P.A** (franc d'avarie particulière), where the owner (armateur) of the ship and the owner (propriétaire) of the cargo both (à eux deux) bear (supporter) the loss in proportion with the values of their lost properties (biens qu'ils ont perdus). For example, if it was necessary to cast overboard (jeter par dessus bord) some of the cargo in order to (afin de) save the ship from sinking, the full loss would not fall on (être imputé à) the owner of the cargo. The loss would be shared (partager, répartir) by the owner of the ship as the latter (celui-ci) might have sunk and thus (donc) be lost if this action (mesure) had not been taken. Claims (dommages et intérêts) would thus be made with (demander à) the insurer of the hull (assureur sur corps) and the insurer of the cargo;

– **PARTICULAR AVERAGE** (avarie simple ou particulière) or **WITH PARTICULAR AVERAGE/W.P.A** (avec avarie particulière), where the loss resulting from damage to the ship or cargo falls on (être imputé à) either (soit) the owner of the hull (coque) or (soit) the owner of the cargo. If a ship strikes a rock and is damaged in the process (ce faisant), the loss will fall only on the hull owner because the cargo is not affected (toucher) as long as (du moment que) the ship can reach (atteindre) port without assistance. Thus the claim will be made against the insurer of the hull only.

☞ See ACCIDENT INSURANCE; INSURANCE; LLOYD'S.

MARINE UNDERWRITER See .... UNDERWRITER.

MARKET CAPITALIZATION See .... STOCK MARKET/EXCHANGE.

MARKET DISRUPTION (désorganisation, perturbation du marché)

The situation which occurs (se produire) when a flood (afflux) of imports of a particular commodity (produit) entails (entraîner) a rapid decrease in sales of similar goods produced on the domestic (intérieur) market, thus (donc, ainsi) jeopardizing (porter préjudice à) the domestic producers.

☞ See DUMPING; ESCAPE CLAUSE; MULTI-FIBRE ARRANGEMENT; ORDERLY MARKETING AGREEMENTS; SAFEGUARDS; SENSITIVE PRODUCTS.

MARKET MAKER (contrepartiste spécialisé ou teneur de marché)

Usually a firm which buys and sells securities (titres) in large quantities (un maison de titres grossiste ou demi-grossiste), is a member of a stock exchange, and guarantees to offer selling and buying prices for a given range of securities (pour une gamme de titres donnée). It is to the market makers that brokers (agent de change/courtier) or broker/dealers (négociant courtier/négociant en titres) go when seeking (chercher à) to buy or sell securities on behalf (pour le compte de) of their clients or for their own account (pour leur propre compte). In the UK prior to the Big Bang in 1986 the market maker was known as a **JOBBER** (marchand de titres), who did not deal directly with investors but always through (par l'intermédiaire de) a broker. The term **"JOBBER"** or **"STOCK JOBBER"** continues to be used from time to time. In the UK now large investors can negotiate directly with a market maker (teneur de marché), and brokers themselves, now called broker/dealers, can also elect (choisir de) to be market makers if they want.

☞ See BID PRICE; BIG BANG, THE; BROKER/DEALER; INTERNATIONAL STOCK EXCHANGE.

MARKET VALUE (valeur marchande)

The value at which something can be sold, which may be different from its nominal or original value.

☞ See PAR VALUE; NOMINAL VALUE; FACE VALUE.

MATERIAL DAMAGE See .... FIRE INSURANCE.

MATERIALS See .... FIRE INSURANCE.

MD See .... BOARD OF DIRECTORS.

MEDIUMS See .... GILT-EDGED STOCKS.

MEMBER BANK (banque ayant adhéré au Federal Reserve System, institution d'émission de la monnaie aux Etats-Unis)

One of the 5,978 reserve banks (banque de la Réserve fédérale) belonging to the Federal Reserve System, abbr. **FED**, the central banking system of the USA. Member banks have the functions of a commercial bank, but as opposed to those in the UK, are mostly single units (i.e. do not have branches [succursale]). Over half of all the US commercial banks are members of the FED.

☞ See BANKING; CENTRAL BANK; COMMERCIAL BANK; FEDERAL RESERVE SYSTEM.

MEMBERS' VOLUNTARY WINDING-UP See .... LIQUIDATION.

MEMORANDUM OF ASSOCIATION See .... AUTHORIZED/REGISTERED ETC. CAPITAL.

MERCANTILISM (mercantilisme)

A word first used by **ADAM SMITH** in his *Wealth of Nations* (1776) to define a prevailing (dominant) economic philosophy from the 16th to the early (début) 18th centuries claiming (affirmer, prétendre) that national wealth (richesse) was essentially acquired not through agriculture but by accumulating and possessing gold and silver through a surplus balance of trade. Some contemporary governments in Central and Eastern Europe, Asia and South America still (encore) apply policies (politique) meant to (destiner à) create trade surpluses (excédent commercial) by means of (au moyen de) import substitution (substitution d'importation) and tariff protection (barrière tarifaire) for domestic (national) industries. Such policies require government control over prices, wages (salaires), exports and imports. They are strongly attacked by the proponents (tenant, partisan) of laissez-faire who follow the tenets (principe) of the **CLASSICAL SCHOOL** originated by **Adam SMITH** and continued by **David RICARDO** and **John Stuart MILL.**

☞ See BALANCE OF TRADE; IMPORT SUBSTITUTION; INDUSTRIAL POLICY; LAISSEZ-FAIRE; PROTECTIONISM.

MERCHANT BANK (banque d'affaires)

This is a bank that specializes in large and wholesale (en gros) financial transactions, as opposed to a retail bank (banque de dépôt). Merchant banks, also known as **HOUSES** or **ISSUING HOUSES** (banque de placement ou d'émission), specialize in raising capital (trouver des capitaux) for industry through issuing (émettre) securities (titres) and loans (emprunt ou prêt), underwriting (souscrire ou garantir) an issue (émission) of securities, investing themselves in venture capital (capital risque/spéculatif) and advising companies on mergers (fusion) and takeovers (rachat de l'entreprise). In the USA many of the activities regarding raising capital for industry are undertaken by **INVESTMENT BANKS** (banque d'investissement/de placement), which will, for example, buy the entire issue of new bonds (obligation) or shares (US, stock) from a company, thus relieving (soulager) the latter (cette dernière) of the risk of not obtaining the capital required, and then sell it on to the public in small parcels (lot). They are also called in to advise on and/or support mergers, takeovers and company reorganizations in general.

They also manage (gérer) unit and investment trusts (SICAV et société de placement à capital fixe), deal in (faire le commerce de) foreign exchange (devises) and gold bullion (or en barres/lingots), arrange Euro-market loans (crédits en euro-devises), and can also deal in securities, insurance and other commercial activities.

Merchant banks play an important role in international trade by accepting (accepter) bills of exchange (lettre de change) and acting as bankers to home (du pays) and foreign companies. Merchant banks carrying out such functions are also referred to as **ACCEPTANCE/ACCEPTING HOUSES** (maison d'acceptation) and in the USA as **ACCEPTANCE BANKS** (banque d'acceptation).

☞ See BILL OF EXCHANGE; COMMERCIAL BANK; EUROCURRENCY MARKET; INTRODUCTION; INVESTMENT TRUST; LEVERAGED BUYOUT; OFFER FOR SALE; PLACING; RISK/VENTURE CAPITAL; SECURITY; SHARE; SPONSOR; TAKEOVER BID; UNIT TRUST.

MERCOSUR See .... FREE TRADE AREA.

MERGER (fusion)

This is when two companies voluntarily join together to form a single (seule) company. This can take place in two ways:

i. the two companies become one single company with a new name (raison sociale); or

ii. the larger company takes over (racheter) the smaller one, which then becomes a subsidiary (filiale) of the former (la première). This contrasts with a takeover, friendly or hostile (OPA amicale ou hostile), where the smaller company becomes absorbed entirely by the larger and can be disposed of at will (et dont le repreneur peut disposer à sa guise).

☞ See LEVERAGED BUYOUT; TAKEOVER BID.

MERGER See .... TAKEOVER BID.

MEZZANINE FINANCE See .... LEVERAGED BUYOUT.

MFA See .... MULTI-FIBRE ARRANGEMENT.

MFN See .... MOST-FAVOURED-NATION TREATMENT.

MICROECONOMICS (microéconomie)

The section of economics concerned with (s'intéresser à) the study of individual decision makers (responsable, décideur), i.e. consumers (consommateur), households (ménage) and companies (entreprise), the way (facon dont) their decisions interrelate (se recouper) to determine relative prices of goods (marchandise) and factors of production as well as the quantities of goods that will be bought and sold.

☞ See MACROECONOMICS.

MILL John Stuart See .... MERCANTILISM.

MINIMUM SUBSCRIPTION See .... OFFER FOR SALE.

MONEP See .... OPTION.

MONETARISTS See .... MONETARY POLICY.

MONETARY COMPENSATORY AMOUNT or **MONETARY COMPENSATION AMOUNT,** abbr. **MCA** (montant compensatoire monétaire/MCM)

A system of compensation employed by the European Union to maintain the common price structure of the Common Agricultural Policy against (vis-à-vis de), par rapport à) exchange rate (taux de change) modifications. The gap (différence) between **GREEN CURRENCY** (monnaie verte), i.e. a fixed rate of exchange for agricultural prices, and real currencies (monnaie ayant réellement cours), is filled (combler) by the MCAs applied (appliquer) on intra-Union and third country (pays tiers) trade. Countries with hard (fort) currencies are rewarded (récompenser) by means of (au moyen de) a positive MCA or subsidy (subvention), while (tandis que) countries with soft (faible) currencies are penalized by means of a negative MCA or tax (impôt), thus (ainsi) offsetting (compenser) the comparative disadvantage, or advantage (avantage ou désavantage comparatif), as the case may be (selon le cas), that would otherwise (sinon) distort (fausser, affecter) the policy of common prices.

☞ See COMMON AGRICULTURAL POLICY; EU; EUROPEAN MONETARY SYSTEM.

MONETARY POLICY (politique monétaire)

Government policy which seeks to influence the level of national economic activity, and in particular inflation and unemployment, by altering (modifier) the money supply (masse monétaire) in the economy. To do this it can adjust interest and exchange rates (taux de change) and control credit. High interest rates, for example, encourage savings as people earn more from saving their money, therefore save more and spend less; where individuals and companies spend and invest through borrowing this becomes more expensive and so they are discouraged to do this, while their existing debts (e.g. house mortgage [hypothèque] or company loan) demand more money to service (payer les intérêts d'un emprunt), leaving less to spend on goods (biens) and services; where future consumer spending and investment depends on borrowing money, which now becomes more expensive, this too inhibits (réduire) consumption; and lastly, credit restrictions can make it more difficult to buy on hire purchase (vente à tempérament) or on credit, dissuading consumers from purchasing in this way. Devaluing (dévaluer) the currency makes imports more expensive (while at the same time encouraging exports, which now become cheaper on foreign markets). The overall effect of such measures is to reduce aggregate demand (demande globale). The danger with such a policy is that businesses may find it difficult to meet (faire face à) their interest payments and may experience cash flow (marge brut d'autofinancement, flux de liquidités) problems, especially as demand has been reduced; they may also be discouraged from investing more, because their financial costs will be greater and this could reduce the profitability (rentabilité) of the proposed investment. If this happens, unemployment is likely to increase, although inflation may have improved. There is also, as regards the latter, the risk that high rates of interest will attract inflows of capital (afflux de capitaux) – so-called **"HOT MONEY"** (déplacements de capitaux cherchant des meilleurs taux d'intérêt ou capitaux spéculatifs/fébriles/flottants) – which actually increase the money supply.

Lowering the rate of interest and making credit more freely available generally encourage consumers and companies to borrow more, increase the money supply and boost aggregate demand (i.e. both private and corporate spending). The danger here, however, is that in boosting demand (and also employment) inflation will increase, as production will lag (être à la traîne) behind demand and imports are likely to increase.
Through open market operations (opérations d'open market sur le marché monétaire) governments can, in a free exchange system, lower or raise the value of their national currency vis-à-vis other currencies. They can, for example, maintain the value of their currency against foreign currencies by buying up vast quantities of the national currency,which increases the demand for the currency vis-à-vis other currencies and therefore the exchange rate or price; this, incidentally, makes exports more expensive and therefore has a tendency to lower them; or the government can devalue the national currency to discourage imports. Interest and exchange rates affect the inflows (afflux) and outflows (sorties) of money and capital. Money supply and interest and exchange rates are all inter-dependent, so it is very difficult for a government to get the right mix (combinaison). It should be noted that **MONETARISTS** (économistes monétaristes) believe that it is possible to control precisely the money supply and hence inflation, but this point of view is disputed.

☞ See AGGREGATE DEMAND; CREDIT CONTROL; EXCHANGE RATE; EXCHANGE RATE MECHANISM; FISCAL POLICY; FREE EXCHANGE SYSTEM; INFLATION; INTEREST RATE; MONEY SUPPLY; OPEN MARKET OPERATIONS; UNEMPLOYMENT.

MONEY AT CALL See .... CALL MONEY.

MONEY AT SHORT NOTICE See .... CALL MONEY.

MONEY MARKET INSTRUMENTS (effets à court terme du marché monétaire)
Short-term fixed interest investments or securities (titres) such as certificates of deposit (certificats de dépôt), treasury bills (bon du trésor), bankers' acceptances (acceptation ou aval) and commercial paper (billet de trésorerie) from blue chip (de premier ordre) companies and which are traded (échanger) in large quantities on the money market.

☞ See BANKERS' ACCEPTANCE; BLUE CHIP COMPANY; CERTIFICATE OF DEPOSIT; COMMERCIAL PAPER; FINANCIAL INSTRUMENTS; INVESTMENT; MONEY MARKET; SECURITIES; TREASURY BILL; WARRANT.

MONEY MARKET/LONDON MONEY MARKET (marché monétaire)
A wholesale market (marché de gros) dealing in large quantities of short-term financial instruments such as bills of exchange (lettre de change), treasury bills (bon du trésor), inter-bank money (prêts interbancancaires) – see **LIBOR** –, bankers' acceptances (acceptation ou aval), certificates of deposit (certificat de dépôt, abbr. CD) and discount house deposits (dépôts de banque d'escompte), as well as gold and foreign exchange. Companies use this market to invest temporary cash surpluses. The main agents in this

market are central and other banks and discount and finance houses. Most transactions involve discounting (escompter) and are made internationally by telephone or telex.

☞ See BANKERS' ACCEPTANCE; BILL OF EXCHANGE; CENTRAL BANK; CERTIFICATE OF DEPOSIT; COMMERCIAL PAPER; DISCOUNT; DISCOUNT HOUSE; FINANCE HOUSE; FINANCIAL INSTRUMENTS; LIBOR; MONEY MARKET INSTRUMENTS; TREASURY BILL; WARRANT.

MONEY ON CALL See .... CALL MONEY.

MONEY SUPPLY (masse monétaire)

Broadly defined, this is the total amount of money held and circulating in the economy. In the UK this is measured in different ways. **M0** is made up mainly of notes (billet) and coins (pièce de monnaie) held by the public and the deposits (dépôt) of banks with the Bank of England. **M1**, the basic measure of money supply, is M0 plus current and some deposit accounts (compte courant et compte de dépôt/d'épargne) held by the public which enable transfers by cheque. **M2** includes M0 and M1 and all private sector (secteur privé) deposit accounts earning interest with banks, finance companies (société/établissement de financement ou de crédit), discount houses (banque d'escompte) and other financial intermediaries operating in the money market (marché monétaire). **M3** is M2 plus all public sector fixed- term deposits (dépôt à terme), as well as all public and private sector foreign currency (devises) deposits with banks etc. **STERLING M 3** is M3 without these foreign currency deposits, and is sometimes referred to as **BROAD MONEY** or **M4**. The UK definition of money supply is similar to that used in other countries. The money supply over the last ten years or so has been the particular target (cible) of UK and US economic policy: if it is excessive this leads to inflation; if it is insufficient this puts a brake (frein) on economic growth (croissance économique) and employment.

☞ See CENTRAL BANK; COMMERCIAL BANK; FINANCIAL INTERMEDIARIES; FOREIGN EXCHANGE; GROSS DOMESTIC PRODUCT;INFLATION; MONETARISTS; MONETARY POLICY; PRIVATE SECTOR.

MONOPOLIES AND MERGERS COMMISSION

This was formerly (précédemment) the UK **MONOPOLIES COMMISSION** and was set up (créé) under the **FAIR TRADING ACT, 1973**. It has the power to investigate (examiner) companies which, as they grow or merge, could occupy a monopolistic position in the market, and prevent them from achieving this. The latter (cette dernière) is defined as controlling a quarter or more of the market, and this is considered as being anti-competitive (i.e. making it very difficult for other companies to compete) and against the public interest. The European Union Commission for Competition has a similar function. The **OFFICE OF FAIR TRADING**, abbr. **OFT**, set up also by this Act with the functions of protecting the consumer and fair trade (pratique commerciale loyale), has the right to refer (soumettre) potential monopoly situations to the EU Commission.

☞ See TAKE-OVER BID.

MONOPOLIES COMMISSION See .... MONOPOLIES AND MERGERS COMMISSION.

MOODY'S See .... CREDIT RATING AGENCY.

MORTGAGE DEBENTURE See .... DEBENTURE.

MORTGAGE PROTECTION See .... LIFE INSURANCE.

MORTGAGE See .... BUILDING SOCIETY.

MOST-FAVOURED-NATION TREATMENT, abbr. **MFN** (Traitement de la nation la plus favorisée)

The GATT policy of non-discrimination that provides to (appliquer à) all trading partners the same customs and tariff treatment (modalités tarifaires et douanières) given to the so-called (que l'on appelle) "Most-Favoured-Nation". All contracting parties (parties contractantes) to GATT apply MFN treatment to one another (les unes aux autres) under (d'après, selon) Article I of GATT. This means that favourable trading conditions granted (accorder) by one country to another must be extended (étendre) to all other GATT signatories (signataire), so that (de sorte que) in fact no nation is more favourably treated than another.

☞ See CUSTOMS; ENABLING CLAUSE; GATT; PRINCIPLE SUPPLIERS; RECIPROCITY; TARIFF.

MULTI-(GB) FIBRE (US) FIBER ARRANGEMENT abbr. **MFA** (Accord multifibres/AMF)

An international agreement according to which (selon lequel) an importing signatory country can apply quantitative restrictions on textiles imports when it considers them necessary to prevent (empêcher) market disruption (perturbation du marché), even when these restrictions would otherwise (par ailleurs) be contrary to GATT rules. The MFA however (cependant) provides that (prévoir, stipuler) such restrictions should not reduce imports to levels (niveau) below those reached (atteindre) the preceding year, and should, if continued (en cas de maintien en place), enable (permettre) trade to expand by specified (défini) percentages. As an importing country may impose these quotas unilaterally, most (la plupart) important textiles exporting countries prefer to try and enter into (conclure) bilateral agreements with the main textiles importing countries.

The MFA went into effect (entrer en vigueur) on January 1st 1974 and was renewed in December 1977, in December 1981 and in July 1986. It applies to cotton, wool and man-made (synthétique) fibre textiles. The objective of the MFA is to reconcile (concilier) the interests of textiles exporting and importing countries by permitting an orderly (ordonné) expansion of this trade while (tout en) avoiding (éviter) market disruption.

The phasing out (démantèlement progressif) of the MFA was decided at the Uruguay Round of GATT talks, whose final act was signed on 15th April 1994.

☞ See GATT; MARKET DISTRUPTION; ORDERLY MARKETING AGREEMENTS.

MULTILATERAL AGREEMENT (accord multilatéral)

An international pact or treaty involving (impliquer, concerner) three or more parties. For example, GATT seeks to (chercher à) promote (promouvoir) trade liberalization (libéralisation du commerce) through multilateral negotiations.

☞ See CODES OF CONDUCT; GATT; LIBERALIZATION; MULTILATERAL TRADE NEGOTIATIONS.

MULTILATERAL TRADE NEGOTIATIONS, abbr. **MTN** (Négociations commerciales multilatérales/NCM)

Most frequently refers to GATT Rounds of talks (pourparlers) which have taken place since 1947.

☞ See GATT; ROUND.

MULTINATIONAL CORPORATION, abbr. **MNC** or **MULTINATIONAL ENTERPRISE,** abbr. **MNE** (société multinationale)

A large commercial concern (établissement commercial) with production and other facilities (infrastructure) operating (fonctionner) in different countries outside the country of origin. MNCs are sometimes called transnational corporations (société transnationale). They are sometimes so large, as is the case with (comme c'est le cas de) some oil companies (société pétrolière), that their revenues are greater than the GDP (PIB) of some national economies.

☞ See EURO-CURRENCY MARKET; SUBSIDIARY.

MULTIPLE VOTING SHARES See .... "A" SHARES.

MULTIPLIER EFFECT See .... UNEMPLOYMENT.

MUNICIPAL BOND See .... BOND.

MUTUAL See .... UNIT TRUST.

MUTUAL FUND See .... UNIT TRUST.

MUTUAL FUNDS COMPANY See .... UNIT TRUST.

MUTUAL SAVINGS BANK, USA (banque/caisse mutuelle d'épargne)

This is a cooperative savings bank owned by the depositors (déposants). It places most of its funds in the mortgage market (marché hypothécaire) and tends to be larger than a savings & loan association. Mutual savings banks are included in the term "thrifts".

☞ See MORTGAGE MARKET; SAVINGS & LOAN ASSOCIATION; SAVINGS BANK; THRIFTS.

N

NAFTA See .... NORTH AMERICAN FREE-TRADE AGREEMENT.

NAIRU See .... UNEMPLOYMENT.

NAMES See .... LLOYD'S.

NASDAQ See .... OVER-THE-COUNTER MARKET.

NATIONAL ASSOCIATION OF SECURITIES DEALERS See .... OVER-THE-COUNTER MARKET.

NATIONAL ASSOCIATION OF SECURITIES DEALERS AUTOMATED QUOTATION SYSTEM See .... OVER-THE-COUNTER MARKET.

NATIONAL INSURANCE (Sécurité sociale)

National Insurance is the name of the social security scheme (régime, système) in the United Kingdom. This scheme provides (assurer) unemployment benefits (allocation ou indemnité de chômage), sickness benefits (allocation ou prestation ou indemnité de maladie), retirement pensions (pension de retraite ou retraite), maternity benefits (allocation de maternité), family or children's allowances (allocations familiales) and other benefits on widowhood (veuvage), incapacity (invalidité) or death (capital décès ou indemnité en cas de décès) in return for (en échange de) regular contributions paid by employees, employers and self-employed persons (travailleurs indépendants).

Contributions are earnings-related (fonction du salaire ou des bénéfices) within (à l'intérieur de) a fixed band (tranche) of earnings. The self-employed pay both earnings-related contributions and a flat-rate contribution (somme forfaitaire, forfait). Payment of these contributions is made to the **NATIONAL INSURANCE FUND** from which benefits are paid. The Government also contributes to the Fund.

☞ See TAX.

NATIONAL INSURANCE FUND See .... NATIONAL INSURANCE.

NATURAL RATE OF UNEMPLOYMENT See .... UNEMPLOYMENT.

NCI See .... NEW COMMUNITY INSTRUMENT.

NEGATIVE (INCOME) TAX See .... TAX.

NEGOTIATING "COIN" See .... CONCESSION.

NEW COMMUNITY INSTRUMENT, abbr. **NCI** (Nouvel instrument communautaire/NIC)
A fund (fonds) controlled by the European Commission, with expert advice from (sur avis autorisé de) the European Investment Bank, which finances priority projects for the development of energy resources (ressources énergétiques), facilities (infrastructures) and small and medium-sized firms (petites et moyennes entreprises). The NCI is also known as the **ORTOLI FACILITY** (Plan Ortoli) after the name of (du nom de) its founder, François Xavier Ortoli, a former (ancien) French European commissioner (commissaire européen).

☞ See EUROPEAN COMMISSION; EUROPEAN INTEGRATED OPERATIONS; EUROPEAN INVESTMENT BANK.

NEW SHARES (actions nouvelles)
Shares issued (émises) by a company to be exchanged for a certain number of old shares. For example, a company might offer to give existing shareholders two new shares for five old shares (i.e. for every five shares that they already possess). Sometimes this offer is made on a purely exchange basis in order to make it easier to divide the capital of the company into smaller parts (in which case the company would offer, say, five new shares for every one old share held by the investor). Sometimes new shares are associated with a rights issue (émission de droit de souscription/d'attribution), whereby the shareholder is offered the right to purchase, say, five new shares at a favourable price for every one that he already holds.

☞ See OLD SHARES; RIGHTS ISSUE; SHARE; SHAREHOLDER; WARRANT.

NEW YORK STOCK EXCHANGE See .... STOCK MARKET/EXCHANGE.

NEWLY INDUSTRIALIZING or **INDUSTRIALIZED COUNTRY,** abbr. **NIC** (Nouveau pays industriel ou industrialisé/NPI)
A relatively advanced country whose industrial production and exports have increased rapidly in recent years. The Organization for Econonic Co-operation and Development includes the following countries in the NIC category: Brazil, Greece, Hong Kong, South Korea, Mexico, Portugal, Singapore, Spain, Taiwan and former (ex) Yugoslavia.

☞ See ORGANIZATION FOR ECONOMIC CO-OPERATION AND DEVELOPMENT.

NIC See .... NEWLY INDUSTRIALIZING or INDUSTRIALIZED COUNTRY.

NIKKEI STOCK AVERAGE See .... SHARE INDEX.

NO-PAR VALUE SECURITIES See .... PAR ETC.

NOMINAL CAPITAL See .... AUTHORIZED/REGISTERED ETC. CAPITAL; SHARE.

NOMINAL VALUE See .... PAR ETC.

NON-ACCELARATING INFLATION RATE OF UNEMPLOYMENT See .... UNEMPLOYMENT.

NON-CUMULATIVE PREFERENCE SHARES (actions priviligiées/prioritaires à dividende non cumulatif/non cumulatives)

Preference shares which do not accumulate any dividends not paid in any one year (i.e. if they are not paid in any one year the shareholder receives nothing afterwards).

☞ See CUMULATIVE PREFERENCE SHARES; PREFERENCE SHARES.

NON-DISCRIMINATION See .... GENERAL AGREEMENT ON TARIFFS AND TRADE.

NON-EXECUTIVE DIRECTORS See .... BOARD OF DIRECTORS.

NON-LIFE INSURANCE See .... INSURANCE.

NON-PARTICIPATING CUMULATIVE PREFERENCE SHARES (actions priviligiées/prioritaires non participantes à dividende cumulatif ou cumulatives sans droit de participation)

Shares which give the holder (porteur ou possesseur) the right to always receive the next year any dividend owing to him in one year but which has not been paid. In other words, the dividend owing to the shareholder but which has not been paid to him accumulates. At the same time these shares give no rights to a share in the profits, as is the case with types of participating preference shares (i.e. there is no participation in any profits left for distribution).

☞ See CUMULATIVE PREFERENCE SHARES; NON PARTICIPATING PREFERENCE SHARES; PARTICIPATING CUMULATIVE PREFERENCE SHARES; PARTICIPATING PREFERENCE SHARES; PREFERENCE SHARES.

NON-PARTICIPATING PREFERENCE SHARES (actions priviligiées/prioritaires non participantes ou sans droit de participation)

Preference shares with no rights to a share in any of the profits.

☞ See PARTICIPATING PREFERENCE SHARES; PREFERENCE SHARES.

NON-PARTICIPATING SHARES (actions sans droit de participation/non participantes ou à dividende fixe)

Preference shares which only give a fixed dividend, but which give no right to a share in the profits, as do participating shares.

☞ See PARTICIPATING SHARES; PREFERENCE SHARES.

NON-PROFITS ASSURANCE See .... LIFE INSURANCE.

NON-TARIFF BARRIERS, abbr. **NTBs,** or **NON-TARIFF MEASURES,** abbr. **NTMs** (barrières/obstacles non tarifaires)

Government measures other than tariffs (tarif douanier) aiming at (viser à) restricting imports. These measures have become all the more (d'autant plus) conspicuous (visible, frappant) impediments (obstacle) to trade as (que) tariffs have been considerably reduced since World War II (Deuxième Guerre Mondiale) through the action of the GATT. Examples of NTBs include (comprendre) regulations on safety, construction and use (utilisation) i.e. standards (normes) in general, as well as deliberate delay (retard) in customs clearance (dédouanement).

☞ See CODES OF CONDUCT; CONCESSION; CONSULAR FORMALITIES AND DOCUMENTATION; EXCHANGE CONTROLS; EXPORT SUBSIDIES; GATT; GOVERNMENT PROCUREMENT POLICIES AND PRACTICES; LICENSING; PACKAGING, LABELING AND MARKING REGULATIONS; PRIOR DEPOSITS; QUANTITATIVE RESTRICTIONS; QUARANTINE, SANITARY AND HEALTH LAWS AND REGULATIONS; ROAD TAX; SERVICES; SPECIAL AND DIFFERENTIAL TREATMENT; SPECIFIC LIMITATIONS ON TRADE; STANDARDS; STRUCTURAL IMPEDIMENTS INITIATIVE; SUBSIDY; TRANSPARENCY.

NON-TARIFF MEASURES See .... NON-TARIFF BARRIERS.

NON-VOTING SHARES (actions sans droit de vote)

Shares which do not give the shareholder the right to vote at the general meetings (assemblée générale) of the company. Examples are: "A" shares, multiple voting and preference shares.

☞ See "A" SHARES; MULTIPLE VOTING SHARES; ORDINARY/COMMON SHARES; PREFERENCE SHARES; SHARE; SHAREHOLDER.

NORTH AMERICAN FREE-TRADE AGREEMENT, abbr. **NAFTA** (Accord de libre échange nord-américain/ALENA)

A pact established between the USA and Canada in 1988 and joined in 1992 by Mexico. The trading bloc thus formed will create a $6.4 trillion giant free-trade area of more than 363 million consumers. The agreement was partly motivated by fears of "fortress" Europe and European competitiveness (compétitivité) as well as protectionism.

At its most basic level, the treaty will reduce and suppress as many as 20,000 different tariffs (tarif douanier) over the next 10 to 15 years.

More important will be NAFTA's moves (action, mesure) to diminish non-tariff barriers (barrière non tarifaire), such as dairy (produits laitiers) and cotton quotas in the US and Canada and various import licences in Mexico.

The pact also aims to (viser à) spur (stimuler) capital investment (investissement de capitaux) across the borders (frontière) of all three countries. However, Mexico will try to continue to prohibit foreign ownership (possession, participation) in its energy industry (secteur énergétique), while Canada will protect its cultural industries (secteur culturel) such as television and publishing (secteur de l'édition).

NAFTA's final aim is to increase growth (croissance) and jobs. It is estimated that Mexico's current (actuel) annual growth rate, 3.6%, could rise to between 6% and 9% and that there could be a net increase of 500,000 Mexican industrial jobs in the near future. The US economy, which is eight times as big as (huit fois plus grand que) the other two combined, cannot expect such a jolt (bond) but will probably see an explosion of exports to Mexico. In the first five months of 1993 Mexico surpassed Japan as the second largest importer of US manufactured goods; Canada is the first. The predicted short-term gain of this export boom is about 130,000 new jobs.

American labour leaders (dirigeant syndical) disagree with these predictions. They contend (soutenir) that tens of thousands (dizaines de milliers) of American workers will be laid off (licencier) as US companies (entreprise) shift (transférer) production south of the Rio Grande to take advantage of (mettre à profit) Mexican industrial wages (salaire) which are about one-sixth of those in the US and Canada. A large majority of Canadians say in opinion polls (sondage) that the pact with the US was a bad deal (mauvaise affaire), and Canadian labour leaders claim (prétendre) that since it took effect in 1989 Canada has lost around half a million manufacturing jobs (emploi dans le secteur industriel), many of which (dont beaucoup) went to the US. However, other sources show that the US multinational corporations operating (fonctionnant, installées) in Canada created more jobs than they eliminated over the same period.

Reasoning in terms of production costs, many American and Canadian plants (usine) that would disappear under NAFTA would probably move away (se délocaliser) in any case, most likely (probablement) to Asia. But manufacturers who move to Mexico are likely to retain (conserver) their US suppliers (fournisseur), while those who move to Asia can be expected to look for supplies near their new locations. So NAFTA may also persuade many US and foreign companies to shift production from low-cost Asia to low-cost Mexico, which could generate business for US suppliers and save or even create US jobs.

Mexico has the most to gain from the treaty because it lags behind (être à la traîne) in industrial development. However, it will have to undergo (subir) an upheaval (bouleversement) and the Mexicans fear that their small and medium-sized firms (petites et moyennes entreprises) will be unable to adapt in NAFTA's competitive climate. Small-scale retailers (détaillant) feel vulnerable to US chains (chaîne de magasins) which have already opened branches (succursale, filiale) on Mexican territory. Farmers also fear to be crushed by America's agricultural giants which will inevitably rush into Mexico to take advantage of liberalized land-ownership rules (règlementation de l'accession à la propriété du sol).

On the whole (en somme) hopes and fears are equally shared:

Canada hopes to improve the competitiveness of its products, to have access to US procurement contracts (marché public) and to develop its exports to Mexico. It fears for a reduction of US investment in Canada and of the competitiveness of Canadian products in the US.

The US hopes to better (améliorer) the competitiveness of its products, to have a better access to Mexican oil, to limit Mexican immigration and to develop its trade with Mexico. It fears Mexico as a Trojan horse (cheval de Troie) for Japanese investors, the too low cost of Mexican labour (main d'oeuvre), the too easy passage of the border and the political risks at home with Congress and labour leaders.

Mexico hopes to modernize its economic structure, to attract foreign investors, to develop its trade with the US and Canada and to improve its competitiveness with the rest of the world. It fears not to be able to control its economic development and to lose its identity. At the moment Mexico is undergoing (subir) a severe financial crisis due to the decision by the Mexican government on December 20, 1994 to let the peso float (flotter), as a consequence of which the latter (celui-ci) declined 35% against the US dollar in spite of (malgré) a 100% rise of Mexican interest rates. Help is being provided by Mexico's NAFTA partners and by the Bank for International Settlements. The price for this support (soutien) will be a greater economic opening of Mexico, with growing privatisations of transport, telecommunication and airport facilities (infrastructures) and maybe even of a part of the famous Pemex, the state-owned Mexican petroleum company, while (tandis que) foreign banks, such as Citicorp and J. P. Morgan, will play a much greater role in the country.

From a more global point of view, some opponents to NAFTA argue that this treaty is managed trade (commerce dirigé) in a regional arrangement, while proponents (défenseur) reply (rétorquer) that it is perfectly compatible with the rules of the GATT.

Like any new institution or organization, NAFTA – ratified by the US Congress in November 1993 – has raised strong reactions on both sides and only time will tell what the advantages and drawbacks (défaut) really are.

☞ See BANK FOR INTERNATIONAL SETTLEMENTS; FREE TRADE AREA; GATT.

NORTH AMERICAN FREE-TRADE AREA See .... FREE-TRADE AREA; NORTH AMERICAN FREE-TRADE AGREEMENT.

NOTICE ACCOUNT See .... DEPOSIT ACCOUNT.

NTBs See .... NON-TARIFF BARRIERS.

NTMs See .... NON-TARIFF BARRIERS.

NYSE See .... STOCKMARKET/EXCHANGE.

O

OECD See .... ORGANIZATION FOR ECONOMIC COOPERATION AND DEVELOPMENT.

OFF-MARKET SHARES. See .... OVER-THE-COUNTER MARKET.

OFFER FOR SALE, (US) PUBLIC OFFERING (offre public de vente)

This is an invitation to the public to buy or to subscribe to (souscrire à) newly issued shares (des action nouvelles qui viennent d'être émises) or other securities, or in other words an offer for **SUBSCRIPTION** (souscription à des actions). The public are partly informed by newspapers which carry a **PROSPECTUS** (prospectus d'émission) and an application form (bulletin de souscription). The prospectus is a legal requirement (obligation légale) and gives details about the company's finances, activities, organization and future prospects such as forecast profits, called **PROSPECTUS FORECAST** (prévision de prospectus). It also contains an estimate of the amount of capital needed to start the business if it is to succeed, known as the **MINIMUM SUBSCRIPTION** (souscription minimale).

There are two kinds of offers for sale:

i. **FIXED-PRICE OFFERS** (à prix fixe), and ii. **TENDER OFFERS** (appel d'offre). In fixed-price offers the sponsors (répondant ou caution), usually merchant banks (banques d'affaires) or other issuing houses (banque de placement ou d'émission) and/or brokers (courtier en bourse), select a price which will ensure as far as possible that the shares are fully subscribed, or all bought. In the case of an **OVERSUBSCRIPTION** (sur souscription ou couverture excédentaire d'une émission de titres), where people want more shares than there are available, the offer is said to be oversubscribed (sursouscrite), and the shares will have to be allotted or allocated (distribuer) to applicants by various methods. In tender offers, used especially where it is very difficult to place a value on the company, and hence fix a price for the shares, the investors are invited to apply for shares, stating the number they want and the price they are prepared to pay. The sponsors then, if the issue is fully subscribed, calculate the price which will best enable all the shares to be sold to the best advantage of the company offering the shares. This is called the **STRIKING PRICE** (cours d'émission/de vente). In both types of offer it is usual for the sponsors to underwrite (garantir) the issue. In acting as **UNDERWRITERS** (soumissionnaire, garant ou syndicataire) it guarantees for (en échange de) a fee (honoraires) to buy up all the shares that have not been sold, that is, in the situation where they have been undersubscribed (non couvert ou non entièrement souscrit); it puts its name and reputation behind the company offering the shares as an added consideration for prospective (potentiel) investors, and ensures the company offering the shares that they will all be sold. The merchant bank, in turn, will pay part of the fee it earns for this service to **SUBUNDERWRITERS** (soumissionnaire sous-traitant) – investors who are prepared to buy a certain number of the new issue, if required to do so.

☞ See MERCHANT BANK; INTRODUCTION; PLACING; SPONSOR.

OFFER LIST (liste d'offres)

A list of measures through which (par laquelle) a country participating in trade negotiations proposes to broaden (élargir) access to its market in exchange for comparable concessions from its trading partners.

☞ See CODES OF CONDUCT; CONCESSION; PRINCIPLE SUPPLIER; ROUND.

OFFER PRICE See .... BID/BUYING PRICE.

OFFERED PRICE See .... BID/BUYING PRICE.

OFFERING PRICE See .... BID/BUYING PRICE.

OFFICE OF FAIR TRADING See .... MONOPOLIES AND MERGERS COMMISSION.

OFFSET REQUIREMENTS (demande de compensation)

Terms (condition) imposed on some large exporters by the public authorities (pouvoirs publics) of importing countries, for the purpose of (dans le but de) reducing outflows of money (sortie de trésorerie). The exporter may be required (se voir demander) to buy goods (marchandise) or services produced in the importing country, establish manufacturing facilities (infrastructure de production) in the country, or use a specified percentage of local content, i.e. locally produced components (composants de fabrication locale), in manufacturing (activité de fabrication).

☞ See COUNTERTRADE; LOCAL CONTENT; TRANSPLANT.

OFT See .... MONOPOLIES AND MERGERS COMMISSION.

OKUN'S LAW See .... UNEMPLOYMENT.

OLD SHARES (actions anciennes)

Existing shares, called "old" to distinguish them from the new shares which are being offered by the company either in exchange for the latter or as part of a rights issue (émission de droits de souscription/d'attribution).

☞ See RIGHTS' ISSUE; NEW SHARES; SHARE; WARRANT.

OMAS See .... ORDERLY MARKETING AGREEMENTS.

OMNIBUS TRADE AND COMPETITIVENESS ACT See .... SECTION 301.

ON CALL MONEY See .... CALL MONEY.

ON CONSIGNMENT See .... IMPORT AGENT.

OPEC See .... ORGANIZATION OF PETROLEUM EXPORTING COUNTRIES.

OPEN GENERAL LICENSE See .... LICENSING.

OPEN INDIVIDUAL LICENSE See .... LICENSING.

OPEN MARKET OPERATIONS (opérations d'open market sur le marché monétaire)

The buying and selling by a central bank of short-term securities (e.g. bonds and bills) as part of a government's monetary policy. Selling securities reduces the amount of money in circulation, as money has to be paid to the central bank in exchange for them, thus withdrawing money from circulation; buying securities increases the money supply (masse monétaire) as the central bank pays the banking system money for their securities, thus increasing the amount of money they can lend (which is always greater than the funds they hold).

☞ See BANKING; BOND; CENTRAL BANK; MONEY MARKET; MONEY SUPPLY; MONETARY POLICY; SECURITIES; TREASURY BILL.

OPEN-ENDED FUND See .... UNIT TRUST.

OPTION (option)

This is a contract which, on paying an option premium (prix de l'option, prime), gives the holder (détenteur) the right to buy from or sell to another party a given amount of a commodity (marchandise) or financial instrument at an agreed price – the exercise/strike/striking price (prix d'exercice, de liquidation) – and within a stated (donnée) period, normally three, six or nine months. A **CALL OPTION** (option d'achat), for example, gives the holder the right to purchase, say (disons), a given quantity of securities at an agreed price within a set period. He has paid a small premium for this right, but he does not necessarily have to exercise (exercer ou lever) it. If, for example, he has a **CALL OPTION** on shares at price X and the market price for these shares is X + Y he will exercise his right to buy at price X because then he can sell those shares at the market price of X + Y and make a profit of Y (minus the premium he paid for the option). If, on the other hand, the market price of these shares falls to X - Y he will not exercise this option as he will have to buy the shares at price X and they are only worth X - Y, which would mean a loss of Y plus the premium on selling the shares. In this case, where he does not exercise his option he only loses the small premium he paid for it. Where the holder has the right to sell at a given price this is known as a **PUT OPTION** (option de vente). Other forms of option exist such as a **PUT AND CALL** or **DOUBLE OPTION** (option de vente et d'achat ou stellage), which gives the holder the right to sell or buy as he wishes, but for this he pays double the premium he would have paid for a simple call or put option.

With options it is the seller who takes most of the risk, while the buyer uses them to minimize his risks of loss. Option contracts which can be bought and sold in the traded options market (bourse des options) are known as **TRADED OPTIONS** (options négociables). In this market it is the option to buy or sell (not the asset itself) which is traded, very much as if it was a share. In the UK the centre for these transactions is the **LONDON TRADED OPTIONS MARKET**, abbr. **LTOM**, which is part of the London International Stock Exchange. The Paris Bourse since 1987 has a special section devoted to traded options, the **MARCHÉ DES OPTIONS NÉGOCIABLES SUR ACTIONS À LA BOURSE DE PARIS**, abrégé **MONEP**.

☞ See ARBITRAGE; BEAR; BULL; COMMODITY; FOREIGN EXCHANGE MARKET; FORWARD CONTRACT; HEDGE; SETTLEMENT OF BARGAINS; SPOT/CURRENT PRICE; WARRANT.

ORDERLY MARKETING AGREEMENTS, abbr. **OMAs** (Accords de commercialisation régulière)

Arrangements (accords) negotiated between two or more countries to restrain the growth of trade (échanges) in certain sensitive (sensible) products – such as steel, textiles, microchips and nuclear-related equipment – generally by imposing export quotas (contingent d'exportation).

☞ See EXPORT QUOTAS; MARKET DISRUPTION; MULTI-FIBRE ARRANGEMENT; SENSITIVE PRODUCT; VOLUNTARY RESTRAINT AGREEMENTS.

ORDINARY DEFERRED SHARES See .... DEFERRED SHARES.

ORDINARY/COMMON SHARES (actions ordinaires)

This is the largest category of shares. Owners of ordinary shares have a right to a share in the profits of a company in the form of dividends before deferred shareholders (actionnaire différé) and after preference shareholders (actionnaire prioritaire). Ordinary shares can also be **PREFERRED** (privilégiée ou de priorité ou à dividende prioritaire) **ORDINARY SHARES**, which give holders the right to be paid an agreed dividend before deferred ordinary shares. Ordinary shareholders take most of the risk – if profits are low they may not earn a dividend – the reward (recompense ou prime) being a chance to receive a higher return (rendement) on their capital (invested in the shares) than do holders of other forms of investment. This return is in the form of a potential increase in share price, so that if the shares are sold at a later date there is a profit or **CAPITAL GAIN** (bénéfice ou plus-value), and while holding the shares, a potentially interesting dividend payment, but neither are guaranteed: the shares can fall in value, the company may decide to pay little or nothing in the way of dividends, or it may even go into liquidation (se mettre en liquidation).

☞ See ANNUAL GENERAL MEETING;DEFERRED SHARES; PREFERENCE SHARES; SHAREHOLDER; SHARE; WARRANT.

ORGANIZATION FOR ECONOMIC COOPERATION AND DEVELOPMENT abbr. **OECD** (Organisation pour la coopération et le développement économique/OCDE)

Created in 1961 and based in Paris, the OECD is an international agency (organisation) whose 24 member countries – Australia, Austria, Belgium, Canada, Denmark, Finland, France, Germany, Greece, Iceland, Ireland, Italy, Japan, Luxembourg, The Netherlands, New Zealand, Norway, Portugal, Spain, Sweden, Switzerland, Turkey, the United Kingdom and the USA – review (examiner) international economic issues (question), collect (rassembler) internationally comparable economic statistics and coordinate their policies (politique), seeking (rechercher) the expansion of world trade and the economic advance of developing countries (pays en voie de développement).

☞ See INTERNATIONAL ARRANGEMENT ON EXPORT CREDITS.

ORGANIZATION OF PETROLEUM EXPORTING COUNTRIES, abbr. **OPEC** (Organisation des pays exportateurs de pétrole/OPEP)

A cartel including (comprendre) 13 major (principal) oil producing countries that mainly (essentiellement) aims at (avoir pour but de) coordinating production and pricing (détermination des prix) policies (politique). The 13 members of the cartel, set up (fonder, mettre sur pied) in 1960, are: Algeria, Ecuador (Equateur), Gabon, Indonesia, Iran, Iraq, Kuwait, Libya, Nigeria, Qatar, Saudi Arabia, The United Arab Emirates and Venezuela. The Organization also determines the level (niveau) of aid granted (accorder) by its members to developing countries (pays en voie de développement). Nowadays, OPEC's share (part) of world oil exports is only about 40% on account of (en raison de) the expansion of supplies (approvisionnements) from non-OPEC producers such as Mexico, Norway, Russia, the United Kingdom and the USA.

☞ See CARTEL; GENERALIZED SYSTEM OF PREFERENCES.

ORTOLI FACILITY See .... NEW COMMUNITY INSTRUMENT.

OVER-THE-COUNTER MARKET, abbr. **OTC** (marché hors cote)

A market outside the stock exchange in which licensed (agréé) dealers (boursiers ou marchands de titres) trade in mainly unlisted securities (valeurs non inscrites à la cote). Shares traded in the over-the-counter market are often referred to as **OFF-MARKET SHARES** (valeurs hors marché). The term originated in the USA, where at the end of the nineteenth century shares were bought in banks over-the-counter (au comptant). It is also used to refer loosely (en gros ou vaguement) to the unlisted securities market. More specifically, in the USA it refers to a type of national market place which trades shares quoted on the six regional markets – the **INTERMARKET TRADING SYSTEM (ITS)**. The system is authorised by the Securities and Exchange Commission and was set up in 1971 by the **NATIONAL ASSOCIATION OF SECURITIES DEALERS (NASD)**, representing brokers (courtier/négociant en titres) and dealers, for dealing in over-the-counter shares. This market functions on the basis of a computerised information services and order execution system (système informatisé d'information et de transactions), known as the **NATIONAL ASSOCIATION OF SECURITIES DEALERS AUTOMATED QUOTATION SYSTEM (NASDAQ).**

☞ See FOURTH MARKET; LISTING; PLACING; SECURITIES AND EXCHANGE COMMISSION; THIRD MARKET; UNLISTED SECURITIES; UNLISTED SECURITIES MARKET.

OVERDRAFT (découvert)

A credit arrangement whereby the bank allows the customer to withdraw (retirer) from his current account more money than he has in it whenever the need arises, but only to an agreed limit. Interest is payable only on the amount overdrawn (tiré à découvert) at the end of each day. This form of credit is widely used by businesses, as on a daily basis very often they must continue to make payments for goods and services received while they have not yet been paid themselves for their sales. Overdrafts can be much cheaper than loans, depending on by how much (de combien) and for how long the account is overdrawn.

☞ See COMMERCIAL BANK; CURRENT ACCOUNT; LOAN.

OVERSUBSCRIPTION See .... OFFER FOR SALE.

P

PACKAGING, LABELING, AND MARKING REGULATIONS (règles en matière d'emballage, d'étiquetage et de marquage)

National requirements (réglementation) compelling (forcer, obliger) exporters to package (emballer) their goods (marchandise) in specified containers (conteneur), identify the contents (contenu) in a certain way, or use a specific type of label (étiquette). These requirements are officially designed (concevoir) to protect consumers but may act as (servir de) non-tariff barriers (barrière non tarifaire).

☞ See NON-TARIFF BARRIERS; QUARANTINE, SANITARY, AND HEALTH LAWS AND REGULATIONS; STANDARDS.

PAID-IN CAPITAL See .... AUTHORIZED/REGISTERED ETC. CAPITAL.

PAID-UP CAPITAL See .... AUTHORIZED/REGISTERED ETC. CAPITAL.

PANEL OF EXPERTS (comité d'experts, commission d'arbitrage)

An ad hoc group of experienced (expérimenté) individuals with specialized skills (qualification) established (constituer) for specified purposes (pour répondre à un besoin précis). Such panels often arbitrate disagreements over (portant sur) trade policy within the framework (dans le cadre) of GATT.

☞ See CODES OF CONDUCT; DISPUTE SETTLEMENT; GATT.

PANEL ON TAKEOVERS AND MERGERS See .... INTERNATIONAL STOCK EXCHANGE.

PAPER OFFER See .... TAKEOVER BID.

PAR/NOMINAL/FACE VALUE (valeur nominale)

The value at which a security (titre) has usually been issued (émettre). If a share has been issued at £10, for example, and then sells on the market at £10, it is said to sell **AT PAR** (au pair ou à la parité); if it sells at less this is **BELOW PAR**, or **AT A DISCOUNT** (au-dessous du pair); if it sells for more than £10, it sells **ABOVE PAR**, or **AT A PREMIUM** (au-dessus du pair). In the USA some securities are issued without a stated par or nominal value, and are called **NO-PAR VALUE SECURITIES** (titre sans valeur nominale).

PARIS CLUB See .... INTERNATIONAL MONETARY FUND.

PARIS INTER-BANK OFFERED RATE See .... LIBOR.

PARTIAL LOSS See .... MARINE INSURANCE.

PARTICIPATING BOND See .... BOND.

PARTICIPATING CUMULATIVE PREFERENCE SHARES (actions priviligiées/prioritaires cumulatives avec participation aux bénéfices ou participantes à dividende cumulatif)

Shares which give the holder the right to a fixed dividend and a limited share in the profits, once the deferred and ordinary shares have been paid, and also the right to have any dividends not paid in one year added to those of the next year.

☞ See CUMULATIVE/NON-PARTICIPATING/PARTICIPATING PREFERENCE SHARES; PREFERENCE SHARES.

PARTICIPATING PREFERENCE SHARES (actions privilégiées/prioritaires participantes/avec participation aux bénéfices)

Shares which give the holder the right to a fixed dividend and also a limited share in the profits, after the ordinary and deferred shares have been paid their agreed proportion.

☞ See DEFERRED SHARES;DIVIDEND; ORDINARY SHARES; PREFERENCE SHARES; SHARE; SHAREHOLDER.

PARTICULAR AVERAGE See .... MARINE INSURANCE.

PARTLY PAID SHARES See .... AUTHORIZED, REGISTERED ETC. CAPITAL; SHARE.

PAY-AS-YOU-EARN (abbr. **PAYE)** See .... TAX.

PAYE (PAY-AS-YOU-EARN) See .... TAX.

PAYEE See .... BILL OF EXCHANGE; CHEQUE; DRAW/DRAFT, TO.

PAYROLL TAX See .... TAX.

P/E RATIO See .... YIELD.

PER See .... YIELD.

PERPETUAL DEBENTURE See .... DEBENTURE.

PERSONAL ACCIDENT POLICY See .... ACCIDENT INSURANCE.

PERSONAL SECTOR See .... PRIVATE SECTOR.

PETITION IN BANKRUPTCY See .... LIQUIDATION.

PHILLIPS' CURVE See .... UNEMPLOYMENT.

PHYSICAL TRANSACTION See .... SPOT/CURRENT PRICE.

PIBOR See .... LIBOR.

PIT, THE. See .... FLOOR, THE.

PLACING, (US) often **PLACEMENT** (placement)

The selling of new shares *not* by invitation to the public through the stock exchange by means of an **INTRODUCTION** or **OFFER FOR SALE**, which involves considerable expense, but to selected institutions (i.e. pensions and insurance companies) and private individuals. This method of raising capital is often used by private companies. Where the shares are sold directly to investors without using the services of a stockbroker this is called a **PRIVATE PLACING** (placement privé). Public companies which are not yet listed (coté) on the stock exchange but perhaps want to be, can use the services of a **SPONSOR** (caution, répondant) to place their shares; this is sometimes referred to as a **PUBLIC PLACING** (placement public). After the shares have been placed permission is given for the shares to be traded (négocier) on the stock market. The Unlisted Stock Market, abbr. USM, is the place in the UK where many shares have been issued via placing. Listed companies in the UK are only allowed to place a small issue (émission) of shares, while large issues require an offer for sale.

☞ See BROKER/DEALER; INTERNATIONAL STOCK EXCHANGE; INTRODUCTION; LISTING; OFFER FOR SALE; PRIVATE and PUBLIC LIMITED COMPANY under LIMITED or LIMITED LIABILITY COMPANY; SPONSOR; UNLISTED SECURITIES MARKET.

PLC See .... LIMITED or LIMITED LIABILITY COMPANY.

POISON PILL See .... TAKEOVER BID.

POLICYHOLDER See .... INSURANCE.

POLL TAX See .... TAX.

PORTFOLIO (portefeuille financier/d'investissements)

This is the different securities (titres) held as an investment by an individual or organization. The act of buying different securities for investment is referred to as **PORTFOLIO INVESTMENTS** (investissements de portefeuille) to distinguish this from direct investment, say (disons), in plant (installations) and machinery.

☞ See BROKER/DEALER; INVESTMENT TRUST; MARKET MAKER; SECURITIES; SHARE; UNIT TRUST.

PORTFOLIO INVESTMENTS See .... PORTFOLIO.

POSTDATED CHEQUE (chèque postdaté)

One which has been signed with a future date on it, giving the drawer (tireur) enough time to put the money in his account to meet the payment, or to ensure the performance (réalisation) of a service or job by the payee (bénéficiaire) by (pour) a given date. In other words, if the payee does not do what he is required to do, the cheque can be stopped (bloquer).

☞ See ANTIDATED CHEQUE; CHEQUE; BOUNCED CHEQUE; STOPPED CHEQUE.

PREFERENCE/PREFERRED SHARES, US PREFERRED STOCK (actions priviligiées/prioritaires/de préférence/de priorité)

A form of lending money to a company in exchange for preference shares. Holders of these get paid a fixed dividend, regardless of whether (sans se préoccuper de savoir si) the company makes any profits and before any dividends get paid to ordinary or deferred shareholders. This dividend can be viewed as a kind of interest payment. They also have prior claim (droit de priorité/préférentiel) over these shareholders on the capital and assets (actif) of the company, should (dans le cas où/ en cas de) it be wound up or go into liquidation (se mettre en liquidation) as they are company creditors. Preference shareholders have limited voting rights.There are various types of preference shares.

☞ See CONVERTIBLE; CUMULATIVE/NON-CUMULATIVE; PARTICIPATING/NON-PARTICIPATING; PARTICIPATING CUMULATIVE/NON-PARTICIPATING CUMULATIVE; IRREDEEMABLE AND REDEEMABLE PREFERENCE SHARES.

PREFERRED ORDINARY SHARES See .... ORDINARY/COMMON SHARES.

PREFERRED STOCK See .... PREFERENCE SHARES.

PREMIUM See .... INSURANCE.

PRESIDENT OF THE BOARD See .... BOARD OF DIRECTORS.

PRICE-EARNINGS RATIO See .... YIELD.

PRIMARY MARKET (marché primaire)

The market for quoted (coté) shares issued (émis) for the first time. On the money market this refers to that part of the market where issuers (émetteurs) of financial instruments sell directly to investors.

☞ See FINANCIAL INSTRUMENTS; FOURTH MARKET; INTERNATIONAL STOCK EXCHANGE; INVESTORS; MONEY MARKET; OVER-THE-COUNTER MARKET; SECONDARY MARKET; STOCK MARKET; THIRD MARKET; UNLISTED SECURITIES MARKET.

PRIME COMMERCIAL PAPER See .... COMMERCIAL PAPER.

PRINCIPAL SUPPLIER (fournisseur principal)

The country which is the most important source of a particular product imported by another country. Principal suppliers mutually grant (accorder) tariff and other barrier concessions to one another (les uns aux autres) facilitating exports of their main (principal, essentiel) production. Contracting parties (partie contractante) to GATT automatically enjoy (jouir de) Most-Favoured-Nation Treatment.

☞ See CONCESSION; GATT; MOST-FAVOURED-NATION TREATMENT; OFFER LIST; ROUND.

PRINCIPLES OF INSURANCE (principes de l'assurance)

In order to be as effective (efficace) as possible and to avoid (éviter) being too wide open to (hypersensible à) abuse (abus), insurance practice (exercice, usage, pratique) is subject to (soumis à) several legal (juridique) principles:

a. **INDEMNITY** (indemnité), i.e. a principle or rule (règle) that provides for (prévoir, stipuler) protection against loss (perte), but only the loss and no more (pas plus). The insured should (devoir) not make (tirer) a profit (bénéfice) out of (de) his misfortune (accident). The insurer never pays out (débourser) more than the full loss (perte totale) even though (même si) a larger sum (somme plus importante) has been insured. This principle does not apply (s'appliquer) to life or personal accident policies (police) where fixed sums are previously (auparavant) agreed (convenir) because such losses cannot be exactly assessed (évaluer) in money terms (en termes financiers). Two sub-principles (principe secondaire) arise out of (découler de) the main one of indemnity: **SUBROGATION** (subrogation) and **CONTRIBUTION** (contribution). These aim at (viser à) making applicable the main rule of full (complet, total) but only fair (juste) compensation for a loss. "Subrogation" makes sure that the insured will not claim (demander) compensation (compensation, dommages) both (à la fois) from his insurance company and the insurance company of the hotel in which his suitcase was stolen (volé). "Contribution" does the same in cases where (dans les cas où) the same property (bien) is insured with (assurer par) two different insurance companies. Each company involved (impliquer, concerner) will only pay a proportion (partie) of the loss, thus (ainsi) giving the insured his fair, but only fair, compensation;

b. **INSURABLE INTEREST** (intérêt pécuniaire), meaning that a person should (devoir) have an interest in what he is insuring, i.e. be liable to (susceptible de) suffer (subir) the loss himself or to be claimed against (se voir réclamer des dommages), due to (à cause de) a loss to (sinistre survenu à) another person. A person cannot insure the property of others (le bien des autres) or other people's lives (la vie des autres). Exceptions are life and marine insurance. Insurance companies consider that husbands and wives (mari et femme) have a sufficient amount of interest in one another (l'un envers l'autre) to insure one anothers' lives (s'assurer mutuellement sur la vie). They also consider that a firm may insure one of its partners (associé) or employees who is of vital importance in the business (affaire, entreprise). This is called a **KEY-MAN INSURANCE** (personnalité ou personnage important) and is also demanded (exiger) by banks and other lenders (prêteur) from the borrower (emprunteur) where large sums (somme) are involved (engager). In those cases, the policy-holder (assuré, détenteur de la police) is free to (avoir la possibilité de) transfer the benefit (indemnité). In any case a real element of risk should exist without which (sans quoi) the principle of indemnity could not apply (s'appliquer);

c. **UTMOST GOOD FAITH** (bonne foi) meaning that insurance must be based on mutual honesty (honnêteté). The insurer must disclose (faire connaître) the exact terms (conditions) of the contract while (tandis que) the intending future insured (celui qui a l'intention de s'assurer) must reveal all necessary details about his particular case, for want of which (sans quoi, faute de quoi) the policy might be invalidated and the insurer refuse to pay when a claim (sinistre) arises (se produire). In order to enforce (faire exécuter, appliquer) this principle, a **CONTRACTUAL DUTY** (avenant) may be added to the proposed contract to the effect that (stipulant que) the information given is correct and that no relevant (d'importance, pertinent) details have been omitted;

d. **PROXIMATE CAUSE** (cause immédiate), i.e. a principle taking into account (tenir compte de) a loss (sinistre) arising from (dû à) an uninterrupted (ininterrompu) chain (enchaînement) of events (événement) started (déclencher) by the occurrence (manifestation) of the event covered by the policy. An example is the damage caused by the water used by firemen (pompier) to extinguish a fire in premises (locaux) covered by a fire policy (police incendie). Experience shows that the validity of such claims (sinistre) is rather difficult to determine and that the decisions are often made by the courts (tribunaux) after tedious (fastidieux) lawsuits (procès).

☞ See INSURANCE.

PRIOR DEPOSITS (dépôts préalables)

A specific sum of money, in domestic (national) or foreign currency (monnaie), an importer is required to (se voir demander de) deposit (mettre en dépôt) by government authorities (pouvoirs publics). This sum corresponds to a certain percentage of the value of the imported product. The purpose (but) of prior deposits is to discourage imports, for balance of payments reasons. Prior deposits are non-tariff barriers (barrière non tarifaire) to trade which also represent a real cost for importers since (puisque) they are held (détenir) without interest for comparatively (relativement) long durations (durée), from the time (depuis le moment où) an order (commande) is placed (passer) and an import licence granted (accorder) until after the importing transaction is completed (effectuer).

☞ See BALANCE OF PAYMENTS; LICENSING; NON-TARIFF BARRIERS.

PRIVATE COMPANY See .... LIMITED or LIMITED LIABILITY COMPANY.

PRIVATE LIMITED COMPANY See .... LIMITED or LIMITED LIABILITY COMPANY.

PRIVATE PLACING See .... PLACING.

PRIVATE SECTOR (secteur privé)

This is the part of the economy owned by private individuals or companies and organizations and based on private enterprise. It includes the **PERSONAL SECTOR** (secteur des personnes), made up of households (ménage) and individuals (individu), and the **CORPORATE SECTOR** (secteur des entreprises), in contrast to the **PUBLIC SECTOR** (secteur public). This comprises government and local government bodies (l'Etat et les collectivités locales) and nationalized industries. **PRIVATIZATION/PRIVATISATION** (privatisation), which is the selling off to the general public of state-owned businesses and so returning them to the private sector, in Britain, France and other European countries has greatly reduced the public sector and enlarged the private. This trend for privatization was started in Britain in the 1980s by Mrs. Thatcher and her Conservative government in the belief that it was necessary to reduce people's dependence on the State and also as a means of reducing the budget(ary) deficit and financing certain policies. Other countries also have followed suit, such as in Latin America and the former Eastern European bloc. In Britain the industries typically affected by privatization have been air and road transport, shipping, telecommunications, gas, electricity and water. The employees have been greatly encouraged to buy shares through employee share ownership plans (actionnariat du personnel), abbr. ESOPs, in the belief that this would create a share-owning democracy.

☞ See EMPLOYEE SHARE/STOCK OWNING PLAN

PRIVATISATION/PRIVATIZATION See .... PRIVATE SECTOR.

PRO FORMA INVOICE (facture pro-forma)

A statement (relevé) of prices for the information of the prospective (éventuel) buyer or for use by (à l'usage de) the customs authorities (administration douanière).

☞ See CUSTOMS AND ADMINISTRATIVE ENTRY PROCEDURES.

PRODUCER GOODS See .... GROSS DOMESTIC PRODUCT.

PRODUCTIVE RESOURCES (ressources de production)

The elements used in production. They include natural resources, land, capital (capital, capitaux), labour (main d'oeuvre) and technology.

☞ See MACROECONOMICS; MICROECONOMICS.

PROFIT-SHARING BOND See .... BOND.

PROGRAMME TRADING (US) **PROGRAM TRADING** (courtage par ordinateur, déclenchement automatique des ordres selon le niveau des cours)

The buying and selling of securities by means of computerised trading systems (systèmes informatisés d'information et de transactions). This means that it is possible to pass an order to a market maker (teneur de marché) to buy or sell securities automatically when they reach a certain price, thus making it unnecessary for anyone to go to the stock exchange to receive or place the order. This is one of the factors that has contributed to the disappearance of the "floor" (la corbeille).

☞ See FLOOR, THE; SAEF; SEAQ; SEAQ INTERNATIONAL; TAURUS; TOPIC;

PROGRESSIVE (INCOME) TAX See .... TAX.

PROMISSORY NOTE (billet à ordre, reconnaissance de dette)

A note written and signed by a person promising unconditionally to pay a certain sum to the holder (détenteur ou porteur) of the note or another named person. It is a form of acknowledgement of debt, an I.O.U. (I owe you), widely used in the U.S.A. but much less so in the U.K. Promissory notes can be sold on (revendu) at a discount (avec escompte).

☞ See COMMERCIAL PAPER; DISCOUNT.

PROMPT/EARLY DELIVERY (livraison rapide)

A trade term or phrase (expression) mentioned on a sales contract (contrat de vente), meaning that the goods (marchandise) can be forwarded (acheminer, expédier) to the buyer within a few days of receiving the order (dans les quelques jours qui suivent la réception de la commande).

☞ See INCOTERMS.

PROMPT CASH (comptant d'usage)

A rather vague trade term meaning that payment has to be made within a reasonable time (dans un délai raisonnable), i.e. varying between (allant de) three and fifteen days from the date of the invoice (facture).

☞ See INCOTERMS.

PROPERTY INSURANCE See .... ACCIDENT INSURANCE.

PROPORTIONAL (INCOME) TAX See .... TAX.

PROSPECTUS See .... OFFER FOR SALE.

PROSPECTUS FORECAST See .... OFFER FOR SALE.

PROTECTED BEAR See .... BEAR.

PROTECTIONISM (protectionnisme)

The use of restrictions on imports such as tariffs and quotas. Reasons for protectionism can be several (divers):

a.. maintain independence of supplies (approvisionnement) in case of war or for political reasons;

b. promote employment by switching (faire passer, transférer) demand from foreign to home suppliers (fournisseur);

c. protect new, developing industries (secteur);

d. apply retaliation (représailles) to counter (riposter à) dumping.

e. restore (redresser, rétablir) the balance of payments.

☞ See DUMPING; INFANT INDUSTRY ARGUMENT; MANAGED TRADE; MERCANTILISM; NON-TARIFF BARRIERS; ORDERLY MARKETING AGREEMENTS; QUANTITATIVE RESTRICTIONS; RETALIATION; SAFEGUARDS; VOLUNTARY RESTRAINT AGREEMENTS.

PROTECTIVE TARIFF See .... TARIFF.

PROTOCOL OF PROVISIONAL APPLICATION, abbr. **PPA** (Protocole d'application provisoire/PAP)

A legal device (instrument juridique) which enabled (permettre) the original Contracting Parties (parties contractantes) of GATT to accept GATT obligations and benefits (avantage) in spite of (en dépit de) local legislation which ruled against (statuer à l'encontre de) imports contrary to GATT provisions (contrairement aux dispositions du GATT). The Protocol was intended to be temporary but has conveniently (par raison de commodité) remained (rester) into effect (en vigueur) since (depuis) the establishment (création) of GATT in 1947.

☞ See CONTRACTING PARTY; GATT; GRANDFATHER CLAUSE.

PROXIMATE CAUSE See .... PRINCIPLES OF INSURANCE.

PUBLIC LIABILITY INSURANCE See .... ACCIDENT INSURANCE.

PUBLIC LIMITED COMPANY See .... LIMITED or LIMITED LIABILITY COMPANY.

PUBLIC OFFERING See .... OFFER FOR SALE.

PUBLIC PLACING See .... PLACING.

PUBLIC PROCUREMENT See .... GOVERNMENT PROCUREMENT POLICIES AND PRACTICES.

PUBLIC SECTOR

PUBLIC SECTOR BORROWING REQUIREMENT, abbr. **PSBR** (besoin de financement du secteur public)

The money needed by the British government to balance the books (équilibrer les comptes) and finance the shortfall (déficit) between its revenue from income tax (impôt sur le revenu), Value Added Tax, abbr. VAT (TVA), corporation tax (impôt sur les sociétés) and other taxes, and its expenses (dépenses de l'Etat). The PSBR is part of fiscal policy (politique budgétaire) and is met by borrowing in three main ways:

i. National Savings schemes and Premium Bonds (plan d'épargne national et obligations avec prime de remboursement);

ii. treasury bills (bons du Trésor); and

iii. gilt edged stocks (fonds d'Etat), also known as "gilts" (dits "valeurs dorées sur tranche").

The government can also finance the PSBR by printing money (faire fonctionner la planche à billets), which could lead to inflation (because of more money available to demand goods), lower interest rates (because of the increase in the money supply [masse monétaire]) and possibly lower exchange rates, depending on the state of the economy at the time. Borrowing, on the other hand (i.e. through the sale of bills and gilts), is expected to reduce the money supply and increase interest rates. This also runs the risk of crowding out (empêchement/interdiction d'accès à l'investissement), i.e. reducing the amount of funds available for investment in productive sectors of the economy. The Conservative government's attempts to reduce the PSBR in the 1980s partly depended on financing current spending through the sale of nationalised industries (privatization). In the early 1990s the budget deficit, and hence the PSBR, has continued to grow.

☞ See EXCHANGE RATE; FISCAL POLICY; GILT-EDGED STOCKS; INFLATION; MONETARY POLICY; MONEY SUPPLY; PRIVATIZATION; TAX; TREASURY BILLS; VALUE ADDED TAX.

PURE LIFE ASSURANCE See .... LIFE INSURANCE.

PUT AND CALL OPTION See .... OPTION.

PUT INTO LIQUIDATION, TO See .... LIQUIDATION.

PUT OPTION See .... OPTION.

Q

QUANTITATIVE RESTRICTIONS, abbr. **QRs** (restrictions quantitatives)

Quotas (contingent) of goods (marchandise) which can be imported or exported, measured by (en) volume or value (valeur). Quotas may vary with (selon) the country of origin selectively or only apply to (s'appliquer à) the total limit (montant ou quantité totales autorisées), thus (ainsi) tending to benefit (avantager) more efficient (performant) suppliers (fournisseur). Licensing (régime de licences) is the most frequent method of administering (appliquer) quotas. Although (bien que) GATT Article XI rules against (se prononcer, statuer contre) the use of quantitative restrictions, Article XIX allows (permettre) quotas for safeguard (sauvegarde) reasons, Articles XII and XVIII permit them for balance of payments purposes (raison, but) as laid out in (comme défini dans) Article XV, Article XX authorizes them in matters (question) of health (hygiène), gold stocks and items (objet) of archeological or historic interest, while (tandis que) Article XXI puts forward (mettre en avant) national security as an undeniable justification for using them.

☞ See BALANCE OF PAYMENTS CONSULTATIONS; GATT; LICENSING; MULTI-FIBER ARRANGEMENT; SAFEGUARDS; SPECIFIC LIMITATIONS ON TRADE.

QUARANTINE, SANITARY AND HEALTH LAWS AND REGULATIONS (législation et réglementation sur la quarantaine et les mesures sanitaires et d'hygiène)

Government measures aimed at (avoir pour but de) protecting consumer (consommateur), animal and plant (végétal) health. An example is the restriction of the use of harmful (nocif) preservatives (produit de conservation) and additives in foods (aliments). The lack (absence, manque) of internationally accepted standards (norme) makes it difficult to distinguish between legitimate measures and those which simply restrict foreign competition. The Tokyo Round GATT Code on Technical Barriers to Trade set up (mettre en place, instaurer) a system through which (par lequel) an exporting country can oppose (s'opposer à) health regulations which appear to discriminate against (traduire une discrimination envers) its products.

☞ See CUSTOMS AND ADMINISTRATIVE ENTRY PROCEDURES; GATT; PACKAGING, LABELING, AND MARKETING REGULATIONS; STANDARDS.

QUOTED COMPANY See .... LISTED/QUOTED COMPANY.

QUOTED SECURITIES See .... LISTED/QUOTED SECURITIES.

QUOTED SHARES (actions cotées)

Shares which are officially quoted (coté) and traded (négocié) on the stock exchange.

☞ See INTERNATIONAL STOCK EXCHANGE; LISTED/QUOTED SECURITIES; LISTING; SHARE; STOCK MARKET;

R

R & D See .... RESEARCH AND DEVELOPMENT.

RAID See .... RAIDER.

RAIDER or **CORPORATE RAIDER** (attaquant, prédateur d'entreprise ou raider ou repreneur de sociétés)

This is an individual or company which has mounted (organiser) a hostile take-over bid – also known as a **RAID** (raid) – (offre public d'achat [abrégé OPA] hostile ou offre de rachat) for a company, whose board of directors (conseil d'administration) are against this – often if the raid succeeds they will lose their jobs. Raiders do this basically for financial reasons. That is to say, once they have succeeded in acquiring the number of shares necessary to have a majority holding (participation majoritaire) they are likely to re-organize the company, sell off non-core parts (parties non essentielles) to reduce the hefty (substantiel) borrowings used for the raid, and later sell their stake (participation) at a higher price. Companies also launch hostile raids, of course, as part of their growth strategy (stratégie de croissance).

☞ See LEVERAGED BUYOUT; TAKEOVER.

RATE OF INTEREST See .... INTEREST.

RATES See .... TAX.

READY DELIVERY (livraison immédiate)

A phrase (expression) mentioned on a sales contract (contrat de vente), meaning that the goods (marchandise) can be forwarded (acheminer, expédier) to the buyer on the very day (le jour même) the order (commande) is placed (passer).

☞ See INCOTERMS.

RECEIVER See .... LIQUIDATION.

RECEIVERSHIP See .... LIQUIDATION.

RECESSION (recession)

This is a temporary fall (chute) in business activity, when consumers spend less, companies invest less and employ less people and in general there is a fall in aggregate demand (demande globale). This is not as severe as a depression. A recession has been defined by economists as existing when Gross National Product, abbr. GNP (Produit National Brut, abrégé PNB), has dropped (baisser) for two or more quarters, i.e. for at least six months. The UK started to experience a recession in 1989, which lasted over three years. Other countries such as the USA, followed by European Union members and other major industrialized nations, have also gone through this. While the USA is said to have come out of the recession, other countries like France by 1994 were still being affected by this. This phenomenon has been aggravated by a decline in world trade. In the UK the severity and duration of the recession (which followed a boom) has been linked with government economic policies which relied predominantly on (s'appuyer essentiellement sur) high interest rates to reduce inflation.

☞ See AGGREGATE DEMAND; BLACK TUESDAY; BOOM; DEPRESSION; UNEMPLOYMENT; INFLATION; MONETARY POLICY; TRADE CYCLE.

RECIPROCITY (réciprocité)

The practice by which (selon laquelle) countries extend (accorder) similar concessions to each other (les unes aux autres). For instance, a government may lower (abaisser) its tariffs (tarif douanier) in exchange for equivalent concessions from a trading partner (partenaire commercial). The mutual acceptance (acceptation) is called a **BALANCE OF CONCESSIONS** (équilibre des concession). Reciprocity has always been a main target (objectif) of GATT's negotiations. Some economists however (cependant) maintain (affirmer, soutenir) that reciprocity is irrational (irraisonnable, déraisonnable), because a country which unilaterally reduces its import barriers will foster (promouvoir) competition (concurrence), encourage the reshuffling (remaniement) of its productive resources and thus (ainsi) enhance (augmenter) its own economic efficiency and national welfare (bien-être) in the long run (à long terme). Reciprocity is also defined as mutuality of benefits (avantages mutuels), quid pro quo (échanges de bons procédés) and equivalence of advantages. Developing countries (pays en voie de développement) are exempted (dispenser) from the strict application of reciprocity in their negotiations with developed countries (pays développés) through (d'après) GATT Article XXXVI and the Enabling Clause of the Tokyo Round.

REDEEMABLE DEBENTURE See .... DEBENTURE.

REDEEMABLE PREFERENCE SHARES (actions priviligiées/prioritaires rachetables/remboursables)

Preference shares which the issuing company (société émettrice) can buy back at any future time it wishes.

☞ See IRREDEEMABLE PREFERENCE SHARES; PREFERENCE SHARES.

REDEEMED, TO BE (racheté, remboursé [être])

To be repaid (rembourser) or paid off, especially with reference to when money is lent to (prêter) or owed by such borrowers as the government, financial institutions and companies (devoir) for a fixed term, and therefore has to be repaid with interest. As proof that he has lent his money the lender (prêteur) holds, bills (traite) or bonds (obligation) indicating the rate of interest and the date they are to be redeemed.

☞ See BILL; BOND; DEBENTURE; SHARE; STOCK.

REDEMPTION YIELD See .... YIELD.

RE-EXPORTATION (réexportation)

Also known as **ENTREPOT TRADE** (commerce franc ou d'entrepôt) it defines the international collection (enlèvement) and distribution of goods (marchandise) which are imported into a country and re-exported in the same or similar form. Although (bien que) these goods or re-exports (produits réexportés) are non-dutiable (non soumis à droits de douane) customs authorities (autorités douanières) carefully check (vérifier) that they will actually (réellement) leave the country and not be fraudulently (en fraude) used for home consumption (consommation intérieure). Some goods may also come into the country and be re-exported in a very different form, for instance tobacco becoming cigarettes. In such cases the duties (droit) paid on importation are reclaimed (réclamer, récupérer) on exportation. A document called **CUSTOMS** or **EXCISE DRAWBACK** (drawback, ristourne) is used for the purpose (à cet effet). Entrepôt trade is conducted (exercer) by importers, exporters and manufacturers (fabricant) in the so-called (appelé, que l'on appelle) free zones (zone franche), free trade zones (zone de libre échange), foreign trade zones (zone de commerce international) or free ports (port franc), of which (dont) here are (voici) a few (quelques-uns): Bremen, Copenhagen, Gdansk, Hamburg, New York City, Rotterdam, Shannon and Singapore.

☞ See BONDED WAREHOUSE; CUSTOMS AND ADMINISTRATIVE ENTRY PROCEDURES; CUSTOMS DUTY; CUSTOMS VALUATION CODE; CUSTOMS DUTY; TRANSIT ZONE.

REGIONAL UNEMPLOYMENT See .... UNEMPLOYMENT.

REGISTERED BOND See .... BOND.

REGISTERED CAPITAL See .... AUTHORIZED/REGISTERED ETC. CAPITAL.

REGISTERED DEBENTURE See .... DEBENTURE.

REGRESSIVE (INCOME) TAX See .... TAX.

REINSURANCE (réassurance)

The insurance which insurers take out (prendre) to protect themselves against big claims (sinistre), odd risks (risque spécial), or just to write (vendre) more business (contrats) than they have capital to support (garantir). If a loss (perte) occurs (survenir), the company that has provided (fournir) direct insurance has to pay, but can in turn (à son tour) claim from (demander indemnité à) the company which has accepted to provide indirect insurance. Reinsurance is indeed (en effet) often called "indirect business". Sometimes the reinsurer (réassureur) will in turn pass on (céder) part of the risk to another reinsurer through a process (par un processus) known as **RETROCESSION** (rétrocession).

☞ See INSURANCE; LLOYD'S; RISK.

REQUIRED RESERVES See .... RESERVE ASSETS.

RESEARCH AND DEVELOPMENT, abbr. **R&D** (Recherche et Développement/R & D)

The continuous development (processus de mise au point ou de développement continu) of a product from the stage (stade) of research to the finished stage, involving (impliquer) the joint (conjoint) activity of scientists (chercheur), engineers (ingénieur) and designers (concepteur).

RESERVE ASSET RATIO See .... RESERVE ASSETS.

RESERVE ASSETS, US REQUIRED RESERVES (réserves obligatoires)

Funds and other liquid assets (actif liquide/disponibilités) held by a commercial bank and not used for lending and other purposes. These can be used, if necessary, when the bank does not have sufficient funds available to meet the demands of its depositors (déposants). The minimum level of reserve assets and definition of what these may compose, particularly as a ratio (rapport) to deposits (dépôts) – the **RESERVE ASSET RATIO** (rapport réserves obligatoires-dépôts) – in most countries is legally laid down (fixer) by the central bank or regulatory authorities, and is a means of ensuring the stability of the banking system and controlling the money supply (masse monétaire). In the UK the term "reserve asset ratio" refers specifically to the ratio of reserve assets to what was known as **"ELIGIBLE LIABILITIES"** (passif défini par les autorités monétaires comme base officielle pour calculer le rapport réserves obligatoires-dépôts) and was part of the measures applied to monetary control during 1971-81, after which the ratio was abandoned. However, banks are still required to deposit a percentage of their "eligible liabilities" – a modified definition – with the Bank of England.

☞ See BANKING; CENTRAL BANK; COMMERCIAL BANK; DEPOSIT; LIQUIDITY; LIQUIDITY RATIO; MONETARY POLICY; MONEY SUPPLY; RUN ON A BANK; SPECIAL DEPOSITS.

RESERVE BANK See .... FEDERAL RESERVE SYSTEM.

RESERVES See .... RETAINED EARNINGS.

RESTITUTIONS See .... COMMON AGRICULTURAL POLICY.

RESTRICTIVE BUSINESS PRATICES, abbr. **RBPs** (Pratiques commerciales restrictives)

The limitation of access to markets and the restriction of competition (concurrence) by means of (au moyen de) such practices as: collusion (entente) to fix export or import prices; allocation (répartition) of markets or customers (client) and discriminatory pricing (politique de prix à caractère discriminatoire). An UNCTAD (CNUCED) non-binding (à caractère non obligatoire) code lists practices to be avoided (éviter) by firms and governments to discourage such activity. Indeed (en effet), free competition (libre concurrence) is supposed to encourage suppliers (fournisseur) to offer the best quality product at the lowest price and encourage innovation, efficiency (efficacité) and the most rational use of economic resources, thus (ainsi) benefiting (profiter à) both consumers and the national economy.

☞ See CARTEL; EU COMPETITION POLICY; UNCTAD.

RETAIL BANK See .... COMMERCIAL BANK.

RETAIL PRICE INDEX See .... INFLATION.

RETAINED EARNINGS/PROFITS or **RESERVES** (bénéfices non distribués)

These are company profits which have not been distributed as dividends but have been put aside as reserves for possible future expenses or needs, or to be invested in additional assets (actif), that is, ploughed back (réinvesti). They belong to shareholders (actionnaire) and can be used to tide over the company (lui permettre de subvenir) when going through a bad period, or even to pay out dividends when profits have been poor. Their level is decided by the board of directors (conseil d'administration).

☞ See ANNUAL GENERAL MEETING; DIVIDEND; ORDINARY SHARE; SHARE.

RETAINED PROFITS See .... RETAINED EARNINGS.

RETALIATION (rétortion, représailles)

Measures adopted by a country to restrain its imports from a trading partner (partenaire commercial) which has augmented tariffs (tarif douanier) or raised other barriers in a manner inconsistent with (contraire à) GATT. The latter (celui-ci) permits retaliatory measures in certain circumstances but above all (surtout) seeks to (chercher à) avoid the causes of their being used (leur utilisation).

☞ See GATT; SECTION 301.

RETROCESSION See .... REINSURANCE.

RETURNED CHEQUE See .... BOUNCED ETC. CHEQUE.

REVENUE TARIFF See .... TARIFF.

REVERSE ENGINEERING (ingénierie à rebours)

A method consisting in (consister à) dismantling (démonter) manufactured goods (produit manufacturé) such as cars, computers etc. to be able to make them oneself or to improve (améliorer) some of their parts (pièces).

RICARDO David See .... MERCANTILISM.

RIGHTS/CASH ISSUE (émission de droits de souscription/d'attribution)

This is an offer by a quoted (coté) company to existing shareholders to buy additional shares at an advantageous price, or at a discount (au-dessous du pair) in proportion to (en proportion de) the number of shares they already hold, before the general public has the opportunity. The right (droit) to purchase these new shares can itself be sold. A rights issue has the advantage for a company of being a relatively cheap way of raising (se procurer de) fresh capital, as all the expenses of listing (être admis à la cote) for the first time are avoided.

☞ See INTRODUCTION; LISTING; OFFER FOR SALE; PLACING; WARRANT.

RISK (risque)

Risk necessarily affects every field of economic activity. Launching (lancer) a loan (emprunt) or a new product is a bet (pari) that has been safely enough calculated but which nonetheless (cependant, néanmoins) involves (comprendre) a good deal of (beaucoup de) uncertainty (incertitude). The greater the risk the higher the interest rate (taux d'intérêt) money lenders (prêteur, créancier) will demand (exiger).

In matters (question) of insurance pure risk (risque pur) is involved (concerner) because there is no possibility of gain, but only the possibility of loss (perte). Some risks are uninsurable or unwillingly (avec réticence) insured because they cannot be properly (de manière adéquate) measured on account of (en raison de) the little information available (disponible) to the insurer (assureur) to calculate the premium (prime), – for example, no sufficient past record (précédent). Trade risks (risques commerciaux) are insured with many precautions by such government agencies (organisme) as the ECGD, EXIMBANK and big companies, because otherwise (sinon) creditors (créancier) would not be encouraged to reclaim from (réclamer son dû auprès de) debtors (débiteur) or would simply give credit indiscriminately. Some trade risks like changes in fashion or consumer taste or the management performance (résultat de gestion) of an executive (cadre) are utterly (tout à fait) uninsurable.

☞ See ECGD; EXIMBANK; INSURANCE; JUNK BOND under LEVERAGED BUYOUT; RISK/VENTURE CAPITAL; SHARE.

RISK-ARBITRAGER See .... ARBITRAGE; TAKEOVER BID.

RISK/VENTURE CAPITAL (capital-risque)

This is capital invested in projects or new companies and therefore entails (comporter) a high level of risk. The investor – the **VENTURE CAPITALIST** (investisseur en capital risque) – is interested over a long term, usually, say (disons) five to ten years, and not only provides a part of the capital needed (the rest may have to be borrowed from other sources such as banks) but actively participates in the development and the management (gestion) of the company. The risks are high because this is a new (and not already established) venture (entreprise hasardeuse) or business, but the potential growth prospects (perspectives de croissance) will also be high, as with high tech ventures. The venture capitalist hopes to be rewarded for his participation by the eventual increase in value of his share of the business (participation), once it has been successfully established – by selling this he could make an enormous capital gain (plus-value en capital). But he could also lose. The impetus (impulsion) for venture capital over the last ten years or so has come from the United States and Britain, but other countries in the past, like France, have been very active in this field. Governments may even take special measures to encourage the growth of venture capital as a means of assuring longterm economic growth.

☞ See MERCHANT BANK; THIRD MARKET; UNLISTED SECURITIES MARKET.

ROAD TAX (taxe routière ou vignette automobile)

A tax imposed by a government on the operation (exploitation) of motor vehicles, generally based on weight (masse) or displacement (tonnage). Such taxes may have the effect of discriminating in favour of one group or type of vehicle over (par rapport à) another.

☞ See EXCISE TAX; NON-TARIFF BARRIERS; TAX.

ROUND See .... GATT.

RPI See .... RETAIL PRICE INDEX under INFLATION.

RUBBER CHEQUE See .... BOUNCED ETC. CHEQUE.

RUN ON A BANK (ruée sur une banque pour demandes de remboursement)

This is a situation when people panic and rush to a bank to take out their money because they are afraid the bank will not be able to give it back to them. If enough people do this the bank could be in danger of collapsing (as it may not be liquid enough to meet its customers' demands). If this happened to enough banks the whole economic system could crash. Therefore central banks impose certain restrictions on the lending capacity of banks and demand they hold certain assets (actif) in liquid form to ensure that this does not happen.

☞ See BANKING; CENTRAL BANK; LIQUID ASSETS; LIQUIDITY; LIQUIDITY RATIO; RESERVE ASSETS; SPECIAL DEPOSITS.

S

S & P 500 See .... SHARE INDEX.

SAD See .... SINGLE ADMINISTRATIVE DOCUMENT.

SAEF acronym for Stock Exchange Automatic Execution Facility (système automatisé de règlement de transactions en titres de sociétés)

The International Stock Exchange (London) computerized system for carrying out (exécuter) buying and selling orders (ordre) for small quantities of shares. The system automatically directs or routes (router) orders to the market maker (contrepartiste) who offers the best price on the TOPIC screens (écran) of the Stock Exchange Automated Quotation System (SEAQ), carries out (exécuter) the order (buy or sell), produces an invoice (facture), called a **CONTRACT NOTE** (bordereau d'achat ou de vente) and then records the transaction in the Exchange's automated settlement system (système informatisé de règlement), TALISMAN. One or two market maker houses (société de contrepartistes) have their own small equivalent computerized system, as does the National Association of Securities dealers, abbr. NASD, in the USA (the **SMALL ORDER EXECUTION SYSTEM**, abbr. S.O.E.S.).

☞ See INTERNATIONAL STOCK EXCHANGE; NASDAQ under OVER-THE-COUNTER MARKET; SEAQ; TALISMAN; TAURUS; TOPIC.

SAFEGUARDS (sauvegardes)

Provisional (provisoire) and selective steps (mesure) meant to (destiner à) slow (ralentir) imports, i.e. increased tariffs (tarif douanier), tariff quotas (contingent tarifaire), or quantitative restrictions, to enable (permettre) a specific industry to adjust to (s'adapter à) rising competition (concurrence) from abroad (de l'étranger). Article XIX of GATT, entitled (intituler) "Emergency Action on Imports of Particular Products", recognizes a country's right (droit) to withdraw (retirer, mettre fin à) or modify concessions granted (accorder) earlier, or to impose new restrictions, if a product is "being imported in such increased quantities... as to cause or threaten serious injury (préjudice) to domestic producers (producteur du pays)", for such time as may be necessary to prevent (empêcher) or remedy (pallier) such injury. Under GATT exporters also have a right not to be deprived (priver) arbitrarily of access to foreign markets. Safeguard actions are also known in the USA as "Escape Clause" (Clause d'exemption) actions.

☞ See CODES OF CONDUCT; CONCESSION; ESCAPE CLAUSE; FRAMEWORK AGREEMENT; GATT; QUANTITATIVE RESTRICTIONS; SPECIAL AND DIFFERENTIAL TREATMENT; TARIFF QUOTA.

SAILING (en route)

A phrase (expression) mentioned on a sales contract (contrat de vente) meaning that the goods (marchandise) will be delivered (livrer) on (à) the ship's arrival (arrivée).

☞ See INCOTERMS.

SALES TAX See .... TAX.

SAVINGS ACCOUNT (compte d'épargne)

In the UK this is an account usually with a commercial or savings bank (caisse d'épargne), building society (société/caisse mutuelle d'épargne de financement immobilier) or other financial institution, in which savings are put and which pays a higher rate of interest than a deposit account. Small sums of money may be withdrawn on demand, but larger ones require notice (préavis). The longer the notice the greater the interest payable. In the USA savings accounts are held with commercial banks and savings and loans associations (caisse d'épargne), abbr. S & Ls, also called thrifts.

☞ See BUILDING SOCIETY; COMMERCIAL BANK; DEPOSIT ACCOUNT; SAVINGS BANK; SAVINGS & LOAN ASSOCIATION; THRIFTS.

SAVINGS AND LOAN ASSOCIATION, USA, abbr. **S & L** (caisse mutuelle d'épargne logement)

Mainly a cooperative savings institution in America originally created purely for financing the building and buying of homes, they have been in existence since the nineteenth century. Since de-regulation (déréglementation) in the early 1980s S & Ls have been allowed to extend their activities into real estate development (promotion immobilière) and other areas for which there was not often the necessary competence, or have become companies in order to compete in the wider money-lending market (as have some building societies in the UK). They are regulated and insured by the US government or by the state where they are located, and are the main source of mortgages (prêt hypothécaire) for Americans (although not the only one). Apart from accepting deposits (dépôts) and granting loans for house purchase, they also now offer a limited range of banking services (e.g. checking account, personal loans, etc.). S & Ls are included in the term "thrifts". In the late 1980s there were about 3,100 S & Ls, out of which 500 went bankrupt (faire faillite) or came very close to it and had to be rescued by the government.

☞ See DE-REGULATION; BUILDING SOCIETY; SAVINGS ACCOUNT; THRIFTS.

SAVINGS BANK (caisse/banque d'épargne)

A bank whose aim is to encourage the general public and particularly small savers (petits épargnants) to save. In the UK the Trustee Savings Bank, abbr. TSB (caisse mutuelle de dépots et de prêts), and the National Savings Bank are savings banks, while in the USA mutual savings banks and stock savings banks carry out (remplir) this function. Until ten or so years ago savings banks were limited to accepting interest-bearing (producteur d'intérêt) deposits from small savers and allowing withdrawals (retraits). But with de-regulation (libéralisation) savings banks in both countries have come to provide more and more of the services offered by commercial banks, such as a cheque book and credit card facility, personal loans, etc., with whom they may compete in the money market.

☞ See COMMERCIAL BANK; DE-REGULATION; MONEY MARKET; MUTUAL SAVINGS BANK; STOCK SAVINGS BANK.

SCHENGEN AGREEMENT See ....EUROPEAN INTERNAL MARKET.

SCORCHED EARTH See .... TAKEOVER BID.

SCREWDRIVER PLANT See .... LOCAL CONTENT.

SCRIP/BONUS/CAPITALIZATION ISSUE, (US) STOCK/DIVIDEND SPLIT (émission d'actions gratuites/données en prime)

This is when a company gives its shareholders additional shares in proportion to (en proportion de) those they already hold. These shares are fully paid up (entièrement libérée) as they are covered by retained earnings (bénéfices non distribués). This step increases the company's paid up capital. If dividends are paid out after a scrip issue they are lower per share than if there had not been such an issue because now for the same total dividend to be distributed there are more shares. After a scrip issue shareholders have more shares, but the total market value of the shares they hold will be virtually (pratiquement) the same, as the market will have adjusted the price of those shares downwards to account for the fact there are now more shares, while the value of the company has remained unaltered (inchangé). Similarly, the proportion of the company owned by the shareholder will have remained unchanged by the scrip issue. Companies do this to lower the share price and hence make the shares more liquid or, in other words, more easily saleable.

☞ See AUTHORIZED/REGISTERED ETC. CAPITAL; DIVIDEND; LIQUIDITY; RETAINED EARNINGS; SHARE; YIELD.

SDR See .... SPECIAL DRAWING RIGHTS under INTERNATIONAL MONETARY FUND.

SEAQ, acronym for STOCK EXCHANGE AUTOMATED QUOTATION SYSTEM (système informatisé de cotation et de transaction)

This is the International Stock Exchange's computerized stock price information service, introduced in 1986. It serves both the domestic (UK) equity market and the international market (through **SEAQ INTERNATIONAL**). It provides competing bid and offer (buying and selling) prices of market makers (teneur de marché) in Alpha stocks, which are the most liquid on the London Stock Exchange, and records all transactions within five minutes on the **TOPIC** television screen system. For Beta stocks it also displays two-way prices, but trades (transactions) are not shown immediately. Two-way prices (prix d'achat et de vente) are shown for Gamma stocks where possible (these, with Delta stocks, are the least frequently traded). Through this system investors, market makers and broker/dealers (négociant en titres) receive up-to-the-minute reliable market information on a screen. This has virtually eliminated the London trading floor (la corbeille), except for traded options dealing (transactions en options négociées), in favour of trading "on screen". **SEAQ INTERNATIONAL** provides the latest competing bid and offer prices (prix offert et demandé) for leading international stocks quoted by international market makers based in London.

Connected with **SEAQ** is a system being perfected which will enable member firms of the ISE to enter orders to buy and sell securities, automatically bringing together the order with the best quote in the system – the SEAQ Automatic Execution Facility, abbr. SAEF.

☞ See ALPHA STOCKS; BROKER/DEALER; FLOOR, THE; INTERNATIONAL STOCK EXCHANGE; LIQUIDITY; MARKET MAKER; SAEF; SECURITIES; TAURUS; TOPIC.

SEASONAL ADJUSTMENT (correction des variations saisonnières)

This is a statistical process to give a more realistic or accurate picture to statistics which vary sharply throughout the period under observation. For example, annual figures for unemployment in agriculture need to be seasonally adjusted to account for the fact that they are much higher in winter than in summer; otherwise (sinon) we would receive a distorted impression of the average tendency over the year for unemployment in agriculture.

☞ See UNEMPLOYMENT.

SEASONAL UNEMPLOYMENT See .... UNEMPLOYMENT.

SEC See .... SECURITIES AND EXCHANGE COMMISSION.

SECOND MARCHE, LE See .... SECONDARY MARKET.

SECONDARY MARKET (marché secondaire)

A market where shares, bonds and other securities (titres) are resold (revendre) and bought. The Stock Exchange, for example, is a secondary (as well as a primary) market. On money markets this refers to that part of the market where dealers (négociants) and investors buy and sell financial instruments (instruments financiers) without involving the original issuer (émetteur). Not to be confused with **"le Second Marché"**, created in

France in 1983, which is the equivalent of the International Stock Exchange's Unlisted Securities Market.

☞ See FINANCIAL INSTRUMENTS; FOURTH MARKET; INTERNATIONAL STOCK EXCHANGE; MONEY MARKET; OVER-THE-COUNTER MARKET; PRIMARY MARKET; SECURITIES; THIRD MARKET; UNLISTED SECURITIES MARKET.

SECTION 22 OF THE AGRICULTURAL ADJUSTMENT ACT OF 1933 (Article 22 de la loi de 1933 sur les réajustements agricoles)

A piece of US legislation authorizing the US President to impose quantitative restrictions on imports of agricultural products when the latter (celles-ci) are likely to (susceptible de) affect price support programmes (programme de soutien des prix) implemented (mettre en oeuvre) by the US Department of Agriculture. Quotas for imports of wheat (blé), flour (farine), cotton, lint (charpie), peanuts (arachide), cheese, butter and other dairy produce (produits laitiers) have thus (ainsi) been imposed by the President. In 1956 GATT Contracting Parties (Parties contractantes du GATT) authorized a waiver of Article XI prohibitions against (dérogation aux interdictions de l'Article XI envers) quantitative restrictions for (en faveur de) US decisions under (au titre de) Section 22. Since that date (depuis lors) the USA has submitted (présenter) an annual report to GATT Contracting Parties on all actions (mesure) in that field (domaine) and the reasons why they were taken.

☞ See ARTICLES OF GATT; CONTRACTING PARTY; GATT; QUANTITATIVE RESTRICTIONS; WAIVER.

SECTION 301 (Article 301)

A provision (disposition) of the US Trade Act (loi sur le commerce) of 1974 enabling (permettre) the President to withdraw (abroger) concessions or restrict imports of specific goods (marchandise) from countries discriminating against US exports, subsidizing (subventionner) their own exports to the USA, or engaging in (se livrer à) other unfair practices (pratique déloyale) against US trade. The so-called (appelé) Omnibus Trade and Competitiveness Act of 1988 made Section 301 more potent (puissant) and added a **SUPER 301**. The latter (celui-ci) is used to accuse countries of a broad range (gamme, éventail, série) of unfair trade practices (pratiques commerciales déloyales). Countries named (désigner) under (au titre de) Super 301 must reach agreement (parvenir à un accord) with the US **TRADE REPRESENTATIVE/USTR** within 12 to 18 months or face (risquer) retaliation (représailles).

☞ See CONCESSION; EXPORT SUBSIDIES; RETALIATION; UNFAIR TRADE PRACTICES; US TRADE REPRESENTATIVE.

SECURED CREDITOR See .... LIQUIDATION.

SECURED DEBENTURE See .... DEBENTURE.

SECURED LOAN See .... LOAN.

SECURITIES (effets/valeurs boursières ou titres)

This is a general word for stocks (obligation), shares (action), bonds, debentures (obligation), bills of exchange (lettre de change) and other commercial paper (effets de commerce ou billets de trésorerie) traded on stock exchanges or secondary markets (e.g. over-the-counter, the USM). Securities provide income, are saleable (vendable) and can be used as security (garantie) for loans.

☞ See BILL OF EXCHANGE; BOND; COMMERCIAL PAPER; DEBENTURE; OVER-THE-COUNTER MARKET; SHARE; STOCK; STOCK MARKET; UNLISTED SECURITIES MARKET; WARRANT.

SECURITIES AND EXCHANGE COMMISSION, USA, abbr. **SEC** (l'équivalent de la Commission des Opérations de Bourse en France, abrégé COB)

This is a US federal body set up in 1934 to regulate (surveiller ou contrôler) the securities market (marché des titres/valeurs), which includes stock exchanges, brokers (négociant en titres), investment advisers (conseiller d'investissement) and other financial intermediaries. Its equivalent in the UK is the Securities and Investment Board (SIB). The SEC requires firms listed (cotées) on any of the national stock exchanges to provide publicly available financial information by filling in **FORM** (formulaire ou imprimée) **10K**. The SEC is also active in protecting the investor and tracking down (traquer) illegal activities such as price-rigging (orgiotage ou fixation illégale des prix) of securities and insider trading (délit d'initié), as witnessed by (comme le prouve) the imprisonment of Ivan Boesky and then Michael Milken, the so-called "junk bond king" in December, 1990. It took the SEC over four years to bring the latter (ce dernier) successfully to trial (parvenir à le faire passer en jugement).

☞ See INSIDER TRADING; LEVERAGED BUYOUT; NASDAQ under OVER-THE-COUNTER MARKET; SECURITIES AND INVESTMENT BOARD; TAKEOVER.

SECURITIES AND INVESTMENT BOARD, UK, abbr. **SIB** (l'équivalent de la Commission des Opérations de Bourse en France, abrégé COB)

A body set up (fondé ou créé) under the Financial Services Act, 1986 with the responsibility for supervising the UK investment and financial subsidiaries sector. The SIB is run (géré ou dirigé) and financed by investment professionals themselves, that is, not by civil servants (fonctionnaires), and is therefore a self-regulating body (organisme indépendant chargé de la réglementation). But it has statutory powers (pouvoirs statutaires) and reports to (être sous les ordres de) the Department of Trade and Industry (l'équivalent du ministère de l'Industrie et du Commerce extérieur en France). All investment business is required by law to be registered (déclarer ou faire enregistrer) either with the SIB or with one of the five Self-Regulatory Organizations, abbr. SROs

(organisation indépendante), for which it is responsible (dont il est responsable). The overall purpose behind the SIB and the SROs is to protect the investor from unfair dealing (transactions déloyales) such as insider trading (délit d'initié) or price-rigging (agiotage ou fixation illégale des prix). The Board also runs a compensation scheme (système d'indemnisation) which covers (protéger) investors against losses of up to £48,000 due to any registered (agréé) investment adviser (conseiller d'investissement) going bankrupt or failing to meet his obligations.
The USA equivalent of the SIB is the Securities and Exchange Commission, abbr. SEC.

☞ See DEPARTMENT OF TRADE AND INDUSTRY; FINANCIAL SERVICES ACT, 1986; FINANCIAL INTERMEDIARIES; INSIDER TRADING; INTERNATIONAL STOCK EXCHANGE; SECURITIES AND EXCHANGE COMMISSION; SELF-REGULATING ORGANIZATIONS.

SECURITIES MARKET See .... STOCK MARKET.

SECURITY or **COLLATERAL** (nantissement, gage ou garantie)

Something of value given temporarily to a lender (prêteur) by the borrower (emprunteur) to protect him against the possibility of the loan not being repaid. This can be in the form of securities (valeurs boursières), insurance policies (police d'assurance), property and company assets (actif) like land, buildings, machinery, plant (biens d'équipement) and stock. If the borrower repays as required the security or collateral is returned to him. Should he fail to meet the terms of the loan and repay it, the lender has the right to sell the security to recover the sum lent, any interest outstanding (à recouvrer) and any other expenses associated with the transaction. In the USA it is common practice for people starting up a business to offer their homes as security in order to borrow the required capital.

☞ See BANKING; CAPITAL; COMMERCIAL BANK; INTEREST; LENDING; LOAN; SECURITIES.

SELF-REGULATING ORGANIZATIONS, abbr. **SROs** (organisations indépendantes)

Organizations set up (fondé/créé) in the UK under the Financial Services Act, 1986 to regulate (contrôler) the investment business and protect investors from unfair trading practices (transactions déloyales). The SROs are managed (dirigé) by professionals (professionnels) from the investment industry itself and are in turn responsible to (responsable devant) the Securities and Investment Board, abbr. SIB (l'équivalent de la Commission des Opérations de Bourse en France, abrégé COB), which is in turn responsible to the Department of Trade and Industry.
The SROs are as follows:

a. **THE ASSOCIATION OF FUTURES** (opérations/contrats à terme) **BROKERS** (courtiers) **AND DEALERS** (marchands/négociants) (**AFBD**) for transactions in traded options (options négociables);

b. **FINANCIAL INTERMEDIARIES** (intermédiaires financiers), **MANAGERS AND BROKERS AND DEALERS**) **REGULATORY ASSOCIATION** (**FIMBRA**) for dealers in securities, unit trusts (**SICAV**), life assurance and other funds belonging to other people;

c. the **INVESTMENT MANAGERS' REGULATORY ORGANIZATION** (**IMRO**) for investment management (gestion des fonds d'investissement) of, for example, pensions funds (caisse de retraite), unit trusts and investment trusts (société de placement);

d. **INTERNATIONAL SECURITIES REGULATORY ORGANIZATION** (**ISRO**) for mainly foreign firms dealing in securities not traded on the International Stock Exchange, such as Eurobonds;

e. **LIFE ASSURANCE AND UNIT TRUST REGULATORY ORGANIZATION** (**LAUTRO**) for insurance companies and unit trusts; and

f. **THE SECURITIES ASSOCIATION** (**TSA**) for companies dealing in securities e.g. market makers (contrepartiste ou teneur de marché).

☞ See BROKER/DEALER; COMMODITIES; DEPARTMENT OF TRADE AND INDUSTRY; EUROBONDS; FINANCIAL INTERMEDIARIES; FINANCIAL SERVICES ACT, 1986; FUTURES; INSURANCE; INTERNATIONAL STOCK EXCHANGE; INVESTMENT TRUST; MARKET MAKER; SECURITIES AND INVESTMENT BOARD; TRADED OPTIONS; UNIT TRUST.

SELLING FOR THE ACCOUNT See .... BULL.

SELLING FORWARD See .... FORWARD CONTRACT.

SELLING IN THE ACCOUNT See .... BULL.

SELLING SHORT See .... HAMMERING.

SENIOR DEBT See .... LEVERAGED BUYOUT.

SENSITIVE PRODUCTS (produits sensibles, névralgiques)

Domestic (national) goods (marchandise) regarded (considérer) as economically and politically important by a country which tries to preserve (conserver) its competitiveness (compétitivité) by imposing protection against the imports of similar goods. The steel (acier) and textile industries are thus (ainsi) protected in many developed countries because the many workers they employ would have no alternative (de remplacement) employment (emploi).

☞ See ESCAPE CLAUSE; GATT; GENERALIZED SYSTEM OF PREFERENCES; LIBERALIZATION; MULTI-FIBRE ARRANGEMENT; ORDERLY MARKETING AGREEMENTS; PROTECTIONISM.

SERVICES (services)

Economic activities like aircraft-landing rights (droit d'atterrissage), advertising (publicité), banking (activités bancaires), data processing (informatique), insurance, telecommunications, tourism and transport – which are intangible (intangible, incorporel), as compared with economic goods (marchandise) which are more tangible (tangible, corporel).

Service industries are often labour-intensive (à fort coefficient de main d'oeuvre) and account for (représenter) a larger and larger share (part) of international trade, so much so that (à tel point que) the Uruguay Round of GATT talks (pourparlers) has tried to set up (instaurer) the framework (cadre) of a so-called (que l'on appelle) **GENERAL AGREEMENT ON TRADE IN SERVICES/GATS**. The purpose of the negotiation on services has been to apply (introduire) some discipline in this sector where the imposition of non-tariff barriers (barrière non tarifaire) to trade had been jealously maintained. Indeed (effectivement) services have become the fastest growing sector in advanced economies at the expense of (aux dépens de) agriculture and manufacturing (production industrielle). Hence (d'où) their potential importance as an export item (article, poste) for large trading blocs like the European Union and the USA, and the discussions on, for example, intellectual property rights (droits sur la propriété intellectuelle).

☞ See BALANCE OF PAYMENTS; GATT; INSURANCE; INVISIBLE TRADE; NON-TARIFF BARRIERS.

SETTLEMENT DAY/DATE See .... SETTLEMENT OF BARGAINS.

SETTLEMENT OF BARGAINS (règlement des transactions)

The payment for securities on stock exchanges according to given rules. The London Stock Exchange, for example, has a business calendar which is divided into fortnightly (bimensuel) periods, each known as **THE ACCOUNT** (liquidation). Payment has to be made normally by the end of the sixth working day (jour ouvrable) after the last day of The Account in which the transaction took place, in other words usually by the second Monday. This payment day is called **THE ACCOUNT DAY**, also known as the **SETTLEMENT DAY/DATE** or **SETTLING DAY** (jour du terme/de liquidation). This allows a credit period of up to ten days, during which the buyer can sell the securities for which he has not yet paid. Should the buyer require to delay payment until the next Account Day, where this is agreed he will have to pay interest – this is called **CONTANGO** (report). In the USA, on the other hand, payment is due after the fifth working day. Should the seller find he cannot deliver the securities he promised on the agreed day, usually a "bear" (baissier ou spéculateur à la baisse), and the buyer agrees to delay acceptance of delivery till the next Settlement Day for a sum of money, this is known as **BACKWARDATION**, **BACKWARDIZATION** or **BACK**, abbr. **bk.** (déport). In commodity markets (bourse des marchandises) **BACKWARDATION** is the situation where the spot price (cours du disponible) is higher than the price quoted for future delivery (livraison à terme).

☞ See BARGAIN; BEAR; BULL; CLOSING PRICE; COMMODITY; FORWARD CONTRACT; HEDGE; OPTION; SPOT/CURRENT PRICE.

SETTLING DAY See .... SETTLEMENT OF BARGAINS.

SHARE, (US) STOCK (action)

Buying a share means contributing money or capital to a company in exchange for ownership (propriété) of part of it, participation in its management through the annual general meeting (assemblée générale annuelle), dependent on (selon) the kind of share, and a right to part of the profits (bénéfice), once all other priority financial obligations have been met (e.g. debt interest). The capital of the company is therefore made up of (constituer de) a given number of equal shares. Those buying shares are called **SHAREHOLDERS** (actionnaires), **US STOCKHOLDERS**. The combined contribution of capital by shareholders to a company is called **NOMINAL CAPITAL** (capital nominatif/social) or **EQUITY CAPITAL** (capitaux propres/capital propre ou actif net d'une société), or in other words, the capital belonging to shareholders once all the company's debts have been paid. The shareholder's reward (récompense ou prime) for risking his money is twofold: a dividend, usually paid twice a year, and a potential increase in the price of his shares if the company does well. If the shares go up in value he can sell them for more than he paid for them and thus make a capital gain (gain en capital ou plus-value). On the other hand, the company could do badly and pay out a very low dividend or nothing at all, go into liquidation or even go bankrupt (faire faillite). In the latter case the shareholder would most probably lose all the money he had paid out (débourser) for the shares.

There are many different kinds of shares, the most common being ordinary (action ordinaire), preference (action prioritaire) and deferred shares (action différée). Where shareholders have paid the full price of shares these are called **FULLY PAID SHARES** (action libérée); where the shares have only partly been paid, they are called **PARTLY PAID SHARES** (action non complètement libérée). When the British government privatised British Telecom the public were invited to buy the shares in instalments (versement échelonné ou à tempérament), enabling more people to subscribe. Thus, after the first instalment the shares remained partly paid. Normally shareholders receive a **SHARE CERTIFICATE** (certificat/titre d'action), from the company issuing the shares. This is legal proof of ownership and gives details of the type of share, serial number (numéro de série) and the quantity of shares held.

While in general the words **SHARES** and **STOCK** or **STOCKS** have come to have the same meaning, in the **UK STOCK** is used to refer specifically to a fixed-interest security (valeur à intérêt fixe); in the USA such securities are called **BONDS**, while other types of securities are known as **STOCKS**.

☞ See "A", "B", BONUS, CONVERTIBLE PREFERENCE, CUMULATIVE PREFERENCE, DEFERRED ORDINARY, DEFERRED, FOUNDERS, IRREDEEMABLE PREFERENCE, MANAGEMENT, MULTIPLE VOTING, NEW, NON-CUMULATIVE PREFERENCE, NON-PARTICIPATING, NON-REDEEMABLE PREFERENCE, NON-VOTING, NO-PAR-VALUE, OLD, ORDINARY, PARTICIPATING PREFERENCE, PREFERENCE, PREFERRED ORDINARY, REDEEMABLE PREFERENCE SHARE; ALPHA SECURITIES; ANNUAL GENERAL MEETING; AUTHORIZED/REGISTERED ETC. CAPITAL; BOND; CREDIT RATING AGENCY; DEBENTURE; DIVIDEND; WARRANT; YIELD.

SHARE CERTIFICATE See .... SHARE.

SHARE EXCHANGE OFFER See .... TAKEOVER BID.

SHARE INDEX (indice boursier)

This measures the average (moyen) percentage change in price of a selected number of shares, considered to represent (jugées répresentatives) the trend (tendance) in the whole market (de l'ensemble du marché), which are weighted (pondérer) according to the size of the company, taking a given year as the starting point for comparison (the first time the prices are noted this is indicated by 100). When the index moves up several points this means that investors have been confident and demanding shares, which has pushed the price up; if the index loses points this indicates they have been less confident, buying less and preferring to sell, all of which lowers the price. In this way share indices (or indexes) are a reflection of the general economic mood of the economy, a barometer, and are quoted daily by the media.

The principle share indices are as follows: the **DOW JONES INDUSTRIAL AVERAGE**, popularly known as the **"DOW JONES"**, covering thirty leading US industrial companies quoted (coté) on the New York Stock Exchange/NYSE, the world's second largest; the **NIKKEI STOCK AVERAGE**, covering 225 equities quoted on the Tokyo Stock Exchange, the world's largest; **STANDARD & POOR'S 500**, abbr. **S & P 500**, covering 500 securities quoted on the NYSE; the **NEW YORK STOCK EXCHANGE COMPOSITE INDEX**, covering minute-by-minute changes in price of more than 1,680 securities traded on the NYSE; the **FINANCIAL TIMES ALL-SHARE INDEX**, covering over 700 shares and calculated daily; the **FINANCIAL TIMES-STOCK EXCHANGE 100 SHARE INDEX**, popularly known as **"FOOTSIE"**, covering 100 leading UK and Irish companies quoted on the London Stock Exchange, the world's third largest, and calculated each minute; the **CAC 40** (CAC veut dire Compagnie des agents de change) covering forty leading French companies considered as representative of the French economy, calculated each minute; and **DAX** (Deutsche Aktienindex), covering thirty leading shares quoted on the Frankfurt Stock Exchange.

☞ See STOCK MARKET.

SHARE WARRANT See .... WARRANT.

SHAREHOLDERS See .... SHARE.

SHARK REPELLANTS See .... TAKEOVER BID.

SHIPOWNER'S LIABILITY INSURANCE POLICY See .... MARINE INSURANCE.

SHIPPING AND FORWARDING AGENT or **BROKER** (commissionnaire expéditeur, agent transitaire ou maritime)

Deals with (s'occuper de) documentation (documentation), shipping space (tonnage nécessaire), insurance and customs (douanes) formalities.

Sometimes acting as (agir en tant que) a **FORWARDING AGENT** or **FREIGHT FORWARDER** (transitaire; chargeur), sees to (s'occuper de) the collection (enlèvement), carriage (transport) and delivery (livraison) of goods (marchandise) between ports and the premises (locaux) of buyers.

☞ See CUSTOMS AND ADMINISTRATIVE ENTRY PROCEDURES; DOCUMENTATION; EXPORT HOUSE; INSURANCE.

SHIPPING DOCUMENTS (documents d'expédition)

Also known as **DOCUMENTATION** or **EXPORT DOCUMENTS**, they consist of: export invoice (facture d'exportation), bill of lading (connaissement), consignment note (bordereau d'expédition), insurance policy (police), insurance certificate and possibly (éventuellement) certificate of origin (certificat d'origine), consular invoice (facture consulaire), sanitary certificate and export licence. The importer needs most of these in order to have the goods delivered (livrer) and cleared through customs (dédouaner). For any claim on insurance (déclaration de sinistre), they will also be necessary. The exporter's bank agent abroad hands them over (remettre) to the importer only once (une fois que) the latter (celui-ci) has paid or accepted a bill of exchange (lettre de change). This system is called **DOCUMENTS FOR COLLECTION** (documents à retirer). The bill of exchange attached to (joindre à) shipping documents is called a **DOCUMENTARY BILL** (traite documentaire). If the bill has to be accepted (accepter) previous to (préalablement à) the delivery (remise) of the documents, it is called a **DOCUMENTS-AGAINST-ACCEPTANCE BILL** or **D/A BILL** (documents contre acceptation). If the bill has to be paid previous to the delivery of the documents, it is called a **DOCUMENTS-AGAINST-PAYMENT BILL** or **D/P BILL** (documents contre paiement). Should (si) the drawee (tiré) fail to (refuser de, manquer de) accept the bill or the acceptor (accepteur) fail to pay for it at maturity (à échéance), it would be a **DISHONOURED BILL** (traite impayée) and the exporter would be liable to (responsable auprès de) the bank for the amount (montant).

☞ See BILL OF EXCHANGE; BILL OF LADING; CERTIFICATE OF ORIGIN; CONSIGNMENT NOTE; CONSULAR INVOICE; EXPORT INVOICE; INSURANCE; LICENSING.

SHORT COVER, TO See .... HAMMERING.

SHORT COVERING See .... HAMMERING.

SHORT POSITION See .... HAMMERING.

SHORT SALE See .... HAMMERING.

SHORT SELLER See .... HAMMERING.

SHORT SELLING See .... HAMMERING.

SHORTING See .... HAMMERING.

SHORTS See .... GILT-EDGED STOCKS; HAMMERING.

SIGHT BILL See .... AT SIGHT; BILL OF EXCHANGE.

SINGLE ADMINISTRATIVE DOCUMENT See ....EUROPEAN INTERNAL MARKET.

SINGLE EUROPEAN ACT, abbr. **SEA** (Acte unique européen)

This act of the European Union, then (alors) called the European Community/EU, was approved in December 1985 at the Luxembourg meeting of the European Council, signed by the twelve member states in February 1986 and came into force (entrer en vigueur) on July I, 1987 after ratification by the twelve national parliaments.

The SEA is composed of four Titles (Titres) including thirty-four Articles. Its main provisions (dispositions) are:

Title 1 contains Articles I-3 that set (fixer) the object of the Act as being to make "concrete progress towards European unity" and to render the status (statut) of the European Council more formal (officiel);

Title 2 contains Articles 4-29 that comprise (comprendre) a number of amendments to the Treaty of Paris – the European Coal and Steel Community – and the two Treaties of Rome – EEC and EURATOM. The main provisions are to establish a first instance court (cour de première instance) to the European Court of Justice, to increase the part played by the European Parliament in the legislative field by setting up (instaurer) a wider cooperation with the European Council of Ministers, to extend the qualified majority system (système de la majorité qualifiée ou pondérée) for the European Council of Ministers on issues (question) regarding (afférent à) the completion (accomplissement, réalisation) of the European Internal Market, and a number of other provisions augmenting the EU's responsibilities as concerns the monetary sphere, social policies, economic and social harmony, research and technology and the environment;

Title 3 contains Article 30 that provides for (prévoir) the creation of a secretariat to promote (promouvoir) cooperation in the field of foreign policy;

Title 4 contains Articles 31-34 that describe the formalities regarding the ratification of the Act, its coming into effect (entrée en vigueur) and translation into all EU languages.

The SEA was a preparatory step (stade) towards the Treaty of Maastricht which was signed in January 1992.

☞ See EU; ECSC; EURATOM; EUROPEAN COUNCIL; EUROPEAN COUNCIL OF MINISTERS; EUROPEAN COURT OF JUSTICE; EUROPEAN INTERNAL MARKET; EUROPEAN PARLIAMENT; MAASTRICHT; TREATY OF PARIS; TREATY OF ROME.

SITUATIONAL CHANGE (changement conjoncturel)

Sudden changes in the political, financial or economic conditions that existed in a country or in the world. Such changes may be brought about (occasionner) by such occurrences (événements) as wars, stock market crashes (krach boursier) bankruptcies (faillite), unexpected (inattendu) rises (montée) in the price of raw materials (matière première) etc.

☞ See STRUCTURAL CHANGE.

SITUATIONAL UNEMPLOYMENT See .... UNEMPLOYMENT.

SITUATIONAL UNEMPLOYMENT See .... UNEMPLOYMENT.

SMALL ORDER EXECUTION SYSTEM See .... SAEF.

SMITH Adam See .... LAISSEZ-FAIRE; MERCANTILISM.

SNAKE See .... EUROPEAN MONETARY SYSTEM.

SOCIAL CHARTER See .... MAASTRICHT.

SOCIAL SECURITY CONTRIBUTIONS/TAXES See .... TAXES.

SOES See .... SAEF.

SPECIAL AND DIFFERENTIAL TREATMENT – for developing country exports – (traitement spécial et différentiel pour les exportations des pays en voie de développement)

The principle that (selon lequel) exports of developing countries should (devoir) be given preferential access to markets of developed countries, and that developing countries participating in trade negotiations (négociations commerciales) need not (ne pas avoir l'obligation de) fully reciprocate (appliquer une pleine réciprocité) the concessions they receive. This principle was first discussed during the Kennedy Round of GATT talks, 1964-1967, and made practicable (rendre applicable) during the Tokyo Round, 1974-1979.

☞ See CODES OF CONDUCT; CONCESSION; FRAMEWORK AGREEMENT; GATT; GENERALIZED SYSTEM OF PREFERENCES; RECIPROCITY; SAFEGUARDS.

SPECIAL DEPOSITS (réserves obligatoires)

In the U.K. these are large sums of money commercial banks are required to deposit with the Bank of England. This amount varies according to the directions (directives) of the government. By forcing the banks to deposit these sums the government controls the level of lending they can carry out. The less a bank has to deposit the more it can lend, and vice versa. Special deposits, therefore, are a tool (instrument) used by the government to regulate the economy and inflation by controlling the money supply (masse monétaire). If banks can lend freely this increases credit and the money supply, giving the economy a boost (coup de fouet). If banks are forced to lend less this reduces credit and the money supply, thus helping to reduce inflation.

☞ See BANKING; CENTRAL BANK; COMMERCIAL BANK; INFLATION; LIQUIDITY RATIO; MONETARY POLICY; MONEY SUPPLY; RESERVE ASSETS.

SPECIAL DRAWING RIGHTS See .... INTERNATIONAL MONETARY FUND.

SPECIFIC DUTY See .... CUSTOMS DUTY.

SPECIFIC IMPORT LICENSE See .... LICENSING.

SPECIFIC LIMITATIONS ON TRADE (Limitations spécifiques aux échanges commerciaux)

Government measures restricting imports or exports of a product over (pendant) a period of time to a specifically stated (établir) volume or value by means of (au moyen de) licensing (régime des licences) or other required (requérir) authorizations.

☞ See EXCHANGE CONTROLS; EXPORT QUOTAS; LICENSING; NON-TARIFF BARRIERS; QUANTITATIVE RESTRICTIONS; TARIFF QUOTA.

SPONSOR (caution ou répondant) or **ISSUING/SECURITIES HOUSE** (institut financier émetteur/d'émission/de placement)

In the UK this is any financial organization such as a merchant bank (banque d'affaires) or stockbroker (sociéte de bourse/courtage) which organizes and usually underwrites (garantir) a new issue of securities (nouvelle émission de titres) for a commission.

☞ See INTRODUCTION; MERCHANT BANK; OFFER FOR SALE; PLACING.

SPOT CASH See .... CASH ON DELIVERY.

SPOT DELIVERY See .... SPOT/CURRENT PRICE.

SPOT MARKET See .... SPOT/CURRENT PRICE.

SPOT/CURRENT PRICE (prix enlevé/sur place/du disponible ou cours du comptant [devises])

The price to be paid for the acquisition of an asset – commodity (marchandise), foreign exchange (devises) or securities (titres) at the moment of purchase, as opposed to one for future delivery (livrable à une date ultérieure) – the forward price. The market for immediate delivery (livraison immédiate) is known as the **SPOT MARKET** (marché au comptant/du disponible). Where contracts are for immediate delivery, called **SPOT DELIVERY** (livraison immédiate), but with specific reference to commodities, they are referred to as **CASH, PHYSICAL** or **ACTUAL TRANSACTIONS** (opération/marché au comptant), while **ACTUALS** (marchandises livrables/disponibles) refers to commodities quickly or readily available for delivery on a commodity market.

☞ See BARGAIN; CLOSING PRICE; COMMODITY; FORWARD CONTRACT; SETTLEMENT OF BARGAINS.

STABEX See .... LOMÉ CONVENTION.

STAG (loup ou chasseur de primes)

This is a speculator who applies (souscrire) for new shares in the hope of quickly selling them at a higher price once trading in these has started. **TO STAG IN NEW ISSUES** (souscrire aux nouvelles émissions pour revendre rapidement) means to speculate as a stag.

☞ See ARBITRAGER; BEAR; BULL.

STAG IN NEW ISSUES, TO See .... STAG.

STAGFLATION See .... INFLATION.

STANDARD & POOR'S See .... CREDIT RATING AGENCY.

STANDARD & POOR'S 500 See .... SHARE INDEX.

STANDARDS (normes)

Technical specifications (description détaillée) that state (préciser, spécifier) characteristics of a product such as size (dimensions), quality, performance (fonctionnement) or safety. These may also cover terminology, testing (essai) methods, packaging (emballage), labeling (étiquetage) or marking (marquage) requirements (réglementation). Through (au moyen de) its Standards Code, GATT seeks to (chercher à) prevent (empêcher) national standards from (de) being used as barriers to trade.

☞ See CODES OF CONDUCT; NON-TARIFF BARRIERS; PACKAGING, LABELING AND MARKING REGULATIONS; QUARANTINE, SANITARY, AND HEALTH LAWS AND REGULATIONS.

STANDING ORDER (prélèvement automatique ou ordre permanent)

An instruction given to a bank by a customer to pay a sum of money regularly to another party. This is very useful where the same payment has to be made, say (disons) each month, for a mortgage (hypothèque) or a credit purchase. The standing order enables the customer to avoid having to write out (tirer) and send a cheque each month.

☞ See DE-REGULATION; SAVINGS BANK.

STANDSTILL See .... TAKEOVER BID.

STATE TRADING NATIONS (pays à commerce d'Etat)

Countries relying (dépendre) heavily (fortement) on government bodies (organisme d'Etat) to conduct trade with other countries. The ex-Soviet Union and its former (ancien) satellites well illustrate this case.

STERLING M3 See .... MONEY SUPPLY.

STOCK/STOCKS See .... SHARE.

STOCKBROKER See .... BROKER/DEALER.

STOCKBROKERS See .... BROKERAGE FIRM ETC.

STOCKBROKING FIRM See .... BROKERAGE FIRM ETC.

STOCKHOLDERS See .... SHARE.

STOCK EXCHANGE AUTOMATED QUOTE SYSTEM INTERNATIONAL (SEAQ INTERNATIONAL) See .... SEAQ.

STOCK EXCHANGE See .... STOCK MARKET.

STOCK EXCHANGE, THE See .... INTERNATIONAL STOCK EXCHANGE.

STOCKHOLDERS' MEETING See .... ANNUAL GENERAL MEEETING.

STOCK EXCHANGE AUTOMATED QUOTATION SYSTEM See .... SEAQ.

STOCK JOBBER See .... MARKET MAKER.

STOCK MARKET/EXCHANGE, SECURITIES MARKET or **BOURSE** (bourse ou marché des titres/valeurs)

This is a market where securities (titres ou valeurs) are bought and sold. In most developed countries there is a stock exchange in the capital city and also in various provincial towns. The size of the stock exchange is measured by its **MARKET CAPITALIZATION** (capitalisation boursière) – the total value at a given moment of all the shares quoted (coté) on it, calculated by multiplying the price of each share by the total volume available (produit du cours par le nombre de titres émis) – and its turnover (chiffre d'affaires) – the value of all the shares sold. The **TOKYO STOCK EXCHANGE** has the world's largest market capitalization, followed by the **NEW YORK STOCK EXCHANGE**, abbr. **NYSE** (America's biggest and oldest, referred to also as **WALL STREET** and **THE BIG BOARD**) and then the **INTERNATIONAL STOCK EXCHANGE**, London, which, incidentally (soit dit en passant ou incidemment), lists more company securities, especially foreign ones, than the other two stock exchanges.

Stock exchanges serve the purpose of bringing together those who need capital and those who possess it; they thus channel (diriger ou canaliser) savings (épargne) gathered by various institutions such as pension funds (caisse de retraite) and insurance companies (compagnie d'assurance) or put aside by individuals, into industry, commerce and government spending (dépenses publiques), and so oil (mettre de l'huile dans les rouages) the economy. To do this they provide first of all a reputable (de bonne réputation) market for first-time issuers (émetteur) of securities, one in which investors have confidence – the primary market –, and another for those investors wishing to sell their securities – the secondary market (le second marché). The latter (ce dernier) is particularly important as it provides the liquidity necessary to encourage investors to buy securities – they know that should they want their money back for whatever reason they can sell their investment, although they will not always be guaranteed the same price they paid for it. Stock exchanges can also provide an opportunity for small companies and potentially promising ideas to raise capital (trouver des capitaux) on a third market, such as London's Unlisted Securities Market (marché hors cote). The reputation of the stock exchange is a very important factor in attracting both seekers and providers of capital. If investors feel they can be easily cheated (tromper/frauder) they simply will not risk their money. So in order to protect them stock exchanges have usually strict rules and regulations concerning which companies may be quoted and the compulsory (obligatoire) information they have to give about their affairs, while at the same time information is continually available about changes in the price of securities, thanks to the electronic revolution. In addition, stock exchanges inevitably attract a great deal of speculative activity, giving the opportunity for some people to get rich very quickly. Therefore strict rules and regulations usually exist to prevent the abuse of investors by professional insiders (initié) who can use their privileged (priviligié) information to the disadvantage of the former (les premiers). For example, insider trading (délit d'initié) and price-rigging (agiotage ou fixation illicite des prix) are illegal in many countries.

Floor trading (opérations boursières à la corbeille) today has been largely replaced by or is in the process of giving way to automated screen information and trading (système informatisé de cotation et de transaction). This, linked with telephone buying and selling, means today that the stock exchanges of the world are all linked (lier) and thanks to time differentials (décalage des fuseaux horaires) trading (opérations) can take place twenty-four hours a day (vingt-quatre heures sur vingt-quatre).

☞ See ARBITRAGER; BEAR; BOND; BULL; DEBENTURE; INSIDER TRADING; INTERNATIONAL STOCK EXCHANGE; LIQUIDITY; LISTING; OVER-THE-COUNTER MARKET; PLACING; PRIMARY MARKET; PROGRAM TRADING; SAEF; SEAQ; SECONDARY MARKET; SECURITIES AND EXCHANGE COMMISSION; SECURITIES AND INVESTMENT BOARD; SECURITY; SHARE; STAG; THIRD MARKET; TOPIC; UNLISTED SECURITIES MARKET.

STOCK SAVINGS BANK, USA (institut/caisse d'épargne)

A privately-owned bank which receives and invests deposits (dépots) from small savers (petits épargnants) and usually offers normal bank facilities (e.g. cheque book, personal loans, etc.). Included in the term "thrifts".

☞ See BANKING; COMMERCIAL BANK; MUTUAL SAVINGS BANK; SAVINGS BANK; THRIFTS.

STOCK SPLIT See .... SCRIP/BONUS ETC. ISSUE.

STOPPED CHEQUE (chèque bloqué ou sur lequel on a fait opposition)

A cheque which has been refused payment by a bank on the instructions (opposition sur un chèque) of the drawer (tireur), who pays a fee (frais) for this.

☞ See CHEQUE.

STORE CARD See .... CREDIT CARD

STREET SWEEP See .... TAKEOVER BID.

STRIKING PRICE See .... OFFER FOR SALE; OPTION.

STRUCTURAL CHANGE (changement structurel)

Long term changes – such as those affecting growth (croissance), inflation or employment – in the general trends (tendance) or development of an economic system. These changes can occur (se produire) within (à l'intérieur de) national economies and are reflected in the interdependence among them and the greater interrelation of the world economy. The causes of these changes may be: developments in comparative advantage (avantage comparatif); technical changes; improved infrastructure and changing consumer (consommateur) preference (goût).

☞ See ADJUSTMENT; COMPARATIVE ADVANTAGE; SITUATIONAL CHANGE; WELFARE.

STRUCTURAL IMPEDIMENTS INITIATIVE, abbr. **SII** (Initiative pour la réforme des barrières structurelles au commerce)

An initiative taken in July 1989 by the Bush Administration (gouvernement) in the USA in order to tackle (aborder) difficulties arising from (découler de) trade (échanges commerciaux) between the USA and Japan. The initiative consists of (consister en) the mutual examination of national practices which directly or indirectly restrict trade between the two countries. At a summit meeting (rencontre au sommet) in Houston in 1990 the two parties agreed (convenir) on the following (de ce qui suit): Japan pledged to (s'engager à) spend more on its infrastructure, to seek (rechercher) ways (moyens) of reforming its land and fiscal system, to improve its import facilities (infrastructure), to shorten (réduire) permission time requirements (délais) for the establishment (implantation) of hypermarkets, to apply (appliquer) legislation against monopolies more strictly, to struggle against unfair business practices (pratique commerciale déloyale) and to reduce price differentials (différentiel). The USA promised to seek to limit its budget deficit by (d'ici) 1993, to take steps (mesure) to promote (promouvoir) savings (épargne) and to maintain free access of foreign capital to its territory, to try and cut capital costs (amortissement fiscal, coût d'immobilisation), to reduce export controls more particularly on energy products, to encourage exports to Japan, to gradually suppress the voluntary restraints (autolimitation) of Japanese exports to the USA, to give a stimulus to research and development, reform its education system and raise (relever) the skill standards (niveau de qualification) of its labour force (main d'oeuvre). Supposing the two parties stick to their word (tenir parole) the effects of these policies can only be felt in the long run (a long terme).

☞ See MANAGED TRADE; USTR; VOLUNTARY RESTRAINT AGREEMENTS.

STRUCTURAL UNEMPLOYMENT See .... UNEMPLOYMENT.

SUBROGATION See .... PRINCIPLES OF INSURANCE.

SUBSCRIBED CAPITAL See .... AUTHORIZED/REGISTERED ETC. CAPITAL.

SUBSCRIPTION See .... OFFER FOR SALE.

SUBSIDIARY (filiale)

A company (société) controlled by another, either (soit) through (par) ownership (détention, possession) of 50% to 100% of its shares (action) or (soit) through other arrangements (disposition) concerning its organization or management (gestion, direction, contrôle).

☞ See MULTINATIONAL CORPORATION; RESTRICTIVE BUSINESS PRACTICES; UNFAIR BUSINESS PRACTICES.

SUBSIDY (subvention)

An economic benefit (avantage) granted (accorder) by public authorities (pouvoirs publics) to producers of goods (marchandise) or services to strengthen (renforcer) their competitive (concurrentiel) position and foster (encourager) employment or simply maintain the income of certain producers. Subsidies may be direct – cash grants (aide pécuniaire, allocation) – or indirect, such as low-interest export credit (crédit à l'exportation) guaranteed by a government agency (organisme). Subsidies may be regarded with disfavour (avec désapprobation, d'un mauvais oeil) as they distort (fausser) the rules of the free market by artificially keeping prices below (au-dessous de) production costs, thus (ainsi) giving subsidized (subventionner) goods an unfair competitive advantage (avantage comparatif déloyal). Hence (en conséquence), the European Union and the GATT, for example, attempt (essayer) to eliminate subsidies in the interests of free competition (libre concurrence) and fair trade. However, subsidies in certain circumstances may be justified, as has been recognized, for instance, by the GATT with its acknowledgement (reconnaissance) of the **INFANT INDUSTRY ARGUMENT**.

☞ See EXPORT SUBSIDIES; GATT; INFANT INDUSTRY ARGUMENT; NON-TARIFF BARRIERS.

SUBUNDERWRITERS See .... OFFER FOR SALE.

SUPER 301 See .... SECTION 301.

SUPPLY AND DEMAND (offre et demande)

Usually referred to in connection with the law of supply and demand (la loi de l'offre et de la demande). In its simplest form this says that prices are determined by the interaction of supply and demand. If there is a shortage (insuffisance, manque ou déficit) in the supply of a commodity or service then prices will increase (augmenter); if supply at a given price is greater than what people demand at that price, then prices will drop. An increase in price because of increased demand will tend to stimulate an increase in production or supply and eventually reduce demand, while a drop in prices will tend to increase demand and reduce production until stocks are cleared. Prices will stabilize where demand equals supply.

☞ See EQUILIBRIUM.

SWAP SCHEMES See .... COUNTERTRADE.

SWITCH TRADING See .... COUNTERTRADE.

SYNDICATED LOAN (prêt en participation consenti par un consortium de banques)
A loan, usually short-term, given by a group of international banks acting together. The interest charged is based on **LIBOR**.

☞ See LIBOR; LOAN.

SYSMIN See .... LOMÉ CONVENTION.

T

TAKE A COMPANY PRIVATE, TO See .... LEVERAGED BUYOUT.

TAKE A COMPANY PUBLIC, TO See .... LEVERAGED BUYOUT.

TAKEOVER PANEL See .... INTERNATIONAL STOCK EXCHANGE.

TAKEOVER/TAKE-OVER BID (offre public d'achat, abrégé OPA ou rachat d'une entreprise)

This is the public offer by an individual or quoted company (coté en Bourse) to the shareholders of another quoted company for their shares, and is made with a view to acquiring over 50% and thus controlling the target company (société/entreprise cible). The takeover is carried out either because it is part of a company's growth strategy (stratégie de croissance) or because the raider (attaquant ou repreneur/prédateur d'entreprise) can see opportunities for profit in the prey (proie) which the latter's management cannot. Takeovers generate much interest in the financial world because they involve increased share prices, which is good for investors, high share dealing volumes (gros volume de transactions en titres), which is good for broker/dealers (négociant en titres) and market makers (contrepartiste), big fees (honoraire) for merchant banks (banque d'affaires) called in to advise the firms concerned, and spin-off benefits (retombées) for lawyers (avocat), accountants (comptable) and other specialists (expert) consulted.

Takeover bids are usually governed by specific sets of rules at different levels. At the national level, in the UK a bid has to be withdrawn (retiré) if it is vetoed (interdire) by the Monopolies and Mergers Commission on the grounds that (sous le prétexte que, pour raison de, à cause de) it could greatly reduce competition. At a European level, the EU Commission for Competition could also stop a bid or merger (fusion) from being realised (effectuer) for the same reasons. Within a country stringent (sévère) rules usually exist to protect the shareholder and enable him to see what is happening before a company changes hands. In the UK such rules have been laid down by the Panel on Takeovers and Mergers, a self-regulating organization (organisation indépendante). The **DISCLOSURE OF SHAREHOLDINGS** rule (l'obligation de divulgation/révélation de possession d'actions), for example, insists that when a buyer has acquired 5% or more of a company's shares he must inform the latter (cette dernière). This level of shareholding is known as a **TRIGGER POINT** (seuil). While a 5% holding may not result in a takeover bid, under this rule the management of a company are warned of a potential danger. Another trigger point is 30% or more: where a raider has acquired a stake (participation) of this size he is obliged to bid (faire une offre) for all the shares in the target company, as this gives him a dominant position which is very close to effective control (contrôle réel). This is known as a **MANDATORY BID** (offre obligatoire). In the USA investors acquiring 5% or more shares in a company are legally bound (sont tenus par la loi) to fill (remplir) and send in to the Securities and Exchange Commission document **THIRTEEN D**, or **13 (D)**. Bids in the UK may be dropped if they have not met certain conditions, such as the bidder having obtained over 50% of the shares in the target company.

The possible manoeuvres in takeover bids are varied and much of their colourful terminology originates from the USA, where the rules are less strict as to what is and is not permissible. To acquire the necessary number of shares, in other words a **MAJORITY HOLDING** (participation majoritaire ou bloc de contrôle), a raider can first obtain shares through market purchases – this is called building up (constituer) a stake (participation) – which can be added to those shareholders have been willing to sell to him. He can buy shares on the market very quickly to acquire up to 15% of the prey – this is known as a **DAWN RAID** (raid à l'aube ou tentative d'OPA surprise). A **STREET SWEEP** (ratissage du marché) is where the raider takes control of a company by the massive purchase of shares without making a public offer. Where a raider persuades friends and associates to buy up shares in the victim on his behalf (de la part de) this is called **WAREHOUSING** (emmagasinage). In this situation the parties are considered to be **ACTING IN CONCERT** (agir de concert) or behaving as a **CONCERT PARTY** (action concertée), which is illegal if shareholders do not know about this. The shares of a concert party must be disclosed (divulguer) if they reach any of the trigger points, but it is not always easy to prove that certain shareholders are acting in concert. Associates of the bidder (e.g. his merchant bank) are required to declare their interests in the shares of either party. A speculator who buys up shares of companies involved in a takeover situation with a view to selling them at a higher price is known as a **RISK-ARBITRAGER** or **ARB** (arbitragiste-risque). Where a company or individual builds up a large stake in a company and then threatens to take it over or sell its stake to another party unless (à moins que) the victim company buys the shares back at a high price this is known as **GREENMAIL** (chantage au billet vert ou financier); this word derives from "green", the colour of dollar bills or cash which will be needed to pay for the shares, and "mail" from the word "blackmail" (chantage).

Where a takeover is agreed by the management of the target company (but not necessarily by the shareholders) this is known as a **FRIENDLY TAKEOVER BID** (OPA amicale) or **MERGER** (fusion). Where the management is against the takeover (often because they fear that they will lose their jobs) this is referred to as a **HOSTILE TAKEOVER BID** (OPA hostile/inamicale/sauvage) and is a **CONTESTED BID** (OPA litigieuse). The raider in this situation is sometimes called a **BLACK NIGHT** (chevalier noir). The attacked company may in this case try to find a more acceptable bidder, who will be prepared to buy the shares at a higher price than that offered by the raider – he is known as a **WHITE KNIGHT** (chevalier blanc). A **STANDSTILL** (trève ou point mort) is generally a short period during the takeover fight when raiders (prédateur ou repreneur d'entreprise) stop buying up the shares of the company they want to take over – the prey (la proie) – and the company in question does not take any further defensive action. **SHARK REPELLANTS** (batterie anti-requins) is a general term for measures taken by companies anticipating takeover bids to discourage them. For example, a company can have stipulated in its articles (statuts) that in the case of takeovers, mergers or sale of assets (actif) the decision has to be approved by 60% or more of the shareholders: this is the **SUPER MAJORITY RULE** (règle de la super majorité). The **POISON PILL** tactic (tactique de la pilule empoisonnée) seeks to discourage the raider by including in its articles a stipulation that under attack the company will issue new capital on favourable terms to existing shareholders, thus making it far more costly and difficult to carry out the takeover; or it can insert a clause which requires enormous compensatory payment to be made to its management, should they be dismissed in the case of a takeover. The **SCORCHED EARTH** tactic (terre brûlée) involves the company selling large parts of its assets in order to look less attractive to the raider. The **FAT MAN** tactic (tactique de l'obèse) relies on frightening off the raider by acquiring heavily indebted (lourdement endetté) assets. Finally, Employee Share/(US) Stock Ownership Plans (actionnariat du personnel), abbr. ESOPs, have been especially used in the USA to prevent hostile takeovers, as employees with shares are less likely to sell them, for fear of (de peur de) losing their jobs, should the company fall under new management.

Takeovers are financed in several ways. First, the raider can offer the shareholders of the target company cash for their shares. Secondly, he can offer to swap (échanger) the shares of his company for those of the target company. This is known as a **SHARE EXCHANGE OFFER** (OPE ou offre publique d'échange), referred to also as a **PAPER OFFER**. He can, of course, make an offer which combines cash and shares. Thirdly, he can raise the finance for the takeover by borrowing heavily (financement à fort degré d'endettement). Where a company is taken over by a raider using this method it is known as a leveraged buyout or LBO (rachat de l'entreprise avec effet de levier, par recours à l'endettement). Takeovers, especially LBOs, were very numerous in the USA in the 1980s, spreading to the UK, and to a lesser extent to continental Europe. In the USA part of the borrowed money has frequently been raised by the issue of junk bonds (obligation de pacotille) and in Europe more by mezzanine finance (financement mezzanine).

☞ See ANNUAL GENERAL MEETING; ARTICLES OF ASSOCIATION and ARTICLES OF MEMORANDUM under AUTHORIZED/REGISTERED ETC. CAPITAL; BOARD OF DIRECTORS; BROKER/DEALER; EMPLOYEE SHARE/(US) STOCK OWNERSHIP PLAN; LEVERAGED BUYOUT, under which also JUNK BOND and MEZZANINE FINANCE; MERCHANT BANK; MARKET MAKER; MONOPOLIES AND MERGERS COMMISSION; OFFER FOR SALE; PANEL ON TAKEOVERS AND MERGERS; RAIDER/CORPORATE RAIDER; RIGHTS ISSUE; SCRIP/BONUS ETC. ISSUE; SECURITIES AND EXCHANGE COMMISSION; SHARE.

TAKER See .... OPTION.

TALISMAN acronym for **TRANSFER ACCOUNTING LODGING FOR INVESTORS AND STOCK MANAGEMENT FOR JOBBERS** (système central informatisé d'enregistrement et de règlement des transactions en titres de sociétés)

This is a computerised system for settling accounts on UK company share transactions on the International Stock Exchange (London), created in 1979. The system registers the shares, allocates them to buyers and registers the new owners. It was due to be superseded (supplanter) by the TAURUS system, which was designed to reduce the circulation of share certificates every time shares changed hands. However, due to practical and technical difficulties the TAURUS system has now been abandoned.

☞ See INTERNATIONAL STOCK EXCHANGE; SAEF; SHARE CERTIFICATE; TAURUS; TOPIC.

TARIFF (droit de douane, tarif douanier)

As regards (en ce qui concerne) international trade, a tariff or **IMPORT TARIFF** is a customs duty (droit de douane) levied (percevoir) upon goods (marchandise) transported from one customs area (zone douanière) to another. Import tariffs can be simply **PROTECTIVE TARIFFS** (droit protecteur) or intended to (destiner à) to bring in revenue – **REVENUE TARIFFS** (droit rémunérateur). The GATT tries to reduce the latter (ceux-ci) more particularly as they are barriers to trade.

☞ See CUSTOMS DUTY; TARIFF QUOTA.

TARIFF QUOTA (contingent tarifaire)

Application of a reduced rate (tarif, taux), or zero duty (franchise, exemption), for a specified quantity of imported goods (marchandise) or for commodities (marchandise, denrée, produit) imported during a given period.

☞ See SPECIFIC LIMITATIONS ON TRADE; TARIFF.

TAURUS acronym for **TRANSFER AND AUTOMATED REGISTRATION OF UNCERTIFIED STOCK** (système informatisé d'enregistrement et de règlement des transactions en titres de sociétés)

This was intended to be a further development of the Stock Exchange's TALISMAN system, which automatically records share transactions and reduces the need for accounting and the material transfer of share certificates (circulation matérielle de titres). TAURUS was recently abandoned by the Stock Exchange, due to technical and practical problems.

☞ See INTERNATIONAL STOCK EXCHANGE; TALISMAN: TOPIC; SAEF.

TAX (impôt)

A sum of money extracted (prélevé) by the government from individuals (personne physique) and organizations and levied (imposé) upon goods (biens), wealth (richesse), income (revenu) or prices as a means of financing its expenditure (afin de financer ses dépenses). Taxes may also be used by a government to encourage or discourage certain forms of behaviour or expenditure such as saving, purchasing homes, etc..

DIRECT TAXES (impôts directs) are those levied directly on the wealth or income of individuals or organizations, who then pay them directly to the tax authorities. Examples of these are: **INCOME TAX** (impôt sur le revenu), which is a tax on wages, salaries and investment income (revenus des capitaux mobiliers); in Britain the tax on earnings (as well as various social charges) is taken out of the wages or salaries of employed people by the employee through the **PAY-AS-YOU-EARN** (abbr. P.A.Y.E.) system (système de prélèvement liberatoire ou de retenue à la source de l'impôt sur le revenu et des cotisations diverses), while there is a separate system for the self-employed (travailleur indépendant), which taxes profits (bénéfices) made at the end of the year; if income tax is very high individuals with large incomes will be very motivated to seek a **TAX HAVEN** (paradis fiscal), such as the Bahamas, Guernsey, and Jersey, where the **TAX RATE** (taux d'imposition) is much lower, or may even prefer to live in another country for the same reason; **SOCIAL SECURITY CONTRIBUTIONS/TAXES (US) PAYROLL TAXES** (charges ou cotisations sociales), which are taxes paid by employers, employees and individuals to cover government expenditure on unemployment benefits (indemnité de chômage), retirement pensions (pension de retraite), sickness (allocation/prestation maladie) and other benefits in what is known usually in the U.K. as **NATIONAL INSURANCE** (Sécurité Sociale), a state insurance scheme; the **POLL TAX** (capitation), which was introduced by the British prime minister Mrs. Margaret Thatcher in the late 1980s, replaced rates (impôts locaux), – see below –, taxed every individual above a certain age in the country, regardless of income, and was extremely unpopular, large numbers of citizens refusing to pay it, has now been abolished; **CAPITAL GAINS TAX** (impôt sur les plus-values), which is raised on the profits made from selling certain assets (actif) such as a building or securities (valeurs mobilières) for more than they cost, thus making a profit; **CORPORATION TAX** (impôt sur les sociétés), which taxes the profits made by businesses; and **INHERITANCE TAXES** (droits de succession), which in the UK prior to 1986 have been known at different times as **DEATH/ESTATE DUTIES** and **CAPITAL TRANSFER TAX**, abbr. CCT (droits de mutation), and which tax inherited wealth.

Income taxes can generally be classified into four types. First, **NEGATIVE (INCOME) TAX** (impôt négatif) is a term used to describe in general subsidies given by the government to families with very low incomes. This is intended to guarantee them a minimum income which replaces various forms of social assistance. Secondly, a **PROGRESSIVE (INCOME) TAX** (impôt progressif) is one in which the proportion of income taxable (imposable) increases with the amount of income earned. In other words, the more a person earns the greater will be the percentage of his income he will have to pay in taxes; for example, a person may not have to pay any taxes on the first £5,000 of his salary; then if he earns not £5,000 but £7,000 he may have to pay 10% on the additional £2,000 in taxes (£7,000 – £5,000), or £200; if he should earn £8,000 he may, in addition to the tax on the £2,000 above £5,000 he has already had to pay, have to pay 15% on the additional £1,000 he has earned above £7,000, and so on. Thirdly, a **PROPORTIONAL (INCOME) TAX** (impôt proportionnel) is one based on the proportion of a person's income, and this always remains the same, regardless of how much the person earns. For example, if the tax rate (taux d'imposition) is fixed at 15%, then 15% of the salary of the managing director and the worker alike is deducted. That is, they both pay the same proportion in tax. Fourthly, a **REGRESSIVE (INCOME) TAX** (impôt régressif) is one where the proportion of income taxable (imposable), in contrast to a progressive tax, diminishes as the income increases. In other words, the more a person earns the lower the percentage he pays in tax; for example, on the first £2,000 above £5,000 he might pay 15%, then on the next £1,000 only 10% and so on.

INDIRECT TAXES (impôts indirects) are taxes on expenditure (dépense) on goods and services Examples are: in the **UK RATES** (impôts locaux), levied on property according to its size, area (superficie) and other criteria; **AD VALOREM** (ad valorem ou proportionnel ou sur la valeur) **TAXES** such as **VALUE ADDED TAX** (abbr. VAT) (taxe à la valeur ajoutée), which is a fixed percentage of the price payable at purchase by the buyer; and **UNIT** or **(US) SALES TAX** (taxe à l'achat), payable on each unit of a product sold, regardless of how much it is sold for; for example, the tax on a bottle of wine costing £ 2 and one costing £ 12, if they are taxed by a unit tax, will be the same.

☞ See FISCAL POLICY; INFLATION; FULL EMPLOYMENT BUDGET BALANCE.

TAX HAVEN See .... TAX.

TAX RATE See .... TAX.

TECHNOLOGICAL UNEMPLOYMENT See .... UNEMPLOYMENT.

TENDER OFFERS See .... OFFER FOR SALE.

TERM ASSURANCE See .... LIFE INSURANCE.

THE SECURITIES ASSOCIATION, abbr. **TSA** See .... SELF-REGULATING ORGANIZATIONS.

THINK TANK (groupe de réflexion)

A group of people of varying expertise (compétences diverses) and backgrounds (origine) assembled to advise (conseiller) governments and other bodies (organisme). A **GOVERNMENT THINK TANK**, for example, may include (comprendre) selected members of various government departments (ministère), businessmen and academics (universitaire) to advise the government on taxation policy (politique fiscale), privatisation or other policy matters (questions d'orientations politiques).

THIRD MARKET (troisième marché, marché hors-cote spécial)

The official market on the International Stock Exchange (London) set up in 1987 for companies wishing to raise capital, but too small for a listing on the Unlisted Securities Market (USM). Such companies may even have no trading record or may just be an idea (à l'état de projet). The Third Market also deals in certain stocks traded off market (hors marché). In the USA this refers to the market in which dealers and clients trade privately in listed securities, by-passing (contourner) the national stock exchanges. One of the major problems with this kind of market is liquidity – it is not always easy to sell shares, and this is discouraging for investors.

☞ See FOURTH MARKET; INTERNATIONAL STOCK EXCHANGE; LIQUIDITY; LISTING; OVER-THE-COUNTER MARKET; PLACING; UNLISTED SECURITIES; UNLISTED SECURITIES MARKET.

THIRD PARTY MOTOR INSURANCE See .... ACCIDENT INSURANCE.

THRIFTS or **THRIFT INSTITUTIONS, USA** (organismes/caisses d'épargne logement)

A popular term from the word "thrifty" (économe) for savings and loan associations (S & Ls), savings banks (mutual savings banks and stock savings banks) and credit unions.

☞ See CREDIT UNION; MUTUAL SAVINGS BANK; SAVINGS & LOAN ASSOCIATION; SAVINGS BANK; STOCK SAVINGS BANK.

TIED LOAN (prêt lié)

A loan made by (accorder) a government agency (organisme officiel) requiring (exiger de) the foreign borrower (emprunteur) to spend the proceeds (montant, produit) in the lender's country (pays du prêteur, du bailleur de fonds). Other conditions may be attached to the loan, to favour (favoriser) the lender, such as preference for other imports from the lending country as opposed to from other countries.

☞ See COUNTERTRADE.

TIED See .... FINANCIAL SERVICES ACT, 1986.

TIGERS See .... DRAGONS.

TIME ACCOUNT See .... DEPOSIT ACCOUNT.

TOKYO ROUND See .... GATT.

TOKYO STOCK EXCHANGE See .... STOCK MARKET/EXCHANGE.

TOPIC - Acronym For Teletext Output Of Price Information By Computer System (système télévisé et informatisé de cours de titres)

The London International Stock Exchange's system of screens (écran ou moniteur), of which there are more than 10,000 in Eire, the UK and USA and which gives up-to-date information on the latest UK buying and selling share prices (cotes d'achat et de vente) offered by market makers (contrepartistes). This information is supplied (fournir) by SEAQ – the Stock Exchange Automated Quotations system (système de cotations automatisé) –, which obliges market makers to enter into the Stock Exchange computer system this information, as well as any deals (transactions) they make within five minutes of being made (dans les cinq minutes qui suivent). This information appears on the TOPIC screens and enables broker/dealers (négociant/courtier en titres) and large investors to telephone the market makers directly with their orders or instructions, thus eliminating the need for broker/dealers to go to the Stock Exchange.

☞ See INTERNATIONAL STOCK EXCHANGE; PROGRAMME TRADING; SAEF; SEAQ; TALISMAN; TAURUS.

TOUCH or **SPREAD** (écart ou marge)

This is the difference between the best buy and sell prices of a security, and represents the profit or loss to be made or actually made on a transaction.

☞ See BARGAIN.

TRADE BALANCE See .... BALANCE OF PAYMENTS.

TRADE CYCLE (cycle économique)

This is a period of economic activity lasting several years which repeats itself regularly and which contains high levels of prosperity, confidence by investors and other economic agents, increasing employment, etc. such as in a boom (période de prospérité ou de haute conjoncture), followed by a slowdown (ralentissement), contraction, recession and slump (crise) or depression. In the latter case economic activity and levels of employment decline sharply and stagnate. This is then followed eventually by a recovery (reprise ou redressement), when business confidence returns, investment picks up again (repartir ou redémarrer) and the economy and employment expand to lead once again into a boom period.

☞ See BLACK TUESDAY; BOOM; DEPRESSION; FISCAL POLICY; INFLATION; MONETARY POLICY; RECESSION; UNEMPLOYMENT.

TRADED OPTIONS See .... OPTION.

TRAINING SCHEMES See .... UNEMPLOYMENT.

TRANSIT TRADE See .... TRANSIT ZONE.

TRANSIT ZONE (zone de transit) sometimes a synonym for **ENTREPÔT TRADE OR TRANSIT TRADE** (commerce transitaire ou de transit) which takes place in a transit zone.

The area surrounding a port of entry (port d'entrée) in a coastal (à façade maritime) country, serving as a storage (stockage) and distribution center for a neighbouring country, for example a land-locked (enclavé) one. Goods (marchandise) in transit to and from the neighbouring country are not subject to (assujettir à) the customs duties (droit de douane), import controls or many of the entry (entrée) and exit (sortie) formalities of the host country (pays hôte). A transit zone has a more limited facility (infrastructure) than a free zone (zone franche). Such zones exist in Africa and in the Persian Gulf (Golfe persique).

☞ See CUSTOMS AND ADMINISTRATIVE ENTRY PROCEDURES; ENTREPÔT TRADE; FREE ZONE; RE-EXPORTATION.

TRANSPARENCY (transparence)

The visibility and clarity (clarté) of laws (loi) and regulations (réglementation). This is one of the fundamental principles of the GATT.

☞ See GATT.

TRANSPLANT (délocalisation, unité de production délocalisée)

A delocalized, often Japanese, factory making, for example, cars in the country, more particularly the USA and Great Britain, where they are to be sold, thus (ainsi) avoiding (éviter) tariff (tarif douanier) or quota (contingent, quota) barriers. Countries receiving transplants insist on a percentage of local content to ensure additional benefits. More generally, the term refers to any foreign company's factory set up (implanter, installer) in a country to escape trade barriers, and take advantage of (profiter de) lower labour costs (coût de la main-d'oeuvre) and cheaper access to markets.

☞ See COUNTERTRADE; LOCAL CONTENT; OFFSET REQUIREMENTS.

TRAVELLER'S CHEQUES, US **TRAVELER'S CHECKS** (chèque-voyage ou chèque de voyage)

Cheques bought in advance by people about to travel, usually abroad (à l'étranger). The cheques are guaranteed payment by the bank or organization issuing them, the most well-known of these being American Express. They are acceptable as payment almost anywhere in the world, by banks, shops, hotels, etc. To be cashed they require the second signature of the holder (porteur) in front of the person agreeing to accept the cheques as payment. This provides security for both the holder (no one else can use the cheques if they are stolen) and the payee (bénéficiaire), who is reasonably assured the cheques do belong to the person who is signing them in front of him. In addition, if the cheques should be lost or stolen, the company issuing them usually guarantees to refund (rembourser) them.

☞ See CHEQUE.

TREASURY BILL (billet/bon du trésor à court terme)

A short-term money market instrument issued (émis) mainly by UK and US central banks to finance shortfalls (déficits) in government income or as a means of influencing credit and the money supply (masse montaire). Treasury bills are always bought and sold at a discount (avec escompte).

In the UK they are issued in denominations (coupure) of £5,000, have a maturity (échéance) of 91 days, and are guaranteed to be entirely bought by the discount houses (banque d'escompte), but can also be bought by banks and brokers (agents de change).

In the USA they are more widely held. In the USA treasury bills have maturities of three, six or twelve months (bon du trésor en comptes courants) and are usually issued in minimum denominations of $10,000, while for longer terms the US government issues treasury notes (bon du trésor à court ou moyen terme) and bonds (bon du trésor à long terme).

☞ See BROKER; CENTRAL BANK; DISCOUNT; DISCOUNT HOUSE; GILT-EDGED STOCKS; MONEY MARKET; MONEY SUPPLY; PUBLIC SPENDING; TREASURY BOND; TREASURY NOTE.

TREASURY BOND, USA (bon du trésor à long terme)

A long-term security (titre) issued (émettre) for the American government by the Federal Reserve (the FED) in denominations (coupure) of $1,000 or more and which has a maturity (échéance) of more than ten years.

Other countries like France issue equivalent borrowing instruments, but not the UK.

☞ See CENTRAL BANK; FEDERAL RESERVE; TREASURY BILL; TREASURY NOTE..

TREASURY NOTE, USA (bon du trésor à court ou moyen terme)

An intermediate security (titre) – i.e. between short-term and long-term – issued (émettre) by the US government with a maturity (échéance) of from one to ten years, usually in denominations (coupure) of $1,000.

☞ See CENTRAL BANK; FEDERAL RESERVE; TREASURY BILL; TREASURY BOND.

TREATY OF PARIS See .... EUROPEAN COAL AND STEEL COMMUNITY.

TREATY OF ROME (Traité de Rome)

Was signed on March 25, 1957 by representatives (représentant) of Belgium, France, West Germany, Italy, Luxembourg and The Netherlands. It established (créer) the European Economic Community/EEC.

On the same day, a separate treaty was signed in Rome by the same signatories (signataire). It established the European Atomic Energy Community/EURATOM), to develop nuclear fuel and power for civilian purposes (à des fins civiles).

Hence (d'où) the occasional use of the phrase (expression, formule) "the two Treaties of Rome". Both (les deux) treaties came into effect (entrer en vigueur) at the same date, on January 1, 1958, after ratification by the six national parliaments.

☞ See EUROPEAN COMMUNITY; MAASTRICHT.

TRIGGER POINT See .... TAKEOVER BID.

TRIPLE A RATING See .... CREDIT RATING AGENCY.

TSA, abbr. **for THE SECURITIES ASSOCIATION** See .... SELF-REGULATING ORGANIZATIONS.

U

UNCALLED CAPITAL See .... AUTHORIZED/REGISTERED ETC. CAPITAL.

UNCLEAN BILL OF LADING See .... BILL OF LADING.

UNCTAD See .... UNITED NATIONS CONFERENCE ON TRADE AND DEVELOPMENT.

UNDERWRITER, abbr. **U/W,** or **UNDERWRITING AGENT** (assureur ou souscripteur de risques ou membre d'un syndicat de garantie ou syndicataire ou garant ou preneur ferme)

In insurance, an insurance company or its representative (représentant) that accepts to insure risks and arranges (mettre au point) the terms (conditions) of the insurance contract. In marine insurance (assurance maritime), the person or firm that accepts marine contracts is known as a **MARINE UNDERWRITER** (assureur maritime). In stock markets (marché des valeurs) the underwriter guarantees to buy the remaining (restant) shares of a new issue (nouvelle émission) which have not been bought.

☞ See CAPITAL MARKET; INSURANCE; LLOYD'S; OFFER FOR SALE; RISK; SPONSOR.

UNDERWRITING AGENT See .... UNDERWRITER.

UNDERWRITERS See .... OFFER FOR SALE; SPONSOR; UNDERWRITER.

UNEMPLOYMENT (chômage)

Broadly speaking this is when more people want work than is available. More precisely, it is measured by taking the number of people able, wanting and available to and looking for work as a percentage of the total **ACTIVE POPULATION** (population active), defined as those wanting and looking for work plus all those already in work – the **ACTIVE WORKING POPULATION** (population active occupée). The **PARTICIPATION RATE** (taux d'activité) is the proportion of the population of working age who have a job or are unemployed but looking for one. This is never 100% because of such categories as students, mothers staying at home, early retirees (retraité anticipé) and others who could work but for various reasons do not.

Unemployment has become a major social and economic problem in most economies. Most governments would like, ideally, to achieve **FULL EMPLOYMENT** (plein emploi). This is generally defined as not more than about 3% unemployed and not zero, which is impossible, because there will always be some workers in the process of changing jobs, or others who cannot find work because they are too old or insufficiently qualified. This "reserve" of unemployed people is called the **UNEMPLOYMENT CUSHION** (volant de chomâge).The government objective of full employment is sometimes sacrificed to other aims such as reducing inflation In the early nineties unemployment has reached as much as over 7% percent in the USA, while in Britain and France it has been 10% or more.

It must be borne in mind that (on doit savoir que) there are actual difficulties in assessing (établir) its level accurately, while governments have an interest in showing a low as possible figure. In Europe the statistics are primarily based on those who register (s'inscrire) as unemployed to obtain unemployment and social security benefits (allocation de chômage et prestations sociales ou de sécurité sociale). In the USA the level of unemployment is measured by two monthly surveys (sondage) – the **CURRENT POPULATION SURVEY/CPS** and the **CURRENT EMPLOYMENT STATISTICS/CES.** The statistics therefore can be under-estimates (sous-estimation), referred to as **DISGUISED** or **CONCEALED UNEMPLOYMENT** (chômage caché), or over-estimates (surestimation). For example, there may be people unentitled to (n'ayant pas droit à) such benefits who do not register; people who are retired early (mis à la retraite anticipée) by their employers but who are not looking for work can register; students can register, but they do this only temporarily, as they will resume (reprendre) their studies; those who may never work again (the injured or handicapped) may be registered; those who are sick (malade) but will return to work may be registered; those who do casual work (travail temporaire) or moonlighting (travailler au noir) may be registered; people on government-created training/employment schemes (action emploi-formation) may be registered as employed, while in fact they do not have a job; finally, any change in the rules defining who can register can affect the number of unemployed.

In order to combat unemployment it is necessary to understand the causes.This leads to a classification of different types of unemployment. **CYCLICAL** or **SITUATIONAL UNEMPLOYMENT** (chômage conjoncturel) is due to a downturn (baisse) in demand in the trade cycle (cycle économique), sometimes referred to as demand deficiency (manque de demande), which results in recession or depression. J. M. Keynes, the English economist, in his classical work *The General Theory of Employment, Interest and Money* (1936) came to the conclusion that cyclical unemployment occurs because the level of spending in an economy is insufficient to absorb all the goods and services that the economy is capable of producing at full employment. As a result firms stockpile (stocker ou entasser), cut back production and lay off (licencier) workers, all of which reduces even more a society's spending power and hence (donc) demand. The Keynesian answer to cyclical unemployment, therefore, is for the government to intervene in the economy by encouraging the total level of spending to increase by enlarging government expenditure and the budget deficit. To finance this implies more government borrowing, which could lead to the **CROWDING OUT** (empêchement d'investissement ou interdiction d'accès à l'investissement) or reduction of investment funds available to other sectors of the economy (because the government has absorbed most of the funds available on the market for borrowing). Monetary policy (politique monétaire) can promote (encourager, stimuler) more spending (and hence demand) by companies and individuals through lower interest rates, which make it easier to borrow or repay existing debt, while fiscal policy (politique budgétaire ou fiscale) can inject more money into the economy through lower taxes and investment incentives (stimulant à l'investissement).

An important part of the Keynesian solution relies on the **MULTIPLIER EFFECT** (effet multiplicateur); this concept simply means that money put into the economy generates far more consumption and demand than the initial amount. This is illustrated by the following table. Say the government spends £1,000 pounds with Company A, a manufacturer of school desks:

Co. A	receives	£1,000	spends with	B	£800	and saves	£200
Co. B	,,	£800	,,,,	C	£640	,,,,	£140
Co. C	,,	£640	,,,,	D	£512	,,,,	£128
Co. D	,,	£512	,,,,	E	£410	,,,,	£102
Co. E	,,	£410	,,,,	F	£328	,,,,	£82
Co. F	,,	£328	,,,,	G	£262	,,,,	£66
Co. G	etc.	etc.					
etc.	etc.	etc.					
TOTAL		£5,000			£4,000		£1,000

In other words, each time a company makes a sale (and therefore receives income) it will spend part of this with another company to renew supplies (it could also employ more people – the effect on the economy broadly being the same –), and it will save or put aside a part of this income for future needs or debt payment (in this example we assume that companies and individuals will tend to spend 80% of their income, or, put in another way, their marginal propensity to consume (propension à consommer) is 80%). Similarly, when individuals receive more income (say through lower taxes) they will save part of it and spend the rest, creating income for other individuals or economic agents. It can be seen, therefore, that an initial investment by the government of £1,000 has generated income of £5,000, which has generated in turn an increase in spending of £4,000 and savings of £1,000. It should be borne in mind, however, that the multiplier effect takes time to work its way through (s'introduire dans) the economy. The example above shows the effects of a **positive multiplier**, but if money was withdrawn from the economic system (e.g. by taxes or a trade deficit) this would have a **negative multiplier effect** much greater than the inital amount withdrawn.

The Keynesian solution to unemployment was successfully adopted by many countries after 1945, but in the 1970s the appearance of high rates of inflation led to a switch (revirement) in the emphasis of government policy to combat this. Earlier in 1958 a British economist, A.W.H. Phillips, indicated a possible relationship between unemployment and inflation, suggesting that lower levels of the latter (ce dernier) corresponded to higher levels of the former (le premier) and vice versa. He demonstrated this with a graph, the **PHILLIPS' CURVE** (la courbe de Phillips). This relationship, however, has not been shown to hold for (être valable) all situations, especially in the 1970s. Nevertheless it presents governments with a dilemma: low inflation and high unemployment or higher inflation and lower unemployment? The question of inflation is linked to the **NATURAL RATE OF UNEMPLOYMENT** (taux naturel de chômage), a theoretical concept which is said to exist when all markets (e.g. labour, capital and goods and services) are in equilibrium (en équilibre) – that is to say, there is neither excess demand nor supply. This is equivalent to the **VOLUNTARY RATE OF UNEMPLOYMENT** (taux de chômage volontaire), so-called because those out of work are considered to have deliberately chosen not to work (for personal reasons or inadequate levels of pay). This **NATURAL RATE OF UNEMPLOYMENT** is sometimes called the **NON-ACCELERATING INFLATION RATE OF UNEMPLOYMENT**, abbr. **NAIRU** (taux de chômage qui n'accélère pas l'inflation) because economists argue à la Phillips that to reduce unemployment even further than this natural rate would result in inflation. In other words, this is virtually a situation of **FULL EMPLOYMENT**.

CLASSICAL UNEMPLOYMENT (chômage classique) is said to exist as a result of wages being too high. According to classical economists unemployment will decrease once wage earners accept a lower wage as employers follow the laws of supply and demand and will therefore be prepared to take on (embaucher) more people at a lower wage. Another factor affecting the general level of unemployment is economic growth (croissance économique). The American economist A.M. Okun in the late 1960s observed that a drop in GNP resulted in an increase in unemployment. This relationship came to be known as **OKUN'S LAW**. Economic growth has come to be seen as a major priority for governments to reduce unemployment and maintain competitiveness.

More specific forms of unemployment will require, in conjunction with general measures as described above, a particular policy. **STRUCTURAL UNEMPLOYMENT** (chômage structurel) springs from developments in the economic situation which change permanently the pattern (structure ou physionomie) of demand. For example, coal has been replaced largely by electricity and other fuels, reducing greatly the numbers employed in the coal industry. The EU's European Social Fund tackles (s'attaquer à) this problem by financing the retraining of workers (recyclage ou reconversion). **TECHNOLOGICAL UNEMPLOYMENT** (chômage technologique) results from a change in the technology used by a given industry. For example, the use of computers and robots in the automobile industry has greatly reduced the need for labour. The trend for technological unemployment is likely to increase with the further use of computer processes, integrated circuits (circuit intégré) and micro-chips (puce électronique). **REGIONAL UNEMPLOYMENT** (chômage régional) describes a situation where structural or technological unemployment are located all in the same area. Whole communities in Europe, for example, depended on coal and steel works for employment; when demand for these products greatly declined, due in part to intensive world competition and the availability (disponibilité) of alternative (de remplacement) fuels such as gas and nuclear energy, these regions faced extremely high unemployment levels. **FRICTIONAL SITUATIONAL UNEMPLOYMENT** (chômage frictionnel conjoncturel) is unemployment of a temporary nature, caused by workers leaving one job and moving into another after a small time lag (intervalle). It may be, of course, linked (lié) to any of the other types of unemployment (e.g. structural, where a worker leaves one industry to enter another). **SEASONAL UNEMPLOYMENT** (chômage saisonnier) is a kind of frictional unemployment found in activities which need extra workers only at particular times of the year (e.g. agricultural workers in summer, tourist guides at Easter and in summer for the tourist industry). The need for seasonal labour is partly supplied by school pupils and students during their holidays, but mainly by others who rely on this employment to earn a living.

Finally, growing **YOUTH UNEMPLOYMENT** (chômage des jeunes) has pushed governments to support (soutenir) or put into place various **TRAINING SCHEMES** (opération ou plan de formation) designed to give young people the education and skills necessary to find work. Apprenticeships (apprentissage), especially the German system, the Youth Training Scheme, abbreviated YTS (opération en faveur de la formation des jeunes) in the UK, Alternance Training (formation en alternance) and the Work-Employment Scheme (emploi-formation) in France and programmes resulting from the 1983 Job Training Partnership Act/JTPA (loi de partenariat emploi-formation) in the USA are only a few examples of the large number of measures in existence to reduce unemployment among the young. Training and re-training schemes have also been created, of course, for older workers faced with unemployment, and especially the long-term unemployed (chômeur de longue durée), such as the UK Restart programme, in which the long-term unemployed are re-interviewed and given more active help in finding training places and jobs. At the same time governments have created various measures to encourage people to start their own businesses. State subsidies (subvention) and tax incentives (mesures d'incitation fiscales) are also used to encourage the unemployed to accept low-paid jobs and the employers to hire hard-to-employ people.

Since President Clinton's special G7 Conference in Detroit in March, 1994 on unemployment and job-creation the international nature of the problem has become more and more recognized. For example, the more a country exports the better this is for jobs. In this way a recovery in the US but a prevailing recession in Europe is bad news for US exports to Europe and hence for US jobs. Therefore countries have an interest in promoting each other's economic welfare. The much-vaunted (mis en avant) low employment rates in the US (about 6-7%) compared with a higher European one (about 10-12%), but much higher in some individual countries like Spain (17-20% or more) hide the qualitative nature of job-creation (are new jobs real jobs or part-time jobs or "Mcjobs" – low-skilled and low-paid?) as well as differences in social security systems and protection for employees. The current debate around unemployment contrasts American labour-market flexibility (in which employees have less protection against dismissal (licenciement) and erosion of earnings, while employers are empowered to adopt and manoeuvre their labour force easily to suit their needs) with European high levels of employment costs (i. e. social charges) and job protection. Current trends in the industrialized world witness: an increase in part-timers and the self-employed; increasing competitive pressures on companies, supported by national and international policies (e.g. European Union competition policy, the GATT), resulting in companies down-sizing (compression de personnel) as much as possible and operating with a minimum labour force; and developments in computers, robotics, automation, telecommunications and other technological areas, all of which also tend to reduce the size of the work force. In addition, it has been noted that despite regular real increases in GDP in the 1970s, 1980s and early 1990s in the European Union there has not been a corresponding percentage increase in jobs growth; the same is true for the USA, but to a lesser extent. This suggests a much higher acceptable level of natural unemployment, which could only be reduced at the risk of increasing inflation. Future solutions to unemployment currently proposed include more investment in education, training (formation), re-training (recyclage, reconversion) and apprenticeship, the de-regulation or liberalization of labour markets, the lowering of labour costs (to employers) and continued reductions in the barriers to trade (essentially the work of the GATT/WTO).

☞ See AGGREGATE DEMAND; DEREGULATION; BLACK TUESDAY; DEPRESSION; EU COMPETITION POLICY; FISCAL POLICY; GENERAL AGREEMENT ON TARIFFS AND TRADE, GROSS DOMESTIC PRODUCT; INFLATION; JOB TURNOVER; MONETARY POLICY; MONEY SUPPLY; RECESSION; SEASONAL ADJUSTMENT; TRADE CYCLE.

UNEMPLOYMENT CUSHION See .... UNEMPLOYMENT.

UNFAIR TRADE PRACTICES (pratiques commerciales déloyales)

Exaggerated government support (soutien, appui) to firms like export subsidies (subvention), or unfair behaviour (attitude, comportement) of firms like dumping, boycotting and discriminatory shipping (expédition) arrangements (mesures), resulting in (avoir pour résultat) an unfair competitive advantage for a country's industry.

☞ See DUMPING; EXPORT SUBSIDIES; RESTRICTIVE BUSINESS PRACTICES.

UNISSUED CAPITAL See .... AUTHORIZED/REGISTERED ETC. CAPITAL.

UNIT TAX See .... TAX.

UNIT TRUST or **OPEN-ENDED FUND, US MUTUAL** or **MUTUAL FUND** or **MUTUAL FUNDS COMPANY** (fonds de placement ouvert ou société d'investissement à capital variable, abrégé SICAV)

This is an organization which invites people to contribute sums of money, which are then used to buy securities (titres). The securities are held in trust (tenir par fidéicommis) by a reliable (solide) financial institution (e.g. bank or insurance company) and the contributors are given units of equal value, which are a fraction of the total value of the securities bought by the trust. The work of deciding in what securities to invest is carried out by a professional investment management company (société d'investissement), which receives for this service a management fee (commission ou commission de chef de file ou frais de gestion). Subscribers (souscripteur) are given units in exchange for their money, and receive from the trust a proportion of the dividends earned from the securities held by the trust (minus management fees and other expenses), or the dividend is not paid out but incorporated in the value of the units; should they wish to sell their units the trust is always willing to buy them back, but at a slightly lower price – the **BID PRICE** (prix offert ou cours/prix acheteur) – than that at which it offers units to subscribers – the **OFFER PRICE** (prix de vente/demandé). The value of the units can go up or down depending on the success of the management company in selecting securities which hold or increase their market value. Unit trusts are called open-ended funds because there is no limit to their size, in contrast to investment trusts, and this depends on how many units the managers succeed in selling. In the UK there are over a thousand of such trusts. Unlike investment trusts, however, unit trusts are not companies, and so the units they issue (émettre) are not traded (négocier) on the stock exchange.

☞ See DIVIDEND; INVESTMENT TRUST; LIMITED or LIMITED LIABILITY COMPANY; SECURITIES; SHARE; STOCK EXCHANGE; YIELD.

UNIT-LINKED ASSURANCE See .... LIFE INSURANCE.

UNITED NATIONS CONFERENCE ON TRADE AND DEVELOPMENT, abbr. **UNCTAD** (Conférence des Nations Unies sur le commerce et le développement/CNUCED)

An agency (organisme) of the United Nations General Assembly which seeks to (chercher à) focus (concentrer) international attention on economic policies (politique) likely to (susceptible de) improve (améliorer) Third World (Tiers Monde) development. The Conference first met in Geneva in 1964 and has been regularly convened (convoquer) since (depuis). Negotiations take place between the so-called (que l'on appelle) Group B – developed countries – and the Group of 77, the original 1964 participating developing countries (pays en voie de développement) together with (ainsi que) an extra 50 nations or so (environ) that have joined (adhérer) since.

Committees (commission) work on such subjects as commodities (denrée, produit), shipping (transports maritimes), manufactures (produit manufacturé), invisibles (échanges invisibles), financing (financement) related to trade, transfer of technology, customs procedures (procédure douanière), regional economic integration etc. UNCTAD has a permanent Secretariat in Geneva.

☞ See INVISIBLE TRADE; GENERALIZED SYSTEM OF PREFERENCES; RESTRICTIVE BUSINESS PRACTICES.

UNITED STATES TRADE REPRESENTATIVE, abbr. **USTR** ("Ministre" américain du Commerce extérieur)

A special representative (représentant) of the White House (Maison Blanche) for foreign trade, with the rank of Ambassador, who negotiates on behalf of (au nom de) the USA at such meetings as the GATT Uruguay Round.

☞ See GATT; SECTION 301; STRUCTURAL IMPEDIMENTS INITIATIVE.

UNLIMITED (LIABILITY) COMPANY See.........................LIMITED or LIMITED LIABILITY COMPANY.

UNLISTED SECURITIES MARKET, abbr. **USM** (Marché hors-cote, l'équivalent du Second Marché en France)

In the UK this is a market created in 1980 for the shares of public companies (société anonyme par actions) which are not yet prepared to meet the stringent (sévère) requirements of a full listing (inscription à la cote officielle) on the Stock Exchange. The USM has been an important stepping stone (marchepied) for companies wishing to have access (avoir accès à) to the main capital markets. Similar organised and regulated lower-tier (de second rang) markets for unlisted shares (valeurs non inscrites à la cote officielle) exist in many other large, advanced countries, as well as informal (officieux) markets for dealing in unlisted shares. The requirements (condition ou exigence) for a listing (cote) on the USM in the UK are: companies must show profitable accounts (exercice bénéficiaire) for the last two years (this is a recent European Union ruling, whereas previously three years were required); they must offer (mettre à disposition) a minimum of 10% of their shares to the public; and that they must be prepared to produce certain financial information regularly. The last requirement is not so onerous as that for fully listed companies. A major problem for unlisted securities markets in general is liquidity – it may not always be easy to sell shares on (revendre), and this can be discouraging for investors. In fact, this very problem is now threatening (menacer) the USM with abolition as there are fewer and fewer market makers (teneur de marché) in small company stocks, many small firms disappeared in the recession and the number of new businesses coming to this market for capital has drastically (radicalement) fallen. So the London Stock Exchange in late 1994 proposed a replacement, referred to as the **ALTERNATIVE**

INVESTMENT MARKET, abbr. **AIM**. This will be screen-based (informatisé) and much easier and cheaper for companies to use.

☞ See FOURTH MARKET; LIQUIDITY; LISTING; INTERNATIONAL STOCK EXCHANGE; OVER-THE-COUNTER MARKET; PLACING; THIRD MARKET; UNLISTED SECURITIES.

UNLISTED/UNQUOTED SECURITIES/SHARES (valeurs non cotées/non inscrites à la cote) Securities (titres) or shares which are not officially listed on the stock exchange, and therefore their prices not officially quoted. There are several markets for such securities.

☞ See FOURTH MARKET; INTERNATIONAL STOCK EXCHANGE; OVER-THE-COUNTER MARKET; PLACING;THIRD MARKET; UNLISTED SECURITIES MARKET.

UNLISTED/UNQUOTED SHARES See .... UNLISTED/UNQUOTED SECURITIES.

UNQUOTED SECURITIES See .... UNLISTED/UNQUOTED SECURITIES.

UNQUOTED SHARES See .... UNLISTED/UNQUOTED SECURITIES.

USECURED CREDITOR See .... LIQUIDATION.

UNSECURED STOCK See .... DEBENTURE.

URUGUAY ROUND See .... GATT.

USANCE BILL See .... AFTER SIGHT; BILL OF EXCHANGE; DRAFT BILL.

USM See .... UNLISTED SECURITIES MARKET.

USTR See .... UNITED STATES TRADE REPRESENTATIVE.

UTMOST GOOD FAITH See .... PRINCIPLES OF INSURANCE.

U/W See .... UNDERWRITER

V

VALUE ADDED TAX (abbrev. VAT) See .... TAX.

VALUE ADDED TAX, abbr. **VAT** (Taxe à la valeur ajoutée/TVA)

An indirect tax on consumption (consommation) levied (percevoir) at each point in the chain of production and distribution. Each processor (intervenant dans la transformation), merchant (commerçant) or user (utilisateur) thus (ainsi) pays a tax proportional to the amount (montant) by which he increases (augmenter) the value of the goods (marchandise) he purchases (acheter) for resale (revente) after making his own contribution. Only the last buyer cannot possibly recover (récupérer) the accumulated added cost from anybody (auprès de qui que ce soit). VAT is imposed throughout (à travers) EU and EFTA countries. Brussels (Bruxelles) EU authorities have had to harmonize rates (taux) in view of (dans la perspective de) the European Internal Market.

☞ See BORDER TAX ADJUSTMENTS; EUROPEAN UNION; EFTA; EUROPEAN INTERNAL MARKET; SALES TAX; TAX.

VAT See .... under TAX, VALUE ADDED TAX.

VENTURE CAPITAL See .... RISK/VENTURE CAPITAL.

VERs See........... VOLUNTARY EXPORT RESTRAINTS under VOLUNTARY RESTRAINT AGREEMENTS.

VISIBLE TRADE or **VISIBLES** (échanges visibles)

Trade in merchandise (marchandises) or physical, tangible (corporel/tangible) goods (biens), as opposed to services and invisibles in general.

☞ See BALANCE OF PAYMENTS; INVISIBLE TRADE.

VOLUNTARY EXPORT RESTRAINTS See............................. VOLUNTARY RESTRAINT AGREEMENTS.

VOLUNTARY RATE OF UNEMPLOYMENT See.. UNEMPLOYMENT.

VOLUNTARY RESTRAINT AGREEMENTS, abbr. **VRAs** (accords d'auto-limitation)

Informal (officieux), protectionist arrangements (entente) through which exporters voluntarily restrain certain exports, generally by means of (au moyen de) export quotas (contingent d'exportation), to avoid (éviter) economic disruption (perturbations) in certain importing countries, and to avert (éviter) the possible (éventuel) imposition of formal (officiel) import restrictions. These export arrangements are known as **VOLUNTARY EXPORT RESTRAINTS/VERs.** They can, in exchange, guarantee the exporter a fixed market share (part de marché) and hence (en conséquence), if his goods are in demand, a higher price. Thus (ainsi), the home manufacturer (producteur national) is protected, but the consumer loses out (être perdant) because there is less competition and higher prices. The USA, the European Union and Japan – as well as other advanced countries – are the biggest users (utilisateur) of VERs and VRAs, especially against developing countries (pays en voie de développement). Such arrangements are a way of by-passing (contourner) the GATT. They are also a form of blackmail (chantage). Those who refuse to voluntarily limit their exports may be threatened (menacer) with retaliation (représailles), like, for example, the European Union and Japan against which the USA uses Section 301.

☞ See COMPENSATION; EXPORT QUOTAS; GATT; ORDERLY MARKETING AGREEMENTS; SECTION 301.

VOTING RIGHTS See .... ANNUAL GENERAL MEETING; "A' SHARES; BOARD OF DIRECTORS.

VRAs See .... VOLUNTARY RESTRAINT AGREEMENTS.

W

W.P.A. See .... WITH PARTICULAR AVERAGE under MARINE INSURANCE.

WAIVER (abandon, désistement, renonciation, dérogation)
A formal (officiel) exemption of a right (droit) or claim (prétention).

WALL STREET See ....STOCKMARKET/EXCHANGE.

WAREHOUSING See .... TAKEOVER BID.

WARRANT or **SHARE WARRANT** (warrant ou bon de souscription)
This is a legal document issued (émis) by a company to shareholders giving them the right to buy from or sell to the former (le premier) a given number of new shares or bonds (obligation) at a given price from (à partir de) a given date. The name of the owner of the warrant is not given and the warrant itself is a negotiable instrument (effet de commerce). The warrant comes attached to the issue of new shares, but more often it is detached (détaché) and in this form is traded (négocier) on the stockmarket. This is because it gives the holder (détenteur) the right to buy or sell at a given price, and this right may be exercised to advantage, for example, when the market price for these shares or bonds is higher than the warrant price. Warrants are offered free (gratuitement) to subscribers (souscripteur) of new shares or bonds in order to give them a bonus and to create a new source of capital (fonds propres).

☞ See BOND; CAPITAL; RIGHTS ISSUE; SHARE.

WELFARE (bien-être)
Economic well-being (bien-être). Classical economists hold (soutenir, prétendre) that advance in the general welfare of a country is the main objective of economic and trade policy. The term was coined (créer, inventer) by a British economist, Arthur Cecil PIGOU (1877-1959) who in his book *The Economics of Welfare*, 1920, insisted that (soutenir la thèse que) the costs of production should (devoir) include social costs.

☞ See COMPARATIVE ADVANTAGE.

WESTERN EUROPEAN UNION See .... MAASTRICHT.

WEU See .... WESTERN EUROPEAN UNION under MAASTRICHT.

WHITE KNIGHT See .... TAKEOVER BID.

WHOLE LIFE ASSURANCE See .... LIFE INSURANCE.

WINDING-UP See .... LIQUIDATION.

WITH PARTICULAR AVERAGE See .... MARINE INSURANCE.

WITH PROFITS ASSURANCE See .... LIFE INSURANCE.

WITHOUT PROFITS ASSURANCE See .... LIFE INSURANCE.

WORLD BANK See .... INTERNATIONAL BANK FOR RECONSTRUCTION AND DEVELOPMENT.

WORLD TRADE ORGANISATION See .... GENERAL AGREEMENT ON TARIFFS AND TRADE.

WRITER See .... OPTION.

WTO See .... GENERAL AGREEMENT ON TARIFFS AND TRADE.

X

X. CP. See .... DIVIDEND.

X.A. See .... DIVIDEND.

X.D. See .... DIVIDEND.

X.D. See .... DIVIDEND.

Y

YIELD (rendement)

The return on money invested in a security (titre). There are various ways of defining and calculating this to take into account the price paid, the current or market value, nominal value (valeur nominale), dividends or interest received and the length of time the security is held. **INCOME** or **DIVIDEND YIELD** on an investment (rendement en intérêts), for example, is calculated by multiplying the annual **GROSS** (brut) **DIVIDEND** or **INTEREST** (i.e. before tax is paid) by 100 and dividing the result by the market price. So, if the gross dividend on a security is £2 and it cost £8, the yield is (2 x 100) ÷ 8 = 25%. If, in addition, after a year the security which originally cost £8 is now worth £10 (i.e. there has been an increase in value of £2, and therefore a **CAPITAL GAIN** (gain en capital) the overall return will be £2 of interest + £2 of capital gain, or £4; The overall yield on the original investment of £8 over one year will then be: [(2 + 2) ÷ 8] x 100 = (0.5 x 100) = 50%. This overall yield with regard to fixed interest securities (valeur à interêt fixe) and stocks, which have to be repaid, is called the **REDEMPTION YIELD** (rendement actuariel brut).

As regards shares, it must be remembered that companies rarely distribute all their profits in dividends – some of these are retained as reserves (provisions) for future possible needs (e.g. a fall in profits, restructuring costs) or for re-investment purposes. Nevertheless (néanmoins), the total profits made by a company reflect its performance, increased wealth and future potential, and so influence the value placed on its shares by investors. The **PRICE-EARNING(S)** or **P/E RATIO**, abbr. **PER** or **P/E** (coefficient de capitalisation des résultats, abrégé CCR ou rapport cours-bénéfice) takes these factors into account. It is calculated by dividing the price of the share at any given moment by the **EARNINGS PER SHARE** (bénéfice par action), which is the after-tax profits of the company (bénéfice net déclaré par la société) divided by the number of shares issued (émises). For example, if a company had issue 10,000 shares and its post-tax profits were £100,000, this would give an earnings per share of £10 (100,000 ÷ 10,000). If the price of the shares on the stock market at the time of the calculation was £30, then the PER would be 3 (£30 ÷ 10). The higher the PER the greater investors estimate the future earning power (capacité bénéficiaire) of the company to be.

☞ See BOND; COUPON; DEBENTURE; GILT-EDGED STOCKS; INTEREST.

YOUNG URBAN PROFESSIONAL, abbr. **YUPPIE** ("yuppie", jeune loup, jeune cadre dynamique)

US young, dynamic executives (cadre).

YOUTH UNEMPLOYMENT See .... UNEMPLOYMENT.

YUPPIE See .... YOUNG URBAN PROFESSIONAL.

Z

ZERO COUPON BOND See .... BOND.

GLOSSAIRE FRANÇAIS-ANGLAIS

À BUT NON LUCRATIF : non-profit making.
À CAUSE DE : on the ground(s) of or that.
À COURT TERME : short term.
À DÉCOUVERT : in a short position (stock market); overdrawn (bank account).
À DOUBLE TITRE : in a dual capacity (London Stock Exchange).
À L'ÉPOQUE : at the time.
À L'ÉTRANGER : overseas.
À LA PARITÉ : at par.
À LONG TERME : long term; long run.
À MOINS QUE : unless.
À MOYEN TERME : medium term.
À PERTE : at a discount.
À PRIX FIXE : fixed price.
À RECOUVRER : outstanding.
À TEMPS PARTIEL : part-time.
À TRAVERS : throughout.
À UN SEUL TITRE : in a single capacity (London Stock Exchange).
À UN TAUX D'INTÉRÊT FIXE : at a fixed rate of interest.
À VUE : at sight.
ABAISSER : to lower.
ABANDON : waiver.
ABATTEMENT FISCAL : tax break or relief.
ABROGER : to abrogate; to repeal; to rescind; to withdraw.
ACCÉLÉRER : to speed up.
ACCEPTATION : acceptance; bank or banker's acceptance.
ACCEPTATION D'EFFETS : acceptance; trade acceptance.
ACCEPTEUR : acceptor; drawee.
ACCIDENT : accident; injury.
ACCOMPLIR : to achieve; to complete.
ACCOMPLISSEMENT : achievement; completion.
ACCORD GÉNÉRAL SUR LE COMMERCE DES SERVICES : General Agreement on Trade in Services/GATs.
ACCORD GENÉRAL SUR LES TARIFS DOUANIERS ET LE COMMERCE : General Agreement on Tariffs and Trade/GATT.
ACCORD INTERNATIONAL SUR LES CRÉDITS À L'EXPORTATION : International Arrangement on Export Credits.
ACCORD INTERNATIONAL SUR LES MATIÈRES PREMIÈRES/AIMP : International Commodity Agreement/ICA.
ACCORD MULTIFIBRES/AMF : Multi-(GB) Fibre (US) Fiber Arrangement regarding international trade in textiles/MFA.
ACCORD : agreement; arrangement; deal; understanding (PARVENIR À UN... : to reach a or an...).
ACCORD CADRE : framework agreement or deal.
ACCORD COMMERCIAL : trade agreement.
ACCORD DE CLEARING OU DE COMPENSATION : clearing agreement.
ACCORD SWITCH : switch arrangement.
ACCORDER : to grant; to yield.
ACCORDS D'AUTOLIMITATION : voluntary restraint agreements/VRAs.
ACCORDS DE COMMERCIALISATION RÉGULIÈRE : Orderly Marketing Agreements/OMAs.
ACCORDS DE TROC : barter/contra or switch-trading.
ACCUSATION : allegation; charge.
ACCUSER RÉCEPTION : to acknowledge receipt.
ACHAT À TERME : buying in/for the account; buying forward or forward buying.
ACHAT ET VENTE EN GROS : wholesale buying and selling.
ACHAT : purchase.

ACOMPTE : advance; down payment.

ACOMPTE SUR DIVIDENDE : interim dividend.

ACQUÉRIR TOUTE LES ACTIONS D'UNE ENTREPRISE AFIN DE LA RETIRER DE LA BOURSE : to go private; to take a company private.

ACQUITTÉ(E) : receipted (bill; invoice).

ACTE : instrument (official document).

ACTE CONSTITUTIF D'UNE SOCIÉTÉ : Memorandum of Association.

ACTE UNIQUE EUROPÉEN : Single European Act/SEA.

ACTIF : assets.

ACTIF LIQUIDE : liquid assets.

ACTIF NET D'UNE SOCIÉTÉ : equity capital.

ACTION CONCERTÉE : concert party.

ACTIONS EMPLOI-FORMATION : government-created training/employment schemes.

ACTION ORDINAIRE : ordinary share.

ACTIONNAIRE : shareholder; stockholder.

ACTIONNARIAT DU PERSONNEL : Employee Share/(US) Stock Ownership Plan/ESOP.

ACTIONS : shares; (US) stock.

ACTIONS À DIVIDENDE FIXE : non-participating shares.

ACTIONS À VOTE MULTIPLE OU PLURAL : multiple voting shares.

ACTIONS ANCIENNES : old shares.

ACTIONS COTÉES : quoted; listed shares.

ACTIONS DIFFÉRÉES : deferred shares or ordinary deferred shares.

ACTIONS ENTIÈREMENT LIBÉRÉES : paid up/ fully-paid capital; (US) paid in/contributed capital.

ACTIONS ÉTRANGÈRES : international equities.

ACTIONS GRATUITES : scrip/bonus/capitalization issue; (US) stock/dividend split.

ACTIONS NON COMPLÈTEMENT LIBÉRÉES : partly paid share.

ACTIONS NON ENCORE ÉMISE/À LA SOUCHE : unissued capital.

ACTIONS NON PARTICIPANTES OU SANS DROIT DE PARTICIPATION : non-participating shares.

ACTIONS NOUVELLES (QUI VIENNENT D'ÊTRE ÉMISES) : new, newly issued shares.

ACTIONS ORDINAIRES AVEC DROIT DE VOTE : "B" shares.

ACTIONS PRIORITAIRES À DIVIDENDE NON CUMULATIF/NON CUMULATIVES : non-cumulative preference shares.

ACTIONS PRIORITAIRES CONVERTIBLES : convertible preference shares or convertibles; (US) convertible preferred stock.

ACTIONS PRIORITAIRES IRRACHETABLES OU IRREMBOURSABLES : irredeemable preference shares.

ACTIONS PRIORITAIRES NON PARTICIPANTES À DIVIDENDE CUMULATIF OU CUMULATIVES SANS DROIT DE PARTICIPATION : non-participating cumulative preference shares.

ACTIONS PRIORITAIRES NON PARTICIPANTES OU SANS DROIT DE PARTICIPATION : non-participating preference shares.

ACTIONS PRIORITAIRES PARTICIPANTES OU AVEC DROIT DE PARTICIPATION AUX BÉNÉFICES : participating preference shares.

ACTIONS PRIORITAIRES OU PRIVILÉGIÉES, OU DE PRIORITÉ OU À DIVIDENDE PRIORITAIRE : preference or preferred shares; (US) preferred stock.

ACTIONS PRIORITAIRES RACHETABLES/REMBOURSABLES : redeemable preference shares.

ACTIONS PRIVILIGIÉES CONVERTIBLES : convertible preference shares or convertibles; (US) convertible preferred stock.

ACTIONS PRIVILIGIÉES CUMULATIVES AVEC PARTICIPATION AUX BÉNÉFICES OU PARTICIPANTES À DIVIDENDE CUMULATIF : participating cumulative preference shares.

ACTIONS PRIVILIGIÉES/PRIORITAIRES À DIVIDENDE CUMULATIF/CUMULATIVES : cumulative preference/preferred shares.

ACTIONS SANS DROITE DE VOTE : non-voting shares.

ACTIONS SOUSCRITES : issued/subscribed capital.

ACTUAIRE : actuary.

ACTUALISER : to revise, to update, to convert to current value (accountancy).

ACTUEL : current.

ADAPTATION : adjustment.

ADAPTER(S') : to adapt; to adjust.

ADÉQUAT : adequate; proper; revelant.

ADHÉRER : to join.

ADHÉSION À : adherence to; membership of.

ADMINISTRATEUR : director; non-executive director.

ADMINISTRATEUR JUDICIAIRE : receiver.

ADVERSAIRE : disputant; opponent.

AFFACTURAGE : factoring or factorizing.

AFFAIRE : bargain (transaction); business (firm); case (legal matters); contract; deal (both used for transaction: like bargain).

AFFAIRES BANCAIRES : banking.

AFFAIRES INTÉRIEURES : domestic or home affairs.

AFFLUX DE CAPITAUX : inflows of capital.

AFFLUX : flood; spate.

AFFRONTER : to tackle.

AFIN DE : in order to; so as to; so that.

AFIN DE FINANCER SES DÉPENSES : as a means of financing its expenditure.

AGENCE : branch (of a bank).

AGENT À LA COMMISSION QUI RECOUVRE LES CRÉANCES DES ENTREPRISES : factor or factoring company.

AGENT DE CHANGE : broker.

AGENT DUCROIRE : del credere agent.

AGENT TRANSITAIRE : shipping and forwarding agent.

AGIOTAGE : price-rigging.

AGIR DE CONCERT : to act in concert.

AGRÉE : accredited; licensed.

AGRÉGAT : aggregate.

AIDE : help; grant (financial).

AIDE FISCALE : tax incentive.

AILLEURS : elsewhere (PAR... : besides; otherwise).

AINSI : so; thus.

AISÉMENT : easily; readily.

AJOUTER(S) : to come on top of.

AJUSTEMENT : adjustment.

AJUSTEMENTS DE LA TAXATION AUX FRONTIERES : border tax adjustments.

ALIGNEMENT ILLICITE DES PRIX : price-rigging.

ALLANT DE... À : varying between... and.

ALLOCATION : allocation; allowance; grant; payment.

ALLOCATION DE CHÔMAGE : unemployment benefit.

ALLOCATION MALADIE : sickness benefit.

AMÉLIORATION : improvement.

AMÉLIORER : to improve.

AMENER : to induce.

AMIANTE : asbestos.

AMORTISSEMENT : capital cost; depreciation.

ANNULATION : cancellation.

ANNULER : to cancel; to nullify.

APPARTENANCE : membership.

APPEL D'OFFRE(S): bid; call or invitation for tenders (LANCER UN... : to invite or solicit bids or tenders).

APPELÉ : so-called.

APPLICABLE : applicable; enforceable; practicable (RENDRE... : to make...).

APPLICATION : enforcement.

APPLIQUER : to administer; to apply; to enforce.

APPRENTISSAGE : apprenticeship.

APPROBATION : approval.

APPROPRIÉ : relevant.

APPROVISIONNEMENT : stock; supply.

ARACHIDE : peanut.

ARBITRAGE : hedge or hedging; arbitrage or arbitraging.

ARBITRAGISTE : arbitrager or arbitrageur.

ARBITRAGISTE-RISQUE : risk-arbitrager or arb.

ARGENT À COURT TERME : call money or money at/on call/at short notice.

ARGENT AU JOUR LE JOUR : call money or money at/on call/ at short notice.

ARMATEUR : shipowner.

ARME : weapon.

ARRIÈRE-PLAN : background.

ARRIÉRÉS : arrears or overdue debts; backlog (of orders).

ARRIVER À L'ÉCHÉANCE : to be redeemed; to come due; to mature.

ARTICLE : item.

ASSEMBLÉE GÉNÉRALE ANNUELLE : annual general meeting/AGM.

ASSEOIR : to assess.

ASSESSEUR : assessor.

ASSISTER : to assit (to help); to attend (to be present).

ASSOCIATION : association; combination; partnership.

ASSOCIATION EUROPÉENNE DE LIBRE ÉCHANGE/AELE : European Free Trade Association/EFTA.

ASSOCIÉ : partner.

ASSUJETTI (ÊTRE... À) : to be liable or subject to.

ASSUJETTISSEMENT : liability

ASSURABLE (AUPRÈS DE) : insurable with (a company).

ASSURANCE : direct business; insurance; assurance (life).

ASSURANCE À DURÉE LIMITÉE OU TEMPORAIRE : term insurance.

ASSURANCE ACCIDENTS : accident insurance.

ASSURANCE AVEC INTÉRESSEMENT : with-profits insurance.

ASSURANCE BIENS ET PERSONNES : non-life; casualty/property insurance.

ASSURANCE BONNE MORALITÉ : fidelity guarantee or bond.

ASSURANCE DE RESPONSABILITÉ CIVILE OU AU TIERS : third-party insurance.

ASSURANCE DES CRÉDITS À L'EXPORTATION : export credit insurance.

ASSURANCE EN CAS DE DECÈS : pure life or whole life insurance.

ASSURANCE EN CAS DE VIE, À CAPITAL DIFFÉRÉ : endowment insurance.

ASSURANCE FRET : freight insurance.

ASSURANCE INCENDIE : fire insurance.

ASSURANCE MARITIME : marine insurance.

ASSURANCE NON-VIE : non-life insurance.

ASSURANCE PERSONNALITÉ OU PERSONNAGE IMPORTANT : key-man insurance.

ASSURANCE PRÊT HYPOTHÉCAIRE : mortgage protection insurance.

ASSURANCE RENTE VIAGÈRE OU ANNUITÉ : annuity.

ASSURANCE RESPONSABILITÉ DE L'ARMATEUR : shipowner's liability insurance (marine insurance).

ASSURANCE SANS INTÉRESSEMENT : non – or without profits insurance.

ASSURANCE SUR CORPS : hull insurance (marine insurance).

ASSURANCE SUR FACULTÉS : cargo insurance (marine insurance).

ASSURANCE TIERS COLLISION : third-party motor insurance.

ASSURANCE TOUS RISQUES : comprehensive; all-in policy.

ASSURANCE VIE OU SUR LA VIE : life insurance/assurance.

ASSURÉ : insured person; policy-holder.

ASSURER (S') : to take out an insurance;... SUR OU CONTRE :... against.

ASSURÉ SINISTRÉ : claimant.

ASSUREUR : insurer; underwriter.

ASTREINT AUX VENTES EXCLUSIVES : tied.

ATTAQUANT : raider or corporate raider.

ATTAQUE DES BAISSIERS : bear raid.

ATTÉNUER : to abate; to ease.

AU COMPTANT : over-the-counter.

AU DÉBUT : to start with.

AU-DESSOUS DU PAIR : below par; at a discount.

AU-DESSUS DU PAIR : above par; at a premium.

AU JOUR LE JOUR : day-to-day.

AU PAIR : at par.

AUDIENCE : hearing.

AUDITEUR : auditor.

AUGMENTATION : increase.

AUGMENTER : to enhance; to increase; to raise.

AU PAIR : at par.

AUPARAVANT : formerly; previously.

AUQUEL CAS : in which case.

AUSPICES : aegis; auspices.

AUSSI : also; too.

AUTOLIMITATION : voluntary restraint.

AUTORISATION : approval; permission.

AUTORISÉ À : entitled to.

AUTORISER À SORTIR : to release (goods; prisoner).

AVAL DE BANQUE : banker's/bank bill or bank/banker's acceptance or bank draft; (US) bankable bill.

AVALISER : to endorse.

AVANCE DE FONDS : loan or advance.

AVANTAGE : advantage; benefit.

AVANTAGE COMPARATIF : comparative advantage.

AVARIE COMMUNE OU FRANC D'AVARIE PARTICULIÈRE : General Average or Free of Particular Average/FPA.

AVARIE SIMPLE OU AVEC AVARIE PARTICULIÈRE : Particular Average or With Particular Average/WPA.

AVEC ESCOMPTE : at a discount.

AVEC LE DIVIDENDE : cum dividend/cum div.

AVEC UNE DÉCOTE : at a discount.

AVENANT : additional clause; endorsement.

AVÈNEMENT : advent.

AVIS : advice (... AUTORISÉ : expert advice).

AVOCAT : lawyer.

AVOIR : (n) asset (s); credit (tax).

AVOIR ACCÈS À : to have access to.

AVOIR POUR CONSÉQUENCE : to result in.

AVOIR TRAIT À : to relate to.

À X JOURS DE VUE : n days after sight.

AYANT DROIT : dependent; representative; rightful claimant.

AYANT DROIT À : entitled to.

BAIL : lease.

BAILLEUR : lessor.

BAILLEUR DE FONDS : lender.

BAISSE : downturn; fall.

BAISSER : to drop.

BAISSIER : bear.

BAISSIER AVEC COUVERTURE : covered/protected bear.

BALANCE COMMERCIALE : balance of trade.

BALANCE DES MOUVEMENTS DE CAPITAUX : balance on capital account.

BALANCE DES PAIEMENTS COURANTS : balance on current account.

BALANCE DES PAIEMENTS : balance of payments.

BANQUE AYANT ADHÉRÉ AU FEDERAL RESERVE SYSTEM : (US) member bank.

BANQUE COMMERCIALE : commercial/retail/deposit/joint-stock bank; US equivalent: member bank; European equivalent: credit bank.

BANQUE D'ACCEPTATION : (US) acceptance bank.

BANQUE D'AFFAIRES : merchant bank.

BANQUE D'AFFAIRES SPÉCIALISÉE DANS L'ACCEPTATION DES TRAITES : accepting house.

BANQUE DE DÉTAIL : retail bank.

BANQUE DE DÉPÔT : commercial/retail/deposit/joint-stock bank; (Europe) credit bank; (US) member bank.

BANQUE D'ÉPARGNE : savings bank.

BANQUE DE PLACEMENT OU D'ÉMISSION : (UK) house, issuing house; (US) investment bank.

BANQUE DE RESERVE FÉDÉRALE : (US) Federal Reserve Bank.

BANQUE D'ESCOMPTE : discount house.

BANQUE DES RÈGLEMENTS INTERNATIONAUX/BRI : Bank for International Settlements/BIS.

BANQUE D'INVESTISSEMENT : investment bank.

BANQUE EUROPÉENNE D'INVESTISSENENT/BEI : European Investment Bank.

BANQUE EUROPÉENNE POUR LA RECONSTRUCTION ET LE DÉVELOPPEMENT/BERD : European Bank for Reconstruction and Development/EBRD.

BANQUE INTERNATIONALE POUR LA RECONSTRUCTION ET LE DÉVELOPPEMENT/BIRD OU BANQUE MONDIALE : International Bank for Reconstruction and Development/IBRD or World Bank.

BANQUE MUTUELLE D'ÉPARGNE : (US) mutual savings bank.

BANQUEROUTE : bankruptcy.

BANQUEROUTIER : a bankrupt.

BARRIÈRE COMMERCIALE : trade barrier.

BARRIÈRES DOUANIÈRES OU TARIFAIRES : tariff barriers or tariff walls.

BARRIÈRES NON-TARIFAIRES : non-tariff barriers/NTBs or non-tariff measures/NTMs.

BÂTIMENTS PUBLICS : administrative buildings.

BATTERIE ANTI-REQUINS : shark repellants.

BÉNÉFICE : profit; (RÉALISER DES BÉNÉFICES : to earn, to make profits).

BÉNÉFICE NET DÉCLARÉ : after-tax profits.

BÉNÉFICES PAR ACTION : earnings per share.

BÉNÉFICES NON DISTRIBUÉS : retained earnings/profits or reserves.

BÉNÉFICIAIRE : beneficiary; payee (bill of exchange, cheque).

BESOIN DE FINANCEMENT DU SECTEUR PUBLIC : Public Sector Borrowing Requirement/PSBR.

BIEN QUE : although.

BIEN-ÊTRE : well-being; welfare.

BIENS : belongings; goods; property.

BIENS D'ÉQUIPEMENT : capital goods; plant.

BIG BANG (BOURSE DE LONDRES EN 1986) : the Big Bang (Stock Exchange).

BILLET À ORDRE : promissory note.

BILLET À VUE : sight bill or bill of sight.

BILLET DE BANQUE : bank-note; (US) bank bill.

BILLET DE TRÉSORERIE : corporate/corporation bond.

BILLETS DE TRÉSORERIE : commercial paper.

BIMENSUEL : fortnightly.

BLÉ : wheat.

BLOC DE CONTRÔLE : majority holding.

BLOQUER UN CHÈQUE : to stop a cheque.

BOIS EXOTIQUE : tropical timber.

BON : bond.

BON DE CAISSE : short-term note.

BON DE SOUSCRIPTION : warrant (Stock Exchange).

BON DU TRÉSOR : government bond or bill.

BON DU TRÉSOR À COURT OU MOYEN TERME : (US) treasury note.

BON DU TRÉSOR À COURT TERME : treasury bill.

BON DU TRÉSOR À LONG TERME : (US) treasury bond.

BONNE FOI : utmost good faith (insurance).

BONS DE CAISSE À COURT TERME : commercial paper.

BORDER : to edge.

BORDEREAU : (detailed) statement or docket.

BORDEREAU D'ACHAT OU DE VENTE : Contract Note (Stock Exchange).

BORDEREAU D'EXPÉDITION : consignment note.

BORDEREAU DE TRANSPORT : freight note.

BOURSE DES MARCHANDISES : commodity market/exchange.

BOURSE DES OPTIONS : traded options market.

BOURSE DES VALEURS : securities exchange; stock exchange; stock market.

BOX : stall.

BRANCHE : branch; line of activity or business; sector of industry.

BRUT : gross.

BRUXELLES : Brussels.

BULLETIN DE SOUSCRIPTION : application form.

BUT : goal; purpose; target (À BUT NON LUCRATIF : non-profit-making; not-for-profit).

CACAO : cocoa.

CADRE : framemork (structure) (DANS LE CADRE DE : under, within the framework of).

CADRE(S) : executive; management (person) (CADRE DÉBUTANT : junior executive; CADRE MOYEN : middle executive; CADRE SUPERIEUR : senior, top, executive) (lower and upper can be used instead of junior and senior or top); CADRE JEUNE, DYNAMIQUE : yuppie/young urban professional.

CADUC : null and void; DEVENIR… : to lapse.

CAISSE D'ÉPARGNE : savings bank; (US) stock savings bank.

CAISSE D'ÉPARGNE LOGEMENT : thrift or thrift institution.

CAISSE D'ÉPARGNE MUTUELLE DE CRÉDIT IMMOBILIER/DE FINANCEMENT IMMOBILIER/D'ÉPARGNE LOGEMENT : building society; (US) equivalent savings and loan association/S & L.

CAISSE DE RETRAITE : pension fund.

CAISSE MUTUELLE D'ÉPARGNE : (US) mutual savings bank.

CAISSE MUTUELLE DE DÉPÔTS ET DE PRÊTS : (UK) Trustee Savings Bank/TSB.

CANALISER : to channel.

CANDIDAT DÉSIGNÉ : nominee.

CAOUTCHOUC : rubber.

CAPACITÉ BÉNÉFICIARE : earning power.

CAPITAL : capital; money.

CAPITAL ACTIONS : share capital.

CAPITAL APPELÉ : called-up capital.

CAPITAL CIRCULANT : floating capital.

CAPITAL LIBÉRÉ : paid up/fully-paid capital; (US) paid in/contributed capital.

CAPITAL NOMINAL : authorized/registered/nominal/subscribed capital or authorized stock/issue.

CAPITAL PROPRE : equity capital.

CAPITAL SOCIAL : authorized/registered/nominal/subscribed capital or authorized stock/issue.

CAPITAL SOUSCRIT : issued/subscribed capital.

CAPITAL SOUSCRIT ET NON APPELÉ : uncalled capital.

CAPITAL VERSÉ : paid up/fully-paid capital; (US) paid in/contributed capital.

CAPITAL VERSÉ : paid-up capital.

CAPITAL-RISQUE : risk/venture capital.

CAPITALISATION BOURSIÈRE GLOBALE : market capitalization (stock exchange).

CAPITATION : poll tax.

CAPITAUX : capital (RÉUNIR, TROUVER DES CAPITAUX : to raise capital) (AFFECTATION DES CAPITAUX; APPROVISIONNENENT EN CAPITAUX : capital appropriation).

CAPITAUX FÉBRILES : hot money.

CAPITAUX FIXES : capital assets.

CAPITAUX FLOTTANTS SPECULATIFS : hot money.

CAPITAUX IMPRODUCTIFS : idle capital.

CARACTÉRISTIQUES : features; specifications (of a product).
CARBURANT : fuel.
CARGAISON : cargo; ship-load (... AÉRIENNE : aircraft cargo).
CARTE DE CRÉDIT : credit card; charge card; store card.
CARTE DE GARANTIE BANCAIRE : cheque/cheque guarantee/bank/banker's card.
CARTEL : cartel.
CAS D'ESPÈCE : case in point; specific case.
CAUSE IMMÉDIATE : proximate cause (insurance).
CAUTION : guarantee; security; sponsor (person).
CÉDER : to yield.
CELUI-/CELLE-/CEUX-CI (DERNIER NOMMÉ) : the latter.
CELUI-/CELLE-/CEUX-LÀ (PREMIER NOMMÉ) : the former.
CENTRE DU COMMERCE INTERNATIONAL CNUCED GATT : International Trade Center /UNCTAD GATT/ITC.
CERTIFICAT D'ACTION : share certificate.
CERTIFICAT D'ORIGINE : certificate of origin C/O.
CERTIFICAT DE DÉPÔT : certificate of deposit/CD.
CESSION-BAIL : lease-back.
CHAMBRE DE COMPENSATION : clearing-house.
CHANGEMENT : shift; change.
CHANGER : to switch.
CHANTAGE : blackmail.
CHANTAGE AU BILLET VERT OU FINANCIER : greenmail (Stock Exchange).
CHANVRE : hemp (... DE MANILLE : abaca).
CHARGE D'AVOUÉ : solicitor's practice.
CHARGE DE TRAVAIL : workload.
CHARGES SOCIALES : social security contributions/taxes; (US) payroll tax.
CHARPIE : lint.
CHARTE DE LA HAVANE : Havana Charter.
CHASSEUR DE PRIMES : stag (stock market).
CHEF D'ÉTAT : head of state.
CHÈQUE : cheque; (US) check.
CHÈQUE ANTIDATÉ : antedated cheque.
CHÈQUE BARRÉ : crossed cheque.
CHÈQUE BLOQUÉ OU SUR LEQUEL ON A FAIT OPPOSITION : stopped cheque.
CHÈQUE DE VOYAGE : traveller's cheque.
CHÈQUE EN BOIS : bounced/rubber/dud/returned/ dishonoured cheque.
CHÈQUE POSTDATÉ : postdated cheque.
CHÉQUIER : cheque book.
CHERCHER À : to seek to.
CHERCHEUR : scientist.
CHEVALIER BLANC : white knight (Stock Exchange).
CHEVALIER NOIR : black knight (Stock Exchange).
CHIFFRE D'AFFAIRES : turnover.
CHOISIR : to opt for.
CHOISIR DE : elect to.
CHÔMAGE : unemployment.
CHÔMAGE CACHÉ : hidden or disguised unemployment.
CHÔMAGE CLASSIQUE : classical unemployment.
CHÔMAGE CONJONCTUREL : cyclical or situational unemployment.
CHÔMAGE DES JEUNES : youth unemployment.
CHÔMAGE FRICTIONNEL : frictional unemployment.
CHÔMAGE RÉGIONAL : regional unemployment.
CHÔMAGE SAISONNIER : seasonal unemployment.
CHÔMAGE STRUCTUREL : structural unemployment.
CHÔMAGE TECHNOLOGIQUE : technological unemployment.
CHÔMEUR DE LONGUE DURÉE : long-term unemployed.
CHUTE : fall.
CI-DESSOUS : below- (mentioned).
CI-DESSUS : above- (mentioned).
CIBLE : target.
CIBLER : to focus.
CIRCUIT INTÉGRÉ : integrated circuit.
CIRCULATION MATÉRIELLE DE TITRES : material transfer of share certificates.
CIRCULATION : movement (LIBRE... : free...).
CIRCULER : to move (goods; people).
CIVIL : civilian (n; adj).
CLASSER : to rate; to classify.

CLAUSE D'ANTÉRIORITÉ : grandfather clause (GATT).

CLAUSE D'AUTORISATION : Enabling clause (GATT).

CLAUSE D'EXEMPTION/DE SAUVEGARDE : escape clause.

CLIENT : customer.

CLUB D'INVESTISSEMENT : investment club.

CODE DES LICENCES : Licensing Code (GATT).

CODE-ANTI-DUMPING : anti-dumping code.

CODE DE CONDUITE : code of conduct.

CODE DE PASSATION DES MARCHÉS DE L'ÉTAT : Government Procurement Code (GATT).

COEFFICIENT DE CAPITALISATION DES RÉSULTATS/CCR : price-earnings ratio/P/E ratio/PER.

COLLECTIVITÉS LOCALES : local administration or communities, local government bodies.

COMBINAISON : mix.

COMMISSAIRE AUX COMPTES : auditor.

COMBLER : to bridge; to fill.

COMITÉ ÉCONOMIQUE ET SOCIAL EUROPÉEN : European Economic and Social Committee.

COMITÉ : board; commission; committee; panel; (... CONSULTATIF : advisory board or commission; ... DE DIRECTION : board of directors; ... D'ENTREPRISE : works council).

COMMANDE : order (... REÇUE DE L'ÉTRANGER : indent).

COMMANDITAIRE : sleeping partner.

COMMANDITÉ : active partner.

COMME LE PROUVE : as witnessed or shown by.

COMMERÇANT : trader.

COMMERCE : trade.

COMMERCE DIRIGÉ : managed trade.

COMMERCE EXTERIEUR : foreign trade.

COMMERCE FRANC : entrepôt trade.

COMMERCE INTÉRIEUR : domestic or home trade.

COMMERCE INVISIBLE : invisible trade.

COMMERCE VISIBLE : visible trade.

COMMERCIALISATION : commercialization; marketing.

COMMISSAIRE EUROPÉEN : European commissioner (European Union).

COMMISSION : fee or panel; commission; board.

COMMISSION D'ARBITRAGE : panel of experts.

COMMISSION DE CHEF DE FILE : management fee.

COMMISSION DES OPÉRATIONS DE LA BOURSE : UK equivalent: Securities and Investment Board/SIB; US equivalent: Securities and Exchange Commission/SEC.

COMMISSION PERMANENTE : standing commission.

COMMISSIONNAIRE : commission agent; ... EN GROS : factor; ... EN DOUANE : customs broker; ... EXPEDITEUR/TRANSPORTEUR : forwarding agent; carrier; ... EXPORTATEUR : export agent; ... D'IMPORTATION : import agent.

COMMISSIONS MINIMUM FIXES : fixed minimum commissions.

COMMODITÉ : convenience.

COMPAGNIE DE TRANSPORTS : shipping company.

COMPARER À : to check against; to compare with.

COMPATIBLE AVEC : compatible with; consistent with.

COMPENSATION : compensation.

COMPENSER : to compensate; to offset.

COMPÉTITIVITÉ : competitiveness.

COMPORTER : to involve; to entail.

COMPOSANT DE FABRICATION LOCALE : local content.

COMPRENDRE : to include.

COMPROMETTRE : to impair; to jeopardize (to endanger; to put in danger).

COMPTABILITE : accountancy; accounting; book-keeping.

COMPTABLE : accountant (EXPERT... : chartered...)

COMPTANT D'USAGE : prompt cash.

COMPTE COURANT : current/cheque account; (US) checking account or demand deposit.

COMPTE D'ÉPARGNE : savings/deposit account; (US) time/notice account.

COMPTE DE COMPENSATION : clearing account.

COMPTE DE DÉPÔT : savings/deposit account; (US) time/notice account.

COMPTE DE DÉPÔT À TERME FIXE : fixed deposit account.
COMPTE FOURNISSEURS : book debts.
COMPTER (À... DE) : as of; from.
CONCENTRER : to direct (to); to focus (on).
CONCEPTEUR : designer.
CONCERNANT : concerning; with respect to.
CONCERNER : to concern; to involve.
CONCESSION : concession; (LISTE DE CONCESSIONS : schedule of concessions).
CONCEVOIR : to design.
CONCILIATION : conciliation; reconciliation.
CONCILIER : to conciliate; to reconcile.
CONCURRENCE : competition.
CONCURRENT : competitor.
CONDITION : requirement.
CONDITIONS : terms (... PRÉALABLES : prior conditions).
CONFÉRENCE DES NATIONS UNIES SUR LE COMMERCE ET LE DÉVELOPPEMENT/CNUCED : United Nations Conference on Trade and Development/UNCTAD.
CONFIER QQE CHOSE À QQUN : to trust someone with something; to vest something in someone (an institution).
CONFLIT D'INTÉRÊTS : conflict of interests.
CONFRONTÉ À : confronted with; facing.
CONJOINT : joint (adj); spouse; wedded partner (n).
CONJOINTEMENT : jointly.
CONJONCTURE : situation.
CONJONCTURE ÉCONOMIQUE : economic climate, situation.
CONJONCTUREL : situational.
CONSEIL D'ADMINISTRATION DE LA RÉSERVE FÉDÉRALE AMÉRICAINE : Federal Reserve Board.
CONMISSION EUROPÉENNE : European Commission.
COMMUNAUTÉ EUROPÉENNE CHARBON ACIER/CECA : European Coal and Steel Community/ECSC.
CONNAISSEMENT : bill of lading B/L.
CONSACRER : to devote.
CONSEIL D'ADMINISTRATION : board of directors.
CONSEIL DE DIRECTION : management/managing board.
CONSEIL DES MINISTRES EUROPÉENS : European Council of Ministers.
CONSEIL EUROPÉEN : European Council.
CONSEILLER : adviser; consultant; counsel; counsellor.
CONSEILLER D'INVESTISSEMENT : investment adviser.
CONSENTEMENT : consent (... EXPRÈS : formal).
CONSERVATEUR : preservative (chemicals).
CONSERVER : hang on to; to preserve; to retain.
CONSIGNATION (EN) : on consignment.
CONSOLIDATION : binding (trade agreement); consolidation (finance).
CONSOMMATEUR : consumer.
CONSOMMATION : consumption.
CONSOMMER : to consume.
CONSTAT : statement (... AMIABLE : agreed).
CONSTITUÉ DE : made up of.
CONSTITUER : to build up; to establish; to form.
CONSTITUTION : formation (establishment); constitution (country); ... DE RÉSERVES : reserving.
CONSULTATION : consultation.
CONTENEUR : container.
CONTENIR : to embody (rules embodied in a treaty).
CONTENU : content(s); subject matter.
CONTINGENT : quota.
CONTOURNER : to by-pass.
CONTRACTER : to incur (debts).
CONTRAT DE COMMERCE INTERNATIONAL : foreign trade contract.
CONTRAT DE CONTRE-ACHAT : counter purchase contract.
CONTRAT DE VENTE : bill of sale; sales contract or agreement.
CONTRATS À TERME : forward or futures contracts.
CONTRATS À TERME D'INSTRUMENTS FINANCIERS : financial futures.
CONTRE EFFETS : secured.
CONTREPARTISTE : market maker.
CONTREPARTISTE GÉNÉRAL EN FONDS D'ETAT : (UK) gilt-edged market maker/GEMM.
CONTRIBUTION : input.

CONTRÔLE DES CHANGES : exchange control.
CONTRÔLE RÉEL : effective control.
CONTRÔLER : to regulate; to check; to control.
CONVENTION DE LOMÉ : Lomé Convention.
CONVERTIBILITÉ : convertibility.
CONVOQUER : to convene.
COQUE : hull (ship).
CORBEILLE : floor; (US) pit (of Stock Exchange).
COREPER/COMITÉ DES REPRÉSENTANTS PERMANENTS (Union européenne) : Committee of Permanent Representatives (European Union).
CORPOREL : tangible (accountancy).
CORRECTION DES VARIATIONS SAISONNIÈRES : seasonal adjustment.
CORRIGER : to correct.
COTATION : quotation.
COTATION EN BOURSE : listing.
COTATION OFFICIELLE : full listing.
COTATIONS À TERME : futures.
COTE : (quoted) price.
COTÉ : quoted; listed.
COTE DE CRÉDIT : rating.
COTE OFFICIELLE : official list, the listed market (Stock Exchange).
COTES D'ACHAT ET DE VENTE : buying and selling prices.
COTISATIONS SOCIALES : social security contributions /taxes.
COULER : to sink.
COUP DE BOURSE : deal.
COUP DE FOUET : boost.
COUPON : coupon.
COUPON ATTACHÉ : cum dividend, cum div.
COUPON DÉTACHÉ : ex dividend, ex div.
COUPURE : denomination (of money).
COUR : court.
COUR DE JUSTICE EUROPÉENNE : European Court of Justice.
COUR DE PREMIÈRE INSTANCE : court of first instance.
COUR DES COMPTES EUROPÉENNE : European Court of Auditors.
COURBE DE PHILLIPS : Phillips' curve.
COURS ACHETEUR : bid/buying price.
COURS BOURSIERS MONDIAUX : world stock market prices.
COURS D'ÉMISSION : striking price.
COURS DE BASE : exercise/strike price.
COURS DE/EN CLÔTURE : closing price.
COURS DE VENTE : striking price.
COURS DU COMPTANT DISPONIBLE: spot price.
COURTAGE PAR ORDINATEUR : (UK) programme (US) program trading.
COURTAGE : brokerage, broking; broker's commission or turn (SOCIÉTÉ DE... brokerage firm).
COURTIER : broker.
COURTIER EN TITRES : broker/dealer.
COÛT : charge; cost.
COÛT ET FRET/C ET F : cost and freight/C & F.
COÛT, ASSURANCE, FRET/CAF : cost; insurance and freight/CIF.
COÛT D'IMMOBILISATION : capital cost.
COUVERTURE DE POSITION À DÉCOUVERT : short covering.
COUVERTURE : cover; coverage; covering (insurance); hedge or hedging (stockmarket dealings).
COUVERTURE EXCÉDENTAIRE D'UNE ÉMISSION DE TITRES : oversubscription.
COUVRIR : to cover.
CRÉANCE : claim (... EN US$: for US$); receivables; ... DOUTEUSE : bad debt.
CREANCIER : creditor (... NANTI ou PRIVILÉGIÉ : secured...; ... SANS GARANTIE ou CHIROGRAPHAIRE : unsecured).
CRÉATION : creation; establishment.
CRÉDIT À LA CONSOMMATION : hire-purchase.
CRÉDIT-BAIL : leasing.
CRÉDIT-BAIL ADOSSÉ : lease-back.
CRÉDIT D'IMPÔT : tax allowance(s).
CRÉDIT RELAIS : stand-by credit.
CRÉDIT SYNDIQUÉ : syndicated loan.
CRÉDITS EN EURO-DEVISES : Euro-market loans.
CRÉER : to create; to establish; to set up.
CRISE : slump.
CROISSANCE : growth.
CROISSANCE ÉCONOMIQUE : economic growth.
CUIVRE : copper.
CYCLE ÉCONOMIQUE : trade cycle.
D'OÙ : hence.
DANS LE CAS OÙ : should.

DANS UN DÉLAI TRÈS COURT : at very short notice.

DATE : date (À UNE... ULTÉRIEURE : at a later date; ... BUTOIR : deadline; target date).

DATE D'ÉCHÉANCE/DE REMBOURSEMENT : maturity/redemption date.

DE BONNE REPUTATION : reputable.

DE L'EXTÉRIEUR : from outside.

DE LA PART DE : on behalf of.

DÉBITEUR : debtor.

DÉBOUCLER SA POSITION : to close one's (short) position; to unwind.

DÉBOURSER : to pay out.

DÉCALAGE DES FUSEAUX HORAIRES : time differentials.

DÉCÈS : death.

DÉCISION : decision (PRENDRE UNE... : to make a...); ruling; step (PRENDRE UNE... : to take a...).

DÉCLARATION D'ENTRÉE EN ENTREPÔT : entry for warehousing.

DÉCLARATION DE SINISTRE : claim on insurance.

DÉCLARATION DE SORTIE D'ENTREPÔT POUR CONSOMMATION : entry for Home Use Ex Ship.

DÉCLARATION EN DOUANE : bill of entry (B/E).

DÉCLARATION POUR MARCHANDISES EXEMPTES DE DROITS : entry for free goods.

DÉCLARÉ AUPRÈS DE : registered with.

DÉCLENCHER : to trigger; to unleash.

DÉCOULER DE : to arise out of.

DÉCOURAGEANT : discouraging; inhibitive.

DÉCOUVERT : overdraft.

DÉDOUANEMENT : clearance.

DÉDOUANER : to clear.

DÉFAILLANCE : default (on a payment); failure to pay (on a contract); sagging (of a market); weakening (of a currency).

DÉFICIT : debit balance; deficit (... BUDGÉTAIRE : budget or budgetary...); shortfall; shortage.

DÉFICITAIRE : adverse; in deficit; passive; unfavourable.

DÉFINIR : to define; to set out.

DÉFLATION : deflation.

DÉLAI : time requirement.

DÉLAI DE CONVERSION : conversion period.

DÉLIT D'INITIÉ : insider trading.

DEMANDE : application; demand; request (À LA... DE QQN : at the request of somebody; at somebody's request).

DEMANDE DE COMPENSATION : offset requirement.

DEMANDE DE DÉPÔT DE BILAN OU DE MISE EN LIQUIDATION JUDICIAIRE : petition in bankruptcy or bankruptcy petition.

DEMANDE GLOBALE : aggregate demand.

DEMANDER : to apply (for); to ask (for); to require.

DÉMANTÈLEMENT PROGRESSIF : phasing out.

DÉMONTER : to dismantle.

DÉMUNIR : to deprive.

DENRÉES ALIMENTAIRES : basic foodstuffs.

DÉPASSER : to be in excess of.

DÉPENDRE DE : to depend on; to rely on.

DÉPENS : legal costs (ÊTRE CONDAMNÉ AUX... : to be ordered to pay costs) (AUX... DE : at the expense of).

DÉPENSE : expenditure.

DÉPENSES PUBLIQUES : public expenditure; expenses.

DÉPIT (EN... DE) : despite; in spite of.

DÉPLACEMENTS DE CAPITAUX CHERCHANT DE MEILLEURS TAUX D'INTÉRÊT : hot money.

DÉPORT : backwardation; backwardization or back; abbr. back (Stock Exchange).

DÉPOSANT : depositor.

DÉPOSER (UN PROJET) : to table (a bill, draft, or project).

DÉPOSER SON BILAN : to file for bankruptcy; to go/be put into liquidation.

DÉPOSITAIRE : trustee.

DÉPÔT : deposit (banking); [EN... : in bond (customs); on consignment (import/export); on sale or return (mail-order business)]; warehouse (store of goods).

DÉPÔT À TERME : fixed-term deposit.

DÉPÔT BANCAIRE : bank deposit.

DÉPÔT DE BILAN : bankruptcy.

DÉPÔT DE BANQUE D'ESCOMPTE : discount house deposits.

DÉPÔT PRÉALABLE : prior deposit.

DÉPRESSION : depression.

DÉPUTÉ : member (assembly; parliament).

DÉRÉGLEMENTATION : de-regulation.

DÉRÉGLEMENTATION DES OPÉRATIONS FINANCIÈRES À LA BOURSE DE LONDRES EN OCTOBRE 1986 : the Big Bang.

DE REMPLACEMENT : alternative.

DÉRIVÉ : by-product.

DERNIER COURS/COURS DE CLÔTURE : closing price.

DÉROGATION : waiver.

DÉROGER À : to waive (a rule).

DE SECOND RANG : lower-tier.

DÉSÉQUILIBRE : disequilibrium; imbalance.

DÉSIGNER : to define; to name; to refer to.

DÉSIGNER POUR UNE CANDIDATURE À UNE ÉLECTION OU À UNE NOMINATION : to nominate.

DÉSINFLATION : disinflation.

DÉSISTEMENT : waiver.

DESTINATAIRE : consignee (of goods); addressee; receiver (fax); sendee (of letters).

DESTINÉ À : intended to; meant to.

DÉTACHÉ : detached.

DÉTAILLANT EN TITRES : retailer of/in shares.

DÉTENIR : to hold (... SUR : against).

DÉTENTEUR : holder.

DÉTENTEUR : holder (of a bank account or insurance policy).

DÉTENTION : ownership (goods; securities).

DÉTÉRIORATION : wear and tear; deterioration.

DÉTERMINATION DES PRIX : pricing.

DETTE : debt.

DETTE DE DEUXIÈME RANG : junior debt.

DETTE DE PREMIER RANG : senior debt.

DÉVELOPPER : to boost; to develop; to promote.

DEVENIR PROPRIÉTAIRE : to legally own (something).

DEVISE : currency (finance) (FAIBLE : soft; weak; FORTE : hard; strong).

DEVISES À TERME : currency futures.

DEVOIR : (n) duty.

DIFFÉRENCE : difference; gap.

DIFFÉREND : difference; dispute.

DIMENSION : size.

DIRECTEUR ADMINISTRATIF : non-executive director.

DIRECTEUR EXECUTIF : executive director.

DIRECTEUR GÉNÉRAL : director general (institution); managing director (business).

DIRECTIVES : directions; directives (European Union).

DIRIGER : to head; to manage; to channel.

DISONS : say.

DISPENSER : to exempt.

DISPONIBILITÉ : availability.

DISPONIBILITÉS : liquid assets.

DISPONIBLE : available; liquid; on hand; spot.

DISPOSER À SA GUISE : to dispose of at will.

DISPOSITION : agreement; arrangement; provision.

DISPOSITIONS DE RACHAT OU DE COMPENSATION : buy-back or compensation arrangements.

DISSOLUTION : liquidation or winding-up.

DISTRIBUER : to allocate; to allot.

DISTRIBUER GRATUITEMENT : give away.

DISTRIBUTEUR AUTOMATIQUE DE BILLETS/DAB : cash dispenser/machine or automatic/automated teller machine/ATM.

DIVERSIFIER SES ACTIVITÉS : to branch out.

DIVIDENDE : dividend.

DIVIDENDE ATTACHÉ : cum dividend/cum div.

DIVIDENDE DÉTACHÉ : ex dividend/ex div./x.d.

DIVIDENDE INTERIMAIRE/PROVISOIRE : interim dividend.

DIVIDENDE SOUS FORME D'OBLIGATION : bond dividend.

DIVULGUER : to disclose; to reveal.

DOCUMENT ADMINISTRATIF UNIQUE/DAU : Single Administrative Document/SAD (European Union customs formalities).

DOCUMENTS À RETIRER : documents for collection.

DOCUMENTS CONTRE ACCEPTATION : documents against acceptance (D/A).

DOCUMENTS CONTRE PAIEMENT : documents against payment (D/P)

DOCUMENTS D'EXPÉDITION : documentation; shipping documents.

DOMAINE : area; field.

DOMINANT : prevailing.

DOMMAGE : loss.

DOMMAGE CORPOREL : personal injury.

DOMMAGE INDIRECT : consequential loss.

DOMMAGE MATÉRIEL : material damage or loss.

DOMMAGES ET INTERÊTS : claims; compensation; damages (DEMANDER

DES... À : to make claims with or against someone).

DONC : thus.

DONNER À BAIL : to lease out (to).

DONNER UNE EXISTENCE LÉGALE : to establish legally.

DOUANE : customs.

DROIT : duty (customs); fee (commission); Law (science); right (prerogative); title to (property).

DROIT COMPENSATEUR : countervailing duty.

DROIT D'ATTERRISSAGE : aircraft-landing right.

DROIT D'ENTRÉE RÉDUIT : introductory trade-in (contract).

DROIT DE DOUANE SPÉCIFIQUE : fixed or specific duty.

DROIT DE VOTE : voting right.

DROIT PRÉFÉRENTIEL OU DE PRIORITÉ : priority claim.

DROIT PROPORTIONNEL : ad valorem duty (customs).

DROIT PROTECTEUR : protective duty (customs).

DROIT RÉMUNÉRATEUR : revenue tariff (customs).

DROITS DE BASSIN : dock charges.

DROITS DE L'HOMME : human rights.

DROITS DE SUCCESSION : inheritance taxes; (formerly) death/estate duties or capital transfer tax.

DROITS DE TIRAGE SPÉCIAUX/DTS : Special Drawing Rights/ SDRs.

DUPLICATA : copy.

DURÉE : duration; life.

DURER : to last.

ÉCART : touch or spread, difference between two prices.

ÉCHANGE : exchange : trading; barter; swap (PLAN D'... : swap scheme) (... DE BONS PROCÉDÉS : exchange of civilities; quid pro quo); (EN... DE : in exchange or return for).

ÉCHANGER : to swap; to trade.

ÉCHANGES COMMERCIAUX : trade.

ÉCHANGES COMPENSÉS : countertrade.

ÉCHANGES INFORMATISÉES : program(me) trading or screen-based trading.

ÉCHANGES INVISIBLES : invisible trade.

ÉCHAPPER À : ward off.

ÉCHÉANCE : date; maturity; term; ARRIVER À... : to come or fall due; À... : at a future date; at maturity; À TROIS MOIS D'... : at three months'date/three months after date; FAIRE FACE À UNE... : to meet a bill; NE PAS POUVOIR FAIRE FACE À UNE... : not to be able to meet one's end of (the) month payments; INTÉRÊT IMPAYÉ À L'... : overdue interest.

ÉCHOUER : to fail.

ÉCONOME : thrifty.

ÉCONOMIE DE MARCHÉ : market economics.

ÉCONOMIES : savings (FAIRE DES... : to save; FAIRE DES... SUR : to economize on).

ÉCONOMISTE MONÉTARISTE : monetarist.

ÉCRAN : screen.

ECU : European Currency Unit (European Union).

EFFECTUER : to achieve; to carry out; to complete; to realize.

EFFET : bill; bill of exchange; draft.

EFFET À USANCE : usance bill.

EFFET BANCABLE : bankable or discountable bill.

EFFET BANCAIRE : bank bill.

EFFET DE COMMERCE : bill of exchange; commercial paper.

EFFET DE LEVIER : leverage.

EFFET ÉMIS PAR UNE SOCIÉTÉ : corporate/corporation bond.

EFFET ESCOMPTABLE : bankable or discountable bill.

EFFET MULTIPLACATEUR : multiplier effect.

EFFETS À COURT TERME DU MARCHÉ MONÉTAIRE : short-term money market instruments.

EFFETS À COURT TERME ÉLIGIBLES SUR LE MARCHÉ MONÉTAIRE : money market instruments.

EFFETS BOURSIERS : securities.

EFFETS DE COMMERCE : commercial paper or negotiable instruments.

EFFETS FINANCIERS : financial instruments.

EFFETS NÉGOCIABLES : negotiable instruments or paper.

EFFICACE : effective; efficient.

EFFONDREMENT DES COURS BOURSIERS : stock market crash.

ÉGIDE : aegis (SOUS L'... DE : under the aegis of).

ÉLABORER : to develop.

ÉLARGIR : to broaden; to enlarge; to promote.

ÉLARGIR OU AGRANDIR LE NOMBRE D'ACTIONNAIRES : to promote wider share-ownership.

ÉLARGISSEMENT : enlargement.

ÉLEVER : to increase; to raise.

ÉLIMINER : to remove.

EMBALLAGE : packaging; packing; wrapping.

EMBALLER : to pack.

EMBARQUEMENT : embarkation; shipment.

EMBAUCHER : to take on; to employ; to hire.

ÉMETTEUR : issuer (of bonds; shares; etc.)

ÉMETTRE : to issue (securities); to put forward (idea); to raise (loan).

ÉMISSION : issue.

ÉMISSION DE DROITS DE SOUSCRIPTION/ D'ATTRIBUTION :
rights/cash issue.

EMMAGASINAGE : warehousing.

EMPÊCHEMENT D'INVESTISSEMENT/
INTERDICTION D'ACCÈS À L'INVESTISSEMENT :
crowding out.

EMPÊCHER : to prevent (... DE : from + present participle); to inhibit.

EMPLOI-FORMATION (PLAN) : employment-training scheme.

EMPLOYER : to employ (person); to use; to utilize.

EMPOCHER : to pocket.

EMPRUNT : loan; (ÉMETTRE UN...; LANCER UN... : to float; to launch a loan); (CONTRACTER UN... : to take up or raise or contract a loan); borrowing (RECOURIR À L'... : to resort to borrowing).

EMPRUNTABLE : loanable.

EMPRUNT À COURT TERME : short-term borrowing.

EMPRUNT À LONG TERME : long term loan.

EMPRUNT GARANTI/GAGÉ/NANTI : secured loan.

EMPRUNT INDEXÉ : indexed or index-linked stock or loan.

EMPRUNTER À : to borrow from.

EMPRUNTEUR : borrower.

EMPRUNTS : borrowing.

EN ARRANGEMENT COLLUSOIRE : in collusion.

EN BLANC : blank.

EN COLLABORATION : in conjunction.

EN ÉQUILIBRE : in equilibrium; in balance.

EN FONCTION DE : according to; in the light of; in line with.

EN FONCTION DE L'ÉLOIGNEMENT DE LEUR ÉCHÉANCE : according to when they are going to be redeemed.

EN GARDE : for safe keeping.

EN GROS : loosely; vaguely; wholesale (trade).

EN LIQUIDATION : in liquidation.

EN MONNAIE CONSTANTE : in real or constant or inflation adjusted terms.

EN PROPORTION DE : in proportion to.

EN TANT QUE : as (... TEL : as such).

EN TOUT : as a whole.

ENCAISSE DISPONIBLE : cash in hand.

ENCLAVÉ : enclosed; land-locked.

ENCORE : still.

ENCOURAGER : to foster; to promote.

ENDETTEMENT : leverage.

ENDOMMAGER : to damage.

ENDOSSER : to endorse.

ENFREINDRE : to breach.

ENGAGEMENT : commitment; pledge.

ENGAGEMENT D'ACHETER OU VENDRE À UNE DATE ULTÉRIEURE À UN PRIX FIXÉ : forward contract.

ENGAGER : to commit; to pledge (one's word); to hire (personnel).

ENGENDRER : to entail; to generate.

ENLÈVEMENT : collection; removal.

ENLEVER : to remove.

ENREGISTRER : to register (... AUPRÈS DE : to... with).

ENSUITE : then.

ENTASSER : to stockpile.

ENTENTE : collusion; concert party (takeover).

ENTÉRINER : to legalize.

ENTIÈREMENT LIBÉRÉE : fully paid up (share).

ENTRAÎNEMENT DE LA BAISSE DES COURS PAR VENTE À DÉCOUVERT : hammering the market.

ENTRAÎNER : to entail.

ENTRAVE : hindrance; impediment; obstacle; shackle.

ENTRAVER : to hinder; to impede; to restrict; to thwart.

ENTREPÔT : warehouse.

ENTREPÔT SOUS DOUANE : bonded warehouse.

ENTREPRISE : business; business concern ; firm (... DE PREMIER ORDRE : leading...; PETITE ET MOYENNE... : small and medium-sized...).

ENTREPRISE CIBLE : target company.

ENTREPRISE HASARDEUSE : venture.

ENTRER DANS : to join (a club; a federation; an organization).

ENTRER EN VIGUEUR : to come into effect; to take effect.

ENTRER EN LIQUIDATION : to pass/go into liquidation.

ENVIRON : about; or so.

ENVOI : consignment; dispatch; shipment (... DE FONDS : remittance).

ÉPARGNE : savings.

ÉPREUVE DE VÉRITÉ : acid test; cash ratio.

ÉQUILIBRE : balance; equilibrium (... DE CONCESSIONS : balance of concessions).

ÉQUILIBRE BUDGÉTAIRE DE PLEIN EMPLOI : full employment budget balance.

ÉQUILIBRER (S') : to balance.

ÉQUILIBRER LES COMPTES : to balance the books.

ÉQUITABLE : fair.

ESCOMPTE : discount.

ESCOMPTE DE RÈGLEMENT : discount (on a bill or invoice).

ESCOMPTER : to discount.

ESPACE ÉCONOMIQUE EUROPÉEN/EEE : European Economic Area/ EEA.

ESPÈCES : physical money.

ESPÉRER : to hope; to look forward to.

ESSENTIEL : essential; primary.

ESTIMER : to estimate; to believe; to think.

ÉTABLI DE LONGUE DATE : longstanding.

ÉTABLIR : to assess; to establish; to lay down (principle); to draw up; to make out (a document); to quote (a price).

ÉTABLISSEMENT DE FINANCEMENT OU DE CRÉDIT : finance house or finance/hire-purchase/credit company.

ÉTABLISSEMENT MUTUEL COLLECTEUR D'ÉPARGNE ATTRIBUANT DES PRÊTS À LA CONSOMMATION : (US) credit union.

ÉTAIN : tin.

ÉTALON : standard.

ÉTANT ENTENDU QUE : on the understanding that.

ÉTAPE : stage, staging post.

ÉTENDUE : scope.

ÉTRANGER (À L'...) : overseas.

ÉTRANGLEMENT DES VENDEURS À DÉCOUVERT : bear squeeze.

ÊTRE À COURT DE : to be short of.

ÊTRE À LA TRAÎNE DE : to lag behind.

ÊTRE ADMIS À LA COTE : to be listed.

ÊTRE AMORTI : to be redeemed.

ÊTRE COMPENSÉ : to be offset.

ÊTRE DÉCLARÉ/MIS EN FAILLITE : to go bankrupt; to be declared bankrupt.

ÊTRE DÛ À : to arise from; to be due to.

ÊTRE EN ÉTAT DE CESSATION DE PAIEMENT : to default.

ÊTRE GAGÉ/GARANTI/NANTI SUR : to be secured on.

ÊTRE INSCRITE À LA COTE OFFICIELLE : to be fully listed (company, share).

ÊTRE MIS À LA RETRAITE ANTICIPÉE : to be retired early.

ÊTRE PERDANT : to lose out

ÊTRE SOUS LES ORDRES DE : to report to.

ÊTRE SUR LE POINT DE : to be about to.

ÊTRE TENU DE : to be required to.

ÊTRE TENU PAR LA LOI : to be legally bound.

ÊTRE VALABLE : to hold, to be valid.

ÉTUDE : survey.

EURO-OBLIGATION : Euro-bond.

EURODEVISES : euro-currencies.

ÉVALUATION APPROXIMATIVE : rough measure, rule of thumb.

ÉVALUATION DES CAPACITÉS D'ENDETTEMENT : rating.

ÉVALUER : to assess (damages); to estimate; to evaluate.

ÉVENTAIL : range (variety).

ÉVENTUALITÉ : possibility, prospect, contingency.

ÉVENTUEL : possible; prospective (CLIENT... : prospect or prospective customer).

ÉVITER : to ward off, to avoid.

ÉVOLUER : to evolve.

EX DIVIDENDE : ex dividend/ex div./x.d; (US) dividend off.

EXCÉDENT : credit balance; excess; surplus.

EXCÉDENTAIRE : active; favourable; in surplus.

EXCLUSION DE LA BOURSE POUR CESSATION DE PAIEMENT : hammering.

EXÉCUTER : to carry out (a decision, an order).

EXÉCUTION : completion.

EXÉCUTOIRE : binding; enforceable.

EXEMPLAIRE : copy (EN DOUBLE... : in duplicate; EN TRIPLE... : in triplicate).

EXEMPT DE DROITS : non-dutiable; with a zero duty.

EXERCER : to carry out.

EXERCER UNE OPTION, UN DROIT : to exercise an option or right.

EXERCICE BÉNÉFICIAIRE : profitable accounts.

EXIGENCE : requirement.

EXIGER : to demand; to require.

EXONÉRATION FISCALE : tax allowance(s).

EXPÉDIER : to forward; to ship.

EXPÉDITEUR : consigner; shipper; shipping firm (of goods); sender (of letters).

EXPÉDITION : shipment.

EXPERT : specialist.

EXPLOITATION : business (firm); operation.

EXPRESSION : phrase.

FABRIQUER : to make; to manufacture.

FAÇADE MARITIME : coast (PAYS À... : coastal country).

FACE (EN... DE) : confronted with (situation); in the face of (situation); in front of, opposite (location).

FACILEMENT : easily, readily.

FACILITER : to ease; to facilitate.

FACTURE : invoice (... CONSULAIRE : consular...; ... EN CONSIGNATION : consignment...; ... PRO FORMA : pro forma...); bill.

FACTURER : to charge; to invoice.

FAILLI : a bankrupt.

FAILLITE : bankruptcy (FAIRE... : to go bankrupt; to go bust); failure.

FAILLITE D'ENTREPRISE/DE SOCIÉTÉ : corporate failure.

FAIRE BAISSER LES COURS EN BOURSE : to bear the market.

FAIRE BAISSER LES PRIX : to hammer the market.

FAIRE ENREGISTRER : to register.

FAIRE FACE À : to meet.

FAIRE FAILLITE : to go bankrupt.

FAIRE FONCTION DE : to act as.

FAIRE FONCTIONNER LA PLANCHE À BILLETS : to print money, to use the printing press or the issuing board.

FAIRE LE COMMERCE DE : to deal in.

FAIRE OPPOSITION À UNE CHÈQUE : to stop a cheque.

FAIRE PAYER : make charges.

FAIRE SAISIR UN ARTICLE OU BIEN NON ENTIÈREMENT PAYÉ : to take back a good.

FAIRE UNE OFFRE : to bid.

FAIRE UNE OPÉRATION SERVANT À COUVRIR UN DÉCOUVERT EN BOURSE : to short cover.

FAIRE VALOIR QUE : to argue that.

FAISANT (CE...) : by so doing.

FAISEUR DE "DEALS" : dealmaker.

FAIT (DU... DE) : because of.

FARINE : flour.

FAUSSER : to distort; to twist.

FAUTE DE QUOI : for want of which.

FERMER : to close down (a business).

FÉROCE : ferocious; fierce (competition).

FERRAILLE : scrap-iron.

FIBRE DE COCO : coir.

FIBRES DURES : hard (GB) fibre (US) fibers.

FILIALE : affiliate; subsidiary.

FINAL : eventual; final.

FINALEMENT : eventually; finally.

FINANCEMENT À FORT DEGRÉ D'ENDETTEMENT : finance by borrowing heavily, leveraged financing.

FINANCEMENT COMPENSATOIRE : compensatory finance or financing.

FINANCEMENT MEZZANINE/INTERMÉDIAIRE/ HYBRIDE/STRAPONTIN : mezzanine finance.

FIXATION ILLÉGALE/ILLICITE DES PRIX : price-rigging.

FIXER : to quote; to set; to set out; to lay down.

FLOTTANT : floating or variable.

FLUX : flow (À... TENDUS : just in time).

FLUX DE LIQUIDITÉS : cash flow.

FONCTION DU SALAIRE OU DES BÉNÉFICES : earnings-related.

FONCTIONNAIRE : civil servant.

FONCTIONNEMENT : operation; running.

FONCTIONNER : to operate.

FOND : the bottom end.

FONDATEUR : founder.

FONDER : to set up.

FONDS CONSOLIDÉS : consols, consolidated stock.

FONDS DE DEVELOPPENENT EUROPÉEN : European Development Fund.

FONDS D'ÉTAT : dits valeurs dorées sur tranche : (UK) gilt-edged stocks or gilts, government bond(s) or stock.

FONDS DE PLACEMENT FERMÉ : investment trust closed-end company/fund/investment company.

FONDS DE PLACEMENT OUVERT : unit trust or open-ended fund; (US) mutual or mutual fund or mutual funds company.

FONDS DE ROULEMENT : (US) operating capital; working capital.

FONDS EUROPÉEN CHARBON ACIER : European Coal and Steel Fund.

FONDS EUROPÉEN D'ORIENTATION ET DE GARANTIE AGRICOLE/ FEOGA : European Agricultural Guidance and Guarantee Fund/ EAGGF.

FONDS EUROPÉEN DE COOPÉRATION MONÉTAIRE/FECOM : European Monetary Cooperation Fund/EMCF.

FONDS EUROPÉEN DE DÉVELOPPEMENT RÉGIONAL/FEDER : European Regional Development Fund/ERDF.

FONDS MONÉTAIRE INTERNATIONAL/FMI : International Monetary Fund/IMF.

FONDS SOCIAL EUROPÉEN : European Social Fund.

FONDS PROPRES : share capital; (US) stockholders'equitity.

FORCÉ : compulsory.

FORCER : to compel.

FORFAIT : flat rate.

FORMALITÉS : arrangements; formalities.

FORMALITÉS DOUANIÈRES ET ADMINISTRATIVES À L'IMPORTATION : customs and administrative entry procedures.

FORMALITÉS ET DOCUMENTATION CONSULAIRES : consular formalities and documentation.

FORMATION : training (... SUR LE TAS : on-the-job...; ... PROFESSIONNELLE : professional or vocational...) (... DES PRIX : market pricing; ... DE RÉSERVES : building up of reserves (in business or banking) (SOCIÉTÉ EN... : developing company).

FORMATION EN ALTERNANCE : (France) alternance training.

FORMATION PLÉNIÈRE (EN) : as a single body or plenary assembly.

FORMULAIRE : form.

FORT DEGRÉ D'ENDETTEMENT : heavy borrowing; leverage.

FOURNIR : to provide; to supply.

FOURNISSEUR : supplier.

FRAIS : charges; costs (... D'EXPLOITATION : working costs; ... DE DOSSIER : administrative costs).

FRAIS DE COURTAGE : brokerage.

FRAIS DE GESTION : management charges/cost/fee.

FRANCHISE : exemption; EN... : duty-free (customs); post-free (post).

FRANCHISE D'ASSURANCE : excess clause.

FRANCO À BORD : free on board/FOB.

FRANCO À QUAI : duty paid; ex dock; ex quay; ex wharf.

FRANCO LE LONG DU NAVIRE : free alongside ship/FAS : free on quay/FOQ.

FRANCO WAGON : free on rail/FOR; (US) free on truck/FOT.

FRAUDE : deception; fraud; misconduct; wilful misrepresentation (... FISCALE : tax evasion; ... DOUANIÈRE : illigal entry; smuggling; EN... : fraudulently; FAIRE ENTRER EN... : to smuggle in(to); to smuggle through the customs).

FRAUDER : to cheat.

FREIN : brake.

FREINER : to put a brake on; to curb; to check; to stem; (US) to damp; to dampen.

FRICHE : fallow; set aside.

FUITE : leakage.

FUSION : merger.

FUSIONNER : to join together; to merge.

GAGÉ : secured.

GAIN EN CAPITAL : capital gain.

GAMME : range.

GARANT D'ÉMISSION : underwriter (securities); SE PORTER GARANT DE : to stand surety for.

GARANTI : secured.

GARANTIE : guarantee (bank; contract; quality); guaranty (payment); security/collateral (funds lodged as security); underwriting; backing (finance); warranty (quality).

GARANTIR : to back; to cover; to guarantee; to secure; to underwrite; to warrant.

GARANTIR : to underwrite.

GARDER : to keep; to retain.

GEL : frost.

GÉRANT : manager.

GÉRANT DE FONDS : fund manager.

GÉRER : to manage; to run.

GESTION DE FONDS D'INVESTISSEMENT : investment management.

GONFLER : to boost.

GOUVERNEMENT : (US) Administration; government.

GRANDE CRISE ÉCONOMIQUE AMÉRICAINE DE 1929 : the Great Depression.

GRANDE SOCIÉTÉ INDUSTRIELLE COTÉE DE PREMIER ORDRE : blue chip company.

GRATUITEMENT : free(ly).

GROS VOLUMES DE TRANSACTIONS EN TITRES : high share dealing volumes.

GROS : bulk; wholesale (FAIRE LE... ET LE DÉTAIL : to deal wholesale and retail; MAISON, COMMERCE DE... : wholesale business; COMMERCANT EN... : wholesaler; PRIX DE... : wholesale price).

GROSSISTE : wholesaler.

GROUPE DE RÉFLEXION : think tank.

GUICHET AUTOMATIQUE DE BILLETS/GAB : cash dispenser/machine or automatic/automated teller machine/ATM.

HARMONISATION : adjustment; approximation; harmonization.

HAUSSE DE SALAIRE : pay awards or rises.

HAUSSIER : bull.

HAUT, LE : the top end.

HONORAIRE NÉGOCIÉ : negotiable commission.

HONORAIRES MINIMUM FIXES : fixed minimum commissions.

HONORAIRES : fee(s).

HORS MARCHÉ : off market.

HÔTELLERIE : hotel industry.

HYPERINFLATION : hyperinflation; galloping inflation.

HYPOTHÈQUE : mortgage.

ICI (D') À : by (in time).

IL FAUT SAVOIR QUE : it must be borne in mind that.

IMMÉDIATEMENT : at once; immediately.

IMMOBILISER : to tie up (capital).

IMPAIR : odd; uneven (figure; number).

IMPLANTATION : establishment.

IMPOSABLE : taxable.

IMPOSER : to levy (tax).

IMPOSITION : taxation; tax levies.

IMPÔT : tax; excise; duty.

IMPÔT INDIRECT : indirect tax.

IMPÔT NÉGATIF : negative (income) tax.

IMPÔT PROGRESSIF : progressive (income) tax.

IMPÔT PROPORTIONNEL : proportional (income) tax.

IMPÔT RÉGRESSIF : regressive (income) tax.

IMPÔT SUR LE REVENU : income tax.

IMPÔT SUR LES SOCIÉTÉS : corporation/corporate tax.

IMPÔTS DIRECTS : direct taxes.

IMPÔTS LOCAUX : (UK) rates.

IMPÔTS SUR LES PLUS VALUES : capital gains tax.

IMPRIMÉ : form.

IMPULSION : impetus.

IMPUTABLE À : chargeable to.

IMPUTER A : to charge to.

INASSURABLE : uninsurable.

INCENDIE : fire.

INCHANGÉ : unaltered.

INCIDEMMENT : incidentally.

INCITATION : incentive; urge.

INCITER : to urge.

INCLURE : to involve.

INCOMPATIBLE AVEC : incompatible or inconsistent with.

INCORPOREL : intangible.

INCOTERMES : incoterms.

INDÉLICATESSE : dishonesty.

INDEMNISATION : compensation.

INDEMNISER : to compensate; to indemnify.

INDEMNITÉ DE CHÔMAGE : unemployment benefit.

INDÉPENDANT : self-employed (tradesman).

INDEXÉ : indexed; index-linked.

INDICE BOURSIER : share index.

INDICE DES PRIX DE DÉTAIL/À LA CONSOMMATION : (UK) Retail Price Index/RPI.

INDIQUER : to state.

INDIVIDU : individual.

INDUSTRIE NAISSANTE : infant industry.

INDUSTRIEL (N) : businessman; industrialist; manufacturer.

INFLATION : inflation.

INFLATION DANS LA STAGNATION : stagflation.

INFLATION GALOPANTE : galloping inflation.

INFLATION PAR (L'AUGMENTATION DE) LA DEMANDE : demand-pull inflation.

INFLATION PAR LES COÛTS : cost-push inflation.

INFORMATION PRIVILIGIÉE : inside information.

INFORMATIQUE : data-processing.

INFRASTRUCTURE : facility (... DE PRODUCTION : manufacturing...).

INGÉNIERIE À REBOURS : reverse engineering.

INGÉNIEUR : engineer.

INITIATIVE POUR LA RÉFORME DES BARRIÈRES STRUCTURELLES ET DOUANIÈRES (EU/JAPON) : Structural Impediment Initiative/SII.

INITIÉ : insider.

INONDATION : flood.

INSCRIPTION EN BOURSE : listing.

INSOLVABILITÉ : insolvency.

INSOLVABLE : insolvent.

INSTABILITÉ D'EMPLOI : job turnover.

INSTALLATIONS : plant.

INSTALLER (S') : to settle.

INSTANCE : body (... CONSULTATIVE : advisory...).

INSTAURER : to set up.

INSTITUT D'ÉMISSION DE LA MONNAIE AUX ETATS-UNIS : (US) Federal Reserve System/FED.

INSTITUT D'ÉPARGNE : (US) stock savings bank.

INSTRUMENT : tool.

INSTRUMENT JURIDIQUE : legal device or instrument.

INSTRUMENT NÉGOCIABLE : negotiable instrument/paper.

INSTRUMENTS D'EMPRUNT : borrowing instruments.

INSTRUMENTS FINANCIERS À TERME : financial futures.

INSTRUMENTS FINANCIERS : financial instruments.

INSUFFISANCE : shortage.

INTENTER UNE ACTION CONTRE : to bring an action against.

INTERDIRE : to forbid; to veto.

INTÉRÊT : interest.

INTÉRÊT COMMERCIAL : trade interest.

INTÉRÊT PÉCUNIAIRE : insurable interest (insurance).

INTÉRIEUR : domestic; interior; À L'... : at home; À L'... DE : within...

INTERMÉDIAIRES FINANCIERS : financial intermediaries.

INTERVALLE : time lag.

INTRODUCTION EN BOURSE : introduction.

INTRODUIRE : usher in.

INTRODUIRE (S') EN BOURSE : to go public.

INVESTISSEMENT : investment.

INVESTISSEMENTS DE PORTEFEUILLE : portfolio investments.

INVESTISSEUR EN CAPITAL-RISQUE : venture capitalist.

INVESTISSEUR INSTITUTIONNEL : institutional investor.

INVISIBLES : invisible trade; invisibles.

ISOLATION : isolation; insulation (against cold, heat, noise).

JETER PAR DESSUS BORD : to cast overboard; to jettison.

JEU (EN) : at stake.

JOINDRE : to attach (a document); to get in touch with (a person).

JOUR DE RÈGLEMENT : settlement day.

JOUR DU TERME/DE LIQUIDATION : The Account Day or the settlement day/date or settling day.

JOUR OUVRABLE : working day.

JUGER RÉPRESENTATIF : to consider to represent.

JUGULER : to curb.

JURIDICTION : jurisdiction.

JURIDIQUE : legal.

JURISPRUDENCE : case law; jurisprudence; statute law.

JUSQU'À : up to.

KRACH : crash (stock market).

KRACH, LE DU LUNDI 19 OCTOBRE 1987 : Black Monday.

KRACH, LE DU MARDI 29 OCTOBRE 1929 : Black Tuesday.

LABEL : trademark.

LAISSER-FAIRE : laissez-faire.

LANCER : to issue; to raise (a loan); to launch (a firm, a product).

LANGUE DE TRAVAIL : working language.

LEASING : leasing.

LÉGÈREMENT : slightly.

LÉGITIME : legal.

LÉSER : to impair; to injure.

LETTRE DE CHANGE : bill of exchange B/E ; b/e; draft; (... SUR L'INTÉRIEUR : inland bill) (... SUR L'EXTÉRIEUR : foreign bill (... LIBRE : clean bill) (... À VUE : (at) sight bill) (... À ÉCHÉANCE : usance bill).

LETTRE DE VOITURE (OU CONNAISSEMENT) : bill of lading.

LETTRE DE VOITURE AÉRIENNE : air consignment note; airway bill.

LEVÉE DE CAPITAUX : capital or fund raising.

LEVÉE D'UNE PRIME : exercise of an option.

LEVER DES CAPITAUX : to raise funds.

LEVER UNE OPTION : to exercise an option

LIBELLER : to draw up; to word (document); to draw; to make out; to write out (a cheque); AU NOM DE QUELQU'UN : to (the order of) someone.

LIBÉRALISATION DU COMMERCE : trade liberalization.

LIBÉRALISATION : de-regulation.

LIBÉRER : to free; to unlock.

LICENCE : (UK) licence or (US) license (... PARTICULIÈRE : open individual...;... PERMANENTE : open general...;... SPÉCIALE : specific...)

LICENCIÉ : laid off; redundant.

LICENCIEMENT : redundancy (PRIME DE... : redundancy payment; (US) severance).

LICENCIER : to dismiss; to lay off; to make redundant.

LIEN : commitment; link.

LIER : to link; to tie; LIÉ AUX RÉSULTATS DE L'INVESTISSEMENT : investment-linked; unit-linked (unit trusts).

LIEU (AU... DE) : instead of.

LIGNES DIRECTRICES : guidelines.

LIMITATIONS SPÉCIFIQUES AUX ÉCHANGES COMMERCIAUX : specific limitations on trade.

LIN : flax.

LIQUIDATEUR : (company) liquidator.

LIQUIDATEUR JUDICIAIRE : official liquidator.

LIQUIDATION : liquidation or receivership or winding-up; ENTRER EN... : to go into receivership; The Account (stock exchange).

LIQUIDATION FORCÉE : compulsory winding-up.

LIQUIDATION PAR LES ACTIONNAIRES : members' voluntary winding-up.

LIQUIDATION PAR LES CRÉANCIERS : creditors' voluntary winding-up.

LIQUIDE : liquid.

LIQUIDITÉ : liquidity.

LISTE D'OFFRES : offer list.

LISTE DE CONCESSIONS : schedule of concessions.

LITIGE : litigation.

LIVRABLE POUR UNE DATE ULTÉRIEURE : for future delivery, forward.

LIVRAISON IMMÉDIATE : spot delivery.

LIVRAISON : delivery (... À TERME : future...; ... IMMÉDIATE : ready or immediate...; ... RAPIDE : prompt or early...).

LIVRAISONS À TERME : futures

LIVRE BLANC : white paper (report).

LIVRE DE BORD : ship's report; ship's papers.

LIVRER : to deliver.

LIVRER (SE... À) : to engage in.

LOCATAIRE : tenant; ... À BAIL : lessee, leaseholder.

LOCATION À BAIL : leasing.

LOCATION AVEC OPTION D'ACHAT/LOA : leasing.

LOCAUX : premises (... COMMERCIAUX : commercial/industrial buildings or premises).

LOGEMENT : lodging.

LOI DE L'OFFRE ET DE LA DEMANDE : the law of supply and demand.

LOIN (DE...) : by far.

LOT : parcel, portion, share, batch.

LOUÉ : leased; rented.

LOUER À BAIL : to lease (to).

LOUEUR : lessor.

LOUP : stag (stock market).

LOURDEMENT ENDETTÉ : heavily indebted.

LOYER : rent.

MACROÉCONOMIE : macroeconomics.

MAIN D'OEUVRE : labour; labour force; workforce (À FORT COEFFICIENT DE... : labour intensive).

MAINTENIR UN SOLDE CRÉDITEUR : to keep (an account) in credit.

MAÏS : maize.

MAISON D'ACCEPTATION : (UK) acceptance/accepting house.

MAISON DE RÉESCOMPTE : discount house.

MAISON DE TITRES : securities firm or house.

MAJORITÉ PONDÉRÉE OU QUALIFIÉE : qualified majority.

MALADIE : illness; disease.

MALADIE PROFESSIONNELLE : industrial disease.

MALADIE TRANSMISSIBLE PAR LES ANIMAUX : animal-borne disease.

MALHONNÊTEMENT : dishonestly.

MANDANT : principal.

MANDAT : commission; mandate; money order; term of office (duration at a post); warrant (to put someone under arrest).

MANDATAIRE : agent.

MANQUE : lack; want (PAR... DE : for... of).

MANQUE DE DEMANDE : demand deficiency.

MANQUEMENT : breach; failure; omission.

MANQUER DE : to be short of.

MANUTENTION : handling.

MARCHAND DE TITRES : jobber or stock jobber.

MARCHANDISE : commodity.

MARCHANDISES : goods (always in the plural).

MARCHANDISES EN MAGASIN : stock in hand.

MARCHANDISES LIVRABLES/DISPONIBLES : actuals.

MARCHÉ : bargain; contract; deal (transactions); market.

MARCHÉ À RÈGLEMENT MENSUEL : forward market.

MARCHÉ À TERME : forward market; futures market (commodities; securities).

MARCHÉ AU COMPTANT/DU DISPONIBLE : spot market or cash; physical or actual transaction.

MARCHÉ BAISSIER/ORIENTÉ À LA BAISSE : bearish market or bear market.

MARCHÉ D'OPTIONS NÉGOCIÉES : traded options market.

MARCHÉ DES CAPITAUX/MARCHÉ FINANCIER :capital market.

MARCHÉ DES CHANGES/DES DEVISES : foreign exchange market.

MARCHÉ DES EURO-DEVISES : eurocurrency market or Euromarket.

MARCHÉ DE GROS : wholesale market.

MARCHÉ DES OPTIONS NÉGOCIABLES SUR ACTIONS À LA BOURSE DE PARIS/MONEP : Paris traded options market.

MARCHÉ DES TITRES/VALEURS : securities/stock market; stock exchange; bourse.

MARCHÉ EN HAUSSE : bull or bullish market.

MARCHÉ EXTÉRIEUR : foreign market.

MARCHÉ HORS COTE : (UK) unlisted securities market USM; (US) over-the-counter market/OTC.

MARCHÉ HORS-COTE SPÉCIAL : Third Market.

MARCHÉ HYPOTHÉCAIRE : mortgage market.

MARCHÉ INTÉRIEUR : domestic or home market.

MARCHÉ MONÉTAIRE : money market or London money market.

MARCHÉ PRIMAIRE : primary market.

MARCHÉ SECONDAIRE : secondary market.

MARCHÉ UNIQUE EUROPÉEN : European Internal or Single Market.

MARCHEPIED : stepping stone.

MARCHÉS DE L'ÉTAT : government procurement.

MARGE : margin (... BÉNÉFICIAIRE : profit margin); touch or spread (Stock Exchange).

MARGE BRUT D'AUTO-FINANCEMENT : cash flow.

MARIEUR D'ENTREPRISES : dealmaker.

MARQUAGE : markings (of cases of goods).

MARQUES D'EXPÉDITION : shipping marks.

MASSE : weight.

MASSE MONÉTAIRE : money supply.

MATÉRIEL : equipment.

MATIÈRES PREMIÈRES : raw materials.

MÉCANISME DU TAUX DE CHANGE : Exchange Rate Mechanism/ERM (European Union).

MEMBRE : member (company; association); limb (part of body).

MÊME : even.

MENACE : threat.

MENACER : to jeopardize; to threaten.

MÉNAGE : household.

MENER À : to lead to.

MERCANTILISME : mercantilism.

MESURE : measure; step; TRAIN DE MESURES : package.

MESURE COMMERCIALE RESTRICTIVE : restrictive trade measure.

MESURE D'ENCOURAGEMENT : incentive.

MESURES SANITAIRES ET D'HYGIÈNE : health laws and regulations.

METTRE À BAIL : to lease (to).

METTRE À COUVERT : to hedge.

METTRE À JOUR : to disclose; to reveal; to uncover; to update (to supply new, recent information).

METTRE À LA DISPOSITION DU MARCHÉ : to offer to the market.

METTRE DE L'HUILE DANS LES ROUAGES : to oil the wheels.

METTRE EN OEUVRE : to implement (MISE EN OEUVRE : implementation).

METTRE EN PLACE : to set out.

METTRE EN PLACE DES RÈGLES DE FONCTIONNEMENT : to set rules.

METTRE EN RELATION : to connect.

METTRE UN POINT D'HONNEUR À : to make a point of doing something.

MICROÉCONOMIE : microeconomics.

MINERAI : ore.

MINISTÈRE DE L'INDUSTRIE ET DU COMMERCE EXTÉRIEUR : equivalent in part of the UK Department of Trade and Industry.

MINISTÈRE DU REDÉPLOIEMENT INDUSTRIEL : (UK) equivalent in part of the Department of Trade and Industry.

MINORITÉ DE BLOCAGE : blocking minority.

MIT : Massachusetts Institute of Technology.

MODALITÉS : arrangements; conditions; terms.

MODIFIER : to alter; to modify.

MOINS (AU...) : at least.

MONEP/MARCHÉ DES OPTIONS NÉGOCIABLES SUR LES ACTIONS À LA BOURSE DE PARIS : Paris traded options market.

MONITEUR : screen.

MONNAIE : currency (... À COURS LÉGAL : legal tender).

MONNAIE DE COMPENSATION : clearing currency.

MONTAGE : arrangement (... EN FAÇADE : fronting...).

MONTANT COMPENSATOIRE MONÉTAIRE/MCM : Monetary Compensatory or Compensation Amount/MCA (European Union).

MOTION DE CENSURE : vote of censure or no confidence.

MOUVEMENT DU PERSONNEL : job turnover.

MOYEN : (n) means; (AU... DE : by means of); (adj) average.

MURS CHINOIS : Chinese walls.

MUTUELLE DE CRÉDIT IMMOBILER/DE FINANCEMENT IMMOBILIER : (UK) building society; (US) equivalent: savings and loan association/S & L.

N'AYANT PAS DROIT À : unentitled to.

NAÎTRE : to be born; to originate.

NANTI : secured.

NANTISSEMENT : collateral; security.

NATALITÉ : birth-rate.

NATIONAL : domestic; home; local; national.

NATIONS UNIES : United Nations.

NAVETTE SPATIALE : space shuttle.

NÉANMOINS : nevertheless.

NE PAS HONORER SES ÉCHÉANCES : to default.

NE PAS PARVENIR À S'ENTENDRE : to fail to agree.

NÉCESSITEUX : needy; (LES... : the needy).

NÉGOCIANT : dealer.

NÉGOCIANT COURTIER EN TITRE : broker/dealer.

NÉGOCIANT EN VALEURSMOBILIÈRES/GROSSISTE OU DEMI-GROSSISTE : jobber.

NÉGOCIATION : bargaining; negotiation; round (of talks) (GATT).

NÉGOCIATIONS COMMERCIALES MULTILATÉRALES/NCM : Multilateral Trade Negotiations/MTN.

NÉGOCIER : to negotiate; to trade.

NIVEAU : level.

NIVEAU DE VIE : standard of living.

NOCIF : harmful.

NOM : name (D'APRÈS LE... DE : after the name of).

NOMINATION : appointment.

NOMMER : to appoint; to name.

NON CONTRÔLÉ : unregulated.

NON COUVERT : undersubscribed.

NON-ESSENTIEL : non-core.

NON-INSCRIT : independent; non-attached (in a political assembly).

NON-RESPECT DE : non-compliance with.

NONOBSTANT : notwithstanding (in spite of).

NORMAL : standard.

NORMALISATION DU TRAVAIL : adoption of labour standards; standardization of labour.

NORME : standard.

NOUVEL INSTRUMENT COMMUNAUTAIRE/NIC OU PLAN ORTOLI : New Community Instrument/NCI or Ortoli facility.

NOUVELLE ÉMISSION DE TITRES : new issue of securities.

NUMÉRO DE SÉRIE : serial number.

NUMERUS CLAUSUS : limited membership; limitation or restriction of numbers.

OBÈIR : to comply with.

OBÈSE : fat man (tactic to avoid takeover).

OBJECTIF : aim; target (FIXER UN... : to assign a target).

OBLIGATAIRE : debenture-holder/bond-holder.

OBLIGATION : bond or debenture; obligation (SOUMIS À... JURIDIQUE : legally binding).

OBLIGATION AU PORTEUR : bearer bond or debenture.

OBLIGATION CONVERTIBLE : convertible bond or debenture.

OBLIGATION À COUPON ZÉRO OU DIFFÉRÉE : zero coupon bond.

OBLIGATION DE DIVULGATION/RÉVÉLATION DE POSSESSION D'ACTIONS : disclosure of shareholdings rule.

OBLIGATION DES COLLECTIVITÉS LOCALES/PUBLIQUES : municipal/local authority bond.

OBLIGATION DIFFÉRÉE : deferred bond.

OBLIGATION ÉMISE EN PAIEMENT DES INTÉRÊTS DÛS SUR UN PRÊT OU DE RENTE: interest bond.

OBLIGATION ÉMISE PAR UNE SOCIÉTÉ : corporate/corporation bond.

OBLIGATION INDEXÉE : indexed bond.

OBLIGATION LÉGALE : legal requirement.

OBLIGATION NANTIE SUR TOUT L'ACTIF DE L'EMPRUNTEUR : floating debenture.

OBLIGATION NANTIE SUR UN ACTIF PARTICULIER : fixed debenture.

OBLIGATION NOMINATIVE : registered bond or debenture.

OBLIGATION DE PACOTILLE/POURRIE : junk bond.

OBLIGATION PARTICIPATIVE : equity bond; participating/profit-sharing bond.

OBLIGATION PERPÉTUELLE OU DE RENTE : irredeemable/perpetual/annuity bond.

OBLIGATION REMBOURSABLE À UNE DATE FIXE OU EN AVANCE À LA DEMANDE DE L'EMPRUNTEUR : redeemable debenture.

OBLIGATIONS À COURT TERME : short-dated bonds.

OBLIGATIONS À INTÉRÊT FIXE : fixed interest securities.

OBLIGATIONS AVEC PRIME DE REMBOURSEMENT : premium bonds.

OBLIGATIONS CONVERTIBLES NON GARANTIES : convertible loan stock.

OBLIGATIONS NON GARANTIES : loan/unsecured stock.

OBLIGATIONS : debentures; debenture stock or industrial debentures.

OBLIGATOIRE : binding; compulsory; mandatory.

OBSTACLE JURIDIQUE : legal restraint.

OBTENIR : to derive; to obtain.

OCTROI : concession; grant.

OFFICIEL : formal; official.

OFFICIEUX : informal; unofficial.

OFFRE : supply.

OFFRE SOUMISSION : tender offer.

OFFRE DE RACHAT : hostile take-over bid.

OFFRE ET DEMANDE : supply and demand.

OFFRE OBLIGATOIRE : mandatory offer.

OFFRE PUBLIQUE D'ACHAT/OPA : take-over bid.

OFFRE PUBLIQUE D'ACHAT AMICALE : friendly take-over bid.

OFFRE PUBLIQUE D'ACHAT HOSTILE/INAMICALE/SAUVAGE : hostile take-over bid.

OFFRE PUBLIQUE D'ACHAT LITIGIEUSE/OPA LITIGIEUSE : contested takeover bid.

OFFRE PUBLIQUE D'ÉCHANGE/OPE : share exchange or paper offer.

OFFRE PUBLIQUE DE VENTE : (UK) offer for sale (shares); (US) public offering.

OLÉAGINEUX : (n) oilseeds; (adj) oleaginous; oil-producing.

OMNIPOTENT : almighty.

OPA AMICALE : friendly takeover bid.

OPA HOSTILE/INAMICALE/SAUVAGE : hostile takeover bid.

OPA/OFFRE PUBLIQUE D'ACHAT : take-over bid.

OPA LITIGIEUSE : contested takeover bid.

OPE/OFFRE PUBLIQUE D'ÉCHANGE : share exchange or paper offer.

OPÉRATEUR EN BOURSE : Stock Exchange trader/dealer/operator; dealmaker.

OPÉRATION AU COMPTANT : cash; physical or actual transaction.

OPÉRATION DE FORMATION : training scheme.

OPÉRATION EN FAVEUR DE LA FORMATION DES JEUNES : (UK) Youth Training Scheme/YTS.

OPÉRATION(S) : deal; dealings (stock market); transactions.

OPÉRATIONS INTÉGRÉES DE L'UNION EUROPÉENNE : European Integrated Operations.

OPÉRATIONS À TERME : futures.

OPÉRATIONS BANCAIRES : banking.

OPÉRATIONS BOURSIÈRES À LA CORBEILLE : floor trading (Stock Exchange).

OPÉRATIONS D'OPEN MARKET SUR LE MARCHÉ MONÉTAIRE : open market operations.

OPÉRER SUR : deal in.

OPPOSITION SUR UN CHÈQUE : instructions to stop a cheque.

OPTER POUR : to exercise an option or right.

OPTION : option.

OPTION D'ACHAT : call option.

OPTION DE VENTE ET D'ACHAT : put and call or double option.

OPTION DE VENTE : put option.

OPTIONS NÉGOCIABLES : traded options.

OR EN BARRES/LINGOTS : gold bullion.

ORDONNANCE : executive order.

ORDONNÉ : orderly.

ORDRE : order.

ORDRE DU JOUR : agenda (À L'... : on the...).

ORDRE PERMANENT : standing order.

ORGANISATION DE COOPÉRATION ET DE DÉVELOPPEMENT ÉCONOMIQUE/OCDE : Organization for Economic Cooperation and Development/OECD.

ORGANISATION DES PAYS EXPORTATEURS DE PÉTROLE/OPEP : Organization of Petroleum Exporting Countries/OPEC.

ORGANISATION INTERNATIONALE DU COMMERCE/OIC : International Trade Organization/ITO.

ORGANISATION INDÉPENDANTE : Self-Regulatory Organization/SRO.

ORGANISATION MONDIALE DU COMMERCE : World Trade Organization/WTO.

ORGANISER : to organize; to mount.

ORGANISME : agency; body; entity; organization.

ORGANISME D'ÉPARGNE LOGEMENT : (US) thrift or thrift institution.

ORGANISME DE CONTRÔLE : regulator.

ORGANISME INDÉPENDANT CHARGÉ DE LA RÈGLEMENTATION : self-regulating body.

ORGANISME PROFESSIONNEL : business organization.

ORIENTÉ À LA HAUSSE/EN HAUSSE : bullish.

OÙ (D'...) : hence.

OUTILLAGE : equipment

OUTRE-MER : overseas.

OUVRIR LA VOIE À : to pave the way to.

PACTE ANDIN : Andean Pact.

PAIEMENT À LA COMMANDE : cash with order/C.W.O.

PAIEMENT À LA LIVRAISON : cash on delivery/C.O.D; spot cash.

PAIEMENT CONTRE REMBOURSEMENT : cash on delivery/C.O.D; spot cash.

PAIEMENT IMMÉDIAT : spot cash.

PAIEMENTS COURANTS : current account (balance of payments).

PAIR : par (AU-DESSOUS DU... : below...; AU-DESSUS DU... : above...) (AU... : at...) (price of securities on the stock market).

PALLIER : to remedy.

PANIER DE MONNAIES : basket of currencies.

PAPIER COMMERCIAL AMÉRICAIN DE PREMIER ORDRE : prime commercial paper.

PAPIER COMMERCIAL/FINANCIER : commercial paper.

PAR/PAR L'INTERMÉDIAIRE DE : through.

PAR LÀ : thereby (by so doing).

PAR QUOI: whereby.

PAR VERSEMENTS ÉCHELONNÉS : by or in instalments.

PARADIS FISCAL : tax haven.

PARITÉ : parity; par value.

PARLEMENT EUROPÉEN : European Assembly or Parliament.

PARRAIN : sponsor.

PARRAINER : to sponsor.

PARTICIPATION : stake.

PARTICIPATION MAJORITAIRE : majority holding.

PARTICULIER : private individual.

PARTIE CONTRACTANTE : contracting party.
PARTIE INTÉGRANTE : integral part.
PARTIES NON ESSENTIELLES : non-core parts.
PARTS DE FONDATEUR : management/managers' shares; founders' shares.
PARVENIR À L'ÉCHÉANCE : to mature.
PARVENIR À FAIRE PASSER QQ'UN EN JUGEMENT : to bring someone to trial.
PASSATION DES MARCHÉS DE L'ETAT : public procurement.
PASSER PAR : to go through.
PASSER UN MARCHÉ : to award or sign a contract.
PASSER UNE COMMANDE : to place an order (*with* a firm *for* goods or services).
PASSIBLE DE : liable to.
PASSIBLE DE DROITS : dutiable.
PASSIF : liabilities.
PAYABLE SUR DEMANDE : repayable on demand.
PAYER À L'AVANCE : to pre-pay.
PAYER LES INTÉRÊTS D'UN EMPRUNT : to service a debt.
PAYS À COMMERCE D'ETAT : State trading nation.
PAYS DÉVELOPPÉ : developed country.
PAYS EN VOIE DE DÉVELOPPEMENT/PVD : developing country or less developed country/LDC.
PAYS TIERS : third country.
PENSION DE RETRAITE : retirement pension;... COMPLÉMENTAIRE :personal/ supplementary.
PÉNURIE : shortage.
PERCEVOIR : to levy (a tax).
PERFORMANT : efficient.
PÉRIODE DE PROSPÉRITÉ/FORTE EXPANSION : boom.
PERMANENT : standing.
PERMETTRE : to allow; to enable.
PERMETTRE À QQ'UN DE SUBVENIR : to tide sb over.
PERSONNE JURIDIQUE/MORALE : legal entity.
PERSONNE PHYSIQUE : individual.
PERSONNEL : staff.
PERSPECTIVE : perspective; prospect; scope; view.
PERSPECTIVES DE CROISSANCE : growth prospects.
PERTE : loss (... TOTALE RÉELLE : Actual Total...; ... CENSÉE TOTALE : Constructive Total...; ... PARTIELLE : partial...).
PERTURBATION : disruption.
PERTURBER : to disrupt; to disturb.
PETIT ÉPARGNANT : small saver.
PEU DISPOSÉ À : reluctant to.
PEUR (DE... DE) : for fear of.
PHYSIONOMIE : pattern.
PIÈCE DÉTACHÉE : component; spare part; spare.
PIED (SUR UN... D'ÉGALITÉ) : on an equal footing; on equal terms.
PIERRE D'ACHOPPEMENT : stumbling block.
PIÉTON : passer-by.
PILULE EMPOISONNÉE : poison pill (Stock Exchange tactic).
PION DE NÉGOCIATION : negotiating coin.
PLACEMENT : placing; (US) often: placement (stocks).
PLACEMENT PRIVÉ : private placing (stocks).
PLACEMENT PUBLIC : public placing (stocks).
PLACER : to invest (money); to place (to sell securities as a broker or an investment bank).
PLAFOND : ceiling (PLAFONNER À : to reach the ceiling of).
PLAIGNANT : complainant; complaining party; plaintiff.
PLAN : plan; scheme.
PLAN D'ÉCHANGE : swap scheme.
PLAN D'ÉPARGNE NATIONAL : National Savings Scheme.
PLANCHER : floor.
PLEIN EMPLOI : full employment.
PLÉNIER : full.
PLUS (DE...) : moreover.
PLUS GRAND CONTACT AVEC : wider exposure to.
PLUS-VALUE EN CAPITAL : capital gain.
POINT (À TEL... QUE) : so much so that.
POINT D'ENTRÉE : port of entry.
POINT MORT : standstill.
POINTE (DE...) : advanced.
POLICE D'ASSURANCE : insurance policy (ÉTABLIR UNE... : to write an...; SOUSCRIRE UNE... : to take out an...).
POLICE D'EXPÉDITION : shipment policy.
POLICE DE CAUTIONNEMENT : finance guarantee policy.

POLICE DE CONTRAT : contract policy.
POLICE FLOTTANTE/OUVERTE : floating policy.
POLICE FRET : freight policy.
POLICE RESPONSABILITÉ DE L'ARMATEUR : ship-owner's liability policy.
POLICE SUR CORPS : hull policy.
POLICE INCENDIE : fire policy.
POLICE SUR FACULTÉS : cargo policy.
POLITIQUE À COURT TERME/À COURTE PORTÉE : short-termism.
POLITIQUE/ORIENTATION POLITIQUE; policy (... AGRICOLE : farm...).
POLITIQUE AGRICOLE COMMUNE/PAC : Common Agricultural Policy/CAP (European Union).
POLITIQUE BUDGÉTAIRE fiscal policy.
POLITIQUE DE DÉFLATION : deflationary policy(ies).
POLITIQUE FISCALE : fiscal policy.
POLITIQUE GOUVERNEMENTALE MONÉTAIRE : monetary policy.
PONDÉRER : to weight.
POPULATION ACTIVE : active population .
POPULATION ACTIVE OCCUPÉE : active working population.
PORT (FRAIS DE PORT): carriage (cost of transport).
PORT D'EMBARQUEMENT : port of loading.
PORT D'ENTRÉE : port of entry.
PORT DE DESTINATION : port of discharge.
PORT FRANC : free port.
PORTE-PAROLE : mouthpiece; spokesman.
PORTEFEUILLE : portfolio (of shares).
PORTEFEUILLE FINANCIER OU D'INVESTISSEMENT : portfolio.
PORTER SUR : to bear upon; to deal with.
PORTER UNE AFFAIRE DEVANT : to refer a case to.
PORTEUR : bearer; holder(of shares or bonds).
POSITION : position; stance.
POSSESSEUR : holder (of shares).
POSSESSION : ownership; possession.
POSTE : item (balance-sheet; budget).
POUR LE COMPTE DE : on behalf of.
POUR LEUR PROPRE COMPTE : on their own account.
POUR RAISON DE : on the ground(s) of or that.
POURPARLERS : talks.
POURVOIR (À) : to provide (for).
POURSUIVRE QQ'UN EN JUSTICE : to take legal action against someone.
POURVU QUE : provided (that).
POUVOIRS PUBLICS : public authorities.
POUVOIRS STATUTAIRES : statutory powers.
PRATIQUE COMMERCIALE DÉLOYALE : unfair trade practice.
PRATIQUE COMMERCIALE LOYALE : fair trade practice.
PRATIQUEMENT : virtually.
PRATIQUES COMMERCIALES RESTRICTIVES : restrictive business practices/RBPs.
PRÉALABLE : previous; prior.
PRÉALABLEMENT : first; previously; to begin with (... À : prior to).
PRÉAVIS : notice.
PRÉCEDEMMENT : formerly.
PRÉCÉDENT : (n) past record.
PRÉDATEUR D'ENTREPRISE : raider or corporate raider.
PRÉÉTABLIR : to predesignate; to predetermine.
PRÉFÉRENCE COMMUNAUTAIRE : Community preference (European Union).
PRÉFÉRENCE TARIFAIRE : tariff preference.
PRÉJUDICE : damage; detriment; injury; prejudice (PORTER... À : to be detrimental or prejudicial to ; to jeopardize; SUBIR UN... : to suffer a damage; an injury; a prejudice; to be adversely affected).
PRÉJUDICIABLE : harmful.
PRÉLÈVEMENT AUTOMATIQUE : standing order.
PRÉLEVER : to extract.
PRENDRE À BAIL : to lease (from).
PRENDRE EN COMPTE : to take into account or consideration.
PRENDRE UNE ASSURANCE : to take out an insurance policy.
PRENEUR À BAIL : lessee.
PRÉPONDÉRANT : prevailing.
PRÉSIDENT : chairman (of a company); (US) president.
PRÉSIDENT DIRECTEUR GÉNÉRAL/PDG : chairman and managing director or chief executive officer /CEO.
PRÉSIDER : to chair; to head.
PRESTATION MALADIE : sickness benefit.
PRESTATIONS DE SÉCURITÉ SOCIALE : social security benefits.

PRÊT : lending ; loan.
PRÊT HYPOTHÉCAIRE : mortgage.
PRÊT INTERBANCAIRE : inter-bank money.
PRÊT LIÉ : tied loan
PRÊT PARTICIPATIF : equity loan.
PRÊT PERSONNEL : personal loan.
PRÊTABLE : lendable.
PRÉTENDRE : to claim; to hold; to insist.
PRÉTENDÛMENT : supposedly.
PRÉTENTION : claim.
PRÊTER : to lend; to loan.
PRÊTEUR : lender.
PRÊTEUR EN DERNIER RECOURS/RESSORT : lender of last resort (central bank).
PRÊTS EN PARTICIPATION : syndicated loan.
PREUVE : evidence; proof.
PRÉVALOIR : to prevail.
PRÉVISION DE PROSPECTUS : prospectus forecast.
PRÉVOIR : to estimate; to forecast; to predict; to provide for (supply); to provide that (to arrange under an agreement).
PRIME : bonus (advantage); premium (insurance; stock exchange) (stock market options); reward (prize).
PRISE D'AVANCE : front-running (stock market).
PRIVATISATION : privatization; privatisation.
PRIVILIGIÉ : favoured; privileged.
PRIX À LA CONSOMMATION : consumer price.
PRIX À TERME : forward/futures price.
PRIX ACHETEUR/OFFERT : bid/buying price.
PRIX CIBLE : target price (European Union).
PRIX D'ACHAT ET DE VENTE : two-way prices.
PRIX D'ÉQUILIBRE : equilibrium price.
PRIX D'EXERCICE/DE LIQUIDATION (OPTION) : exercice/strike/striking price.
PRIX D'INTERVENTION : intervention price.
PRIX DE RÉFÉRENCE OU INDICATIF : target price (marketing).
PRIX DE SOUTIEN : support price; guaranteed price; pegged price (European Union).
PRIX DE VENTE DEMANDÉ : seller's price; selling price; offer/offered price; (US) offering price.
PRIX DÉPART QUAI/ENTREPÔT MARITIME : ex wharf.
PRIX DU DISPONIBLE/ENLEVÉ/SUR PLACE : spot price.
PRIX DU MARCHÉ : market price.
PRIX MARCHANDISES DÉBARQUÉES : ex ship; ex quay-duty on buyer's account.
PRIX OFFERT ET DEMANDÉ : bid and offer prices.
PRIX SORTIE D'ENTREPÔT; DE MAGASIN : ex warehouse.
PRIX SORTIE D'USINE : ex factory; ex mill; ex store; ex works.
PRIX SUR PLACE : spot price.
PROCÉDÉ : device; means; way.
PROCÉDURE : action; proceedings; procedure.
PROCESSUS : process.
PRODUCTION : output; production.
PRODUCTEUR D'INTÉRÊT : interest-bearing.
PRODUCTION INDUSTRIELLE "MAIGRE" : lean manufacturing.
PRODUIRE (SE) : to arise; to occur.
PRODUIT : commodity; product; proceeds (amount of money derived from a commercial transaction).
PRODUIT INTÉRIEUR BRUT/PIB : Gross Domestic Product/GDP.
PRODUIT NATIONAL BRUT/PNB : Gross National Product/GNP.
PRODUIT DE BASE : primary product.
PRODUIT DU COURS PAR LE NOMBRE DE TITRES ÉMIS : multiplying the price of each share by the total volume of shares available.
PRODUIT ESSENTIEL : key commodity.
PRODUITS FINIS/MANUFACTURÉS : manufactured goods.
PRODUITS INTERMÉDIAIRES : intermediate goods/products or producer goods.
PRODUITS LAITIERS : dairy produce or products.
PROFITER DE : to benefit from; to profit by; to take advantage of.
PROGRAMME INTÉGRÉ DES MATIÈRES PREMIÈRES/PIMP : Integrated Program for Commodities/IPC.
PROGRAMME DE SOUTIEN DES PRIX : price support programme (UK) or program (US).
PROGRAMMES INTÉGRÉS MÉDITERRANÉENS/PIM : Integrated Mediterranean Programmes (European Union).
PROIE : prey.
PROJET : bill; draft (... DE LOI : bill or draft legislation).

PROMOTION IMMOBILIÈRE : real estate development.

PROMOUVOIR : to promote.

PRÔNER : to advocate.

PROPENSION À CONSOMMER : propensity to consume.

PROPOSER : to offer; to propose; to recommend (for a post).

PROPOSITION : proposal; proposition; nomination (for a post).

PROPRIÉTAIRE : owner.

PROPRIÉTÉ : ownership; property.

PROSPECTUS D'ÉMISSION : prospectus.

PROTECTION/REFUGE : hedge.

PROTECTIONNISME : protectionism.

PROTÉGER : to cover; to protect.

PROTOCOLE D'APPLICATION PROVISOIRE/PAP : Protocol of Provisional Application/PPA.

PROVENANCE : location; origin.

PROVENIR DE : to originate from.

PROVISIONS : reserves.

PROVISOIRE : interim; provisional.

PUBLICITÉ : advertizing; publicity (DONNER DE LA... À : to publicize).

PUCE ÉLÉCTRONIQUE : micro-chip.

PUREMENT ET SIMPLEMENT : utterly.

QUAI : dock; quay; wharf (À... : duty paid; ex dock; ex quay; ex wharf; À..., DROITS À LA CHARGE DE L'ACHETEUR : ex quay duty on buyer's account; ex ship).

QUALIFICATION : skill (NIVEAU DE... : ... standard).

QUARANTAINE : quarantine.

QUATRIÈME MARCHÉ : (US) fourth market.

QUESTION : issue; matter; question.

RABAIS : discount (on a bill or invoice).

RACHAT D'ENTREPRISE AVEC EFFET DE LEVIER :
leveraged buyout/buy-out/LBO.

RACHAT D'UNE ENTREPRISE : takeover bid.

RACHAT D'UNE ENTREPRISE PAR LES CADRES EXTÉRIEURS : management buy-in.

RACHAT DE L'ENTREPRISE PAR SES CADRES : management buyout.

RACHAT DE L'ENTREPRISE PAR SES SALARIÉS/RES : management-employee buyout.

RACHAT DE SES PROPRES ACTIONS PAR L'ENTREPRISE : management buyback.

RACHATS DE VENDEURS À DÉCOUVERT : short covering.

RACHETER À DÉCOUVERT : to short cover.

RACHETER : to buy; to buy back; to redeem (shares); to take over.

RADICALEMENT : drastically.

RADIER : to strike off.

RAID : raid; hostile take-over bid.

RAID À L'AUBE OU TENTATIVE D'OPA SURPRISE : dawn raid.

RAIDER : raider.

RAISON (EN... DE) : because of; due to; on account of; through.

RAISON SOCIALE : name; title.

RALENTISSEMENT : slowdown.

RAMASSER : to harvest (crop).

RAPPORT (PROPORTION) : proportion; ratio (PAR... À : against; in proportion with; in terms of).

RAPPORT RESERVES OBLIGATOIRES-DÉPÔTS : reserve asset ratio.

RATIO DE LIQUIDITÉ (IMMÉDIATE) : liquidity or acid test ratio.

RATIONNEMENT : rationing.

RATISSAGE DU MARCHÉ : street sweep (Stock Exchange).

RÉALISATION : achievement; completion; performance.

RÉALISER : to achieve; to reach.

RÉASSURANCE : indirect business; reinsurance.

RÉCEPTION : receipt (DÈS... : immediately on receipt).

RECESSION : recession.

RECETTES : earnings; receipts.

RECHANGE (DE...) : alternative.

RECHERCHE ET DÉVELOPPEMENT : Research and Development/R&D.

RÉCIPROCITÉ : reciprocity (APPLIQUER LA... : to reciprocate).

RÉCLAMATION : claim.

RÉCLAMER DES DOMMAGES ET INTÉRÊTS À : to make claims against.

RÉCLAMER DES MARCHANDISES : to claim goods.

RÉCOLTE : crop; harvest.

RÉCOMPENSE : reward.

RECONDUIRE DANS SES FONCTIONS : to reappoint.

RECONNAISSANCE : acknowledgement; recognition; IOU (for "I owe you") (debt).
RECONNAISSANCE DE DETTE : equivalent of an IOU ("I owe you") : in some cases a promissory note.
RECONVERSION : redeployment; re-training.
RECONVERTIR : to redeploy.
RECOURIR À : to resort to.
RECOUVREMENT : collection.
RÉCUPÉRER : to reclaim; to recover.
RECYCLAGE : re-training.
REDÉMARRER : to pick up again.
REDÉPLOIEMENT : reallocation (resources); redeployment (firm, business).
REDEVANCE : fee.
REDRESSEMENT : recovery.
REDRESSER : to restore, to turn around.
RÉDUCTION : cut.
RÉDUCTION D'IMPÔTS : tax cuts or rebate.
RÉDUIRE : to cut; to decrease; to inhibit; to lower..
RÉEL : actual; real.
RÉESCOMPTER : to re-discount.
RÉFORME : reform.
RÉFUGE : hedge.
RÉGIME DES LICENCES : licensing.
RÉGIME FISCAL : tax system; tax bracket.
RÈGLE : rule.
RÈGLE DE LA SUPER MAJORITÉ : the super majority rule.
RÈGLEMENT (RÉGLEMENTATION) : regulation.
RÈGLEMENT : payment; settlement (... FORFAITAIRE : global; lump sum settlement).
RÈGLEMENT DE TRANSACTIONS : settlement of bargains.
RÈGLEMENT JUDICIAIRE : receivership (ÊTRE MIS EN... : TO GO INTO... ; METTRE EN... : to put into).
RÉGLER : to pay for; to remit; to settle.
RÉINVESTIR : to plough back; to reinvest.
RELAIS : staging post.
RELANCER : to relaunch.
RELATIF À : relevant (to).
RELATIONS D'AFFAIRES : business dealings or relations.
RELEVÉ : statement.
RELEVER : to increase; to raise.
RELIER À : to link with.
REMANIEMENT : rearrangement; reshuffling.
REMANIER : to rearrange; to reshuffle.
REMBOURSABLE : redeemable; repayable.
REMBOURSEMENT : redemption; refund(ing); repayment (... GLOBAL EN ESPÈCES : lump cash refund).
REMBOURSER : to redeem (bonds); to refund; to repay.
REMBOURSER LE MONTANT TOTAL DE LA SOMME EMPRUNTÉE À UNE DATE SPÉCIFIÉE : to repay the stocks on maturity.
REMETTRE : to hand over (to give); to postpone : to put off (to a later date); to remit (to pay money due); to cancel, to write off (debt).
REMISE : delivery (letter, goods); discount (rebate on a bill or invoice); remission (debt, tax); remittance (payment).
REMISE D'IMPÔT : tax rebate.
REMONTER : to pick up (demand, prices); ... À : to date back to.
REMPLACER : to replace; to substitute for; (... QQ'UN : to take over from someone).
REMPLIR : to fill in (a form); to perform or to carry out (a function) (... CERTAINES CONDITIONS : to meet specific requirements).
RENDEMENT : yield (... ACTUARIEL BRUT : redemption...).
RENDEMENT ÉLEVÉ : high returns.
RENDEMENT EN INTÉRÊTS : dividend or income yield.
RENDU SOUS PALAN : free alongside ship/FAS : free on quay/ FOQ.
RENFORCER : to strengthen.
RENONCIATION : disclaimer; waiver.
RENOUVELABLE : renewable.
RENTABILITÉ : profitability; earning power/capacity.
RENTE : annuity (... AVEC REMBOURSEMENT EN ESPÈCES : cash-refund; ... ALÉATOIRE, CASUELLE, CONDITIONNELLE, CONTINGENTE : contingent...; ... CERTAINE : certain; terminable...; ... DIFÉRÉE : deferred...; ... IMMÉDIATE : immediate...; ... RETRAITE : retirement...; ... RÉVERSIBLE : reversionary or in reversion...; ... TEMPORAIRE : temporary...; ... VARIABLE : variable...; ... VIAGÈRE : life...; ... VIAGÈRE AVEC REVERSION : survivorship...).

RENTE CONSOLIDÉE : consols, consolidated stock.

RENTIER : annuitant.

RÉPANDU : widespread.

RÉPARATION : legal redress.

RÉPARTIR : to allocate (costs, charges); to distribute (funds, profits), to spread 'risks).

REPARTIR : to pick up again.

RÉPARTITION : allocation; distribution; spreading.

RÉPERCUSSION : aftermath; repercussion.

RÉPONDANT : sponsor.

REPORT : contango (Stock Exchange).

REPRENDRE POSSESSION D'UN ARTICLE OU BIEN NON ENTIÈREMENT PAYÉ : to repossess a good.

REPRENDRE : to resume (meeting, negotiation); to go back to work; to take over (firm).

REPRENEUR D'ENTREPRISE : rescuer (friendly); (corporate) raider (hostile).

REPRÉSAILLES : reprisal(s); retaliation; (EXERCER DES... : to retaliate).

REPRÉSENTANT : agent.

REPRÉSENTER : to account for (a share of something, wealth); to represent.

REPRIS(E) : taken over (firm); returned (goods).

REPRISE : recovery.

RÉPUTATION : (quality) rating; reputation; repute.

REQUÉRIR : to require.

RÉSEAU : network.

RÉSERVE : reservation; reserve; SOUS TOUTES... S : without prejudice; SOUS... DE :
subject to; SANS... : clean (bill of exchange); SOUS... : claused, dirty, foul, unclean (bill of lading).

RÉSERVES : reserves.

RÉSERVES OBLIGATOIRES : special deposits and/or reserve assets; (US) required reserves.

RÉSOLUTION : resolution.

RESPONSABILITÉ : liability; responsibility.

RESPONSABILITÉ CIVILE : public liability.

RESPONSABILITÉ DE L'EMPLOYEUR : employer's liability.

RESPONSABILITÉ LIMITÉE : limited responsibility.

RESPONSABLE : (n) decision maker; official; ... DE : (adj) responsible for; ÊTRE... DEVANT : to report to, to be responsible to.

RESSOURCES DE PRODUCTION : productive resources.

RESSOURCES ÉNERGÉTIQUES : energy resources.

RESTAURATION : catering; (food industry).

RESTITUTION : export subsidy; restitution (European Union).

RESTREINDRE : to restrict.

RESTRICTIONS QUANTITATIVES : quantitative restrictions/QRs.

RÉSULTATS : performance.

RETARD : delay (EN... : back; late; outstanding; overdue (debts)).

RETIRER : to withdraw.

RETOMBÉES : spin-off.

RETORTION : retaliation.

RETRAIT : withdrawal.

RETRAITÉ ANTICIPÉ : early retiree.

RÉTROCESSION : retrocession.

RÉUNIR : to convene; to muster (people); to muster; to raise (funds).

REVENDRE : to sell on; to re-sell..

REVENIR À : to revert/return to.

REVENU : earnings; income.

REVENUS DES CAPITAUX MOBILIERS : investment income.

REVIREMENT : switch; turn around.

RICHESSE : wealth.

RICHESSE ACCUMULÉE : accumulated wealth.

RISQUE : hazard; risk (... DIRECT : direct risk) (insurance); venture (business).

RISTOURNE : discount (to sell at a discount).

ROTATION DU PERSONNEL : job turnover.

ROUTE (EN...) : sailing (incoterm).

ROUTER : to dispatch.

RUÉE SUR UNE BANQUE POUR DEMANDES DE REMBOURSEMENT : run on a bank.

S'APPUYER ESSENTIELLEMENT SUR : to rely predominantly on.

S'ATTAQUER À UN PROBLÈME : to tackle a problem.

S'EFFONDRER : to fall (sharply).

S'ENGAGER À : to guarantee to.

S'INSCRIRE : to register.

S'INTRODUIRE DANS : to work one's way through.

S'OCCUPER DE : to deal with; to see to.

SAIN : sound.

SALARIÉS : workforce.

SALLE DE COTATIONS : the floor; (US) the pit.

SANS SE PRÉOCCUPER DE SAVOIR SI : regardless of whether.

SAUVEGARDE : safeguard.

SCRUTIN : election; vote (... MAJORITAIRE : majority vote).

SE CONFORMER À : to comply with.

SE CONFORMER À DES CONDITIONS SÉVÈRES : to comply with stringent requirements.

SE COUVRIR, SE METTRE À COUVERT : to hedge oneself.

SE METTRE EN LIQUIDATION : to go/be put into liquidation.

SE PASSER DE : to dispense with.

SE PRÉSENTER : come in (a certain form, shape or size); to introduce oneself (person).

SE PROCURER DES CAPITAUX : to raise capital.

SECOND MARCHÉ : equivalent of the UK Unlisted Securities Market/USM.

SECTEUR DES ENTREPRISES : corporate sector.

SECTEUR DES PERSONNES : personal sector.

SECTEUR PRIVÉ : private sector.

SECTEUR PUBLIC : public sector.

SECTEUR : industry; sector.

SÉCURITÉ : safety.

SÉCURITÉ SOCIALE : (UK) National Insurance.

SEIN (AU... DE) : within.

SELON : according to; dependent or depending on; through.

SELON LE CAS : as the case may be.

SELON QUE : according to whether.

SEMESTRE : half year (economy); semester (academic).

SEMESTRIELLEMENT : bi-annually.

SENSIBLE : sensitive.

SERVICES : services.

SERVICES FINANCIERS : financial services.

SERVIR DE : to act as; to serve as.

SERVIR DE RÉFÉRENCE : to be used as the basis for.

SEUIL : threshold; trigger point.

SEUL ET UNIQUE : one; single.

SEVÈRE : stringent.

SI, DANS LE CAS OÙ : if/should.

SICAV/SOCIÉTÉ D'INVESTISSEMENT À CAPITAL VARIABLE : unit trust; (US) mutual fund.

SIÈGE : base; headquarter; seat (AVOIR SON... À : to be based or headquartered in).

SIÉGER : to sit.

SIGLE : acronym.

SINISTRE : claim; damage; loss; FAIRE UNE DÉCLARATION DE... : to put in a claim (on one's own or somebody else's insurance); INDEMNISER LES... S : to pay claims.

SINON : otherwise.

SISAL : sisal.

SITUER : to locate.

SOCIÉTÉ À RESPONSABILITÉ ILLIMITÉE : unlimited (liability) company.

SOCIÉTÉ À RESPONSABILITÉ LIMITÉE/SARL : limited or limited liability company or private limited company.

SOCIÉTÉ ANONYME PAR ACTIONS : joint-stock company; public limited company/PLC; (US) corporation, incorporated company.

SOCIÉTÉ CIBLE : target company.

SOCIÉTÉ COTÉE EN BOURSE : listed or quoted company.

SOCIÉTÉ D'ÉVALUATION DU CRÉDIT/DE LA SOLVABILITÉ : credit rating agency.

SOCIÉTÉ D'INVESTISSEMENT : investment or investment management company.

SOCIÉTÉ D'INVESTISSEMENT/DE PLACEMENT À CAPITAL FIXE : investment trust or investment (trust) company or closed-end company/fund/investment company.

SOCIÉTÉ D'INVESTISSEMENT À CAPITAL VARIABLE/SICAV : open-end unit trust; (US) mutual or mutual fund or mutual funds company.

SOCIÉTÉ DE BOURSE : brokerage firm or stockbroking firm or stockbrokers.

SOCIÉTÉ DE CONTREPARTISTES : market maker house.

SOCIÉTÉ DE COURTAGE : brokerage firm or stockbroking firm or stockbrokers.

SOCIÉTÉ DE CRÉDIT/DE FINANCEMENT/DE PRÊT : finance house or finance/hire-purchase/credit or leasing company.

SOCIÉTÉ DE PLACEMENT/D'INVESTISSEMENT EN VALEURS MOBILIÈRES : securities firm.

SOCIÉTÉ DE TOUT PREMIER ORDRE : blue chip company.

SOCIÉTÉ ÉMETTRICE : issuing company.

SOCIÉTÉ MULTINATIONALE : multinational corporation.

SOCIÉTÉ MUTUELLE D'ÉPARGNE DE CRÉDIT IMMOBILIER/ DE FINANCEMENT IMMOBILIER : building society; (US) equivalent: savings and loan association/S & L.

SOCIÉTÉ PAR ACTIONS : joint-stock company.

SOCIÉTÉ SPÉCIALISÉE DANS LE COMMERCE EXTÉRIEUR GARANTISSANT LA SOLVABILITÉ DE L'ACHETEUR : confirming house.

SOCIÉTÉ TRANSNATIONALE : transnational corporation.

SOIT DIT EN PASSANT : incidentally.

SOLDE : balance.

SOLDE CRÉDITEUR : credit balance.

SOLDE DE DIVIDENDE : final dividend.

SOLDES : sales.

SOLIDE : reliable.

SOLVABILITÉ : solvency.

SOLVABLE : solvent.

SOMME FORFAITAIRE : lump sum.

SOMMET : summit (meeting).

SONDAGE : survey.

SORTIE DE TRÉSORERIE : outflow of money.

SORTIES : outflows.

SOULAGER : to relieve.

SOUMETTRE À QQ'UN : to bring before or to refer to or to submit to someone.

SOUMIS À : subject to.

SOUMISSION : tender offer.

SOUMISSIONNER POUR : to bid for; to tender for.

SOUMISSIONNAIRE : bidder; tenderer (allocations); underwriter (finance).

SOUMISSIONNAIRE SOUS-TRAITANT : sub-underwriter.

SOUPLESSE D'EMPLOI : flexibility (labour market).

SOUS LE PRÉTEXTE QUE : on the grounds that.

SOUSCRIPTEUR : subscriber.

SOUSCRIPTION À DES ACTIONS : subscription.

SOUSCRIPTION MINIMALE : minimum subscription.

SOUSCRIRE À : to subscribe to; to apply for.

SOUSCRIRE À UNE NOUVELLE ÉMISSION POUR REVENDRE RAPIDEMENT : to stag in a new issue.

SOUS-ESTIMATION : underestimate.

SOUTENIR : to claim, to insist that; to support.

SOUTIEN : incentive; support.

SPÉCIFIER : to indicate; to state.

SPÉCULATEUR À LA BAISSE : bear.

SPIRITUEUX : spirits.

STAGFLATION : stagflation.

STATUER SUR : to rule on.

STATUER À L'ENCONTRE DE : to rule against.

STATUT : articles; statute (company, body); status (condition, financial situation); ... JURIDIQUE : statutory basis.

STATUTS : Articles of Association.

STELLAGE : put and call or double option.

STIMULANT À L'INVESTISSEMENT : investment incentive.

STIMULER : promote.

STIPULER : to provide (... QUE : ... that); STIPULANT QUE : providing that; to the effect that).

STOCK : inventory; stock; stockpiles; store; STOCKS REGULATEURS : buffer stocks.

STOCKABLE : storable.

STOCKAGE : storage.

STOCKER : to stockpile; to store.

STRATÉGIE DE CROISSANCE : growth strategy.

STRUCTURE : pattern; structure.

STRUCTUREL : structural.

SUBIR : to suffer.

SUBROGATION : subrogation.

SUBSTANTIEL : hefty.

SUBSTITUTION AUX IMPORTATIONS : import substitution.

SUBVENTION : subsidy.

SUBVENTIONNER : to subsidize.

SUCCESSION : estate.

SUCCURSALE : branch.

SUFFRAGE UNIVERSEL : direct election.

SUITE (... À, À LA... DE) : further to; in reply to; in response to; with reference to; DONNER... À : to carry out or deal with (an order); to follow up (a letter).

SUIVRE (L'EXEMPLE) : to follow suit.

SUPERFICIE : area.

SUPPLANTER : to supercede.

SUPPLÉMENTAIRE : additional; extra; supplemental; supplementary (FAIRE DES HEURES... (S) : to work overtime).

SUPPRESSION : removal; suppression.

SUPPRIMER : to remove; to suppress.

SUR : out of (e.g.: UNE PERSONNE... TROIS : one person... three).

SUR DEMANDE : on demand.

SUR PRÉSENTATION : at sight.

SURCHAUFFER : to overheat.

SURESTIMATION : over-estimation/evaluation.

SURFACE FINANCIÈRE : financial position or standing.

SURNOMMER : to dub; to nickname.

SURPASSÉ : oversubscribed (securities issue).

SURSOUSCRIT : oversubscribed (securities issue).

SURVEILLANCE : monitoring; supervision.

SURVEILLER : to monitor; to regulate; to supervise.

SURVENIR : to arise; to happen; to occur.

SUSCEPTIBLE À : likely to.

SUSCEPTIBLE DE : liable to; likely to.

SYNDIC DE FAILLITE : receiver.

SYNDICAT : trade union.

SYNDICAT DE FAILLITE : receivership.

SYNDICATAIRE : underwriter (securities issue).

SYNTHÉTIQUE : man-made; synthetic.

SYSTÈME : system; scheme; plan.

SYSTÈME AUTOMATISÉ DE RÈGLEMENT DE TRANSACTIONS EN TITRES DE SOCIÉTÉS : Stock Exchange Automatic Execution Facility/SAEF.

SYSTÈME MONÉTAIRE EUROPÉEN/SME : European Monetary System/EMS.

SYSTÈME CENTRAL INFORMATISÉ D'ENREGISTREMENT ET DE RÈGLEMENT DES TRANSACTIONS EN TITRES DE SOCIÉTÉS : (UK) Transfer Accounting Lodging for Investors and Stock Management for Jobbers/TALISMAN. Also Taurus : now dead.

SYSTÈME D'INDEMNISATION : compensation scheme.

SYSTÈME DE PRÉLÈVEMENT LIBÉRATOIRE OU DE RETENUE À LA SOURCE DE L'IMPÔT SUR LE REVENU ET DES COTISATIONS DIVERSES : (UK) Pay-As-You-Earn/PAYE.

SYSTÈME DE TAUX DE CHANGES FIXES : fixed exchange rate system.

SYSTÈME DE VIREMENTS INFORMATISÉS : electronic funds transfer/EFT.

SYSTÈME DE VIREMENTS INFORMATISÉS AU POINT DE VENTE : electronic funds transfer at point of sale/EFTPOS.

SYSTÈME GÉNÉRALISÉ DE PRÉFÉRENCES/SGP : Generalized System of Preferences/GSP.

SYSTÈME INFORMATISÉ DE COTATIONS : computerised quotations system.

SYSTÈME INFORMATISÉ DE COTATION ET DE TRANSACTION : (UK) Stock Exchange Automated Quotation System/SEAQ.

SYSTÈME TÉLÉVISÉ ET INFORMATISÉ DE COURS DE TITRES : Teletext Output of Price Information by Computer System/TOPIC.

SYSTÈMES INFORMATISÉS D'INFORMATION ET DE TRANSACTIONS : electronic information and trading systems.

TARIF DOUANIER : tariff.

TARIF EXTÉRIEUR COMMUN/TEC : common external tariff/CET or CXT.

TAUX : rate.

TAUX CONSOLIDÉ : bound rate.

TAUX D'ACTIVITÉ : participation rate.

TAUX D'ESCOMPTE : discount rate; ... OFFICIEL : minimum lending rate/MLR.

TAUX D'IMPOSITION : tax rate.

TAUX D'IMPOSITION ZÉRO : zero rating system of taxation.

TAUX D'INTÉRÊT : interest rate.

TAUX D'INTÉRÊT DIRECTEUR SUR LE MARCHÉ DES EURODEVISES DE LONDRES : London Inter-Bank Offered Rate/LIBOR or inter-bank rate.

TAUX D'INTÉRÊT FIXE : fixed interest rate.

TAUX DE CHANGE : exchange rate.

TAUX DE CHÔMAGE QUI N'ACCÉLÈRE PAS L'INFLATION : non-accelerating inflation rate of unemployment/NAIRU.

TAUX DE CHÔMAGE VOLONTAIRE : voluntary rate of unemplyment.

TAUX DE DIVIDENDE CONVENU : agreed dividend rate.

TAUX DE NON-PAIEMENT : default rate.

TAUX DE RÉFERENCE : target rate.

TAUX EFFECTIF GLOBAL/TEG : annual percentage rate/APR.

TAUX INTERBANCAIRE OFFERT À LONDRES/TIOL : London Inter-Bank Offered Rate/LIBOR or the inter-bank rate.

TAUX NATUREL DE CHÔMAGE : natural rate of unemployment.

TAUX PIVOT MOYEN : central rate or value.

TAXE AD VALOREM OU PROPORTIONNELLE OU SUR LA VALEUR : ad valorem tax.

TAXE À L'ACHAT : unit or (US) sales tax.

TAXE À L'IMPORTATION : import levy.

TAXE À LA VALEUR AJOUTÉE/TVA : value added tax/VAT.

TAXE DE CORESPONSABILITÉ : co-responsibility levy.

TAXE ROUTIÈRE : road tax.

TEMPÉRAMENT (À...) : by/in instalments (credit terms).

TEMPÊTE : gale; storm.

TEMPS DE RÉPONSE/LATENCE : time lag.

TENDANCE : trend.

TENEUR DE MARCHÉ : market maker.

TENIR COMPTE DE : to bear in mind.

TENIR PAR FIDÉICOMMIS : to hold in trust.

TENIR PAROLE : to stick to one's word.

TENIR SES ENGAGEMENTS : to meet current commitments.

TENTATIVE D'OPA SURPRISE : dawn raid.

TERME (AU... DE) : at the end of (time); by; under (law, rule, treaty).

TERME, À COURT/LONG : short/long range (forecasts); short term; short-dated/long-term; long-dated (banking, finance); ARGENT À COURT... : money at short notice or at call; DÉPÔT À... : fixed deposit; DETTES À COURT... : current liabilities; COURS/TAUX À... : forward rate/price for the account (for forward/future(s) transactions); MARCHÉ À... : futures/forward market; ACHETER À... : to buy forward/for the account; VENDRE À... : to sell forward; ... DE GRÂCE : extra time to pay; ... DE RIGUEUR : latest (possible) date; PAIEMENTS À... : instalments.

TERRE BRÛLÉE : scorched earth (stock market tactic).

THÈSES DIVERGENTES : opposing claims.

TIERCE PERSONNE/TIERS : tiers; third party or person; person outside a vehicle; LES TIERS : third party risks.

TIRAGE D'UN CHÈQUE PAR UNE BANQUE SUR ELLE-MÊME : bank/banker's draft.

TIRÉ : acceptor; drawee (bank account, bill of exchange).

TIRER : to draw or draft or write out (a cheque or bill).

TIRER SON NOM DE : to be named after.

TIREUR : drawer (bank account : bill of exchange).

TITRE : security (stocks and shares).

TITRE À TAUX FIXE : fixed-interest security.

TITRE D'ACTION : share certificate.

TITRE MUNI DE DIVIDENDE : cum dividend/cum div. security.

TITRES NON REMBOURSABLES : undated stock.

TITRES SANS VALEUR NOMINALE : no-par value securities.

TITULAIRE : holder (of a bank account or insurance policy).

TONNAGE : displacement; shipping space; tonnage.

TOUR À TOUR : in turn.

TOUR DE TABLE : introduction of participants (meeting); (list of) partners (deal); capital invested, equity (deal).

TOUS RISQUES : all-in or all-risks or comprehensive (insurance policy).

TOUT À FAIT : utterly.

TOUTE INFORMATION NOUVELLE DE NATURE À MODIFIER LE COURS DES TITRES : price-sensitive information.

TRAITE : draft bill or bill of exchange.

TRAITE À ÉCHÉANCE : usance bill.

TRAITE BANCAIRE/SUR UNE BANQUE : bank/banker's draft.

TRAITE DOCUMENTAIRE : documentary bill.

TRAITE IMPAYÉE : dishonoured bill.

TRAITÉ COMMERCIAL : trade pact.

TRAITEMENT : processing (goods).

TRAITEMENT DE LA NATION LA PLUS FAVORISÉE : Most-Favoured-Nation Treatment/MFN (GATT).

TRAITER : to process.

TRANCHE D'IMPOSITION : tax bracket.

TRANSACTION : bargain; contract; deal; dealing; business; transaction.

TRANSACTIONS COMMERCIALES LOYALES : fair trade.

TRANSACTIONS DÉLOYALES : unfair dealing.

TRANSACTIONS EN BOURSE PAR MOYEN D'ORDINATEUR : program(me) trading.

TRANSACTIONS EN OPTIONS NÉGOCIÉES : traded options dealings.

TRANSACTIONS MALHONNÊTES : dishonest dealing.

TRANSFER ÉLÉCTRONIC DE FONDS : electronic funds transfer/EFT.

TRANSFER ÉLÉCTRONIQUE DE FONDS AU POINT DE VENTE : electronic funds transfer at point of sale/EFTPOS.

TRANSFÉRER : to transfer.

TRANSFÉRER SUR LE MARCHÉ BOURSIER UNE PARTIE DU CAPITAL D'UNE SOCIÉTÉ, QUI

DEVIENT COTÉE EN BOURSE : to go public; to take a company public.

TRANSFERT : transfer.

TRANSFERT DE FONDS : money transfer.

TRANSFORMATION : processing.

TRANSFORMER : to process.

TRANSITOIRE : transitional.

TRANSMISSIBLE : transferable.

TRANSPARENCE : transparency.

TRANSPLANT : transplant.

TRANSPORT : carriage; freight; transport.

TRANSPORT MARITIME : shipping.

TRAQUER : to track down.

TRAVAIL TEMPORAIRE : casual/temporary work.

TRAVAILLER AU NOIR : to moonlight.

TRAVAILLEUR TEMPORAIRE : temporary worker or "temp".

TRAVAILLEURS INDÉPENDANTS : self-employed.

TRAVERSÉE : voyage.

TREMBLEMENT DE TERRE : earthquake.

TRÈS PROBABLEMENT : more than likely.

TRÊVE : standstill.

TRIBUNAL : court.

TRIER : to sort (out).

TRIMESTRIELLEMENT : quarterly.

TRIPARTITE : three party.

TROC : barter.

TROISIÈME MARCHÉ : Third Market (of the International Stock Exchange in London).

TROMPER : to cheat.

TROQUER : to barter.

TROUBLES DE L'ORDRE PUBLIC : civil disturbances.

TROUVER DES CAPITAUX : to raise capital.

TYPE D'ACTIVITÉ : form of business.

UNION DOUANIÈRE : customs union.

UNION EUROPÉENNE : European Union.

UNIQUE : once-only; single.

UNITÉ DE COMPTE : unit of account.

UNITÉ DE PRODUCTION DÉLOCALISÉE : transplant.

UNIVERSITAIRE (N, ADJ) : academic.

USINE CLÉS EN MAIN : turnkey factory.

USURE : wear and tear.

UTILISATION : operation; use.

VAGUEMENT : loosely; en gros.

VAISSEAU : ship; vessel.

VALEUR (SANS...) : without any market value; worthless.

VALEUR À INTÉRÊT FIXE : fixed-interest security.

VALEUR AU PAIR : face or par value.

VALEUR MARCHANDE : commercial or market or transaction value.

VALEUR NOMINALE : face or nominal or par value.

VALEUR PONDÉRÉE : weight.

VALEUR REFUGE : hedge or hedge security.

VALEURS À COURT TERME : shorts.

VALEURS À MOYEN TERME : mediums.

VALEURS À LONG TERME : longs.

VALEURS BOURSIÈRES : securities.

VALEURS COTÉES : listed/quoted securities.

VALEURS DE PÈRE DE FAMILLE : blue chips.

VALEURS HORS MARCHÉ : off-market shares.

VALEURS MOBILIÈRES DE PREMIER ORDRE : blue chips.

VALEURS MOBILIÈRES VENDUES À DÉCOUVERT : shorts.

VALEURS NON COTÉES : unlisted or unquoted securities/shares.

VARIABLE : floating or variable.

VARIER : to vary.

VÉGÉTAL : (n-adj) vegetable.

VEILLER AU RESPECT DES NORMES DE QUALITÉ : to enforce standards.

VENDABLE : saleable.

VENDEUR À DÉCOUVERT : bear; short seller.

VENDEUR DE L'OPTION : writer or taker (of an option).

VENDRE À DÉCOUVERT : to sell short; to short sell; to short; to go short.

VENDRE À TERME : selling forward.

VENTE : sale.

VENTE À DÉCOUVERT : selling short; short selling; short/bear sale or shorting.

VENTE À TEMPÉRAMENT : hire-purchase; (US) instalment/credit buying.

VENTE À TERME : selling in/for the account/ forward.

VÉRIFIER : to audit (accounts); to check; to cross-check.

VERSEMENT : payment.

VERSEMENT À TEMPÉRAMENT : instalment.

VERSEMENT ÉCHELONNÉ : instalment; (PAR S ... S : by instalments).

VERSER DES ARRHES : to pay a deposit.

VIGNETTE AUTOMOBILE : road tax.

VINGT-QUATRE HEURES SUR VINGT-QUATRE : around the clock or twenty-four hours a day.

VIREMENT : transfer.

VIS-À-VIS DE QUELQU'UN : regarding someone.

VISER À : to aim at or to.

VISIBLE : conspicuous; visible.

VOIES : channels.

VOIX : vote (UNE... PAR PERSONNE : one man one vote).

VOL : burglary; theft.

VOLAILLE : poultry.

VOLANT DE CHÔMAGE : unemployment cushion.

VOLONTAIRE : voluntary.

VOLUME DES TRANSACTIONS : trading.

VOTE À L'UNANIMITÉ : unanimity; unanimous vote.

VOTER : to pass (with success); to vote.

WARRANT : warrant.

Y : therein (within).

ZINZINS : institutional investors.

ZONE DE COMMERCE INTERNATIONAL : foreign trade zone.

ZONE DE LIBRE ÉCHANGE : free-trade area.

ZONE DE TRANSIT : transit zone.

ZONE DOUANIÈRE : customs area.

ZONE FRANCHE : free zone.

SUGGESTED FURTHER READINGS

(ORIENTATIONS BIBLIOGRAPHIQUES)

ADAM J. H. : *Longman Dictionary of Business English;* Harlowe, Essex, 1989.

ANDERTON A.G. : *Economics : a New Approach;* Unwin Hyman Ltd.; London; 1990.

BANNOCK, GRAHAM, BAXTER, R. E. and DAVIS, E. : *The Penguin Dictionary of Economics*; Penguin Books ltd, London, 1987.

BANNOCK, GRAHAM and MANSER WILLIAM : *The Penguin International Dictionary of Finance*; Penguin Books ltd, London, 1990.

BANNOCK GRAHAM ET AL. : *Dictionary of Economics;* Hutchinson; London; 1989.

BERNARD YVES ET AL. : *Dictionnaire économique et financier;* Éditions du Seuil; Paris; 1975.

BRÉMOND JANINE ET GÉLÉDAN ALAIN : *Dictionnaire économique et social;* Hatier; 4e édition; Paris; 1990.

BRÉMOND JANINE : *Mieux comprendre l'économie;* Éditions Liris; Paris; 1991.

BRETT MICHAEL : *How to Read The Financial Pages : a Simple Guide to The Way Money Works and The Jargon;* Hutchinson Business Books; 2nd edit.; London; 1989.

CABINET SAXÉ : *Dictionnaire comptable; fiscal et financier : French-English, (USA)/English (USA)-French*; Paris; 1986.

CENECO : *Dixeco de l'économie pour comprendre le langage économique;* Dunod; 2e édition; Paris; 1991.

COLLIN PETER : *Dictionary of Banking and Finance;* Peter Collin Publishing Ltd.; Middlesex; 1991-1993.

CONSO PIERRE ET AL. : *Dictionnaire de gestion financière*; Dunod/Entreprise; Bordas; Paris; 1979.

DEBOUZY MARIANNE : *Travail et travailleurs aux États-Unis;* Repères; La Découverte; Paris; 1990.

DÉFOSSÉ GASTON ET BALLEY PIERRE : *La Bourse des valeurs;* Presses universitaires de France; 16e édition; Paris; 1990.

EYRAUD FRANÇOIS : *Travail et travailleurs en Grande-Bretagne;* Repères; La Découverte; Paris; 1985.

FOUET MONIQUE : *L'économie des États-Unis;* Repères; La Découverte; Paris; 1989.

FREYSSINET JACQUES : *Le chômage;* Repères; La Découverte; Paris; 1991.

HAMILTON MARIE-JUDITH AND PHILIPPE; SMITH NANCY : *Glossary of Financial English;* Armand Collin-Longman; Paris; 1989.

HEN CHRISTIAN; JACQUES LÉONARD : *L'Europe;* Repères; La Découverte; Paris; 1990.

HINDLE TIM : *Pocket Banker;* Basil Blackwell and The Economist; Oxford; London; New York; 1985.

Le Robert et Collins du Management; Dictionnaires Le Robert; Paris; 1992.

LEBRAS MICHEL ET FONTENILLES ALFRED : *Glossary of Accounting/Glossaire d'anglais comptable;* Armand Collin-Longman; Paris; 1985.

LEONARD DICK : *Pocket Guide to the European Community;* Basil Blackwell and The Economist; Oxford; London; New York; 1988.

LES PUBLICATIONS DU QUÉBEC : *Lexique de la Bourse et des valeurs mobilières anglais-français;* Cahiers de l'Office de la langue française; 2e édition; Québec; 1988.

LOBLEY DEREK T. : *Applied Economics Made Simple;* W.H. Allen & Co.; Ltd.; 4th edit.; London; 1980.

MARCHETEAU MICHEL ET AL. : *Dictionnaire de l'anglais économique, commercial et financier*; Presses Pocket; Paris; 1989.

MCCULLOUGH VINCE : *Pocket Guide to the City;* Basil Blackwell and The Economist; Oxford; London; New York; 1988.

NOBES CHRISTOPHER : *Pocket Accountant;* Basil Blackwell and The Economist; Oxford; London; New York; 1985.

PAXTON JOHN (ED.) : *The Stateman's Year-Book;* Macmillan; London and Basingstoke; latest edition. *RAMSES;* édition de l'année en cours.

PENNANT-REA, RUPERT & EMMOTT, BILL : *Pocket Economist;* The Economist Publications; 2nd edit.; London; 1987.

RAINELLI MICHEL : *Le commerce international;* Repères; La Découverte; Paris; 1992.

RIVOIRE JEAN : *Les techniques bancaires;* Presses universitaires de France; 2e édition; Paris; 1988.

ROSIER BERNARD : *Les théories des crises économiques;* Repères; La Découverte; Paris; 1988.

SAMUELSON PAUL A. : *Economics;* Tenth Edition; McGrawHill; New York; 1955.

TEULON FRÉDÉRIC : *Vocabulaire monétaire et financier;* Presses universitaires de France; Paris; 1991.

THOMAS MICHAEL : *Pocket Guide to Marketing;* Basil Blackwell and The Economist; Oxford; London; New York; 1986.

TORRINGTON DEREK & EARNSHAW JILL : *Pocket Employer;* Basil Blackwell and The Economist; Oxford; London; New York; 1988.

Aubin Imprimeur
LIGUGÉ, POITIERS

Achevé d'imprimer en juillet 1995
N° d'impression L 49591
Dépôt légal juillet 1995
Imprimé en France